UNCOMMON PEOPLE

ALSO BY ERIC HOBSBAWM

UNCOMMON PEOPLE

RESISTANCE, REBELLION AND JAZZ

Eric Hobsbawm

Weidenfeld & Nicolson
LONDON

First published in Great Britain in 1998 by
Weidenfeld & Nicolson

The Orion Publishing Group Ltd
Orion House
5 Upper Saint Martin's Lane
London WC2H 9EA

A catalogue reference is available from the British Library.

ISBN 0 297 81916 X

Typeset in Monophoto Photina
by Selwood Systems, Midsomer Norton

Printed in Great Britain by
Butler & Tanner Ltd, Frome and London

CONTENTS

PREFACE

This book is almost entirely about the sort of people whose names are usually unknown to anyone except their family and neighbours, and, in modern states, to the offices registering births, marriages and deaths. Occasionally they are also known to the police and to journalists in search of a 'human story'. In some cases their names are entirely unknown and unknowable, like those of the men or women who changed the world by cultivating crops imported from the recently discovered New World through Europe and Africa. Some played a role on small or local public scenes: the street, the village, the chapel, the union branch, the council. In the era of the modern media, music and sport have given personal prominence to a few who, in earlier times, would have remained anonymous.

They constitute most of the human race. The arguments among historians about how important individuals and their decisions are in history, do not concern them. Writing such individuals out of the story would leave no significant trace on the macro-historical narrative.

The point of my book is not just that such people should be rescued from oblivion or from what E. P. Thompson called, in his memorable phrase, 'the enormous condescension of posterity'. Of course they should, and I hope some chapters in my book – for instance, 'Political Shoemakers' and 'Peasant Land Occupations' – have helped to do so. As the late Joseph Mitchell, of the *New Yorker*, wrote in protest against those who talked, however sympathetically, about 'the little people': 'They are as big as you and I'. Their lives are as interesting as yours and mine, even if nobody has written about them. My point is rather that, *collectively*, if not as individuals, such men and women are major historical actors. What they do and think, makes a difference. It can and has changed culture and the shape of history, and never more so than in the twentieth century. That is why I have called a book about ordinary people, the ones that are traditionally known as 'the common people', *Uncommon People*.

They are not 'featureless and commonplace', like the crimes which Sherlock Holmes found so unusually difficult to deal with. How they are shaped by their past and present, what is the rationale of their beliefs and actions, how they in turn shape their societies and history: these are the central concerns of my book. I hope they give it a basic unity of theme.

Three of the sections of this book deal with particular social groups or milieux: The Radical Tradition (chapters 1–10) with the working class and the ideologies associated with its movement, Country People (chapters 11–13) with traditional peasantries, and Jazz (chapters 19–25) with one of the few developments in the major arts entirely rooted in the lives of poor people. A fourth section, Contemporary History (chapters 14–18), is relevant to my theme, inasmuch as it deals mainly with situations to which conscious human intentions and decisions are hardly relevant, though conventionally they are usually discussed in such terms. However, I cannot conceal that it gives me pleasure to reprint at least one successful exercise in contemporary analysis. Nor have I been able to resist including a brief coda on a wrongly forgotten villain of the USA in the strange Cold War era, published in the series 'Heroes and Villains' of the young *Independent* newspaper. It is, of course, based on Nicholas von Hoffmann's unanswerable *Citizen Cohn: The Life and Times of Roy Cohn* (New York, 1988).

In one way or another, as the present essays demonstrate, these questions have preoccupied me throughout my career as a historian. They continue the lines of enquiry pursued in my early studies of labouring people and in my first books, published almost forty years ago, *Primitive Rebels* and *The Jazz Scene*. *Uncommon People* brings together a number of studies written between the early 1950s and the middle 1990s. Eleven out of the twenty-six essays have previously appeared in earlier books: *Labouring Men*, *Revolutionaries* and *Worlds of Labour* (in the American edition: *Workers*); the rest have not previously been published in books under my name, at least in the United Kingdom.

Further details are given at the head of each chapter.

London, 1998   Eric Hobsbawm

CHAPTER 1

Thomas Paine

This chapter was first published as a review of a biography of Tom Paine in the New Statesman *in 1961. There have been several, and better, lives of Paine since, notably the one by John Keane (London 1995), but they cannot but inspire the same reflections.*

A moderate revolution is a contradiction in terms, though a moderate putsch, coup or pronunciamento is not. However limited the ostensible aims of a revolution, the light of the New Jerusalem must shine through the cracks in the masonry of the eternal Establishment which it opens. When the Bastille falls, the normal criteria of what is possible on earth are suspended, and men and women naturally dance in the streets in anticipation of utopia. Revolutionaries, in consequence, are surrounded by a millennial halo, however hard-headed or however modest their actual proposals may be.

Tom Paine reflected this rainbow light of an age 'in which everything may be looked for'. He saw before him 'a scene so new and transcendently unequalled by anything in the European world, that the name of revolution is diminutive of its character, and it rises into a regeneration of man'. 'The present age', he held, 'will hereafter merit to be called the Age of Reason, and the present generation will appear to the future as the Adam of the new world.' America had become independent, the Bastille had fallen, and he was the voice of both these marvellous events. 'A share in two revolutions', he wrote to Washington, 'is living to some purpose.'

And yet the actual political proposals of this profoundly and instinctively revolutionary man were almost ridiculously moderate. His goal, 'universal peace, civilization and commerce', was that of most Victorian free traders. He deliberately disclaimed any intention of 'mere theoretical reformation' in economic matters. Private enterprise was good enough for him and 'the most effectual process

1

is that of improving the condition of man by means of his interest'. His analysis of the evils of society, namely that war and high taxes were at the bottom of it all, is still sound doctrine in the Sussex executives' belt, except at times when the profits of armament and the fear of communism outweigh the horror of high government spending. Paine's most radical incursion into the economic process was a proposed 10 per cent inheritance tax to finance old-age pensions. When he came to France, he – like other English 'Jacobins' – joined the Gironde, and was a moderate even in that group.

That he should nevertheless have been a revolutionary is not surprising. There was, after all, a time when the sound industrialists were prepared to raise barricades (or, more precisely, to support raising them) against the forces of iniquity which prevented 'the general felicity of which civilization is capable' by preferring kings and dukes to businessmen. What is surprising is Paine's extraordinary, and indeed probably unparalleled, success as a spokesman of revolt. This is what turns him into a historical problem.

Other pamphleteers have sometimes pulled off the coup which justifies the agitator's life and which turns him for a moment into the voice of everyman. Paine did it three times. In 1776 *Common Sense* crystallized the half-formulated aspirations for American independence. In 1791 his defence of the French Revolution, *The Rights of Man*, said all most English Radicals would ever wish to say on its subject. It is said to have sold 200,000 copies in a few months, at a time when the entire population of Britain, including children and other illiterates, was less than that of Greater London today. In 1794 his *Age of Reason* became the first book to say flatly, in language comprehensible to the common people, that the Bible was not the word of God. It has remained the classic statement of working-class rationalism ever since. Clearly such a triple triumph is not due to accident.

It is due in part to the fact that Paine *was* the people for whom he wrote, the self-made, self-educated, self-reliant men as yet not finally divided into employers and hired hands. The man who was successively apprenticed stay-maker, teacher, petty official, tobacconist, journalist and 'an ingenious person, hoping to introduce his mechanical contrivances in England', could speak for all of them. He had, incidentally, the same uncanny rapport with the public as inventor and as journalist. The most popular single structure of the industrial revolution, to judge by its innumerable reproductions on jugs, is the iron bridge over the Wear, built to Paine's pioneer design, though – characteristically – not to his profit. The discovery of revolution as a

2

fact gave him, like his readers, the enormous confidence in a future which was theirs.

Indeed, the discovery made him. But for the struggle in America, in 1776, he might have become a minor literary figure, or more likely an inventor and failed industrialist, for applied science remained his first and last passion. His friends – but few others – would have admired him as a wit, a charming star of small-town society, a sportsman and a good man at chess or piquet. They would have mildly deplored his fondness for brandy, and might occasionally have commented on the absence of any sex-life in one apparently so sensible to the charms of the fair. Had he not emigrated to America with a recommendation from the astute Franklin, he would be forgotten. Had he not been reborn in the Revolution, he would be remembered only in a rare PhD thesis.

But he is unforgotten, and, typically enough, not in the world of orthodox liberalism, but in the partisan universe of political and theological rebellion; and this in spite of his uniform political failure, except as a journalist, and his lack of extremism. (He was the only member of the French Convention who fought openly against the death sentence on Louis XVI, though he had been the first to call for a republic.) Most of the lives of Paine are by left-wingers; a communist has edited his collected works.

Why? Because for most of Paine's readers salvation by private enterprise was not the answer, whatever he or they may have thought. His and their opposition was ostensibly against 'privilege' which stood in the way of 'freedom'; but in fact it was also against unrecognized and new forces which pushed men such as themselves into poverty. They were independent enough – as skilled artisans, small shopkeepers or farmers – to see themselves as the future, not because (like the Marxian proletariat) the very degree of their oppression destined them for revolution, but because it was ridiculous and irrational that independent men should not triumph. Not for another twenty-five years did rationalist artisans of the Painite type seek their salvation through 'general union' and a co-operative commonwealth. But already poverty was for them a collective fact, to be solved and not merely escaped.

For and to these self-reliant poor Paine spoke. His analysis matters less than his unswerving and arrogant devotion to them, expressed with that 'profound reason and energy' which Condorcet so admired in him. When he spoke of human felicity, it was the end of poverty and inequality that he had in mind. The great question of the Revolution, in spite of his devotion to low taxes and free enterprise, was 'whether man shall inherit his rights and universal civilization take place. Whether the fruits of his labour shall be enjoyed by himself ... Whether robbery shall be banished from courts and wretchedness from countries.' It was that 'in countries which we call civilized we see age going to the workhouse and youth to the gallows'. It was that aristocracy ruled over 'that class of poor and wretched people who are so numerously dispersed all over England, who are to be told by a proclamation that they are happy'.

But Paine not only told his readers that poverty was incompatible with felicity and civilization. He told them that the light of reason had dawned in men like themselves to end poverty, and that Revolution showed how reason must triumph. He was the least romantic of rebels. Self-evident, practical, artisan common sense would transform the world. But the mere discovery that reason can cut like an axe through the undergrowth of custom which kept men enslaved and ignorant was a revelation.

Throughout the pages of *Age of Reason*, as through generations of working-class discussion groups, there glows the exaltation of the discovery how *easy* it is, once you have decided to see clearly, to discover that what the priests say about the Bible, or the rich about society, is wrong. Throughout *The Rights of Man* there shines the *obviousness* of the great truth. For Burke this revolutionary reason meant that 'all the decent drapery of life is to be rudely torn off' to leave 'our naked, shivering nature' revealed in all its defect. Paine was not afraid of a nakedness which revealed man, self-made, in the glory of his infinite possibilities. His humanity stood naked, like the Greek athletes, because it was poised for struggle and triumph. Even now, as we read those clear, simple sentences in which common sense rises to heroism and a cast-iron bridge spans the distance between Thetford and the New Jerusalem, we are exhilarated and moved. And if we believe in man, how can we fail, even now, to cheer him?

CHAPTER 2

The Machine-Breakers

The purpose of this essay is clearly stated on its first page. It was to defend British labour movements against what E. P. Thompson was later to call 'the enormous condescension of posterity'; and, one might add, against ideologists of our own times. It was first published in 1952 in the first issue of a historical journal that had been recently founded by the author and a group of friends, and is still flourishing, Past & Present.

It is perhaps time to reconsider the problem of machine-wrecking in the early industrial history of Britain and other countries. About this form of early working-class struggle misconceptions are still widely held, even by specialist historians. Thus, an excellent work, published in 1950, can still describe Luddism simply as a 'pointless, frenzied, industrial *Jacquerie*', and an eminent authority, who has contributed more than most to our knowledge of it, passes over the endemic rioting of the eighteenth century with the suggestion that it was the overflow of excitement and high spirits.[1] Such misconceptions are, I think, due to the persistence of views about the introduction of machinery elaborated in the early nineteenth century, and of views about labour and trade union history formulated in the late nineteenth century, chiefly by the Webbs and their Fabian followers. Perhaps we should distinguish views and assumptions. In much of the discussion of machine-breaking one can still detect the assumption of nineteenth-century middle-class economic apologists, that the workers must be taught not to run their heads against economic truth, however unpalatable; of Fabians and Liberals, that strong-arm methods in labour action are less effective than peaceful negotiation; of both, that the early labour movement did not know what it was doing, but merely reacted, blindly and gropingly, to the pressure of misery, as animals in the laboratory react to electric currents. The conscious views of most students may be summed up as follows: the triumph of mechanization was inevitable. We can understand and sympathize with the long rearguard action which all but a minority of favoured workers fought against the new system; but we must accept its pointlessness and its inevitable defeat.

The tacit assumptions are wholly debatable. In the conscious views there is obviously a good deal of truth. Both, however, obscure a good deal of history. Thus they make impossible any real study of the methods of working-class struggle in the pre-industrial period. Yet a very cursory glance at the labour movement of the eighteenth and early nineteenth century shows how dangerous it is to project the picture of desperate revolt and retreat, so familiar from 1815 to 1848, too far into the past. Within their limits – and they were intellectually and organizationally very narrow – the movements of the long economic boom which ended with the Napoleonic Wars were neither negligible nor wholly unsuccessful. Much of this success has been obscured by subsequent defeats: the strong organization of the West of England woollen industry lapsed completely, not to revive until the rise of general unions during the First World War; the craft societies of Belgian woollen workers, strong enough to win virtual collective agreements in the 1760s, lapsed after 1790 and until the early 1900s trade unionism was for practical purposes dead.[2]

Yet there is really no excuse for overlooking the power of these early movements, at any rate in Britain; and unless we realize that the basis of power lay in machine-wrecking, rioting and the destruction of property in general (or, in modern terms, sabotage and direct action), we shall not make sense of them.

To most non-specialists, the terms 'machine-wrecker' and Luddite are interchangeable. This is only natural, for the outbreaks of 1811–13, and of some years after Waterloo in this period, attracted more public attention than any others, and were believed to require more military force for their suppression. The 12,000 troops deployed against the Luddites greatly exceeded in size the army which Wellington took into the Peninsula in 1808.[3] Yet one's natural preoccupation with the Luddites tends to confuse the discussion of machine-breaking in general, which begins as a serious phenomenon (if it can be properly said to have a beginning) some time in the seventeenth century and continues until roughly 1830. Indeed, the series of farm-labourers' revolts which the Hammonds baptized the 'last labourers' rising' in 1830 was essentially a major offensive against farm-machinery, though it incidentally destroyed a fair amount of manufacturing equipment too.[4] In the first place, Luddism, treated as a single phenomenon for administrative purposes, covered several distinct types of machine-breaking, which for the most part existed independently of each other, but before and after. In the second place, the rapid defeat of Luddism led to a widespread belief that machine-breaking never succeeded.

Let us consider the first point. There are at least two types of machine-breaking, quite apart from the wrecking incidental to ordinary riots against high prices or other causes of discontent – for instance, some of the destruction in Lancashire in 1811 and Wiltshire in 1826.[5] The first sort implies no special hostility to machines as such, but is, under certain conditions, a normal means of putting pressure on employers or putters-out. As has been justly noted, the Nottinghamshire, Leicestershire and Derbyshire Luddites 'were using attacks upon machinery, whether new or old, as a means of coercing their employers into granting them concessions with regard to wages and other matters'.[6] This sort of wrecking was a traditional and established part of industrial conflict in the period of the domestic and manufacturing system, and the early stages of factory and mine. It was directed not only against machines, but also against raw material, finished goods and even the private property of employers, depending on what sort of damage these were most sensitive to. Thus in three months of agitation in 1802 the Wiltshire shearmen burned hay-ricks, barns and kennels of unpopular clothiers, cut down their trees and destroyed loads of cloth, as well as attacking and destroying their mills.[7]

The prevalence of this 'collective bargaining by riot' is well attested. Thus – to take merely the West of England textile trades – clothiers complained to Parliament in 1718 and 1724 that weavers 'threatened to pull down their houses and burn their work unless they would agree with their terms'.[8] The disputes of 1726–7 were fought, in Somerset, Wiltshire and Gloucestershire as well as in Devon, by weavers 'breaking into the houses [of masters and blacklegs], spoiling of wool, and cutting and destroying the pieces in the looms and the utensils of the trade'.[9] They ended in something like a collective contract. The great textile workers' riot at Melksham in 1738 began with workers 'cut[ting] all the chains in the looms belonging to Mr Coulthurst ... on account of his lowering of the Prices';[10] and three years later anxious employers in the same area were writing to London for protection against the men's demands that no outsiders should be employed, on pain of destroying wool.[11] And so on, throughout the century.

Again, where coalminers had reached the point of aiming their demands against employers of labour, they used the technique of wrecking. (For the most part, of course, miners' riots were still directed against high food prices, and the profiteers believed to be responsible for them.) Thus in the Northumberland coalfield the burning of pit-head machinery was part of the great riots of the 1740s, which won the men a sizeable wage-rise.[12] Again, machines were smashed, and coal set on fire in the riots of 1765, which won the miners the freedom to choose their employers at the end of the annual contract.[13] Acts of Parliament against the burning of pits were passed at intervals through the later part of the century.[14] As late as 1831 the strikers at Bedlington (Durham) wrecked winding-gear.[15]

The history of the frame-breaking in the East Midlands hosiery trade is too well known to need retelling.[16] Certainly the wrecking of machines was the most important weapon used in the famous riots of 1778 (the ancestors of Luddism), which were essentially part of a movement to resist wage-reductions.

In none of these cases – and others might be mentioned – was there any question of hostility to machines as such. Wrecking was simply a technique of trade unionism in the period before, and during the early phases of, the industrial revolution. (The fact that organized unions hardly as yet existed in the trades concerned does not greatly affect the argument. Nor does the fact that, with the coming of the industrial revolution, wrecking acquired new functions.) It was more useful when intermittent pressure had to be put on masters than when constant pressure had to be maintained: when wages and conditions changed suddenly, as among textile workers, or when annual contracts came up for simultaneous renewal, as among miners and seamen, rather than where, say, entry into the market had to be steadily restricted. It might be used by all sorts of people, from independent small producers, through the intermediate forms so typical of the domestic system of production, to more or less fully fledged wage-workers. Yet it was, in the main, concerned with disputes which arose from the typical social relationship of capitalist production, that between employing entrepreneurs and men who depended, directly or indirectly, on the sale of their labour-power to them, though this relationship existed as yet in primitive forms, and was entangled with the relationships of small independent production. It is worth noting that riot and wrecking of this type seem more frequent in eighteenth-century Britain, with its 'bourgeois' Revolution behind it, than in eighteenth-century France.[17] Certainly the movements of British weavers and miners are very different from the superficially trade-union-like activities of journeymen's associations in many more old-fashioned continental areas.[18]

The value of this technique was obvious, as a means both of

putting pressure on employers and of ensuring the essential solidarity of the workers.

The first point is admirably put in a letter from the town clerk of Nottingham in 1814.[19] The framework knitters, he reported, were now striking against the firm of J. and George Ray. Since this firm employed mainly men who owned their own looms, they were vulnerable to a simple withdrawal of work. Most of the firms, however, rented out the looms to knitters 'and through them acquire entire control of their workmen. Perhaps the most effectual manner in which the combination could coerce them was their former manner of carrying on war by destroying their frames.' In a domestic system of industry, where small groups of men, or single men, work scattered in numerous villages and cottages, it is, in any case, not easy to conceive of any other method which could guarantee an effective stoppage. Moreover, against comparatively small local employers, destruction of property – or the constant threat of destruction – would be pretty effective. Where, as in the cloth industry, both the raw material and the finished article were expensive, the destruction of wool or cloth might well be preferable to that of looms.[20] But in semi-rural industries even the burning of the employer's ricks, barns and houses might seriously affect his profit-and-loss account.

But the technique had another advantage. The habit of solidarity, which is the foundation of effective trade unionism, takes time to learn – even where, as in coalmines, it suggests itself naturally. It takes even longer to become part of the unquestioned ethical code of the working class. The fact that scattered framework knitters in the East Midlands could organize effective strikes against employing firms, for instance, argues a high level of 'trade union morale', higher than could normally be expected at that period of industrialization. Moreover, among badly paid men and women without strike funds, the danger of blacklegging is always acute. Machine-wrecking was one of the methods of counteracting these weaknesses. So long as the winding-gear of a Northumbrian pit was broken, or the blast-furnace of a Welsh iron-works out, there was at least a temporary guarantee that the plant would not be operated.[21] This was only one method, and not everywhere applicable. But the whole complex of activities which eighteenth- and early-nineteenth-century admin-istrators called 'Riot' achieved the same purpose. Everyone is familiar with the bands of militants or strikers from one works or locality, touring the whole region, calling out villages, workshops and factories by a mixture of appeals and force (though few workers needed much persuasion in the early stages of the fight).[22] Even much later mass demonstrations and meetings were an essential part of a labour dispute – not only to overawe the employers, but to keep the men together and in good heart. The periodic riots of the North-eastern seamen, at the time when hiring contracts were fixed, are a good example,[23] strikes of modern dockers another.[24] Clearly the Luddite technique was well adapted to this stage of industrial warfare. If British weavers in the eighteenth century (or American lumber-men in the twentieth) were a proverbially riotous body of men, there were sound technical reasons why they should be so.

On this point too we have some confirmation from a modern trade-union leader who, as a child, lived through the transition of a woollen industry from domestic to factory system. 'It is necessary to remember', writes Rinaldo Rigola,

> that in those pre-socialist times the working-class was a crowd, not an army. Enlightened, orderly, bureaucratic strikes were impossible.* The workers could only fight by means of demonstrations, shouting, cheering and cat-calling, intimidation and violence. Luddism and sabotage, even though not elevated into doctrines, had nevertheless to form part of the methods of struggle.[25]

We must now turn to the second sort of wrecking, which is generally regarded as the expression of working-class hostility to the new machines of the industrial revolution, especially labour-saving ones. There can, of course, be no doubt of the great feeling of opposition to new machines – a well-founded sentiment, in the opinion of no less an authority than the great Ricardo.[26] Yet three observations ought to be made. First, this hostility was neither so indiscriminate nor so specific as has often been assumed. Second, with local or sectional exceptions, it was surprisingly weak in practice. Lastly, it was by no means confined to workers, but was shared by the great mass of public opinion, including many manufacturers.

(i) The first point will be clear if we consider the problem as it faced the worker himself. He was concerned, not with technical progress in the abstract, but with the practical twin problems of preventing unemployment and maintaining the customary standard of life, which included non-monetary factors such as freedom and dignity, as well as wages. It was thus not to the machine as such that he objected, but to any threat to these – above all to the whole change in the social relations of production which threatened him. Whether this threat came from the machine or from elsewhere depended on circumstances. The Spitalfields weavers rioted against machines by which 'one man can do as much ... as near twenty

---

* Rigola was an extreme conservative among union leaders.

without them' in 1675, against wearers of printed calicoes in 1719, against immigrants working below the rate in 1736; and they wrecked looms against rate-cutting in the 1760s:[27] but the strategic objective of these movements was the same. Around 1800 the western weavers and shearmen were simultaneously in action; the former organized against the flooding of the labour market by extra workers, the latter against machines.[28] Yet their object, the control of the labour market, was the same. Conversely, where the change did not disadvantage the workers absolutely, we find no special hostility to machines. Among printers, the adoption of power-presses after 1815 seems to have caused little trouble. It was the later revolution in typesetting which, since it threatened wholesale down-grading, provoked a fight.[29] Between the early eighteenth and the mid-nineteenth century mechanization and new devices greatly increased the productivity of the coalminer; for instance, the intro-duction of shot-firing. However, as they left the position of the hewer untouched, we hear of no important movement to resist technical change, though pitmen were proverbially ultra-conservative and riotous. Restriction of output operated by workers under private enterprise is a different matter altogether. It can and does occur in wholly unmechanized industries – for instance, the building trade; nor does it depend on overt movements, organizations or outbreaks.

In some cases, indeed, the resistance to the machine was quite consciously resistance to the machine in the hands of the capitalist. The Lancashire machine-wreckers of 1778–80 distinguished clearly between spinning-jennies of twenty-four spindles or less, which they spared, and larger ones, suitable only for use in factories, which they destroyed.[30] No doubt in Britain, which was more familiar with social relations of production which anticipated those of industrial capitalism, this kind of behaviour is less unexpected than elsewhere. Nor should we read too much into it. The men of 1760 were still a good way from understanding the nature of the economic system they were about to face. Nevertheless, it is clear that theirs was not a simple fight against technical progress as such.

Nor is there, for the most part, any fundamental difference in the attitude of workers towards machines, taken as an isolated problem, in the earlier and later phases of industrialism. It is true that in most industries the object of preventing the introduction of undesirable machines has given way, with the coming of full mechanization, to the plan to 'capture' them for workers enjoying trade union standards and conditions, while taking all practicable steps to minimize tech-nological unemployment. This policy seems to have been adopted patchily after the 1840s[31] and during the Great Depression, more generally after the middle 1890s.[32] Nevertheless, there are plenty of examples of the straightforward opposition to machines which threaten to create unemployment or to downgrade labour even today.[33] In the normal working of a private-enterprise economy the reasons which led workers to distrust new machines in the 1810s remain persuasive in the 1960s.

(ii) The argument so far may help to explain why, after all, the resistance to machines was so small. The fact is not widely recognized, for the mythology of the pioneer age of industrialism, which men like Baines and Samuel Smiles reflected, has magnified the riots which actually occurred. The men of Manchester liked to think of themselves not only as monuments of enterprise and economic wisdom, but also – a more difficult task – as heroes. Wadsworth and Mann have reduced the riots of eighteenth-century Lancashire to more modest proportions.[34] In fact we have record of only a few really widespread wrecking movements such as that of the farm-labourers, which probably destroyed most threshing-machines in the areas affected,[35] the specialized campaigns of the small body of shearmen in Britain and elsewhere,[36] and perhaps the riots against power-looms in 1826.[37] The Lancashire wreckings of 1778–80 and 1811 were confined to limited areas and limited numbers of mills. (The great East Midland movements of 1811–12 were not, as we have seen, directed against new machinery at all.) This is not only due to the fact that some mechanization was regarded as harmless. As has been pointed out,[38] most machines tended to be introduced in times of rising prosperity, when employment was improving and opposition, not fully mobilized, could be temporarily dissipated. By the time distress recurred, the strategic moment for opposing the new devices was past. New workers serving them had already been recruited, the old hand-operatives stood outside, capable only of random destruction of their competitor, no longer of imposing themselves on the machine. (Unless, of course, they were lucky enough to possess a specialized market which was not affected by machine-production, as hand-bootmakers and tailors did in the 1870s and 1880s.) One reason why the wrecking by the shearmen was so much more persistent and serious than that by others was that these highly skilled and organized key-men retained much control over the labour market, even after partial mechanization.[39]

(iii) The mythology of the pioneer industrialists has also obscured the overwhelming sympathy for machine-wreckers in all parts of the population. In Nottinghamshire not a single Luddite was denounced, though plenty of small masters must have known perfectly well who broke their frames.[40] In Wiltshire – where the cloth-finishing middlemen and small masters were known to sympathize with the shearmen[41] – the real terrorists of 1802 could not be discovered.[42] The merchants and woollen manufacturers of Rossendale themselves passed resolutions against power-looms some years before the men smashed them.[43] During the 1830 labourers' rising the clerk to the magistrates in Hindon, Wiltshire, reported that 'where the mobs have not destroyed the machinery, the farmers have exposed the same for the purpose of being destroyed',[44] and Lord Melbourne had to send a sharply worded circular to magistrates who had 'in many instances recommended the Discontinuance of the Employment of Machines used for thrashing out Corn and for other Purposes'. 'Machines', he argued, 'are as much entitled to the protection of the Law as any other Description of Property.'[45]

Nor is this surprising. The fully developed capitalist entrepreneurs formed a small minority, even among those whose position was technically that of profit-makers. The small shopkeeper or local master did not want an economy of limitless expansion, accumulation and technical revolution, the savage jungle pursuit which doomed the weak to bankruptcy and wage-earning status. His ideal was the secular dream of all 'little men', which has found periodic expression in Leveller, Jeffersonian or Jacobin radicalism, a small-scale society of modest property-owners and comfortably-off wage-earners, without great distinctions of wealth or power; though doubtless, in its quiet way, getting wealthier and more comfortable all the time. It was an unrealizable ideal, never more so than in the most rapidly evolving of societies. Let us remember, however, that those to whom it appealed in early-nineteenth-century Europe made up the majority of the population, and outside such industries as cotton, of the employing class.[46] But even the genuine capitalist entrepreneur could be in two minds about machines. The belief that he must inevitably favour technical progress as a matter of self-interest has no foundation, even if the experience of French capitalism and of later British capitalism were not available. Quite apart from the possibility of making more money without machines than with them (in sheltered markets and so on), only rarely were new machines immediate and obvious paying propositions.

There is, in the history of any technical device, a 'threshold of profit' which is crossed rather late – the larger the capital that has to be sunk in a machine, the later. Hence, perhaps, the proverbial lack of business success of inventors, who sink their own and other people's money in their projects while they are still inevitably imperfect and by no means clearly superior to their non-mechanized rivals.[47] Of course, the free-enterprise economy could overcome these

obstacles. What has been described as the 'vast secular boom' of
1775–1875 created situations, here and there, which provided entrepreneurs in some industries – for instance, cotton – with the impetus
to leap across the 'threshold'.[48] The very mechanism of capital
accumulation in a society undergoing revolution provided others. So
long as competition operated, the technical advances of the pioneer
section were spread over quite a wide field. Yet we must not forget
that the pioneers were minorities. Most capitalists took the new
machine in the first instance not as an offensive weapon, to win
bigger profits, but as a defensive one, to protect themselves against
the bankruptcy which threatened the laggard competitor. We are not
surprised to find E. C. Tufnell in 1834 accusing 'many of the masters
in the cotton trade ... of the disgraceful behaviour of instigating
workmen to turn out against those manufacturers who were the
first to enlarge their mules'.[49] Petty producer and run-of-the-mill
entrepreneur were in an ambiguous position, but without the independent power to change it. They might dislike the need for new
machines, either because they disrupted their way of life, or because,
on any rational accounting, they were not really good business at
the moment. In any case they saw them as strengthening the position
of the large modernized entrepreneur, the main rival. Working-class
revolts against machines gave such men their chance; often they
took it. One may reasonably agree with the student of French
machine-wrecking who observes that 'sometimes the detailed study
of a local incident reveals the Luddite movement less as an agitation
of workmen, than as an aspect of competition between the backward
and the progressive shop-owner or manufacturer'.[50]

If the innovating entrepreneur had the bulk of public opinion
against him, how did he succeed in imposing himself? By means of
the state. It has been well remarked that in Britain the Revolution of
1640–60 marks a turning-point in the state's attitude towards
machinery. After 1660 the traditional hostility to devices which take
the bread out of the mouths of honest men gave way to the
encouragement of profit-making enterprise, at whatever social cost.[51]
This is one of the facts which justifies us in regarding the seventeenth-
century Revolution as the real political beginning of modern British
capitalism. Throughout the subsequent period the central state apparatus tended to be, if not ahead of public opinion on economic matters,
then at least more willing to consider the claims of the fully capitalist
entrepreneur – except, of course, where these clashed with older and
bigger vested interests. The Squire Westerns in some counties might
still toast the shadow of a vanished feudal hierarchy in an unchanging
society: there was no significant trace of feudal policy in the Whig

governments, at any rate after 1688. London sympathy was to prove of inestimable value to the new industrialists when, in the last third of the century, their meteoric rise began. On issues of agrarian, commercial or financial policy Lancashire might be in conflict with London, but not on the fundamental supremacy of the profit-making employer. It was the unreformed Parliament in its most ferociously conservative period which introduced full *laissez-faire* into the relations between employer and worker. Classical free-enterprise economics dominated the debates. Nor did London hesitate to rap its more old-fashioned and sentimental local representatives over the knuckles if they failed 'to maintain and uphold the rights of property of every description, against violence and aggression'.[52]

Yet until the latter part of the eighteenth century the support of the state for the innovating entrepreneur was not unqualified. The political system of Britain from 1660 to 1832 was designed to serve manufacturers only insofar as they bought their way into the ring of vested interests of an older type – commercially minded landlords, merchants, financiers, nabobs and so on. At best they could only hope for a share of the pork barrel proportionate to their pressure, and in the early eighteenth century the 'modern' manufacturers were as yet only occasional groups of provincials. Hence, at times, a certain neutrality of the state in labour matters, at any rate until after the middle of the eighteenth century.[53] Western clothiers complained bitterly that the majority of local JPs was biased against them.[54] The attitude of the national government in the weavers' riots of 1726–7 contrasts strikingly with that of the Home Office from the 1790s on. London regretted that the local clothiers needlessly antagonized the men by arresting rioters; pooh-poohed suggestions that these were seditious; suggested that both parties get together amicably, so that a proper petition might be framed and Parliament could take action.[55] When this was done, Parliament sanctioned a collective agreement which gave the men very much what they wanted, at the cost of a perfunctory 'apology for past riots'.[56] Again, the frequency of *ad hoc* legislation in the eighteenth century[57] tends to show that no systematic, consistent and general attempt was made to enforce it. As the century progressed, the voice of the manufacturer increasingly became the voice of government in these matters; but earlier it was still possible for the men occasionally to fight sections of the masters on more or less fair terms.

We now come to the last and most complex problem: how effective was machine-breaking? It is, I think, fair to claim that collective bargaining by riot was at least as effective as any other means of bringing trade union pressure, and probably *more* effective than any other means available before the era of national trade unions to such groups as weavers, seamen and coalminers. That is not to claim much. Men who did not enjoy the natural protection of small numbers and scarce apprenticed skills, which might be safeguarded by restricted entry to the market and strong hiring monopolies, were in any case bound normally to be on the defensive. Their success therefore should be measured by their ability to keep conditions stable – for example, stable wage-rates – against the perpetual and well-advertised desire of masters to reduce them to starvation level.[58] This required an unremitting and effective fight. It may be argued that stability on paper was constantly undermined by the slow inflation of the eighteenth century, which steadily rigged the game against wage-earners;[59] but it would be asking too much of eighteenth-century activities to cope with that. Within their limits, one can hardly deny that Spitalfields silk-weavers benefited from their riots.[60] The disputes of keelmen, sailors and miners in the North-east, of which we have record, ended, as often as not, with victory or acceptable compromise. Moreover, whatever happened in individual engagements, riot and machine-wrecking provided the workers with valuable reserves at all times. The eighteenth-century master was constantly aware that an intolerable demand would produce, not a temporary loss of profits, but the destruction of capital equipment. In 1829 a leading colliery manager was asked by the Lords' Committee whether a reduction of wages in the Tyne and Wearside coalmines could 'be effected without danger to the tranquillity of the district, or risking the destruction of all the mines, with all the machinery, and the valuable stock vested in them'. He thought not.[61] Inevitably, the employer faced with such hazards paused before he provoked them, for fear that 'his property and perhaps his life [might] be endangered thereby'.[62] 'Far more masters than one might expect', Sir John Clapham noted with unjustified surprise, supported the retention of the Spitalfields Silkweavers' Acts, for under them, they argued 'the district lived in a state of quietude and repose'.[63]

Could riot and machine-breaking, however, hold up the advance of technical progress? Patently it could not hold up the triumph of industrial capitalism as a whole. On a smaller scale, however, it was by no means the hopelessly ineffective weapon that it has been made out to be. Thus, fear of the Norwich weavers is supposed to have prevented the introduction of machines there.[64] The Luddism of the Wiltshire shearmen in 1802 certainly postponed the spread of mechanization; a petition of 1816 notes that 'in time of War there was no giggs nor Frames at Trowbridge but sad to relate it is now Increasing Every Day'.[65] Paradoxically enough, the wrecking by the helpless farm-labourers in 1830 seems to have been the most effective of all. Though the wage-concessions were soon lost, the threshing machines did not return on anything like the old scale.[66] How much of such successes was due to the men, how much to the latent or passive Luddism of the employers themselves, we cannot, however, determine. Nevertheless, whatever the truth of the matter, the initiative came from the men, and to that extent they can claim an important share in any such successes.

CHAPTER 3

Political Shoemakers*
Co-written with Joan W. Scott

The members of certain trades and professions are traditionally regarded as having common characteristics, but historians, while observing this, have rarely asked why. This is an attempt to explain the proverbial radicalism of shoemakers. The two authors discovered their common interest in this subject at the wonderful international Round Tables on Social History organized by Clemens Heller of the Maison des Sciences de l'Homme in the 1970s. Their co-operative effort was published in Past & Present, no. 89, in 1980 and is reprinted by permission of Joan Wallach Scott.

'He had gone deeper into Arminianism and politics than any of his fellows. The *Methodist Magazine* and the *Weekly Dispatch* were regularly sent to him by his brother. He always had plenty of shoemaking, and was more independent than either the farmers or labourers. He used to make uncivil remarks about the landlords and the House of Lords, the House of Commons, the new poor law, bishops, parsons, Corn laws, the church, and class legislation.'[1]

'A very curious thing is that each trade develops in the artisans practising it, a specific character, a particular temperament. The butcher is generally serious and full of his own importance, the house painter is thoughtless and a rake, the tailor is sensual, the grocer stupid, the porter curious and prattling, the shoemaker and cobbler, finally, are gay, sometimes even lively, with a song always on their lips ... Despite the simplicity of their tastes, the makers of new and old shoes are always distinguished by a restless, sometimes aggressive spirit and by an enormous tendency to loquacity. Is there a riot? Does an orator emerge from the crowd? It is without doubt a cobbler who has come to make a speech to the people.'[2]

---

* We would like to thank William Sewell Jr, E. P. Thompson and Alfred Young for their helpful comments.

I

The political radicalism of nineteenth-century shoemakers is proverbial. Social historians of a variety of persuasions have described the phenomenon and assumed it needed no explanation. A historian of the German Revolution of 1848, for example, concluded that it was 'not accidental' that shoemakers 'played a dominant role in the activities of the people'. Historians of the 'Swing' riots in England referred to the shoemakers' 'notorious radicalism' and Jacques Rougerie accounted for the shoemakers' prominence in the Paris Commune by referring to their 'traditionally militancy'. Even so heterodox a writer as Theodore Zeldin accepts the common view on this point.[3] The present paper attempts to account for the remarkable reputation of shoemakers as political radicals.

To say that shoemakers, or any other trade, have a reputation for radicalism may, of course, mean one or more of three things: a reputation for militant action in movements of social protest, whether confined to the trade in question or not; a reputation for sympathy or association with, or activity in, movements of the political left; and a reputation as what might be called ideologists of the common people. Though very likely to be associated, these are not the same. Apprentices and unmarried journeymen in traditional corporate crafts were likely to be mobilized readily, without any necessary connection with whatever counted at the time as political radicalism. French *universitaires* have, at least since the Dreyfus period, had a reputation for standing well to the left of their students. This did not necessarily imply, though it did not exclude, militant collective action. Australian sheep-shearers, though often both militant and associated with the left, are not generally thought of as greatly interested in ideology,* whereas village schoolteachers often are.

Shoemakers as a trade had, in the nineteenth century, a reputation for radicalism in all three senses. They were militant both on trade matters and in wider movements of social protest. Though shoemakers' unions were limited to certain sections or localities of a very large trade, and only intermittently effective, they were organized on a national scale rather early in both France and Switzerland, not to

---

* The late Ian Turner of the Australian National University, Canberra, cited the case of a large number of these men, arrested after the October Revolution for holding a meeting in favour of insurrection and soviets. A careful search for subversive literature produced no printed matter of any kind, except a leaflet which a number carried in their pockets. It read: 'If water rots your boots, what will it do to your stomach?'

mention England where the London union, founded in 1792, was said to extend nationally in 1804. Shoemakers and carpenters were the first members of the Federation of Workers of the Argentine Region (1890), the first attempt at a national union body for that country. They occasionally struck on a large scale and were among the most strike-prone trades in France during the July monarchy. They were also prominent in revolutionary crowds. Their role as political activists can be documented amply. Of the persons active in the British Chartist movement whose occupations are known, shoemakers formed much the largest single group after the weavers and unspecified 'labourers': more than twice the number of building-trade workers and more than 10 per cent of all occupationally described militants. In the taking of the Bastille, or at least among those arrested for it, the twenty-eight shoemakers were exceeded only by the cabinet-makers, joiners and locksmiths – and in the riots of the Champ de Mars and in August 1792 by no other trade.[4] Among those arrested in Paris for opposing the *coup d'état* of 1851, shoemakers were most numerous.[5] The workers involved in the Paris Commune of 1871 who suffered the highest proportion of deportations after its defeat were, as Jacques Rougerie observes, 'of course, as always, the shoemakers'.[6] When rebellion broke out in the German city of Konstanz in April 1848, the shoemakers provided by far the largest single component of the rioters, almost as much as the next most riotous trades (the tailors and joiners) put together.[7] At the other end of the world, the first anarchist ever recorded in a provincial town in Rio Grande do Sul in Brazil was an Italian shoemaker in 1897, while the only craft union reported as participating in the first (anarchist-inspired) Workers' Congress of Curitiba (Brazil) was the Shoemakers' Association.[8]

Militancy and left-wing activism alone, however, do not distinguish shoemakers as a group from some other craftsmen, who were at times at least as prominent in these respects. Among the casualties of the March Revolution of 1848 in Berlin, joiners were more than twice as numerous, and tailors distinctly more numerous than shoemakers, though the trades were of comparable size.[9] Carpenters and tailors were as 'strike-prone' as shoemakers during the July monarchy. French revolutionary crowds included proportionately more printers, joiners, locksmiths and building workers than were in the Parisian population. If eleven shoemakers formed the largest group among the forty-three anarchists arrested in Lyon in 1892, construction workers were not far behind.[10] Tailors are associated with shoemakers as typical activists in the 1848 Revolution in Germany, and if both were prominent among the German travelling journeymen who made up the bulk of the Communist League ('the workers' club is small and consists only of shoemakers and tailors', Weydemeyer wrote to Marx in 1850),[11] it seems clear that the tailors were more prominent. Indeed the apparently large number of shoemaker activists may sometimes merely reflect the size of a trade which, in Germany and Britain, constituted much the largest single artisan occupation.[12] The collective actions of the group do not therefore account for the shoemakers' radical reputation.

There can be little doubt, however, that as worker–intellectuals and ideologists shoemakers were exceptional. Once again, they were obviously not unique although, as we shall see, in rural villages and small market towns they had less competition from other settled artisans. Certainly their role as spokesmen and organizers of country people in nineteenth-century England is clear from any study of the 'Swing' riots of 1830 or of rural political radicalism. Hobsbawm and Rudé report that in 1830 the average riotous parish had from two to four times as many shoemakers as the average tranquil one.[13] The local shoemaker quoting Cobbett – John Adams in Kent, William Winkworth in Hampshire – is a familiar figure.[14] The craft's character as 'red-hot politicians' was proverbial. In the shoemaking centre of Northampton, election days were celebrated as 'traditional holidays' as much as the spring and autumn race meetings.[15] Yet the striking fact is the connection between politics and articulate literacy. Who says cobbler surprisingly often says journalist and versifier, preacher and lecturer, writer and editor. This impression is not easy to quantify, though shoemakers form the largest single group – three – in a sample of nineteen French 'worker–poets' of the period before 1850, all of radical views:[16] Sylvain Lapointe of the Yonne, who stood as a candidate in 1848; Hippolyte Tampucci, the editor of Le Grapilleur; and Gonzalle of Rheims, the editor of Le Républicain.[17] The list could be easily added to – one thinks of Faustin Bonnefoi, editor of the Fourierist newspaper in Louis-Philippe's Marseille,[18] of the autodidact 'Efrahem', who wrote pamphlets urging 'an association of workers of every corps d'état',[19] and of Citizen Villy, a boot-maker who spoke at the first Communist Banquet in 1840 and who had published a pamphlet on the abolition of poverty.[20]

Of course nobody would claim that all or even the majority among shoemaker activists were artisan-intellectuals. Indeed we have examples of militant shoemakers who were distinctly not great readers, at least in their days of activity, such as George Hewes, the last survivor of the Boston Tea Party.[21] Though as a craft shoemakers seem to have been more literate than the average, a fair percentage of bad readers would not be surprising in so large a trade containing so many proverbially poor men.[22] The less literate shoemaker may even have become more common as the trade expanded and was diluted during the nineteenth century. And yet the existence of an unusually, perhaps a uniquely, large number of shoemaker–intellectuals is impossible to deny, even if it may be supposed that such persons would draw special attention to themselves in a largely non-literate society. When ideology took a primarily religious form, they pondered the Scriptures, sometimes coming to unorthodox conclusions: it was they who brought Calvinism into the Cevennes,[23] who prophesied, preached (and wrote) messianism, mysticism and heresy.[24] In the secular era the majority of the (largely Spencean communist) Cato Street conspirators were shoemakers, and their attraction to anarchism was notorious. Emile Pouget's *Le Père Peinard* symbolically carried on its cover the picture of a cobbler in his workshop.[25] More generally there is, at least in English, a substantial literature of collective shoemaker biography in the nineteenth century, such as, to our knowledge, exists for no other craft.[26] The overwhelming majority of its subjects are commemorated for intellectual achievements. Their success in this field may explain the appearance of such compendia in the age of self-improvement.

It may even be argued that such proverbs as 'Shoemaker stick to your last', which are found in many countries from antiquity to the industrial revolution, indicate precisely this tendency of shoemakers to express opinions on matters which ought to be left to the officially learned – 'Let the cobbler stick to his last and let the learned men write the books'; 'Preaching cobblers make bad shoes'; and so on. Certainly similar proverbs are distinctly less common with reference to other crafts.[27]

Even if we leave such indirect evidence aside, the number of shoemaker–intellectuals is impressive. They were not necessarily radicals, though their eighteenth- and nineteenth-century eulogists preferred to dwell on their achievements in fields which would impress socially superior readers – learning, literature and religion – while not concealing their reputation as folk-politicians. Still, the historians will not fail to note that the religion in which shoemakers distinguished themselves when not associated with anticlericalism and atheism[28] was often heterodox and radical by contemporary standards. One thinks of Jakob Boehme, the mystic, persecuted by the Lutheran Church of his city, and George Fox, the Quaker. One also notes the combination of radicalism and literary activities, as in Thomas Holcroft, the ex-shoemaker playwright and English Jacobin, in Friedrich Sander, the founder of the Vienna Workers' Union in 1848, who also wrote poems,[29] and in the anarchist Jean Grave, shoemaker-turned-printer, and editor of magazines with a distinct literary–artistic bent.[30]

We cannot of course allow the shoemakers a monopoly of plebeian intellectual activities. Samuel Smiles, always the apostle of self-help, in an essay on 'Astronomers and Students in Humble Life: A New Chapter in the "Pursuit of Knowledge under Difficulties"' lists examples from other trades also.[31] Nevertheless the fact that 'in country places, it is very common to find the situation of parish clerk held by a shoemaker' suggests an uncommon degree of literacy.[32] In any case the intellectualism of shoemakers as a trade impressed more than one observer, and could not readily be explained. Both W. E. Winks and the *Crispin Anecdotes* confessed themselves baffled by it, but agreed 'that more thinking men are to be found shoemakers, as a fraternity, than most others'.[33] In his autobiography the radical shoemaker John Brown commented that: 'Persons possessing the advantages of a more refined education would hardly guess what an amount of knowledge and book-learning is to be met with amongst the members of my ancient trade.'[34] In France shoemakers were said to be 'thinkers ... [they] think about things they have seen or heard ... they fathom more than most the concerns of the workers'.[35] In England an eighteenth-century verse recorded that:

> A cobbler once in days of yore
> Sat musing at his cottage door.
> He liked to read old books, he said,
> And then to ponder, what he'd read.[36]

In Russia a character in a work of Maxim Gorki is described as 'like so many other shoemakers, easily fascinated by a book'.[37]

The shoemaker's reputation as popular philosopher and politician predates the era of industrial capitalism and extends well beyond the typical countries of the capitalist economy. Indeed one has the sense that the nineteenth-century radical shoemakers were fulfilling a role long associated with members of their trade. The patron saints of the craft, Crispin and Crispinian, were martyred because they preached unorthodoxy to their customers in their workshop in Soissons – in this instance Christianity under the pagan Emperor Diocletian.[38] In Act I of Shakespeare's *Julius Caesar* a cobbler appears leading a crowd of protesters through the streets. The journeymen in Dekker's *Shoemaker's Holiday*, an Elizabethan exercise in public relations on behalf of the 'gentle craft' of London, appear characteristically militant: they threaten to leave their master if a travelling journeyman is not given a job. Almost contemporary with these theatrical allusions, we find the following reference to the shoemakers Robert Hyde and a certain Lodge of Sherborne:

And he further sayeth that a little before Christmas one Robte Hyde of Sherborne shomaker seinge this depont passinge by his doore, called to him & desyered to have some conference with him and after some speches, he entered into these speches. Mr Scarlet you have preachett vnto vs that there is a god, a heaven & a hell & a resurreccion after this Liffe, and that we shall geive an accompte of or worckes, and that the soule is immortall; but nowe sayeth he here is a companye aboute this towne that saye, that hell is noe other but povertie & penurye in this worlde; and heaven is noe other but to be ritch, and enioye pleasueres; and that we dye like beastes, and when we ar gonne there is noe more rememberance of vs &c. and such like. But this Examint did neither then demande whome they were; neither did he deliuer any particulers vnto him And further saieth That it is generally reported by almost euery bodye in Sherborne, and the sayd Allen & his man aforesayde ar Atheistes. And alsoe he sayeth there is one Lodge a shomaker in Sherborne accompted an Atheiste.[39]

The shoemaker, as what the poet Gray called a 'village Hampden', is commemorated in an engraving of Timothy Bennett (died 1756) of Hampton Wick, Middlesex. He challenged the king's closing of a right of way through Bushy Park by threatening to bring a prosecution – and won. The engraving represents him in 'a firm and complacent aspect, sitting down in the attitude of his conversation with ... [Lord Halifax]' (the ranger of the royal park), symbolizing a democratic confrontation with, and triumph over, privilege.[40] Another source describes a shoemaker walking 'from village to village with his kit in a basket on his back. On getting a job he would drop down on the doorstep, and while at work, he and his customer would strike up with a song, or talk politics'.[41] The notoriety of shoemakers as leaders led Sir Robert Peel to ask some shoemakers, who had come to him to press the demands of their trade society: 'How is it ... that you people are foremost in every movement? ... If there is a conspiracy or political movement, I always find one of you in it.'[42] E. P. Thompson quotes a Yorkshire satirist's 1849 portrait of a 'Village Politician':

He is, typically, a cobbler, an old man and the sage of his industrial village: 'He has a library that he rather prides himself upon. It is a strange collection ... There is the 'Pearl of Great Price' and 'Cobbett's Twopenny Trash' ... 'The Wrongs of Labour' and 'The Rights of Man', 'The History of the French Revolution' and Bunyan's 'Holy War' ... It warms his old heart like a quart of mulled ale, when he hears of a successful revolution, – a throne tumbled, kings flying, and princes scattered abroad...'.[43]

Englishmen believed, moreover, that French shoemakers shared these traits. More than one account of the French Revolution described 'cobblers ... haranguing under the splendid domes of the Valois and the Capets' and then leading crowds to torture and murder the king.[44] In France as well as in England the shoemaker was known for his love of liberty and his role as village politician. Shoemakers were admired for 'independence of their opinions'. 'The freedom of the people', said one writer, 'is expressed in their demeanour.'[45] The revolt of the Maillotins in 1380 was said to have been sparked by a shoemaker, whose impassioned oration inflamed a crowd.[46] And the downfall of Concini, the Italian statesman, in 1617, was said to have been assured by one Picard, a shoemaker and popular orator, who insulted the admiral when he was alive and defiled him when dead by roasting and eating his heart.[47] Anthropophagy is not a characteristic usually associated with shoemakers, unlike a taste for strong drink, but the shoemakers' reputation for radicalism was deserved and it was not limited to France.

II

To what extent was the shoemaker as philosopher and politician a product of his craft? There seem to be two aspects of this question, one having to do with literacy, the other with independence.

The question of literacy and the shoemaker's proverbial fondness for books and reading is difficult to explain, as there is nothing in the nature of the craft to suggest any occupational connection with the printed word – as among printers. The desperate guesses that their skills with leather were often called upon to bind or repair books, and that sometimes their stalls adjoined those of booksellers, appear to be unsupported by any evidence.[48] Moreover, so far as we can tell, there is nothing in the customs and traditions of the craft journeymen which stresses or even implies a special interest in reading; and though Hans Sachs of Nuremberg was, as every opera-lover knows, the most famous of the *Meistersinger*, there is no evidence that shoemakers were disproportionately represented among these poetic artisans. The link between shoemakers and books could not have been established before the invention and popularization of printing, since the written word could hardly have been directly accessible to the poor before then. The general character of the shoemakers' journeymen customs suggests that they have been largely formed by this time.[49] It may, of course, be argued that once books were available they were naturally likely to attract a profession given to speculation and discussion. Nevertheless the question remains.

It may be that the relatively primitive division of labour in shoe-making allowed or compelled vast numbers of shoemakers to work entirely alone. Certainly Mayhew surmised that it was 'the solitude of their employment developing their internal resources' which accounted for their being 'a stern, uncompromising and reflecting race'.[50] Itinerant cobblers were, of course, isolated workers. But even in his workshop the lonely shoemaker was typical. In Germany in 1882 two-thirds of them employed no assistants at all.

Yet even the single cobbler was not culturally isolated. He might receive his training in a small establishment. The master, a few journeymen and one or two apprentices, as well as the master's wife, seems to have constituted the ideal-typical artisan establishment. In the most traditional regions of nineteenth-century Germany there were on average only 2.4 or 2.6 journeymen per apprentice.[51] The rapid turnover of journeymen, however, would widen both the masters' and the apprentices' horizon, and journeymen were notori-ous and prolonged travellers. A Swabian rural shoemaker describes their impact on him as an apprentice: 'There were much-travelled and intelligent people among the journeymen. So I heard and learned a good deal.' And he in turn worked in seventeen establishments in fifteen different places between finishing his apprenticeship and setting up as a small master and social-democratic activist.[52] If, as was the case in Jena, journeymen stayed only six months on average in a shop, the typical apprentice would, in the course of three years, have close contact with perhaps fifteen widely travelled men, and the typical travelling journeyman with a great many more.

The journeymen would meet each other not only in workshops but on the road and in the inns which functioned as houses of call, where jobs and relief, asked for and received in highly ritualized form,[53] were to be found. There was plenty of occasion for discussing the problems of the trade, the news of the day and the diffusion of information generally. In larger cities shoemakers, like most other tradesmen, might live and work in specialized shoemakers' rows or streets. In centres of market shoemaking, urban or rural, there was no shortage of others in the trade. Since the work took little space, several semi-proletarian outworkers or garret-masters might share a workshop together. Even the loneliest cobbler had probably been socialized in the culture of the 'gentle craft' at some time.

That 'shoemaker culture', which Peter Burke has recently described as stronger than any other craft culture except the weavers'[54] was unusually marked and persistent. In Scotland, for instance, its Catholic patron saint survived the Calvinist reformation as 'King Crispin', and in England St Crispin's Day was celebrated as a shoemakers' holiday, often with processions of the craft, until well into the nineteenth century, or was revived by journeymen for political purposes, as in Norwich in 1813. It was still alive or remembered in some purely rural areas at the end of the century. The early decline of organized gilds and corporations in England makes such survivals all the more impressive.[55]

Yet there appears to be nothing in the formal or informal craft traditions that linked shoemakers specifically to intellectualism, or even to radicalism. They stressed pride in the trade, based largely on its indispensability to high and low, young and old. This is the commonest theme of journeymen shoemakers' songs.[56] They stressed independence, especially journeyman independence, as proved by the shoemaker's control over his time of work and leisure – his capacity to celebrate Saint Monday and other holidays as he chose.[57] Since social leisure and drink were inseparable, they also stressed drinking, an activity for which shoemakers were celebrated, and that other by-product of bar-room culture, settling disputes by fighting. 'Look for the best beer where carters and shoemakers drink,' says a Polish proverb. Johann Nestroy's farce *Lumpazivagabundus* (1836), which follows the fortunes of three ideal-typical journeymen, presents its shoemaker both as an amateur astronomer (his interest in comets may be inspired by the reading of almanacs) and as a spectacular and quarrelsome soak. But these are not particularly intellectual associations.

Perhaps the most plausible explanation of the trade's intellectualism derives from the fact that a shoemaker's work was both sedentary and physically undemanding. Probably it was physically the least taxing labour for men in the countryside. As a result small, weak or physically handicapped boys were habitually put to this trade. Such was the case of Jakob Boehme, the mystic,[58] of Robert Bloomfield, author of *The Farmer's Boy*,[59] of William Gifford, later editor of the *Quarterly Review*, who was 'put ... to the plough' but 'soon found ... too weak for such heavy work', of John Pounds, pioneer of the 'Ragged Schools', who became a shoemaker when an accident maimed him and drove him out of his original trade as a shipwright,[60] of John Lobb, founder of a celebrated firm in St James's which still exists,[61] and almost certainly of numerous others. In Pomeranian Loitz 'almost the only people who devote themselves to this trade are crippled or unsuited to agricultural or industrial work'. Hence the tendency of village shoemakers unable to make ends meet by their craft to

27

take (as in the town of Heide, Schleswig) such second jobs as nightwatchmen, school caretakers, messengers, waiters, town criers, assistants to the pastor or assistant postmen and street sweepers.[62] American naval recruiting orders in 1813 insisted on recruiting 'none but strong, healthy, able men. Landsmen may be entered as ordy. seamen ... but on no account ship Tailors, Shoemakers or Blacks [sic] as these from their accustomed occupations rarely possess physical force.'[63]

The number of deformed shoemakers and tailors ('crooked, hump-backed, lame') in the Italian corporate processions of these crafts was noted by Ramazzini.[64] Unlike the tailors, however, the shoemakers were not proverbially associated with feebleness, an observation supported by nineteenth-century statistics of British occupational mortality.[65] On the other hand the *lame* cobbler is recorded as early as the Latin dramatist Plautus. Perhaps the frequency of rural shoemakers who combined their trade with agricultural activities is relevant here. Nevertheless the craft was at least to some extent selected by boys incapable of competing with other labouring men of their age in the conventionally valued physical activities. This may have provided an incentive to acquire other kinds of prestige. And here the semi-routinized nature of much of their work, which could readily be combined with thinking, watching and conversation, may have suggested intellectual alternatives. Shoemakers working together in larger workshops were among those crafts (tailors and cigar-makers are others) which developed the institution of the 'reader' – one of the men taking turns to read newspapers or books out aloud, or an old soldier being hired to read, or the youngest boy having the duty to fetch and read the news. (George Bloomfield, a minor shoemaker–poet, not unreasonably suggested that this was the point to which 'those who say that "Shoemakers are politicians" might trace the solution of their wonder'.)[66] Such quiet and unde-manding indoor occupations existed in towns, but in the villages it is difficult to think of others – certainly not the blacksmiths or the wheelwrights.[67]

The shoemaker's work thus permitted thinking and discussion while working; his frequent isolation during working hours threw him on his own intellectual resources; he was selectively recruited from boys with a likely incentive to compensate for their physical handicaps; the training of apprentices and the tramping of jour-neymen exposed him to the culture of the trade and to the culture and politics of a wider world. We may perhaps add that the lightness of his tool-kit actually made it easier than in some other trades to carry books with him – a fact for which there is also some evidence.

Whether all this provides an adequate, still more a testable, explanation of his bookishness, we cannot be certain. Nevertheless three things are clear.

First, the more literate artisan crafts shoemakers, as we shall shortly see, were unusual in being widely distributed in predominantly illiterate rural and small-town environments, where they could become unofficial clerks or labourers' intellectuals. They had little competition. Secondly, once the popular image of the shoemaker as intellectual and radical existed (as it undoubtedly did) it must have affected reality in several ways. Every time a shoemaker fitted the role, he confirmed popular expectations. As a result shoemakers' behaviour in this role was probably more often noted, recorded and commented upon. The popular image may have attracted young men with literary or philosophical tastes and political interests; or conversely, boys brought into contact with philosophic and radical cobblers might acquire an interest in these matters. Finally, the culture of the trade might develop some of these traits among its practitioners not only because material conditions facilitated them, but because its mores did not stand in the way. In many occupations a 'reading man' would have such tastes knocked or mocked out of him. Among shoemakers they might be more easily accepted as one version of behaviour compatible with group norms.

The shoemaker's independence was clearly tied to the material conditions of his trade and from it stemmed his ability to be a village politician. In addition the humble status of the trade and the relative poverty of its recruits, at least in the nineteenth century, help to explain its radicalism.

The two characteristics are linked. The trade was essentially based on leather, whose preparation (skinning, cleaning, tanning and so on) is noisome and dirty, and therefore often confined to persons of low social status or outcasts (as in India and Japan). In their origins shoemakers and tanners were closely linked, since shoemakers often tanned their own leather, as they still did until the mid-nineteenth century in the Pomeranian shoemaker community of Loitz.[68] In Leipzig the tanners and shoemakers originally formed a single gild.[69] The low status of shoemakers and the contempt in which they were often held in antiquity – at any rate by writers[70] – may be partly due to this association with 'uncleanness' or the memory of it. Conversely it is not unreasonable to suppose that the craft (which emphasized its indispensability and gentility) was inclined towards radicalism by resentment. Certainly an element of low status seems to have persisted, possibly also influenced by the shoemaker's reputation for physical neglect, possibly a reason for this reputation. Even in the late nineteenth century an author could write of the traditional (pre-factory) trade: 'As a class ... the common shoemakers were neither clean nor tidy in their habits and persons, and the calling was looked down upon as one of low social grade; a fitting employment to which to apprentice the boy inmates of workhouses.'[71]

Moreover, as the costs of apprenticeship were minimal, families which could not afford to bind their sons to a more prosperous, exclusive (and more costly) trade could scrape together the fees required for learning shoemaking. Indeed the association of the craft with poverty was also proverbial.[72] 'All shoemakers go barefoot,' goes a Yiddish saying. 'The shoemaker always wears torn shoes.' A mixture of leftover scraps of food was known, around Hamburg, as 'shoemaker's pie'.[73]

The coexistence of independence and poverty in the trade is partly due to its peculiar ubiquity. It was organized early in both town and country, at least in temperate zones where it had long been recognized that 'there's nothing like leather' for tough outdoor labouring foot-wear. The shoemakers, often of humble origin themselves, served a clientele which included large numbers of humble people. The making and repairing of leather footwear requires specialists of some kind, unlike a good deal of other making and mending. At the end of the nineteenth century there were still shoemakers who specialized in going round the Alpine farms of Austria (*Störschuster*) to make and mend the year's footwear from the hides and leather provided by the farmers.[74] Shoemakers and cobblers were therefore not only a craft organized as such at an uncommonly early date (they are among the earliest documented craft gilds in both England and Germany),[75] but one of the most numerous and widely distributed crafts in town and country. In eighteenth-century Seville, as in nineteenth-century Valparaiso, they exceeded in numbers all other crafts.[76] So did they in Prussia in 1800 (followed by tailors and smiths). In Bavaria in 1771 they were exceeded in numbers only by weavers, but in market villages they were first, followed by brewers and weavers.[77] In rural Friesland in 1749 there were 5.79 of them per 1,000 inhabitants, compared to 4.53 weavers, 4.48 carpenters, 3.70 bakers, 2.08 smiths, 1.76 clergymen, 1.51 innkeepers and 1.45 tailors; shoemakers were to be found in 54 per cent of all settlements, carpenters in 52 per cent, smiths in 40 per cent and innkeepers in 32 per cent.[78] It seems clear that people found it harder to manage without specialized shoemakers and menders within close reach than without other specialized craftsmen and services.

The shoemaker's trade, though it extended over a very wide range of skill and specialization, remained sufficiently primitive in technology and division of labour, and with a sufficiently homogeneous product, to continue essentially as a single craft. There is no equivalent in it to the growing fragmentation of metalworking into specialized separate crafts so often found in the medieval gild economy. Broadly speaking, once the trade had separated from the tanners, leather-sellers and other producers and suppliers of its raw material, its main internal fissures were commercial – between shoemakers and shoe-merchants (whether or not these also made shoes). There was also a division between those who made and those who merely repaired shoes, defined in various ways – cordwainers and cobblers (*savetiers*, *Flickschuster*, *ciabattino*), though it must be noted that the merchants developed essentially from among the cordwainers. The separation between makers and menders was sometimes institutionalized in separate gilds, though cobblers' gilds had difficulty in emancipating themselves completely from cordwainers' control or in remaining viable.

Cobbling was clearly the inferior branch, and the term (in English) is used for any work of poor quality. However, the line between the two was and had to be unclear, especially in times and regions (like eighteenth-century Germany) where fairly static demand confronted growing supply in the towns.[79] To live only by *making* shoes was hardly possible for more than a few. In fact it was assumed that makers cobbled. Thus to reach a 'decent' income (91 gulden a year) it was claimed, no doubt rhetorically, that a master 'would have to work up one pair of new shoes or three pairs of soles and patches every day, and in addition rely on customers paying'. It is thus not surprising that in the eighteenth and nineteenth centuries the terms seem to have become interchangeable in English,[80] while in French the word *cordonnier* came to mean both maker and mender, as *Schuster* did in popular German usage, in spite of the tendency for the more high-class *Schuhmacher* to gain ground at its expense.[81] And indeed, outside strongly gild-controlled cities, which were becoming weaker, how was it possible to keep the making and mending of shoes strictly apart?

The widespread demand for specialized shoemakers and menders made it impossible for corporate cities to monopolize the craft. Village shoe-mending could hardly be banned, and though this type of countryside cobbling was (no doubt inevitably) free of gild control and qualifications, it had almost always to be learned from some kind of shoemaker. There was no way of preventing the local cobbler from also supplying the local demand for shoes, especially of the rough working kind, until the rise of large-scale production and distribution. So journeymen with poor chances of becoming masters in the controlled trade of the city might well prefer to set up on their own in some village or country town. Indeed a growing tendency to do so in Germany was noted as late as the nineteenth century. When in 1840 the prohibition on rural shoemakers (as distinct from cobblers) was finally lifted in the countryside of Saxony, a single master (without apprentices) being henceforth permitted per village, a considerable number of rural shoemakers immediately appeared.[82] It is a good guess that many of them had simply changed their official title.

On the other hand, if there was no sharp line between the best and most specialized shoemaker and the most modest cobbler, the enormous size of the trade suggests that it must generally have included an unusually large section of the marginal, who could not live by their craft alone, especially as shoe-mending – from which German village cobblers might draw half their income – was notoriously unremunerative. Pre-industrial data are hard to find, but a calculation for a Swabian village in the nineteenth century suggests that because of insufficient demand a shoemaker there could not, on average, have made more than seven pairs of footwear in a year,[83] so that for most of them the craft could not have been more than a source of supplementary earnings, possibly taken up as such. The reputation of the trade for poverty thus had a sound base, though the reasons for its overcrowding are not quite clear. Perhaps this is partly explained by the cheapness of the basic equipment and the possibility of practising it at home; perhaps also by the fact that shoemakers were recruited externally, outside the ranks of practising craftsmen and their families. Printers and glass-workers restricted recruitment to their sons, relatives and a few privileged outsiders; shoemakers could rarely do so.* As a result shoemakers controlled neither entry into nor the size of their trade, hence its overcrowding.

The trade was therefore far from homogeneous. Yet so long as it remained essentially a manual artisan trade – and until the 1850s not even the domestic sewing-machine entered it – the divisions within it were vague and shifting. Hence, though there were 'aristocrats' or favoured sectors among shoemakers as among tailors (for example, in the high-class bespoke trade of the cities), neither trade as a whole stood high in the pecking order of the crafts, as the artisan communist Wilhelm Weitling observed.[84] For both, and especially the shoemakers, were unusually numerous, and therefore contained an unusually high proportion of the marginal and unprosperous. Among

* We are informed, however, that among eighteenth-century London cordwainers intergenerational continuity in the trade was unusually high.

the hundreds of journeymen artisans who flocked into industrializing Wiener Neustadt in the 1840s and applied for permission to stay there, no less than 14.7 per cent (17 per cent of those from Bohemia) were shoemakers, followed at some distance by 10 per cent (14.6 per cent among Bohemians) of tailors and 8.3 per cent (9.1 per cent among Bohemians) of joiners.[85]

The village shoemaker was self-employed. His business required little capital. Equipment was cheap, light and portable, and he only required a modest roof over his head to work and live, in the worst case in the same room. While this made him unusually mobile, it did not distinguish him from a number of other crafts. What did distinguish him was his contact with large numbers of humble people and his independence from patrons, wealthy clients and employers. Farmers depended on landlords; wheelwrights and builders relied on orders from farmers and persons of substance; tailors served the wealthy since the poor made their own clothes. The shoemaker also served the wealthy, since they needed him; but his main clientele must, in most cases, have been among the poor, since they could not do without him either. That fact is undeniable, even if we know less than we might about the actual use of leather footwear among the poor, which was certainly more restricted than in our prosperous times.* Indeed there is evidence that, as wealthier villagers in the later nineteenth century advanced to store-bought shoes manufactured elsewhere, if not to high-class bespoke footwear, the village shoemaker became increasingly dependent on the custom of those who needed tough footwear for outdoor labour.

He could thus express his opinions without the risk of losing his job or his customers – if he were good enough, even his respectable customers.[86] Moreover he was closely linked with his clients by bonds of confidence. This was in part because they were likely to be his debtors, since farm-workers and perhaps peasants could only pay at rare intervals when they received lump sums, for example, after the harvest (pay-day in Pomerania was St Crispin's Day, 25 October)† or between Easter and Whitsun, when annual hirings were renewed. He had to trust his clients, but they had no reason to distrust him. Unlike so many with whom the poor had dealings – the miller, the baker, even the tavern-keeper, who could give short weight or measure – the shoemaker produced a new or mended shoe which could be readily judged, and variations in quality were most likely

---

* We need to know more, in particular, about the extent of the practice of going barefoot (widespread among women and children) and the use of alternative footwear – clogs, felt or bast boots and shoes, and the like.

† Is there a connection between this agricultural rhythm and St Crispin's Day on 25 October?

due not to cheating but to variations in skill.[87] The shoemaker thus had licence to express his opinions, which there was no reason to distrust.

That these opinions were heterodox and democratic should cause no surprise. The village shoemaker's life was akin to that of the poor, not the rich and powerful. He had little use for hierarchy and formal organization. There was little enough in his trade, and in many cases he found work outside and in spite of gild or craft regulation. He knew the value of independence and had ample opportunity to compare his relative autonomy with that of his clients. How far this ability to articulate independent views was confined to the minority of relatively successful craftsmen rather than the (presumable) majority of marginal part-time cobblers, we cannot say, since it is difficult or impossible to compile a representative sample of the radicals in the craft. The question must be left open. However, in the specific context of the late eighteenth and early nineteenth centuries it is natural to find radical shoemakers reading Cobbett, who cried out against the demolition of all small tradesmen and who denounced a system which replaced 'master and man ... every one was in his place and every one was free' with 'masters and slaves'.[88] Nor is it surprising to find them in the ranks of sansculottes and later of anarchists. In all cases the insistence on modest means, hard work and independence as solutions to problems of injustice and poverty were within the experience of village shoemakers.

Much of this argument might also apply to other village artisans. But while, say, the blacksmith's shop was noisy and his labour made conversation at work difficult, the shoemaker was strategically well placed to pass on city ideas and mobilize action. His village shop provided an ideal setting for the purpose, and articulate men who worked alone most of the time might grow loquacious in company, and could do so while they worked. The rural shoemaker was always present, his eyes on the street, and he knew what went on in the community, even when he did not happen to double as parish clerk or in some other municipal or communal capacity. Moreover their quiet workshops in villages and small towns were social centres second only to the inn, open and ready for conversation all day. Not surprisingly in the French countryside of 1793–4 shoemakers, together with tavern-keepers, 'seem to have had had a veritable vocation for revolution'. Richard Cobb stresses:

the role of the shoemakers, those village revolutionaries who, installed as mayors by the revolutionary upsurge of summer 1793, or at the head of the committees of surveillance, led the sansculotte minorities against *les gros* ... On the lists of 'terrorists to be disarmed' which were drawn up in the year III in the countryside, they formed a majority. We have here an undeniable social phenomenon.[89]

Of course the cobbler's shop and the tavern differed as meeting-places in one important respect. Men gathered to drink in groups, but in cobblers' shops in ones and twos. Taverns were only for adult males, but women, or more likely children, had access to the village intellectual. In how many village and small-town lives did the shoemaker as educator play a role! Thus Hone's *Every-Day Book* recalls 'an honest old man who patched my shoes and my mind, when I was a boy ... my friend the cobbler, who, though no metaphysician, was given to ruminate on "causation"'. He lent the boy books 'which he kept in the drawer of his seat, with ... the instruments of his "Gentle Craft"'.[90] And as late as the 1940s a future distinguished Marxist labour historian was introduced to politics in boyish conversations in a small-town cobbler's workshop in his native Rumania.[91]

The shoemaker was thus a key figure in rural intellectual and political life: literate, articulate, relatively informed, intellectually and sometimes economically independent, at least within his village community. He was constantly present in the places where popular mobilization was likely to take place: on the village street, at markets, fairs and feasts. Whether this is sufficient explanation for his frequently attested role as crowd-leader is not so clear. Under the circumstances, however, we are hardly surprised to find him on occasion in such a role.

III

Among social historians the reputation of shoemakers as radicals is associated mostly with the late eighteenth and early nineteenth centuries, the period of the transition to industrialism. We cannot measure whether or not there was an increase in the number of militant shoemakers, but it seems likely that two developments stimulated an intensified radicalism. The first stemmed from the slow decline of shoemaking as an essentially artisan occupation and a consequent period of extreme tension within the trade. Specific problems varied from place to place (relations between masters and journeymen were different in Northampton and London) but it is undeniable that the trade as a whole was politicized. Thus a young journeyman experienced strikes and participated in discussions of alternate political and economic systems as he acquired his skills.

Those who ended up in small village shops knew about Jacobinism and carried radical ideas from cities to small towns. The second development was tied to the growing discontent of village populations as they faced the consequences of the growth of agricultural capitalism. Villagers were increasingly open to the ideological formulations for their grievances which shoemakers were in a position to provide. The combination of trade and village circumstances could readily turn the village philosopher into a village politician, as it most certainly did during the 'Swing' riots.

What changes affected the shoemaking trade during the period which extended, roughly, from 1770 to 1880?

The first point to recall is the sheer numerical size of the trade which, until mechanization and factory production transformed it, grew with urbanization and population. The number of shoemaking workers in Vienna (where factories were negligible) more than trebled between 1855 and 1890, most of this increase occurring before the early 1870s.[92] In Britain the number of adult males in the trade grew from 133,000 to 243,000 between 1841 and 1851, when there were more shoemakers in the country than miners.[93] Between 1835 and 1850 an annual average of between 250 and 400 shoemakers entered Leipzig and, since the city was growing, a somewhat smaller number left each year. Over this fifteen-year period there was a minimum number of 3,750 arrivals and 3,000 departures.[94]

The second point to note is the spread of manufacture for the market as distinct from individual clients and the ubiquitous repair-work. The 'market shoemaker', making rough ware for sale on local and regional markets, might in many places still have as close a relationship with his clients as the bespoke shoemaker, since he could be found regularly at his stall on market day by men and women he knew well and who knew him. His was probably a closer relationship than that of his growing rival, the shoemaker–hawker, who went from house to house.[95] Both these arrangements, however, lent themselves to various forms of putting-out system – hence the development of both rural and urban shoemaking communities, which might range from agglomerations of traditional craft workshops with minimal workshop division of labour to larger centres which were, in effect, unmechanized factories working with operatives confined to special processes supplemented by urban or village out-workers with their own subdivision of labour.[96] Here large-scale production for export or army and navy contracts could be undertaken. It is possible that many such semi-skilled handworkers came to the trade untrained or unsocialized in the craft, especially when drawn from agriculture.[97] It may well be that apprentices at this period were largely drawn from the rural poor. In Europe, however, the nucleus of apprenticed shoemakers around whom this semi-skilled labour force grew was substantial. This is suggested even for factory operatives in (the radical) J. B. Leno's handbook of shoemaking, and certainly in Erfurt, one of the main German centres of mechanized factory production, one-third of a sample of 193 workers had learned the trade, and half of these were the sons of shoemakers.[98] Since, outside the United States and a little later Britain, no technical innovation other than the small sewing-machine (which spread between the mid-1850s and the early 1870s) was of significance until very late in the nineteenth century, this is not surprising.[99]

The third point is that the press of numbers and the proliferation of putting-out manufacture (referred to by honourable craftsmen as 'dishonourable' or 'junk' work) undermined the independence of the trade and also depressed wages. An enquiry into employment in Marseille in the 1840s revealed that shoemakers were the largest occupational group, notoriously underpaid. They earned an average daily wage of only 3 francs, and an average annual wage of 600 francs, which placed them lower in earnings than many unskilled labourers.[100] The worker–poet Charles Poncy protested in 1850 to St Crispin:

> Hunger harnesses us to its black wagon: our wages are so reduced. For bread and rags we burn the midnight oil.
>
> My children, piled pell-mell on ancient bedding, have sucked dry their mother's scrawny breast. We eat the seed-corn that should grow food for the young.[101]

The English shoemaker John Brant attributed his part in the Cato Street conspiracy to low wages and the loss of independence that entailed. His statement suggests that he sought to strike back at those in power, asserting his ability to think and act independently:

> He had, by his industry, been able to earn about £3 or £4 a-week, and while this was the case, he never meddled with politics; but when he found his income reduced to 10s a-week, he began to look about him ... And what did he find? Why, men in power, who met to deliberate how they might starve and plunder the country ... He had joined the conspiracy for the public good.[102]

The spread of manufacture for a remote market rather than known clients affected the trade in different ways. At one extreme it might, at least temporarily, lead to a reassertion of the values and claims of the craft as such, shared by both masters and journeymen, against slopwork or 'dishonourable' work locally or in large-scale manu-

facturing centres like Northampton. At the other extreme, journeymen or proletarianized small masters who perceived that they
had become permanent wage-workers, might find their way to trade
unionism and conflict with employers, which sharpened the edge of
shoemaker radicalism. Thus the Parisian shoemaker 'Efrahem' spoke
of the day when 'on the signal being given, all workers will simultaneously leave their workshops and abstain from labour in order
to obtain the rise in the price-list they have demanded from the
masters'.[103] As already observed, shoemakers took rapidly to forming
militant unions. In Britain, at least, the roots of unionism went deep.
James Hawker, who occupies a modest place in history as a brilliant
and politically conscious poacher and village radical in Leicestershire,
was the son of a poor tailor, apprenticed to the Northampton shoe
trade. In the intervals of joining and deserting from the army, he
drifted into any job he could in the Eastern Midlands. Yet he joined
a union whenever one was available: 'I ran home as quick as I Could
and Drew my Travelling Card. For by this time I was a Trade
unionist – almost before I knew what it Meant ... Had I not been a
union man I might have been compelled to Beg or Steal.'[104]

The line between craft and wage-work, between economic and
political militancy, was as yet vague enough to discourage excessive
classification. Not until 1874 did traditional shoemakers and manufacturing operatives diverge sufficiently in Britain for the latter to
break away from the Amalgamated Cordwainers' Association to form
the National Union of Boot and Shoe Riveters and Finishers – the
future National Union of Boot and Shoe Operatives. The union of
1820 contributed to the cause of the defendants in the Cato Street
conspiracy. And the unions in putting-out and manufacturing centres
drew on the old craft tradition in their protests. At Nantwich in
Cheshire, for example, a strong union of this sort celebrated St
Crispin's Day in 1833 with:

> a grand procession – King Crispin on horseback attired in royal regalia
> ... attended by train-bearers in appropriate costume. The officers
> were attired in vestments suitable to their rank, and carrying the
> Dispensation, the Bible, a large pair of globes, and also beautiful
> specimens of ladies' and gents' boots and shoes ... Nearly 500 joined
> in the procession, each one wearing a white apron neatly trimmed.
> The rear was brought up by a shopmate in full tramping order, his kit
> packed on his back and walking stick in his hand.[105]

The union's banner, 'emblematical of our trade, with the motto "May
the manufactures of the sons of Crispin be trod upon by all the world"

...' was much admired.[106] A gild procession would not have looked very different.

However, the lines leading to our village radicals in the late eighteenth and early nineteenth centuries originate more often from contexts like London, where masters and journeymen shared Jacobin positions such as those articulated by the London Corresponding Society and members of the Cato Street conspiracy, or Paris, where shoemakers were among the most numerous followers of Etienne Cabet. The village shoemaker shared with honourable urban shoemakers the cause of the independent small artisan. In defence of that cause he offered a critique of the economy and the government which could focus the grievances of other workers and spur them to action. The call to action rested upon the assumption that men like himself were capable of action; indeed it assumed that small groups of intelligent 'citizens' could act to remedy injustice independently – without the leadership of more learned men or the support of central formal organizations.

Nevertheless, if changes in the trade itself heightened the awareness of its members to the inequities of society, we cannot simply say that shoemaker radicalism emerged in the late eighteenth century as a response to early industrial capitalism. As we have tried to show, the cobbler as a labouring man's intellectual and heterodox philosopher, as the common people's spokesman, as a trade militant, long antedates the industrial revolution – at least if the argument of this paper is accepted. What the early stages of industrialization or pre-industrialization did was to broaden the base of shoemaker radicalism by increasing the numbers of shoemakers and menders and by creating a large body of at least intermittently pauperized semi-proletarian outworkers. Many craft journeymen were forced out of the traditional framework of corporate artisan activities and expectations, and towards the trade-union militancy of skilled workers.

But what this period did above all was vastly to increase both the tool-kit of political radicalism and its repertoire of ideas, demands and programmes. Secular democratic, Jacobin, republican, anticlerical, co-operative, socialist, communist and anarchist ideologies of social and political criticism multiplied, and supplemented or replaced the ideologies of heterodox religion which had previously provided the main vocabulary of popular thought. Some had greater appeal than others, but aspects of all of them spoke to experiences of shoemakers, old or new. The media for popular agitation and debate also multiplied: newspapers and pamphlets providing greater scope for the writing of labouring intellectuals could be read and discussed in the shoemaker's shop. And as the philosophic or heretical shoemaker turned into the

Reichstag election of 1912: occupational groups as a percentage of candidates and deputies*

Occupational group	Candidates	Deputies
Metalworkers	15.6	15.2
Woodworkers	14.8	10.9
Builders	12.8	3.6
Printers	6.6	7.3
Shoemakers	6.6	4.5
Tobacco-workers	3.8	6.4
Tailors	2.7	4.5
Textile-workers	0.8	2.7

* Note and source: W. H. Schröder, 'Die Sozialstruktur der sozialdemokratischen Reichstagskandidaten, 1898–1912', in *Herkunft und Mandat: Beiträge zur Führungsproblematik in der Arbeiterbewegung* (Frankfurt and Cologne, 1976), pp. 72–96. All figures are percentages.

politically radical shoemaker, the emergence of movements of protests and social liberation, of a world turned upside down by great revolutions attempted, achieved and anticipated, gave him a vastly increased public ready to listen, perhaps to follow, in town and village. No wonder that the century beginning with the American Revolution was the golden age of shoemaker radicalism.

IV

There is a final question which should be asked. What eventually happened to the radicalism of the gentle craft? We have been concerned overwhelmingly with the period before shoemaking became a fully mechanized and factory industry and before the rise of the modern socialist and communist working-class movements. During this lengthy period shoemakers were associated with virtually any and all movements of social protest. We find them prominent among religious sectarians and preachers, in republican, radical, Jacobin and sansculottes movements, in artisan co-operative, socialist and communist groups, among atheist anticlericals, and not least among the anarchists. Were they equally prominent among the socialist movements in the new era?

The answer is no. In Germany they were indeed among the six groups of skilled workers who provided at least two-thirds of the social democratic worker–candidates for the Reichstag elections before 1914: together with woodworkers, metalworkers, printers, cigar-makers and, later, building workers. Nevertheless by 1912 they were well behind all these (except the builders) in elected members, and very far indeed behind metalworkers, builders and woodworkers, though level with the much smaller printers and ahead of the smaller cigar-makers in providing candidates (see table on p. 40). The shoemakers' union, though as usual early off the mark as an organization, declined from the eighth position in size-ranking in 1892 to ninth in 1899 and twelfth in 1905–12. In the German Communist Party after 1918 they were negligible, for out of 504 leading members only 7 were apprenticed shoemakers. Among the 107 skilled trades (omitting the overwhelmingly predominant metal trades) they were far behind printers (17) and woodworkers (29), though on the same level as tailors (7), bricklayers (7) and plumbers (8). Apart from the unskilled and unapprenticed shoe factory worker Willi Münzenberg, the great propagandist, the German Communist Party contained no eminent shoemaker.[107]

In France the shoemakers were clearly somewhat over-represented in the Parti Ouvrier Français of the 1890s compared to their share in the occupied population (3.6 per cent), with 5.3 per cent of party members and 7.7 per cent of party candidates (1894–7), but local data do not show them unduly prominent except in a few localities.[108] Nobody would have chosen them, as seemed reasonable for the anarchists, to symbolize the militants of the socialist movement. Indeed the most prominent left-wing shoemakers were certainly Jean Grave the anarchist and Victor Griffuelhes the revolutionary syndicalist, both with their trade's characteristic bent for political writing. There is not much doubt that the role of the shoemaker diminished as the movement's centre of gravity shifted to the large-scale industries and public sector employment. Though the most prominent communists in 1945 contained two former joiners and a former pastry-cook, shoemakers were absent from the list, whose centre of gravity lay in metals and railways. Among the fifty-one former artisans elected to the French chamber in 1951 there was only one shoemaker (a socialist).[109]

If any occupations were typical of Austrian Socialist Party activists, they were those of locksmiths/mechanics and printers.[110] Prominent shoemakers are hard to find in this party, and though the Spanish Socialist Party had Francisco Mora, a shoemaker, at one time as its secretary and eventually (and characteristically) its historian, the occupation that clearly dominated that body of craftsmen was the printing trade. We can no doubt discover a few prominent shoemakers in lesser socialist parties such as the Hungarian, where two of them, not unexpectedly, became editors of its newspaper, and in the (Marxist) Social Democracy of the Kingdom of Poland and Lithuania, where cobblers 'remained throughout its history, the main stronghold' of its support.[111] But the only brands of modern socialism and communism in which the radical cobbler seems genuinely to have been prominent are those which notably failed to become mass parties, or even typical parties of the industrial working class. The general secretary of the tiny Austrian Communist Party and its (symbolic) presidential candidate were both former journeymen shoe-makers from provincial Carinthia and Bohemia respectively, and much the most eminent shoemaker–radical of the twentieth century is doubtless President Ceausescu of Rumania, whose party, at the time he joined it, probably contained a mere handful of ethnic Rumanians.

In industrialized Britain the shoemakers, so prominent between the days of the London Corresponding Society and the election of the atheist radical Charles Bradlaugh for the shoemaking constituency of Northampton in 1880, played no marked role in the era of the Labour Party, except in their own union. They were barely represented among Labour MPs, nor were they especially visible in other ways. The only man with some (unskilled) shoemaking experience early in his chequered career who became at all prominent is the transport workers' leader Ben Tillett.[112]

There seems little doubt that, on the whole, the role of the radical shoemaker was no longer as prominent in the era of the socialist mass labour movements as it was before them. No doubt this is partly due to the transformation of shoemaking from a numerically large artisan or semi-artisan craft into a numerically much smaller industry distributing its products through shops. There were no longer so many members of the most characteristic of 'those sedentary crafts which allow a man to "philosophize" while carrying on with familiar tasks of work' among whom the anarchists found so many of their supporters.[113] Most men and women manufacturing shoes increasingly became a sub-species of the factory operative or out-worker of developed industrialism; most who sold shoes had no connection with their making. The radical shoemaker as a type belongs to an earlier era.

His period of glory lies between the American Revolution and the rise of the mass socialist working-class parties, whenever that occurred in any particular country (insofar as it did). During this period his bent for democratic and self-confident thinking, talking and preaching, hitherto expressed chiefly through religious heterodoxy and rad-icalism, found theoretical formulations in secular egalitarian rev-olutionary ideologies, and his practical militancy in mass movements of social protest and hope. The association with such specifically political ideologies of radicalism turned the age-old 'philosophic cob-bler' into the 'radical cobbler' – the poor village intellectual into the village sansculotte, republican or anarchist.

42

The combination of ubiquity with occasional large concentrations of semi-proletarianized craftsmen gave the shoemaker his universal and prominent role as poor man's advocate, spokesman and leader. He was rarely in the front rank of national movements as an individual. Even among manual workers who gained a reputation as theorists and ideologists, people like Tom Paine the staymaker, Weitling the tailor, Proudhon and Bray the printers, Bebel the wood-turner, Dietzgen the tanner are more likely to be remembered than any shoemaker. His strength lay at the grassroots. For every Thomas Hardy or Mora or Griffuelhes, there were hundreds of men whom even the specialist in the history of radical and labour movements has difficulty in rescuing from the anonymity of the local militant, for little is known about them except that they spoke and fought locally for other poor men: John Adams, the Maidstone cobbler in the 1830 farm-labourers' riots; Thomas Dunning, whose deter-mination and ingenuity saved the Nantwich shoemakers from what might well have been the fate of the Dorchester labourers; the lone Italian shoemaker anarchist who brought his ideas into a Brazilian provincial town. His milieu was that of face-to-face politics, of *Gemein-schaft* rather than *Gesellschaft*. Historically he belongs to the era of workshop, small town, city neighbourhood and above all village, rather than that of factory and metropolis.

He did not disappear totally. One of the authors of this paper still recalls as a student attending Marxist classes given by an admirable Scottish member of the species, and first had his attention drawn to the problem of shoemaker radicalism in the workshop of a Calabrian cobbler in the 1950s. There are no doubt still places where he survives, not least to inspire the young to follow the ideals of liberty, equality and fraternity, as the shoemaker uncle of Lloyd George taught his nephew the elements of radical politics in a Welsh village of the 1880s. Whether or not he is still a significant phenomenon in the politics of the common people, he has served them well. And he has, collectively and through a surprisingly large number of indi-viduals, made his mark on history.

CHAPTER 4

Labour Traditions

This paper is an enquiry into the contribution of specific national histories to the character of labour movements. Though not published until 1964, it is based on a lecture in a course on 'British and French Labour Movements Compared' in Cambridge around 1951. College Fellows (as I was then) had the right to offer lecture courses, even when (like me) refused jobs by both the Economics and the History faculties of the University.

What part do custom, tradition and the specific historical experience of a country play in its political movements? So far as the labour movement is concerned, the problem has been more frequently discussed by politicians (Marx versus Wesley) than by historians. I propose in this essay to illustrate it from a comparison of the experience of France and Britain, the countries with the longest history of the labour movement.

The labour movement, whether politically or industrially considered, is, of course, a novel phenomenon in history. Whether or not there is continuity between journeymen's associations and early trade unions, it is mere antiquarianism to think of the movement of the 1870s or even of the 1830s in terms of, say, the early hatters' and curriers' trade societies. However, historically speaking, the process of building new institutions, new ideas, new theories and tactics rarely starts as a deliberate job of social engineering. Men live surrounded by a vast accumulation of past devices, and it is natural to pick the most suitable of these, and to adapt them for their own (and novel) purposes. The historian, of course, who traces these processes, must not forget the specific function which the new institutions are expected to fulfil; neither must the functional analyst forget that the specific historical setting must colour (and perhaps assist, hamper or divert) them.

Let us take a pair of extreme examples. In 1855 the slate-quarrymen

44

of Trelazé, discontented with their economic conditions, decided to take action: they marched on Angers and proclaimed an insurrectionary Commune,[1] presumably with the memory of the Commune of 1792 in their minds. Nine years later the coalminers of Ebbw Vale were equally agitated. The lodges from the valley villages marched on to the mountains, headed by bands. Speeches were made, tea provided by the Ebbw Vale lodge at 6d a head and the meeting ended with the singing of the Doxology.[2] Both Welsh miners and Breton quarrymen were engaged on rather similar economic agitations. Clearly they differed, because the histories of their respective countries had differed. The stock of past experience, upon which they drew when learning how to organize, what to organize for, where to pick their cadre of leaders, and the ideology of those leaders embodied, in part at least, specific French and British elements: broadly speaking we may say, in the former case, the revolutionary, in the latter the radical–nonconformist traditions.

Again, concrete illustrations may be useful. The Lyon weavers and subcontractors, wishing to organize a trade union in 1828, naturally organized their society of 'Mutualists' on the revolutionary model. Thus they described their foundation year as 'Year One of Regeneration', an obvious echo of Jacobinism, and organized in small conspiratorial groups, which seem to have owed something to Babouvist devices,[3] though perhaps also to the old Compagnonnages,[4] and to the practical need to circumvent the Chapelier Law. Again, under the Second Empire, the labour programme was patently derived from classical Jacobin–radical doctrine; the left-wingers merely went to Robespierre and St Just, if not to Hébert and Jacques Roux for inspiration, while the liberals sought theirs further on the right. As late as the 1890s Emile Pouget the anarchist and later leader of the Confédération Générale du Travail (CGT) modelled his journal *Le Père Peinard* in title and style on Hébert's *Père Duchêne*. Moreover, it was the revolutionary ideology which automatically commended itself to the advanced workers and intellectuals who formed the core of the movement's leadership. The porcelain workers of Limoges were republicans, and easily switched from trade unionist to political methods; thus when their union was held up, they promptly organized an insurrectionary commune.[5] The left in the Nièvre department opposed Louis Napoleon's *coup d'état*, and was organized in a secret society known as the 'Jeune Montagne'.[6]

In Britain the situation is more complex, because the original radical–democratic tradition had developed two wings, the line between them being (I oversimplify) largely that between the artisans and craftsmen unionists in the older towns, and the new factory and mining centres: radical–secularist on one hand, dissenting–Methodist on the other. In London, for instance, the nonconformist tradition never really took root as a left-wing one, which may explain the relatively greater influence of Marxism here in later times. Even so naturally religious a worker as George Lansbury found himself in the Marxist Social Democratic Federation at the outset of his political career, and was never drawn to the dissenting chapels, but to the Church of England – a most unusual state of affairs. In the provinces the road led much more naturally to ILP or Methodist lay-pulpit. We have, in fact, two lines of intellectual descent. One goes from men like Tom Paine, through men like the atheist radicals of the Owen-Carlile period, to mid-Victorian secularists like Holyoake and Brad-laugh, and, after 1880, the Marxists. From this tradition the British labour movement derives some of its most important organizational devices: the 'Corresponding Society' of the 1790s, the pamphlet, the working-class newspaper, the petition to Parliament, the public meeting and public debate, and so on; also, of course, what little interest it takes in theory.

In a sense this first tradition goes back to that branch of the seventeenth-century dissenters which, in the eighteenth, evolved towards deism and later agnosticism. Part of the other tradition – especially in Calvinist Scotland – goes back directly to that sev-enteenth-century revolution which was still fought out in terms of religious ideology. Even in England the independent sectarian persisted as a pure type – for example, in Mark Rutherford's Zechariah Coleman.[7] In the main, however, the labour tradition of dissent derives from the Methodist revival; more specifically, from the series of breakaways after 1810 of which the Primitive Methodist is the best known. It was in this school that the new factory proletarians, rural labourers, miners and others of the sort learned how to run a trade union, modelling themselves on chapel and circuit. One has merely to read the district report of an East Anglian farm-labourers' union[8] to see how much they owed to it. From Methodists too, as Dr Wearmouth has shown, came important devices of mass agitation and propaganda: the camp meeting, the class meeting and others. Above all, however, dissent provided the ideological rallying-ground for the leadership of the movement, especially in the mining areas. When Lord Londonderry evicted the leaders of the Durham miners' agitation in 1843, two-thirds of the local Primitive Methodist circuit found themselves victimized,[9] and when in the 1870s a Lincolnshire farm-labourers' union found itself in difficulties, it considered merging with the Primitive Methodists. Clearly this sect was to the Durham miners of the 1840s or the Lincolnshire labourers of the 1870s what the Communist Party was to the French workers for fifty years, the cadre of leadership.

Such a religious phenomenon is not quite unknown in France. In parts of the South the Huguenot minority has always been, for obvious reasons, inclined to anti-conservatism, and has therefore provided a disproportionate number of left-wing leaders. But on the whole this is not of great importance for the French labour movement. It is easy to explain the different degrees of political radicalism in Britain and France by such difference in tradition. But is the explanation true?

A revolutionary tradition may be politically moderate; a religious one need not be so. When the leading Communards returned from exile in 1880 they found themselves in the main[10] on the extreme right wing of a movement which was rapidly coming under socialist influence. A willingness to raise barricades does not necessarily indicate an extremist programme. For most of the nineteenth century the French revolutionary tradition was merely an aspect of French liberal–radicalism, whose supporters were ideologically quite on a par with respectable British secularist republicans like George Odger. It is significant that the modern form of revolutionism, the Communist Party, in some ways marked as great a break with French traditions as with British ones, though in others it continued both.

The fortunes of what is ostensibly one of the most violent trends in French labour, the anarchist, illustrate the point. In general the small craftsmen and artisans who formed the mainstay of French anarchism were extremely militant. (However, their spiritual father, Proudhon, was markedly pacific.) They fought, often with no holds barred – as did their counterparts in the small Sheffield metal crafts – and they easily attracted radical intellectuals. But, just as the Sheffield terrorists were extremely moderate in their politics,[11] so the French anarchists were essentially on the moderate wing of their movement. Their greatest triumph, the CGT, moved from apparent ultra-revolutionism to a careful social democracy with remarkable speed after the outbreak of the First World War. Moreover, that section of French socialism which was later to support the policy of appeasement most passionately, and to collaborate with Pétain – Dumoulin, Belin and others – drew its strength largely from the anarchizing wing of the pre-1914 movement. By and large the French political system had long learned to cope with these older, and often intrinsically moderate, forms of revolutionism. When the French Communist Party was formed in 1920, it was immediately joined by large numbers of respectable middle-class figures for 'the tradition that the son of the family begins his career on the extreme left, under the indulgent eye of the clan, to end it in the most respectable of postures'[12] was well established. Indeed, a group of revolutionary railwaymen who were to provide several leaders of the new party (Sémard, Monmousseau, Midol) at first refused to join it for this reason. It was not 'bolshevized' until some years later.[13]

A religious tradition, on the other hand, may be very radical. It is true that certain forms of religion serve to drug the pain of intolerable social strains, and provide an alternative to revolt. Some, like Wesleyanism, may do so deliberately. However, insofar as religion is the language and framework of all general action in undeveloped societies – and also, to a great extent, among the common people of pre-industrial Britain – ideologies of revolt will also be religious.

Two factors helped to maintain religion as a potentially radical force in nineteenth-century Britain. First, the decisive political event of our history, the revolution of the seventeenth century, had been fought out at a time when the modern secular language of politics had not as yet been adopted by the common people: it was a Puritan revolution. Unlike France, therefore, religion was not primarily identified with the *status quo*. Moreover, habits die hard. As late as the 1890s we find an almost pure example of the medieval or puritan approach: the Labour Churches. John Trevor, who founded them, was a misfit springing from one of those small and super-pious sects of working-class or lower-middle-class hellfire puritans which were always splitting away to form more godly communities. Like other mid-Victorian intellectual movements, dissent was slowly cracking under the impact of political and social change after 1870, and during the Great Depression Trevor was drawn towards the labour movement after various crises of conscience and a somewhat chequered spiritual career. Incapable of conceiving a new political movement which should not also have its religious expression, he turned labour into a religion. He was *not* a Christian Socialist; he believed the labour movement to be God, and built his apparatus of churches, Sunday schools, hymns and so on round it. Of course the dour dissenting artisans of Yorkshire and Lancashire did not follow his peculiar theology, which can best be described as a very etherealized unitarianism. However, they had been brought up in an atmosphere in which chapel was the centre of their social and spiritual life. The Great Depression (and such things as the McKinley Tariff of 1891) made them increasingly aware of the cleavage of interests within chapels between employer and worker brethren; and nothing was more natural than to suppose that the political split should take the form of a chapel secession, just as earlier the split between Wesleyan and Primitive Methodists had been one between politically radical and conservative groups. So the Labour Churches, with their familiar paraphernalia of hymns, Sunday schools, chapel brass bands and choirs, dorcas clubs and so on, sprang up in the North. In fact, they were a halfway house between orthodox political liberal–radicalism and the ILP, with which the Churches soon merged.[14] This phenomenon would clearly have been impossible in a country in which pre-secular traditions of politics had not sunk particularly deep roots.

The second factor was the extraordinary psychological strain of early industrialism in the pioneer industrial country – the rapid transformation of a traditional society, based on custom; the horror; the sudden tearing-up of roots. Inevitably the masses of the uprooted and the new working class sought an emotional expression of their maladjustment, something to replace the old framework of life. Just as today Northern Rhodesian copper-miners flock to Jehovah's Witnesses, and among the Basutos the cataclysm of social change finds expression in a revival of magic and witch-cults, so all over Europe the early nineteenth century was an age of overcharged, intense, often apocalyptic religious atmosphere, which expressed itself in revivalist campaigns in mining areas, giant camp meetings, conversions and so on. Now wherever organized religion was, by and large, a strongly conservative force – as was the Roman Catholic Church – the active labour movement necessarily developed independently of it. In France, moreover, the great emotional experience of the Revolution had generated, out of purely secular fuel, its own emotional fire to heat the cold life of the workers. We remember the old man of the 1840s dying with the words, 'Oh sun of 1793, when shall I see thee rise again?' The great image of the Jacobin Republic beckoned, and it was round the personified republic that the emotions of struggling men and women most easily gathered, just as later in Germany and Austria they gathered round the personification of their own struggles, the Marxist parties and their leaders. In Britain there was no such living experience; but there were the dissenting conventicles and sects, independent of the state, comparatively democratic, and alive. Hence that experience which is so typical of the British labour movement, the young worker 'seeing the light', often as a Primitive Methodist, and translating his political aims into the terms of the New Jerusalem.[15]

This did not necessarily make him any less class-conscious or militant. Evidence of the strongly militant nature of the Primitive Methodists in some regions abounds; and on occasion – as in far-off Dorset – even the conservative Wesleyans could find themselves the rallying-point for local labour leaders. Nor did this tradition prevent men from making further political advances. In our own days Arthur Horner (a boy-evangelist) and William Gallacher (whose first political experience was in that by-product of dissent, the teetotal movement) both became communists.

Are we then to regard our two traditions as so many lumps of plasticine, to be moulded to fit the shape of their movements' mood and practical situation? No theory could be less suited to conversion into a doctrine of the 'inevitability of gradualness' than Marx's; yet between the end of the Great Depression and the First World War this was done, tacitly or by startling pieces of exegetical acrobatics, in a number of countries. The Roman Catholic Church has insisted on few maxims of social politics more firmly than on the undesirability of organizing masters and workers separately; yet, without significant exceptions, the joint organizations it has sponsored in industrial countries have either drifted out of the labour movement or – after some struggles – turned into ordinary trade unions.[16] Ideas, in truth, are more elastic than facts. Yet a political or ideological tradition, especially if it sums up genuine patterns of practical activity in the past, or is embodied in stable institutions, has independent life and force, and must affect the behaviour of political movements. The plasticine theory is patently an oversimplification.

When, however, we try to estimate the real part which such traditions play, we tackle one of the most difficult tasks of the historian. A few points may, however, be legitimately suggested. Thus, in the first place, the dissenting tradition, being politically rather imprecise, was far more malleable than the revolutionary. Behind it there was no such specific historical experience as the French Revolution, with its programmes, lessons of tactics and political slogans, however unsuitable. It was extremely difficult to get away from the fact that the revolutionary tradition glorified the armed revolt of the 'people' against the 'rich'; or from the hallowed methods of such a revolt – insurrectionary communes, revolutionary dictatorships and so on. If it was to be turned into its opposite, a theory of gradualism and social collaboration, for example, this could only be done indirectly; for instance, by using its liberal–radical aspects against the communists, as the inter-war CGT and the post-1945 Catholic Church have attempted to do in idealizing its Proudhonian as against its Babouvist and Blanquist traditions; or – as Gambetta did[17] – by stressing the common interest of all classes of the 'people' against some common outside enemy, like 'Reaction' or 'Clericalism'. But the very process of rounding off its edges in practice could be achieved only by glorifying revolution in theory. The genuine conservative had, sooner or later, to make a clean break with it. But the dissenting tradition, insofar as it was religious, was not tied to any special programme or record, though long associated with particular political demands. The fallacy of the modern claim that 'British Socialism derives from Wesley, not from Marx' lies precisely in this. Insofar as socialism (or for that matter radical liberalism) was a specific critique of a particular economic system, and a set of proposals for change, it derived from the same secular sources as Marxism. Insofar as it was merely a passionate way of stating the facts of poverty, it had no intrinsic connection with any particular political doctrine. In any case, only a slight shift of theological emphasis was needed to turn the actively revolutionary dissenter into the quietist (both Anabaptists and Quakers had made it in the past), or to allow the militant left-winger to become the moderate. The difference between the elasticity of the two traditions may be illustrated by individual cases: John Burns' change from revolutionary agitator to Liberal Minister inevitably implied a breach with his former Marxist beliefs. On the other hand, Mr Love the mine-owner of Brancepeth, a union man in his youth, who wrecked the Durham Miners' Association in 1863–4, could end his life as he had started it, as an active and pious Primitive Methodist.[18]

A second point follows from the first. A revolutionary tradition is by its very existence a constantly implied call to action, or to sympathy with action. The Newport Rising of 1839 was, numerically speaking, a much more serious, though a much worse-managed affair than the Dublin Easter Rising of 1916; yet its effect on the ten years following was much smaller than that of the Irish venture, and its impact on the British or even the Welsh popular tradition incomparably less. The one fitted into a picture in which pride of place had long been reserved for the 'rebel'; the other did not.

The one therefore easily became inspiration or myth, the other merely an obscure historical incident. The difference is of considerable importance, for it is not the willingness to use violence, but a certain political way of using or threatening violence which makes movements revolutionary. No other European country has so strong a tradition of rioting as Britain, and one which persisted well past the middle of the nineteenth century. The riot as a normal part of collective bargaining was well established in the eighteenth century.[19] Coercion and intimidation were vital in the early stages of trade unionism, when the immorality of blacklegging had not yet become part of the ethical code of organized labour. It would be foolish to claim that, had Britain possessed a revolutionary tradition, it would therefore also have had a revolution. It is, however, fair to claim that episodes like the Derbyshire and Newport Risings might well have occurred more frequently, and extremely tense situations, like that in Glasgow in 1919, might not have been so easily settled.[20]

It is, of course, quite true that in the normal day's work of the labour movement the presence or the absence of a revolutionary tradition is not of immediate importance. From the point of view of getting higher wages and better conditions, the Trelazé quarrymen's willingness to proclaim the social republic at the drop of a hat was no more and no less than a specially militant form of mass demonstration. It might not even be the most effective way of achieving their immediate economic demands. Or else, it might merely be useful, because in organizing weak and unorganized workers against strong opposition aggressive and flamboyant tactics are always the most effective. (Hence political revolutionaries have always done a disproportionately large share of such organizing, whether in the British 'new unionist' movements of 1889 and 1911, the sardine canners of Douarnenez, the British light engineering of the 1930s, or even the American and Canadian unions of the same decade.) At times of rapid political change and great tension, however, its presence or absence may well be a serious independent factor; for instance in Germany after 1918.

The revolutionary tradition, then, was by its very nature political; the dissenting tradition much less directly so. How much this fact contributed to the much more political character of the French labour movement, it is not easy to say. Weak trade union movements generally tend to draw on political campaigning for additional strength, while strong ones tend not to worry about it; and the French trade unions were throughout the nineteenth and twentieth centuries vastly weaker than the British. Nevertheless, this does not wholly account for two striking phenomena: the much greater speed with which French working-class opinion turned socialist, and the much greater interchangeability of political and industrial agitation.

Thus in France the labour and socialist movement began to capture municipalities about twenty years before it did so in Britain. The first British borough to have a labour–radical–Irish majority was West Ham in 1898. Yet as early as 1881 the Parti Ouvrier won its first majority in Commentry. By 1892, when socialist councillors (often not even elected as such) were still exceedingly rare in Britain, the revolutionary Marxists alone – not counting the Possibilists, Allemanists and the various other bodies sporting the socialist label – commanded over twelve municipalities, among them places like Marseille, Toulon and Roubaix. The disparity is even more marked in parliamentary elections.

Again, the political activities of the British trade unions have always been extremely limited, though this has been obscured by the fact that those who took part in them were often also trade unionists. They finance the Labour Party, though it is far from clear (except in certain rather special cases) how far trade unionists vote for Labour *because* their unions are supporters of the party, or whether they are both unionists and Labour voters because they are 'working-class people'. Certainly *pure* trade-union candidates have rarely been successful. In the London of the 1870s and 1880s the candidates put forward by the London Trades Council polled notably worse than those put forward by political organizations like the National Secular Society,[21] and in the 1950s the elected (communist) convenor of shop-stewards at a great motor-factory might poll a derisory vote in an area full of men who, in their factory, voted for him and – what is even more important – followed him. The sharpness of the distinction is specially clear in the case of a man like Arthur Horner, who was both a political figure and a trade unionist – a combination which is very rare. (Aneurin Bevan, for instance, was a political figure of major importance, but never played a part of any great consequence in the miners' union.) Horner's career falls into two distinct segments: the early period, when he was primarily a political leader, with a powerful local base in Maerdy, and the later, when – after his extrusion from leading positions in the Communist Party – he concentrated on his union work. But the Horner who became the ablest leader the British miners have ever had, though he was an ornament of his party, was not in any significant sense a leader of it.[22]

Similarly, it is hard to think of any successful or even seriously attempted political strikes in Britain, though sympathy and solidarity strikes (which enter into the narrowest terms of reference of trade unionism) are common. The General Strike of 1926 belongs to this class. It is hard to conceive of a British equivalent for the general strikes in favour of electoral reform which the Marxist-led movements on the continent organized, often with much success, between 1890 and 1914, as in Belgium and Sweden. Political strikes are not inconceivable in Britain, especially at times of intense and almost revolutionary excitement, as in 1920, when one was threatened against British intervention in the Russo-Polish War. Yet the existence of a political tradition almost certainly favours them more, though of course their scope is always more limited (except during times of revolution) than their advocates have often supposed.

Third, and most important, a revolutionary tradition by definition envisages the transfer of power. It may do so so inefficiently, as among the anarchists, that it need not be taken seriously. But its possibility is always explicit. The historian of Chartism, for instance, can hardly fail to be saddened by the extraordinary feebleness of this greatest of all the mass movements of British labour; and, what is more, by the equanimity with which the British ruling class regarded it, when not frightened by *foreign* revolution.[23] This equanimity was justified. The Chartists had no idea whatever of what to do if their campaign of collecting signatures for a petition were to fail to convert Parliament, as of course it inevitably would. For even the proposal of a general strike ('sacred month') was, as its opponents pointed out, merely another way of expressing an inability to think of anything to do:

> Are we going to let loose hundreds of thousands of desperate and hungry men upon society without having any specific object in view or any plan of action laid down, but trusting to a chapter of accidents as to what the consequences shall be? ... I shall oppose fixing a day for the holiday until we have better evidence, first as to the practicability of the thing, or the probability of its being carried into effect; and next as to the way in which it is going to be employed.[24]

Moreover, when something like a spontaneous general strike did occur in the summer of 1842, the Chartists were incapable of making any use of it, and it was less effective than the spontaneous rioting of the agricultural labourers in 1830, which did, in fact, largely succeed in its limited object of holding up the progress of mechanization on the farms. And the reason for the ineffectiveness of Chartism was, in part at least, due to the unfamiliarity of Englishmen with the very idea of insurrection, of the organization needed for insurrection, and of the transfer of power.

Conversely, the French Resistance movement during the Second World War was deliberately *not* an attempt to take power, at all events on the part of the communists who, as usual, formed by far its most important and active contingent. The argument that it was, put forward as an excuse for propagandist purposes after 1945 and during the Cold War is a canard, and has been conclusively disproved.[25] It never had any plausibility or evidence to back it, except conceivably the independent activities of a few local groups which either went against central policy or were unaware of it. Yet the point is that in the conditions of the French movement a special effort was needed to *prevent* the Resistance from taking what would have appeared to be the logical (though not necessarily the best-advised) form of a bid for power; that Resistance groups, left to their own devices, might well have followed their noses into local attempts to seize power.[26] It is extremely unlikely that any British movement, however militant and radical, would spontaneously do so.

How important such differences of tradition are in practice must remain a matter of speculation. Clearly they are not decisive. They affect the *style* of a movement's activities rather than their, or its, nature. Yet style may be of more than superficial interest, and there may well be times when it is the man, or rather the movement. Obviously this will rarely be so where – for instance – movements conform to rigidly determined patterns of organization, ideology and behaviour, as among communist parties. Yet everyone with knowledge of communist movements knows that the extreme international uniformity which was imposed on them from the mid-1920s on ('bolshevization') no more prevented striking differences in the national atmosphere and style of communists than the uniformity of the Catholic priesthood makes the Irish Church identical with the Italian or Dutch. Where the conscious forces shaping the movement are less strong, the stylistic effects of tradition may be even more obvious.

An instructive example is that of the 'peace movement', which has always been abnormally strong in Britain, and relatively weak in France. (It is not to be confused with the anti-militarist movement, which sometimes runs parallel with it.) An aggressive and sometimes militant patriotism has, since the Jacobins, been deeply engrained on the French extreme left, and indeed had dominated it except at certain historical periods (for example, from *circa* 1880 to 1934) when the tricolour was seized by other hands. One might go so far as to suggest that the periods of maximum unity and power of French labour have been those when it could stigmatize the ruling classes not merely as exploiters but also as traitors: as during the Paris Commune, during the Popular Front period and especially during the Resistance. (In a sense this is merely another expression of the built-in aspiration to power in a revolutionary tradition: the Jacobins and their heirs have always seen themselves as potentially or actually a state-carrying or governing force.)[27] On the other hand, a moral dislike for aggression and war as such has always been deeply ingrained in the British labour movement, and is plainly one of the most important parts of its liberal–radical – and often specifically of its dissenting – heritage. It is no accident that in 1914 the ILP was the only non-revolutionary socialist party in a belligerent country – and indeed almost the only socialist party in any country – which as a body refused to support the war; but then Britain was the only belligerent country in which two ministers – both Liberals – resigned from the cabinet for the same reason. Time and again opposition to aggression or war has been the most effective method of unifying or dynamizing the British left: in the late 1870s, at the time of the Boer War, during the 1930s and again in the late 1950s.

The contrast between the peace movements of France and Britain after 1945 is particularly illuminating, because it is difficult to find any factors other than those of tradition to explain it. France has had no spontaneous mass peace movement, but only a phase when the Communist Party put its energies behind an anti-nuclear appeal, and therefore collected a great many signatures. The British have had no important political organization willing to mobilize public opinion against nuclear war or capable of doing so. (The close connection between the 'World Peace Movement' and the communists probably postponed the emergence of a broadly based mass peace movement in Britain until after the end of the worst hysteria of the Cold War.) On the other hand, an unofficial group of people could improvise the implicitly pacifist Campaign for Nuclear Disarmament, which has not merely become the most massive anti-nuclear movement in the world, with the possible exception of that of the Japanese, and a model for (less successful) foreign imitators, but a major force in British politics outside its narrow terms of reference. For it was largely on the issue of 'peace' that the left wing within the labour movement rallied to overthrow the long domination of a right-wing party leadership.

CHAPTER 5

The Making of the Working Class, 1870–1914

This paper was originally given as a Ford Lecture at Oxford University in 1981 and first published in 1984. It is an enquiry into the comparatively recent historical origins of the so-called 'traditional' British working-class way of life of the first half of the twentieth century.

I

If I call this chapter 'The Making of the Working Class' it is not because I wish to imply that the formation of this or any other class is a once-for-all process like the building of a house. Classes are never made in the sense of being finished or having acquired their definitive shape. They keep on changing. However, since the working class was historically a new class – not recognized as a social or institutional collective by itself or others before a specifiable period – there is some point in tracing its emergence as such a social group during some period. That is what E. P. Thompson attempted to do in a book which instantly and rightly became a classic.[1] On the other hand the working class of the 1820s and 1830s – assuming the name is already applicable – was patently very different from the so-called 'traditional' working class about which cultural observers, sometimes of proletarian parentage like Richard Hoggart, began to write bitter-sweet elegies in the 1950s. The famous fustian jackets of Chartism were still a long way from Andy Capp. It is the emergence of the Andy Capp working class which is my subject here: the British proletariat which came to be recognizable not only by its headgear, about which I shall have something to say, but by the physical environment in which it lived, by a style of life and leisure, by a certain class consciousness increasingly expressed in a secular tendency to join unions and to identify with a class party of Labour. It is the

57

working class of cup finals, fish-and-chip shops, palais-de-danse and Labour with a capital L. Since the 1950s this class has both contracted and changed, though the 1950 theorists of 'classlessness' and 'embourgeoisement' were wrong in predicting its dissolution. A lot of it is still there. The transformations since 1950 have been profound, nevertheless. However, these more recent developments of and within the working class are not my subject here. I have joined a number of people in the labour movement in discussing the nature and implications of these changes elsewhere.[2]

But my title is also both a tribute to and a critique of E. P. Thompson's remarkable book. In one sense Thompson was right to date the emergence of the working class in British society in the early nineteenth century, for by the time of Chartism the image of British society expressed in Asa Briggs' 'language of class' was already formulated, and it was formulated as a trinitarian image of landlords, bourgeoisie and labour. And this image already implies the conceptual absorption into the working class of all sorts of social strata which still existed in fact, but had, as it were, become socially invisible. The considerable body of people who played so large, and often so conscious, a part on the social stage of other countries under such names as peasantry, petty-bourgeoise and small craftsmen appear to be absent in Britain. By the time of Chartism, such terms as 'artisan', 'journeyman', 'craftsman' and for that matter virtually all terms associated with the ancient world of independent small producers and their organizations, denote something like the skilled wage-worker rather than the independent producer, while, conversely, the term 'manufacturer', which previously referred vaguely to the labour force, came to be monopolized by the industrial employer. Polarization of terminology indicates economic transformation. If the words 'trade' and 'tradesman', when used by workers, came to mean primarily industrial skill, the same terms in middle- and upper-class usage came to denote exclusively the function of retailing. The classic *Handwerker*, *artisan* or *artigiano* who both made and sold disappeared into the gap between.

But if the Thompson period is in this and some other ways crucial for the emergence, the 'making', of the English working class, Thompson seems to me to be wrong to suggest – for he does no more than this – that the labour classes of the period before, or even during, Chartism *were* the working class as it was to develop later. In spite of the striking and, by international standards, quite exceptional continuity of the trade-union movement with its pre-industrial artisan past, most of the work since Thompson has shown how dangerous it is to read the proletariat, the labour movements and the ideologies of our century back into the post-Napoleonic decades. Indeed, the lack of continuity between the labour movements before and after Chartism, the generation gap between the socialism of Owen and the socialist revival of the 1880s, is so obvious that attempts to explain it still keep historians busy. Some of our organizations may be very old and the occasional bit of folklore may have survived, but the truth is that the continuous history of British labour movements, including their historic memory, begins long after the Chartists. If the living tradition of the movement reaches back beyond this, it is because labour historians have disinterred the remoter past and fed it into the movement, where it has become part of the intellectual baggage of the activists. Owenism, Chartism and the rest, and the working classes of that early period, are of course the ancestors of the later British working class and its movements, but they are in crucial respects different phenomena. In this sense the working class is not 'made' until long after Thompson's book ends.

II

It is hardly surprising that the working class of the powerful and broad-based late-Victorian economy was very different from the labouring classes of the period before the railway network had been built. We need not waste time in establishing so obvious a point. In 1851 there were more shoemakers than coalminers, two and a half times as many tailors as railwaymen, and more silkworkers than commercial clerks.[3] The workshop of the world was not yet what Clapham called 'the industry state', either in scale, pattern or technology and industrial organization. If Lancashire had found its industrial pattern, Birmingham, Sheffield, Tyneside and South Wales were only finding it or about to find it. The question is rather how the development of the new and broadened industrial economy affected the working class. It did so in a number of ways.

In the first place, it greatly increased in absolute size and concentration. If total percentage employed in manufacture, mining and industry did not increase much between 1851 and 1911, and hardly at all until the 1890s – but transport did – it now constituted a much larger and more concentrated mass.[4] In 1911 there were thirty-six cities of over 100,000 inhabitants in Britain, compared to ten in 1851; and they contained 44 per cent of the total population compared to 25 per cent. Between 1871 and 1911 Merseyside increased by about three-quarters, and Tyneside almost trebled in population. The mean size of the establishments in which people worked also increased, though in industries which had established their pattern early, this may not have altered the general order of magnitude. Whether or not the 400 or so miners who formed the mean labour force in a Yorkshire and Glamorgan–Monmouth mine in 1912 were much bigger than before, pits of that size had long been familiar; and the 220 operatives in the average cottonmill of 1906, though larger by a quarter than in 1871, hardly transformed the character of such establishments.[5]

On the other hand we cannot but be struck by the rise of large industrial concentrations where none had existed before. There is nothing before the 1850s to compare with mid-Victorian Tyneside where we already find in the 1860s perhaps twelve shipyards employing a minimum of 1,500 men each; Armstrongs already had 6,000 to 7,000 in their Elswick works. But by 1914 it was to be 20,000, or about three times as many. Just so the Great Western Railway's works in Swindon trebled its 1875 labour force to reach 14,000 by 1914. There is a qualitative and not only a quantitative difference between Barrow-in-Furness in 1871–2, when the town's largest shipyard and engineering works employed 600 men each, and the Barrow of the First World War, in which Vickers employed 27,000 engineers and 6,000 shipbuilders.[6]

In the second place the occupational composition of the working classes changed substantially, as witness the rise of the railwaymen from less than 100,000 in 1871 to 400,000 in 1911, and of miners from half a million to 1.2 million in the same period, while the total male population of England, Wales and Scotland increased by only 60 per cent. And so, plainly, did its age- and sex-composition, with the decline of school-age employment from 30 per cent of all children in 1851 to 14 per cent in 1914[7] and the modest, but novel, penetration of women into factory industries other than textiles. The changes in the manual skills of workers are less plain, and are still the subject of much debate. Yet it is undeniable that in 1875 the largest national trade unions by far were the Amalgamated Engineers and the Operative Stonemasons, followed, in that order, by the Boilermakers, the Amalgamated Carpenters and Joiners, the Amalgamated Tailors and the Cotton Spinners. After 1895 the TUC was notoriously dominated by the big battalions of coal – now nationally organized – and cotton, and by 1914 by the Triple Alliance of Coal, Transport and Railways. Moreover, even the powerful groups of labour aristocrats relied increasingly, and necessarily, not on the indispensability of irreplaceable manual skills, but on job monopolies guaranteed by the strength of organizations which kept out others who might quite easily have done their work. Hence the crucial issue for labour during the First World War was to be 'dilution'.

In the third place, the growing national integration and concentration of the national economy and its sectors, and the growing role of the state in both, transformed the conditions of industrial conflict. Let us merely remind ourselves that the industrial dispute as a *national* strike or lock-out does not exist for practical purposes before the 1890s. Indeed, Cronin has shown that the strike itself only came into its own after 1870.[8] For that matter the negotiated *nationwide* collective agreement is absent before 1890, except in parts of the cotton industry where the 'nation' coincided with sections of Lancashire. By 1910, as Clegg, Fox and Thompson point out,[9] there were such agreements in engineering, shipbuilding, printing, iron and steel, and footwear, as well as equivalent mechanisms elsewhere. Moreover, the direct and urgent interest of government in industrial relations is shown not only by the establishment of the Labour Department of the Board of Trade (1893) and the growing scope of its activities, but by the direct intervention of senior politicians in labour disputes, Rosebery's incursion into the coal lock-out of 1893 being the first major example.[10]

In the fourth place – and here we leave economics for politics – there was the widening of the franchise and mass politics. What proletarian voters might think and want was henceforth a major preoccupation of politicians, and conversely what central government could be got to do was of much more practical concern to workers, even though they took a while to wake up to this fact. When politicians – I am quoting the Edwardian Churchill – thought that the main problem was how to stop party politics turning into class politics, workers were also more likely to be struck by the potential of national class politics. Belonging to 'Labour', that is to manual labour, took on a political dimension it had not had since Chartism.

These developments are important, because without them it is difficult to understand how that aggregate of microcosms which constituted the British world of labour, that collection of often strictly self-contained little worlds, could transform itself into a national phenomenon. Take a late and rather extreme example, that of W. P. Richardson (1873–1930). He was born and lived all his life in Usworth, County Durham, worked for thirty years in Usworth colliery, married a local miner's daughter, presided over Usworth parish council, directed the Usworth Colliery Primitive Methodist Chapel choir and wrote a column on poultry for the local paper. It is safe to say that if, say, Manchester had been wiped out by an earthquake, it would have made no practical difference to him. Yet this man, who was as rooted in his village as any Herefordshire milkmaid, helped to found the local ILP branch, joined the board of the *Daily Herald*, championed the nationalization of all mines and was to become the national treasurer of the Miners' Federation. This is by no means as natural a development as it may seem in retrospect. For miners of Richardson's generation it became both easier, and in many ways essential, to see Usworth as part not only of the Durham coalfield, but of a national coal industry, and that being a miner implied being a member of a national working class whose specific political and social aspirations were expressed in an independent party of Labour with its own newspapers and specific programmes. An older figure like Henry Rust (1831–1902) never really reconciled himself to the fact that the miners of West Bromwich and Darlaston had anything to gain from joining the rest of the Midland miners, let alone the national Miners' Federation.[11]

Given all this, we should expect the working class itself to change. But how and when? Let me take the simple and apparently frivolous case of Andy Capp. When did this particular headgear – the flat cap – become characteristic of the British proletarian? It was certainly not so in the 1870s in London, for Jules Vallès, the Communard refugee, specifically complained about the lack of the local workers' class consciousness, because they did not, unlike the Paris artisans, wear 'la blouse et la casquette' when off work.[12] The illustrations and photographs of the 1870s and 1880s show a mixture of headgear and, incidentally – as Keir Hardie's deerstalker demonstrates – even caps were not yet standardized. Yet by 1914 any picture of masses of British workers anywhere, on or off duty, reveals the familiar sea of flat peaked caps. The detailed chronology of this transformation awaits research on the rich iconographic material. But it is evident that, within a matter of a couple of decades or so, the British male workers had taken to wearing a badge which immediately stamped them as members of a class. Moreover, they knew that it did. The argument of my paper is that the so-called 'traditional' working class with its specific patterns of life and views of life did not emerge much before the 1880s and took shape in the next couple of decades. I should perhaps also add that this was also the period of the emergence of the 'middle class' as we know it, which is very different indeed from its early- and mid-Victorian predecessors and from the upper bourgeoisie of the 'Establishment'. The sudden rise of the cap is parallelled by the equally rapid rise of the old-school tie[13] and the even more sudden rise of the golf club. Twenty-nine golf courses were laid out in Yorkshire in 1890–5: before 1890 there had been just two.[14] However, though the restructuring of each of the two main social strata of Britain is not separable from the other, this is not my subject here.

III

The 1880s are familiar to every labour historian as the decade of the so-called rebirth of socialism in Britain, but the phenomena I am here concerned with are statistically more significant than the ideological shifts among the few hundred people who, in the 1880s, constituted the British socialist organizations and their sympathizers. They are more massive even than the beginnings of the transformation of trade unionism in this decade, known as the 'new' unionism. I pick out the 1880s because the substantial transformation of the material conditions of working-class life and of what might be called the social and institutional compass-bearings of the working-class course across the territory of national life were hardly visible before then. I am not claiming that they were not present. It is easy to play the well-known historian's game of pushing origins backwards, especially into a period as curiously lacking a definable working-class profile as the decades after Chartism, a period when it is often still hard to decide whether time off for working men meant the weekend – the famous *semaine anglaise* of which continentals dreamed, or the traditional Saint Monday.[15] Thus, to take a familiar landmark on the map of the 'traditional' working class, the fish-and-chip shop originated, probably in Oldham, in the 1860s, and a local firm began to manufacture ranges exclusively for fish-frying in the first half of the 1870s. In 1876 this was still described as 'a petty trade', whereas by 1914 there were something like 25,000 fish-fryers.[16] Other innovations of the 1880s can be traced back to the 1870s. Football already had a modest subterranean life as a proletarian spectator sport in the later 1870s.[17] Professional agents and national booking of music-hall artistes seem to have developed in that decade, which also saw the birth of a professional trade press for the pop music business.[18] It is not my intention to claim patent rights on the basis of priority for any decade, but simply to point out that, whatever may be the case in the 1870s, the new pattern emerged on the national scene in the 1880s and cannot any longer be overlooked, though both contemporary middle-class observers and subsequent historians have long succeeded in overlooking it.

Three factors affected the workers' material conditions of life after 1870: the dramatic fall of the cost of living during the so-called Great Depression of 1873–96, the discovery of the domestic mass market, including that of the well-paid or at least regularly employed workers

63

for industrially produced or processed goods, and (after 1875) the so-called 'by-law housing' (under section 157 of the Public Health Act), which in fact created so much of the environment of working-class life, the rows of terraced houses outside the old town centres. All imply or were based on the modest, patchy but plainly undeniable improvement in the standard of life of the bulk of British workers, which is not a matter of dispute even among historians. The crucial point about this improvement is not the mere rise in real incomes and consumer expenditures, but the structural changes which mediated them. These are most spectacular in distribution, that is in the relative decline of retail markets and small shops and the rise on the one hand of the Co-ops, whose membership increased from about half a million in the late 1870s to about one million around 1890, and three million in 1914, and, on the other, the rise of the multiple shops which were to give the British high streets their character-istic appearance between the 1890s and the rise of the modern supermarket since the 1950s.[19] Nor should we forget the rise and institutionalization of hire-purchase, which made possible the trans-formation of the working-class interior. Its history has been neglected, though work is in progress. Here again the 1880s and 1890s seem to have been crucial. The dates of the key cases which cleared up the legal and financial confusions surrounding this growing practice are 1893 and 1895.[20] But distribution and manufacture cannot be separated. The mass production of tea in standardized packets dates from 1884,[21] and the new jams and preserves which changed the working-class diet were manufactured in those factories which are chiefly known to labour historians as the scene of the early struggles of women factory workers.

As for housing, the major development was not only that somewhat bigger and better houses were now built, but that there was growth of segregated working-class streets and quarters, and indeed, especially with the massive development of cheap public transport in the 1880s, even some segregated working-class suburbs – mainly inner suburbs. I shall say something about the effect of this growing residential segregation later. As for working-class suburbanization, we may as well note that it tended to fray or cut one of the strongest existential links of the working-class community, that between where people lived and worked, but probably only in London. By 1905 the LCC estimated that 820,000 workmen were making extensive journeys to work every day in London.

The most spectacular transformation, of course, was in the pattern of working-class leisure and holidays. I need hardly remind you today of the rise of football as a national, and increasingly proletarian, spectator sport and of the development of a male football culture, finally consecrated by the attendance of the king at the Cup Final from 1913. Nor that the emancipation of football from – or rather against – middle- and upper-class patronage took place in the 1880s, with the triumph of Blackburn against the Old Etonians, the open professionalization of the game in 1885, and the formation of the League in 1888, incidentally on the model of the system established earlier in the USA for professional baseball.[22] The 1880s are clearly equally crucial in the development of the working-class holiday. The first volume of *Herapath's Railway Journal* in which the index lists 'holiday traffic' as such is 1884, and the paper's comments deserve to be quoted:

> Year by year the holiday traffic at Easter, Whitsun and August is growing in importance. Its dimensions have not yet swelled so far as seriously to affect dividends, but it is easy to foresee a time when this will be the case ... We may never turn Easter into a carnival, but our toiling masses seem determined to turn it to account as a substantial holiday.[23]

The growth of the links between the mill-towns and Blackpool can be traced through Bradshaw. In 1865 there were only two trains with third-class carriages daily between Bolton and Blackpool, in 1870 four, in 1875 twelve, in 1880 thirteen, in 1885 fourteen and in 1890 twenty-three. But there is at least one more general and less labour-intensive way of estimating the growth of the holiday business, for an annual return by the Board of Trade under an act of 1861 enables us to measure the amount of proposed investment in piers and harbourworks, many of which can be identified as pleasure or promenade piers, those characteristic structures of English seaside holidays.[24] The table (overleaf) breaks down the proposed investment into that destined for primarily middle-class and working-class resorts, omitting doubtful cases.[25] This necessarily crude index shows the rise of working-class resorts from the later 1870s, but above all the enormous spurt in proposed investment in the 1890s which, for the first time, pushed the plans for investment in working-class holiday entertainment massively above those for middle-class resorts.

We may illustrate this by the classic example of Blackpool, where the first real signs of action are in the 1860s, with the opening of the North Pier (it cost little more than half of what was spent on that of Ventnor, Isle of Wight), the second pier and the first theatre. With the 1870s we are clearly getting into substantial business: the Winter Garden (which was to cost £107,000) was started in 1878. But the Blackpool we know best is that of the 1890s: that of the

Projected investment in pleasure piers 1863–1899

Period	Middle class		Working class	
	total £000s	annual mean £000s	total £000s	annual mean £000s
1863–5	78	26	30	10
1866–70	112.5	22.5	25	5
1871–5	98.5	19.7	30	6
1876–80	184.4	36.9	83.8	16.8
1881–5	292	58.4	70	14
1886–90	174.5	34.9	75.5	15.1
1891–5	172	34.4	291.5	58.3
1896–9	158	39.5	191.9	48

Tower, the Great Wheel, the Victoria Pier on the South Shore, the extended promenade, the Opera House (1889), the new market, free library, town hall and, for good measure, a special bench of magistrates and a coat-of-arms.

Now everyone knows that British workers, unlike the English middle class, which developed a high degree of standardization in this period – notably in its speech – did not lose its regional or even local identity, its local peculiarities, tastes and pride. And yet it is equally clear that the new pattern of life was more nationally homogeneous than anything before. At the coalface miners might insist on wearing the working-clothes of regional custom. Even in the Second World War, the Board of Trade's attempt to replace these by standard 'utility' garments caused a considerable uproar from the unions. Yet outside work the miner, like most of the rest of male workers, wore the same clothes from Blyth to Midsomer Norton. The worker identified with his local team against the rest of the world – indeed in sufficiently large towns with one of the two moieties – City or United, Forest or County – which between them defined the citizen of Manchester or Nottingham or wherever. Yet the pattern of the football culture was the same everywhere – give or take an extra dose of emotion – and it was a *national* pattern, or to be more precise a pattern of the proletarian nation, since the map of the Football League was virtually identical with the map of industrial England. It was national even in the symbolic annual conquest of the public space of the national capital by the two local proletarian armies which invaded London for the cup final. Since the later 1860s there had been regional collective rituals of the same kind, notably the miners' annual demonstrations of which the Durham Miners' Gala has survived – perhaps just because, unlike the others, it had exactly this characteristic of a symbolic occupation of a local capital by the miners – but not yet national ones.

A single, fairly standardized, national pattern of working-class life: and at the same time one increasingly specific to the working class. It is the segregation of the British manual worker's world which is so striking.[26] In the first place it was a growing residential segregation, due both to the exodus of the middle and lower-middle strata from formerly mixed areas – the process has been traced for the East End of London – and to the construction of new and *de facto* single-class urban quarters and suburbs. Some of these new quarters, buildings or estates were intended for the working class, such as the Queen's Park Estate in Paddington, most for the new 'suburbanites' who were, quite correctly, identified with the new white-collar lower-middle class; and 'Villa Toryism': the sort of people who, as the *Cornhill Magazine* supposed in 1901, would naturally live, if they could, in one of the 'clerks' suburbs' of London – Clapham, Forest Gate, Wandsworth, Walthamstow or Kilburn.[27] Others would not be specifically designed for a social stratum and a class lifestyle, but would become so either because the rents precluded poorer tenants or, more likely, because in fact the lifestyles of manual workers and black-coated employees of comparable income increasingly diverged. By the early 1900s the residential separation of the better-paid workers (the 'artisans') and the new lower-middle class was by no means universal. The better type of popular dwellings – five- or six-room houses – were still reported as being inhabited indifferently by 'artisans, clerks, insurance agents, shopmen' and the like in Birkenhead, Bolton, Chester, Crewe, Croydon, Darlington, Derby, Hull, Newcastle, Oldham, Portsmouth, Preston, Sheffield, South Shields and Wigan, but in a number of places the absence of workers from such accommodation is specifically noted, or it is described as being inhabited 'more frequently by clerks, shop-assistants and the like than by people of the kind usually included in the term "working classes"'.[28] These included Birmingham, Bradford, Bristol, Burton-on-Trent, Gateshead, Grimsby, Halifax, Hanley, Huddersfield, Kidderminster, Liverpool (or at least Bootle), Manchester, Middlesbrough, Northampton, Norwich, Nottingham, Plymouth, Reading, Southampton, Stoke on Trent, Walsall, Wolverhampton and most of outer London. Since the better housing was commonly the more recent housing, we may reasonably suppose that segregation was increasing.

So, of course, and for the same reason, was the segregation between the better-paid artisans and the lower-paid, even though their cohabitation is still noticed in several towns – Norwich, Nottingham, Preston and Stockport for instance – and though the concentration of the working class in the inner zone of cities and their reluctance

to move too far away from work, which is noted in various towns –
meant that the working-class belts, though residentially stratified,
formed a coherent quarter. The Shaftesbury buildings in Battersea,
which were a stronghold of artisans (and of Battersea socialism),
were, after all, part of that area between Lavender Hill and the river
in which 'the bulk of the working *class* ... are housed'.[29]

In the second place, workers were segregated by expectations. As
Robert Roberts says, before 1914 'skilled workers generally did not
strive to join a higher rank',[30] but in fact even the chance of
improvement within the stratum below the accepted middle class
was diminished by two developments: the increasing use of formal
schooling as a class criterion, not to mention a way out of the manual
working class, and the decline of the alternative way forward to self-
respect and pride, the training and experience of the all-round
craftsman. Workers were increasingly defined as those who had no
education or got nothing out of it; and the contrast between those
who left school and those who stayed, or those who got jobs on the
strength of schooling and those to whom it was irrelevant – a contrast
sometimes between fathers and sons, though not so much between
mothers and sons (see D. H. Lawrence) – intensified the felt differences
between manual and non-manual workers. On the other hand the
fairly extensive de-skilling which took place in the last thirty years
before 1914 created the frustration which Askwith, the government's
chief industrial conciliator in those years, thought so important. The
young worker:

> does not like to admit to himself that he is not being trained as an
> engineer or a shipbuilder or a housebuilder, but to become an operative.
> But in a brief time to the majority comes disillusionment; and when
> once a man is disillusioned, bitterness is a very natural result, and
> antagonism to the system which he deems to be the cause.[31]

The horizons of the skilled worker were thus increasingly bounded
by the world of manual labour, and those of the less skilled even
more so. In spite of their differences they were pressed into a single
class by their exclusion from the rest of society.

In the third place, workers were segregated by the divergence of
lifestyles, of 'what workers do' from those of other classes. Thus it
seems clear that as football gained mass support, it became increasingly a proletarian activity, for both players and supporters. No doubt
primarily an activity of the more skilled or respectable workers, but
insofar as support for the team united all who lived in Blackburn or
Bolton or Sunderland, and insofar as football became the main topic
of social conversation in the public bar,[32] a sort of lingua franca of

social intercourse among men, it was part of the world of *all* workers. Again, the peculiar working-class form of betting which plainly increased enormously from the 1880s on was spectacularly pro-letarian. It was, as McKibbin suggests, 'the most successful form of working-class self-help in the modern era':[33] an illegal but almost totally honest network of financial transactions stretching into every proletarian street and every workshop. The same class distinction increasingly separated the Sunday paper (of which the *News of the World* became the ideal type, until the later rise of the proletarian daily) both from the quality press and from the new lower-middle-class press pioneered by Northcliffe. And then, as I have already noticed, there is the cap.

And, finally, the working class was not so much segregated as alienated from the ruling class by two developments which, together with the fall in real wages, Askwith made responsible for the labour unrest of 1910–14. These, he told the cabinet confidentially, were the conspicuous display of luxury by the rich, especially demonstrated by the use of the motor-car, and the growth of the mass media, which made for greater national co-ordination of news – and activity.[34] I quote Askwith not as proof that the plutocracy – the phrase belongs to the Edwardian political vocabulary – flaunted itself any more in the Belle Epoque than under Queen Victoria, though this is possible; but as evidence for the belief that the wealth of the rich was now more visible and more resented.

What all this amounts to is a growing sense of a single working class, bound together in a community of fate irrespective of its internal differences. A class in the social and not merely in the classificatory sense: a body within which it would be absurd any longer to speak of 'the class of miners' as distinct from 'the class of cotton-workers', as Keir Hardie had still done in the early 1880s.[35] And this indeed explains how a period which provided plenty of reasons for growing sectionalism and infighting among groups of workers – one thinks of the shipbuilding industry – could also be a period when workers increasingly saw themselves and acted as Labour, with a capital L. The history of that capital L remains to be written, like the history of the working class as a singular rather than a plural noun, but there is little doubt that the transformation becomes noticeable in the twenty-five years before 1914. And indeed, even in purely economic terms, from 1900, and even more from 1911, a con-vergence rather than a divergence between local, regional, skilled and unskilled wage-rates becomes observable. As Hunt has shown, until 1890 trade unions and the whole environment of industrial relations in Britain helped to sustain differentials, between 1890 and

1910 they exercised no clear influence in either direction, but by 1911 they were a force helping to reduce differentials.

Politicians were aware of this class consciousness – of what Chamberlain, in 1906, called 'the conviction, born for the first time in the working classes, that their social salvation is in their own hands'.[36] If party politics was not to be identified with class conflict, one now had to pay one's respects to the supremacy of class when appealing to workers on the grounds of party. The Rhondda, as both its MP, the Lib–Lab Mabon, and the local paper proclaimed, was 'Labour in every aspiration', but the point of this observation was of course to argue that it was not *only* Labour: 'Since men cannot live by bread alone, the Rhondda mining electors are Nationalists, they are Nonconformists', and so on. Edwardian political rhetoric 'had to use a language, and in particular the word "Labour" to bind their supporters into the established pattern of politics',[37] from which they threatened to escape. Where, as in Ulster and in Salvidge's Liverpool, the appeal to religion and nationality was sufficient, class did not loom large – or to much effect – in the language of local politics.[38]

Paradoxically, class initially made its way into Labour politics by a back door. Insofar as a man was seen as 'a class representative' he was in fact seen as 'outside the arena of "party politics"', even though as an individual he might be Liberal, Tory or, more rarely, socialist.[39] This meant not merely that socialists and non-socialists could collaborate happily in the new Labour Party, or that the solidly Liberal miners could transfer to Labour without changing their views. It also meant that Tory workers who would not vote for Liberals could vote for Labour men. This was commented on when Will Crooks won Woolwich in 1903, a seat so hopeless that the Liberals had not even fought it in 1900, and it was significant in Lancashire, where workers were politically divided, even though Joyce's 'factory politics' were already in rapid decline in the 1890s. It was the Lancashire coalfield which had much the largest majority for affiliation to Labour, and in 1913[40] the notoriously unradical cotton unions voted in favour of the political levy by a substantial majority everywhere except in the Tory working-class stronghold of Oldham.[41]

Yet we must ask whether this could have happened if the common interests of workers as a class did not already seem, even in politics, *more* important, or at least more immediately relevant, than other loyalties; as they clearly were not in Liverpool and Belfast. Very soon a choice for Labour had to become a choice *against* other parties, not a way of bypassing party politics. It may well be that the stagnation of the Labour vote after 1906 reflects the difficulty of taking this next step. The 1914 war was to remove this difficulty.

For this step implied the socialists' view of the independent party of Labour, which was fundamentally different from the earlier struggle for independent labour representation in Parliament. This had essentially been a demand that there should be *some* workers in Parliament who could speak directly for the special interests of manual labour, as railway directors spoke for the railway interest or shipowners for shipping. The trouble with the Liberal Party was not that, as a national party, it opposed this – on the contrary – but that it could not understand that the new concept of independent Labour implied more than a handful of authoritative workers or ex-worker MPs: a Joseph Arch, a Burt, even – why not? – a John Burns, who spoke for Labour as Cobden and Bright had spoken for Lancashire manu-facturers. It implied that workers should *only* vote for class-rep-resentatives. As Ramsay MacDonald explained in 1903, 'so soon as there is a Labour movement in politics, the very meaning of Labour representation must change', for 'Labour politics was the expression of the needs of the working class'. *Not*, he added characteristically, 'as a class, but as the chief constituent of the nation'.[42] But the class struggle could not be so easily eliminated from working-class politics, least of all at a time when it was conducted with growing acrimony on both sides.

This brings me to my last point: class consciousness. I have deliberately avoided identifying the sentiments and opinions of the mass of workers, so far as we know them, with those of the avant-garde of activists and militants, because the two were plainly not the same. Activists were imbued with the spirit of nonconformity at a time when dissent was on the decline. They actively disliked much of the new working-class way of life – notably the football culture. One could compile a large anthology from the writings of contemporary socialists expressing hatred, ridicule and contempt for the stupidity and sluggishness of the proletarian masses. Whatever the implications of class consciousness for the militants, the masses were not living up to their expectations. And yet it is equally wrong to see the working class simply as an apolitical stoic underworld, a ghetto comprising most of the nation, or at best as a force which could be mobilized in defence of their narrow economic interests as potential or actual trade unionists. They also acquired a consciousness of class. I do not want to make too much of the conversion of a smallish minority of workers to socialism, though this is not negligible; nor even of the astonishing success of this minority and its organizations in getting itself accepted as a cadre of leaders and a brains-trust from the 1890s on. Labour movements need leaders and leaders need training. Since the revival of socialism, the organizations of the socialist left have provided by far the most effective mechanisms for bringing together the self-selected elite of able, intelligent, dynamic and innovatory workers – mainly young workers – and by far the best schooling for them. In our period such people started their careers as SDFers or ILPers or Syndicalists, just as between the wars the future leaders of national trade unionism started in the Communist Party. They were accepted as leaders by people who did not share their views, because they were the best and they had relevant as well as apparently irrelevant ideas. But there is clearly more to the political transformation of Labour than this. What we have to explain is the transformation of the miners from a body notoriously immune to the appeal of the socialists to what has been called 'the Praetorian guard of an explicitly socialist Labour Party'.[43] What we have to explain is why this happened not only in areas of embittered class battle like South Wales, but in areas of no notable industrial militancy like Yorkshire; not only in coalfields where miners were doing poorly, like Lancashire, but in some where they were doing well.

Unlike the progress of the trade-union movement in our period, which doubled in numbers and then, after a couple of decades, doubled again to reach over four million in 1914, the progress of class consciousness is almost impossible to chart. The rise of what is even by our standards mass unionism – and in 1910–14 mass militancy – certainly indicates some transformation, but its exact nature is unclear. Electoral indicators fail us, partly because other workers are not so identifiable as voters as the miners, but mainly because the statistics of the independent Labour vote are obscure before 1906 and not significant from then till 1914. It is only from 1918 on, when Labour suddenly appears with 24 per cent of the total votes cast, rising to 37.5 per cent in 1929, that voting Labour can reasonably be used as an index of political class consciousness. At that point it becomes possible to say that large and growing masses of British workers regard voting Labour as an automatic consequence of being workers. Before 1914 this is not yet so. In 1913 even 43 per cent of the miners still voted against paying the union's political levy to the Labour Party.[44]

Yet if the making of the working-class consciousness before 1914 cannot be quantified, it is still there. In 1915 Beatrice Webb could say: 'The power of the Movement lies in the massive obstinacy of the rank-and-file, every day more representative of the working class. Whenever this massive feeling can be directed for or against some particular measure, it becomes almost irresistible. Our English governing class would not dare overtly to defy it.'[45] In 1880 nobody could or would seriously have made such a statement. The two nations of Disraeli were now no longer the rich and the poor, but the middle class and the working class, a working class which, in its physical environment, its practices and reflexes, is recognizable, at least in the industrial areas, as Richard Hoggart describes it from inter-war experience. Insofar as it was not deferential, apolitical and apathetic, its politics were no longer implicit in a general belief in the rights of man, workers being merely one large section of a comprehensive 'the people'. The politics of Chartism, whether as an independent mass movement or as part of liberal–radicalism, fade out. The last movement of this type was founded very nearly at the same moment as the Labour Representation Committee. It united the mid-Victorian left of *Reynolds News*, which inspired it, powerful Lib–Lab figures like Howell, Fenwick and Sam Woods, with New Unionists on the socialist left: Tom Mann, Bob Smillie. John Burns blessed it. Yet this National Democratic League disappears by 1906 after a few years of by no means negligible influence. I doubt whether any general history of Britain in this period so much as mentions its name. Even labour historians treat it as little more than a footnote. The future lay with the Labour Representation Committee, and the essence of its programme, whatever it was, was that it specifically served the demands and aspirations of the working class.

Let me conclude with yet another miner. I choose Herbert Smith, 1862–1938, because he was neither a chapel activist nor a man one would associate with ideology or, in spite of his enthusiasm for education, with much reading. He was probably as close to the average pitman as any leader, even among miners, even in South Yorkshire, has even been: a slow, hard, reliable man, keener on cricket and Barnsley Football Club, whose matches he attended religiously, than on ideas; a man more inclined to ask opponents to step outside than to argue. Herbert Smith advanced steadily from checkweighman to the presidency of the Yorkshire miners and eventually, in the 1920s, of the Miners' Federation. In 1897, at the age of thirty-five, he decided to support the ILP. It is the late age of this decision, which makes his conversion significant. Henceforth he remained a socialist, and while in the 1920s he hammered the communists, by Edwardian standards he was a rather left-wing ILPer. It was clearly not ideology that attracted him. It was the experience of the miners' struggle, and that the socialists demanded what he thought the miners needed, a legal eight-hour day, a guaranteed minimum wage and better safety.

But his choice also expressed a visceral, militant and profound class consciousness which found visible expression in his dress. Herbert Smith was famous for his cap. A biography of him has been written under the title *The Man in the Cap*.[46] He wore it like a flag. There is a photograph of him in old age, as mayor of Barnsley, with Lord Harewood in the elongated elegance, bowler and furled umbrella of *his* class and the Chief Constable in a frogged uniform. Herbert Smith, a stocky, rather fat old man, wore the Mayor's chain and insignia, but above them he wore his cap. One could say a lot about his career, not all of it complimentary, though I defy anyone to withhold all admiration from the man who, in 1926, sat at the negotiating table in his cap, minus his false teeth, which he had put on the table for comfort, and said 'no' on behalf of the miners to the coalowners, the government and the world. All I want to say here is that Herbert Smith as a labour leader and his career would have been unthinkable in any earlier period of labour history – perhaps also in any later one. He was made by, and he helped to make, the new working class whose emergence in the decades before 1914 I have tried to sketch. Among the millions of men in caps he was certainly exceptional; but he was exceptional only as a particularly majestic tree is in a large forest. There were innumerable others, less prominent, less political, less active, who recognized themselves in his image, and we should recognize them also.

CHAPTER 6

Victorian Values

This chapter is, among other things, a threnody for the skilled manual worker. It was originally given as the Tawney Lecture to the Economic History Society in 1983. Hence the reference, at the end, to R. H. Tawney (1880–1962) a key figure in British economic history, socialism and the fight for – to name the title of two of his books – 'Equality' and against 'The Acquisitive Society'.

This chapter is essentially an argument about the fortunes and transformations of the skilled manual wage-worker in the first industrial nation. His characteristics, values, interests and, indeed, protective devices had their roots deep in the pre-industrial past of the 'crafts' which provided the model even for skilled trades that could not have existed before the industrial revolution, such as the Journeymen Steam Engine Makers. Skilled labour continued to bear the marks of this past until well into the twentieth century; in some respects it survived strongly until the Second World War. It is now generally accepted that the British industrial economy in its prime relied extensively, and often fundamentally, on skilled hand-labour with or without the aid of powered machinery. It did so for reasons of technology – insofar as manual skill could not yet be dispensed with; for reasons of productive organization – because skilled labour supplemented and partly replaced design, technological expertise and management; and, more fundamentally, for reasons of business rationality. So long as it did not stand in the way of making satisfactory profits, the heavy costs of replacing it, or incidental to its replacement, did not seem to be justified by the prospects of the profits to be made without it. This applied not only to special cases like Fleet Street. Sir Andrew Noble of Armstrong's argued, no doubt correctly, that there was more money to be made from building one river boat than from producing 6,000 cars.[1] Unlike the United States, skilled manual labour was not in short supply. And the major incentive to replace it, namely the mass production of standardized goods, was unusually weak or patchy in the British home market until the last decades of the century, while the commanding position of British goods on the world market, or more precisely in the markets of what today would be called the third world and the white empire, kept old methods of production viable. Moreover, it may be suggested that, in terms of money wages, British skilled labour was probably not expensive. It may well have charged less than the traffic could have borne.

The British skilled worker thus occupied a crucial position of considerable strength, and the longer he occupied and exploited it, the more troublesome and expensive it would be to dislodge him. Skill could indeed have been toppled. Skilled men were defeated in pitched and apparently decisive battles between the early 1830s and the 1850s – even the powerful engineers. Yet what followed in the 1850s and 1860s was, in most industries, a tacit system of arrangements and accommodations between masters and skilled labour, which satisfied both sides. The position of the skilled men was reinforced to such an extent that the much more systematic later attempt to displace them by a new and more sophisticated mechanization and 'scientific management' also largely failed. The nineteenth-century artisan was indeed doomed. Except in some small if crucial patches of the industrial economy, and in the undergrowth of the black economy, he – for even in our days it is very rarely a she – no longer counts for much. But then neither does British industry.

The history of the artisan is thus a drama in five acts: the first sets him in his pre-industrial heritage, the second deals with his struggles in the early industrial period, the third with his mid-Victorian glories, the fourth with his successful resistance to renewed attack. The last sees his gradual but far from smooth decline and fall since the end of the first post-war boom.

I shall begin with a simple observation. In most European languages the word *artisan* or its equivalent, used without qualification, is automatically taken to mean something like an independent craftsman or small master, or someone who hopes to become one. In nineteenth-century Britain it is equally automatically taken to refer to a skilled wage-worker, or indeed sometimes initially (as in Gaskell's *Artisans and Machinery*) to any wage-worker. In short, artisan traditions and values in this country became proletarianized, as nowhere else. The term *artisan* itself is perhaps misleading. It belongs largely to the world of nineteenth-century social and political discourse, probably entering the public vocabulary in the course of the ill-fated campaigns, almost the last collective endeavours of both craft masters and journeymen – the latter already vastly predominating – for putting life back into the Elizabethan labour code at the end of the Napoleonic Wars. The term seems rarely to be used for social description or classification in the eighteenth century. The actual word almost universally used in working-class circles is 'tradesman'. While in nineteenth-century middle-class usage it came to mean almost without exception a, generally small, retailer (a man who was 'in trade'), in working-class usage it retained, and perhaps among older men still retains, the ancient craft usage of the man who 'has a trade': here language and the differentiation of the estate of artificers into those who make and those who sell go together. We may note in passing that while 'being in trade' develops connotations of contempt or deference, 'having a trade', at least for those who have it or compare themselves to its possessors, maintains its connotations of self-satisfaction and pride.

As the word 'master' shows an analogous development, becoming in nineteenth-century usage a synonym for 'employer', so conversely 'journeyman' becomes synonymous with a wage-working tradesman. Indeed, in the dawn of industrialization it is sometimes used for any wage-worker. Trade societies and trade unions, in which the name of the old artisanate survives, are now not only bodies of traditional crafts like hatters or brushmakers, but unprecedented ones like journeymen steam engine makers and boilermakers. While unions gradually dropped the word 'journeyman' from their titles, the word itself continued as a description of the skilled man, no longer in contrast to the 'masters' in his trade, but rather in contrast to the apprentices whose numbers he sought to control, and especially the 'labourers' or 'handymen' against whom he defended his job monopoly. Nineteenth-century class differentiation and stratification is thus deeply rooted in the vocabulary and hence the congealed memories, of the pre-industrial craft world.

What is more, the term 'the trade' becomes essentially identified with the skilled workers who practise it. 'The men of every trade speak of their trade among themselves as "the trade".'[2] 'In connexion with labour affairs,' says an early-twentieth-century labour dictionary, 'this term denotes either 1) a specific craft or occupation in the field of manual employment, or 2) the collective body of workers engaged at a single specific craft or occupation.'[3] Indeed 'the trade' may actually become a synonym for the union. Thus as late as the Second World War we find a cooper's apprentice, outraged by seeing a labourer doing skilled work, successfully threatening the boss to bring the matter to the attention of 'the trade', if he is not told to stop.[4]

I do not wish to labour the linguistic point, though the question of language is significant and would repay systematic research. At all events, it is clear that not only the vocabulary and institutions of pre-industrial craft organization passed over to the working class almost *en bloc*, but the basic Victorian classificatory distinction within the working classes also derived from craft tradition. It is common ground that the Victorian division of workers into either 'artisans' (or some similar term such as 'mechanics') and 'labourers' was unrealistic, and had always been descriptively inadequate. Yet it was very generally accepted, and not only by skilled workers, as representing a real dichotomy, which caused no major classificatory problems until the expansion of groups which could neither be realistically fitted into either pigeon-hole, nor overlooked and who, from the 1890s, came to be known vaguely as 'semi-skilled'.[5] From the masters' point of view it represented the difference between all other labour and skilled labour, that is 'all such as requires a long period of service, whether under a definite contract or agreement, and in a single firm, or with no such agreement, the learner moving about from firm to firm'.[6] This was also essentially the men's definition.[7]

From the men's point of view it represented the *qualitative* superiority of the skill so learned – the professionalism of craftsmanship – and simultaneously of its status and rewards. The apprenticed journeyman was the ideal type of labour aristocrat, not only because his work called for skill and judgment, but because a 'trade' provided a formal, ideally an institutionalized, line of demarcation separating the privileged from the unprivileged. It did not much matter that formal apprenticeship was, almost certainly, not the most important gateway to many trades. George Howell estimated in 1877 that less than 10 per cent of union members were properly apprenticed.[8] They included so firm a pillar of the crafts as Robert Applegarth, secretary of the ASCJ (Amalgamated Society of Carpenters and Joiners). The basic fact was that good fitters – even good carpenters and bricklayers, who were much more vulnerable to interloping – were not made in a day or a month. So long as genuine skill was indispensable, artisans – the kind who would never be out of a job if jobs were going – were less insecure than has been sometimes suggested. What they had to protect themselves against was not so much labourers or even handymen who could immediately take over their jobs, as a long-term over-supply of trained tradesmen – and of course the insecurity of both trade cycle and life cycle. In many trades, for example in engineering, the risk of an uncontrolled generation of a reserve army of tradesmen was small, though in some of the building trades, with their large influx of country-trained men, it was significant.

Such, then, were the artisans we are dealing with. I may note in passing that they are not to be confused with the so-called 'intelligent artisan' of the mid-Victorian debates on parliamentary reform, or of Thomas Wright, that 'hero of a thousand footnotes', to quote Alastair Reid. Artisans were indeed apt to be more adequately schooled than most non-artisans and, as the history of most labour movements shows, far more apt than the rest to occupy responsible and leading positions. Even in the 1950s skilled workers provided the same proportion of full-time union officials – about 95 per cent – in former craft unions with a heavy admixture of the semi-skilled, as in unions still described as skilled unions.[9] Yet, as Thomas Wright correctly observed, the reading artisans with intellectual interests – at least in England – were a minority among their mates, whose tastes did not differ notably from the rest of the proletariat.[10] An analysis of a sample of what might be considered 'intelligent artisans' by definition confirms the point. In the first three years' intake of the London Mechanics Institution such groups as, say, hatters, coopers and shipwrights were grossly under-represented, though they would scarcely have considered themselves less skilled, or lower in the artisanal pecking-order, than say the somewhat over-represented woodworking trades.[11] The truth, confirmed by later attendance statistics at evening schools,[12] is that some trades found it professionally more useful to make written calculations and use or produce designs than others, and therefore tended to be more studious. We may therefore safely leave the 'intelligent artisan' to one side.

What did they derive from their pre-industrial craft heritage? Academics should have no difficulty in grasping the assumptions behind the thinking and action of corporate crafts, since we largely continue to act upon those assumptions ourselves. A craft consisted of all those who had acquired the peculiar skills of a more or less difficult trade, by means of a specific process of education, completed by tests and assessments guaranteeing adequate knowledge and performance of the trade. In return such persons expected the right to conduct their trade and to make what they considered a decent living corresponding to its value to society and to their social status. It is quite easy to translate this last requirement into the terms of market economics, and indeed much of what the crafts did served to restrict entry to the trade, to exclude competition by outsiders (possessing their own trade or not) and to restrict output and labour supply in such a manner as to keep the average income at the required level. In our days market economics have indeed taken over, but the basic assumptions of crafts had only a peripheral relation to the discourse of business schools. They spoke the ancient language of a properly structured social order, or in E. P. Thompson's terms, a 'moral economy':

> The obvious intention of our ancestors in enacting the Statute [of Artificers] ... was to produce a competent number and perpetual succession of masters and journeymen, of practical experience, to promote, secure and render permanent the prosperity of the national arts and manufactures, *honestly wrought by their ability and talents* [italics added], inculcated by a mechanical education.

And this in turn meant that they had 'an unquestionable right ... [to] the quiet and exclusive enjoyment of their several and respective arts and trades which the law has already conferred upon them as a property'.[13] That labour was the working man's 'property' and to be treated as such was, of course, a commonplace of contemporary radical political debate.

Conversely, the duty to work properly was assumed and accepted: the London Operative Tinplate Workers who left their job were obliged to return to complete any unfinished work, or to pay for it to be completed, on pain of fine by their Society.[14] In short, the trade was not so much a way of making money; rather the income it provided was the recognition by society and its constituted authorities of the value of decent work decently done by bodies of respectable men properly skilled in the tasks which society needed. The ideal, and indeed the expected, situation was one in which the authorities left or conferred these rights on the body of the trade, but in which the trade collectively ensured the best ways in which they were carried out and safeguarded.

In the classical, or if you prefer the ideal-typical, corporate crafts of the pre-industrial period, such regulation and safeguarding were essentially in the hands of the craft masters, whose enterprises formed the basic units of the collectivity, as well as of its educational and reproductive system. It is clear that artisan interests represented essentially by hired workers would be formulated rather differently. It is less evident that a 'trade' so identified would not be the same as a self-contained stratum of craft journeymen within a craft economy, even when organized in specific journeymen's gilds, brotherhoods or other associations. The difference between the latter type of organization and the British 'trade society' which developed directly into the craft union deserves more analysis than it has received, though some recent work has advanced it significantly. It has been suggested that such forms of collective journeyman action tended to stress 'honour' and the social prestige of the journeymen *outside*, and often at the expense of, their economic interests, often by a sort of hypertrophy of symbolic practices such as the well-known journeymen rituals, fights and riots.[15] All we need note here is that this road of journeyman development – which has no British parallel, so far as I know – could not easily lead directly into trade unionism.

The economic interests of wage-workers were clearly fundamental in British journeyman trades organizations even before the industrial revolution. That is to say, they were designed to safeguard them against the primary life risks to manual workers, namely accident, sickness and old age, loss of time, underemployment, periodic unemployment and competition from a labour surplus.[16] Whereas the core of German or French journeyman collectivity was to be found outside the workshop – in the institutionalized period of travel, the journeymen's hostel or lodging-house where the rituals of initiation took place – the essential locus of the British apprentice's socialization into the ways of the journeyman was patently the workplace. There he was 'taught both by the precept and the example of his mates, that he must respect the trade and its written and unwritten laws, and that in any matter affecting the trade generally he must sacrifice personal interest, or private opinion, to what the trade has rightly or wrongly ruled for the general good'.[17] There was thus no clear distinction between the 'custom of the trade' as tradition or ritualized practice and as the rationale of collective action of workers on the job or the sanction of concessions won by it. Thus some formalized rituals could be allowed to atrophy without weakening the force of the 'custom of the trade'.

The basic journeyman institutions, as Prothero's *Artisan Politics* shows, were the friendly benefit society, the house of call, the tramping system – which gave artisans a nationwide dimension – and apprenticeship. To these research has rightly insisted we must add the unorganized, yet by no means totally informal, work group in the shop or on the site.[18]

They protected the interests of hired men – yet it must never be forgotten that this was seen to be 'the trade', composed essentially of hired men, that is to say a specific body of respectable and honourable men defending their 'craft', that is, their right to independence, respect and a decent livelihood which society owed them in return for the proper performance of socially essential tasks which required their education in skill and experience. The 'right to a trade' in the original constitution of the ASE (Amalgamated Society of Engineers) was compared to the right belonging to the holder of a doctor's diploma.[19] The qualification for the job was identical with the right to exercise it.

The artisan's sense of independence was, of course, based on more than a moral imperative. It was based on the justified belief that his skill was indispensable to production; indeed on the belief that it was the *only* indispensable factor of production. Hence the artisan's objection to the capitalism which, in the early nineteenth century, increasingly denied the moral economy which gave the trades their modest but respected place, was not so much to working masters, whom they had long known, or to machinery as such, which could be seen as an extension of hand tools, but to the capitalist seen as an unproductive and parasitic middleman. Masters who belonged to the 'useful classes' both insofar as – to quote Hodgskin – 'they are *labourers* as well as their journeymen' and insofar as they were needed 'to direct and superintend labour, and to distribute its produce'[20] were fine: only, unfortunately, 'they are also' – Hodgskin again – 'capitalists or agents of capitalists, and in this respect their interest is decidedly opposed to the interests of their workmen'. Small masters raised no problem at all, and indeed could often be, or remain, members of unions. The theoretical foundations of early socialism, misnamed 'utopian', are to be found in this attitude. Essentially it envisaged the elimination of competition and the capitalist by means of co-operative production by artisans. Prothero has shown how artisans who began simply by trying to defend or re-establish the old 'moral economy' could find themselves driven, under the pressure of the economic transformations of the early nineteenth century, to envisage a new and revolutionary way of re-establishing the moral social order as they saw it, and in so doing to become social innovators and revolutionaries. And Prothero has also, rightly, drawn attention to the fact that in this respect the evolution of the British journeyman artisan runs parallel with that of the continental, or rather French, ones.[21] Both tended to become politically active as artisans and in doing so to transform themselves into the 'working classes' or essential sectors of these.

Yet there is a vital difference. Utopian socialism, or rather mutualism and producers' co-operation, became and long remained the core of French socialism. But in Britain, in spite of occasional surges of popularity and an attraction for journeymen cadres, co-operative socialism was always a peripheral phenomenon, on the way to oblivion even as Chartism swept the country, the first mass working-class movement, in which journeymen artisans, like all others under economic pressure, took their share. Socialism declined in the Britain of the 1840s, as it rose on the continent. Whatever the reasons for this difference – and they remain to be fully explained – they will probably have to be sought partly in the political conditions of the country, but chiefly in the very advance of the British capitalist economy over the rest, which already made an economy of small commodity producers, individual or collective, somewhat implausible or economically marginal. Journeymen were workers. They lived in a world of employers. Characteristically, the only form of co-operation which proved to have genuine appeal from the start was that which sought to replace an economic sector of small independents, namely the co-op shop.

Thus the tradesman had no difficulty in coming to terms with an economy of industrial capitalism, once that economy decided to accept his modest claims to skill, respect and relative privilege, and plainly offered expanding opportunities and material improvement. And this clearly came to be the case in the 1850s and 1860s. Their position may be symbolized in the anniversary dinner of the Cardiff branch of the Amalgamated Society of Carpenters and Joiners in 1867, in the Masons Arms, 'nicely decorated with evergreens etc. and over the head of the president's chair was a design portraying the friendship existing between employer and workman, by their cordially shaking hands'.[22] This iconographic theme appears frequently at the time.[23] 'In the background was represented the commerce of all nations and in the corner were busts of ancient philosophers etc. This design bore the following inscription: "Success to honourable competition" and "the prosperity and wealth of nations are due to science, industry and a just balance of all interests".' It would be an error to suppose that such sentiments were incompatible with going on strike.

It may be worth noting, as Richard Price reminds us, that if the artisan certainly required collective organization, his collective force is normally not yet to be measured by the membership of trade unions. The general assumption, by Mayhew and others, was that 'society men' represented perhaps 10 per cent of all but exceptional trades. Powerful bodies like the masons had perhaps 15 per cent of the trade organized in 1871, the carpenters and joiners perhaps 11 to 12 per cent, the plasterers under 10 per cent.[24] The Amalgamated Engineers with perhaps 40 per cent in 1861 were quite exceptional.[25] Whether or when society men in unorganized trades acted as pacemakers of economic advance, is today a reopened question. At all events, in wage and hours movements there was no sharp distinction between the organized and the unorganized, inasmuch as both had the same interest in restriction against non-tradesmen. Thus among the bricklayers of poorly organized Portsmouth, where there were no indentured apprentices and 70 per cent of the men had just 'picked up' the trade, there was nevertheless no piece-work, and the advancement of labourers, once frequent, had become rare.[26] In Glasgow, where the Webbs found poor relations with employers, no working rules, no limit on apprentices and far from dominant unions, there was no piece-work, and labourers did not 'encroach'.[27] The truth is that craftsmanship was not only the criterion of a man's identity and self-respect, but the guarantee of his income. The best men, said a student of unemployment in the London building trade, always get work.[28] In the Amalgamated Carpenters and Joiners it was taken for granted that 'the success of the society depends on the members being invariably competent workmen',[29] and they were recruited accordingly, and indeed kept up to the mark. 'If a man's not worth 36 shillings a week,' said the ASE *Monthly Record* proudly, though perhaps in 1911 no longer with total sincerity, 'the union has rules to deal with incompetence.'[30] Just so James Hopkinson had observed in the 1830s: 'Our shop was a strong union shop and the leading workmen in the town worked there.'[31] The small-arms fire with which the artisans fought the big guns of the employers derived its effectiveness from the ramparts of skill which protected it as well as the solidarity of the marksmen.

The skill, and the artisan's independence, were symbolized by the possession of personal tools,[32] those small but vital means of production, which enabled him to work anywhere at his trade. Broadhurst, the union leader and Lib–Lab MP, kept his mason's tools packed and ready throughout his time of political eminence: they were his insurance.[33] Many years later, in 1939, when the boiler-maker Harry Pollitt was deposed from his post in the Communist Party, his mother proudly wrote: 'Your marking-off tools are here, and I have kept them in vaseline, ready for use at any time.'[34] At a more modest level, when Jess Oakroyd, in J. B. Priestley's *Good Companions*, lost his job and went on tramp, the most important thing he took with him was his bag of tools.

The highest skills did not necessarily require the most expensive or elaborate tool-kit, though proud tradesmen – notably in woodworking – spent heavily on tools and luxury containers as status symbols. The ASCJ in 1886 limited benefit for the loss of a tool-chest, on the grounds that 'if a member takes a more valuable chest to work [that is, than is necessary] he should do so at his own risk'.[35] Tool insurance by the union was usual among woodworkers, though less so among metalworkers, presumably because their personal tools were ancillary to shop equipment.[36] The 'tool benefit' of the ASCJ was clearly intended as a major selling-point for the union – it insured against theft, and not only against fire and shipwreck – and its importance is indicated by the frequency of branch resolutions and notices on the subject.[37] Indeed, in their first thirty years the amount of tool benefit paid per member was roughly comparable to accident benefit, and amounted to about 55 per cent of funeral benefit.[38]

Yet the value of implements was secondary to their symbolic importance. London shipwrights, than whom few were more skilled, owned perhaps 50 shillings' worth in 1849, according to Mayhew,[39] and in the 1880s the union paid 50 per cent of replacement costs up to a maximum of £5.[40] Mayhew estimated cabinet makers' tools at £30 to £40, joiners' tools at up to £30, coopers' at £12. These figures, except for carpenters and joiners, are rather higher than those quoted in the Royal Commission on Labour or derivable from the lists of stolen tools in the carpenters' reports; and, according to both Mayhew and probability, tools were bought piecemeal in a man's last years of apprenticeship, and usually secondhand to begin with.[41] But they symbolized independence. Hence the disputes about 'grinding-time'. Since the tradesman brought to the job his skill and his tools, both must be absolutely ready for action. He and only he must sharpen them – at a weekly expense which was not negligible.[42] Logically the moment for this was at the end of the last job, and in the employer's time, which (or money in lieu) was expected to be made available.[43] Even today, as Beynon shows for Ford's, tools still imply some independence for tradesmen as against production workers.[44]

But, if personal tools symbolized independence for the artisans, conversely control of the tools symbolized the superiority of management. We know that management was about to transform its plant organization, where emery wheels were taken from the shop and workers were no longer allowed to sharpen tools in their own way and to their own specifications, but must have this done to angles determined by others in a special tool-room.[45] And characteristically the tool-room was to remain the last stronghold of the craftsman in the semi-skilled mass-production engineering works of the twentieth century. Even in the non-union motor industry between the wars, management would be careful of the susceptibilities of the tool-room and turn a blind eye to the unionism of toolmakers. In the nineteenth century such control was most visible in the giant railway companies, enterprises which employed and trained numerous artisans and, though recognizing that their foremen were essentially drawn from among them, and hence were likely to have the artisan view,[46] saw no need for a symbiosis with partly autonomous labour. Thus the Great Western and the Great Eastern turned craftsman's pride into an obligation, by *obliging* workmen, in the unilaterally imposed Working Rules, to buy and insure their personal tools. Foremen in Stratford were to examine the men's tool-chests before they were taken out of the works, and in Derby they needed a special pass to do so.[47] The labour policies of the railway companies, which deserve more study than they have so far received in Britain, sometimes look as though they had been specifically designed to replace craft autonomy and exclusive control by managerial control of hiring, training, promotion to higher grades of skill and workshop operations.

For tools symbolized not merely the relative independence of the artisan from management, but, even more clearly, his monopoly of skilled work. The standard expression for what the unskilled or the not specifically trained men must be prevented from doing at all costs, that is 'encroaching' or 'following the trade', is some variant of the phrase 'taking up the tools', or 'working tradesmen's tools' or 'getting hold of the tools for himself'.[48] Bricklayers' labourers, in more than one set of working rules, are prohibited specifically from the 'use of the trowel'.[49] Coopers' labourers were only allowed to use some specified coopers' tools such as hammers.[50] Conversely, artisans recognized each other's status by lending each other tools.[51] In short, they may be defined essentially as tool-using and tool-monopolizing animals.

The right to a trade was not only a right of the duly qualified tradesman, but also a family heritage.[52] Tradesmen's sons and relations did not only become tradesmen because, as among the professional middle classes, their chances of doing so were notably superior to the rest, but also because they wanted nothing better for their sons, and fathers insisted on privileged access for them. Free apprenticeship for at least one son was provided for in many a set of Builders' Working Rules.[53] The formidable Boilermakers Society was largely recruited from sons and kin,[54] and in Edwardian London hereditary succession was considered usual among boilermakers and engineers, in some printing trades, though among the builders only for the favoured masons, plasterers and perhaps plumbers. Here it was also pointed out that the attractions of office jobs for tradesmen's sons were small.[55] This is confirmed by the analysis of some 200 biographies from the *Dictionary of Labour Biography*[56] (mainly of those born between 1850 and 1900) which shows that, though the number of sons of non-tradesmen was only about 75 per cent of that of tradesmen, the number of tradesmen's sons who went into white-collar or similar jobs was not much more than half of that of non-tradesmen's sons. In short, for the Victorian artisan workshop learning rather than schooling was what still counted, and a trade was at least as desirable as or better than anything else effectively on offer. Indeed, the largest single group in the *Dictionary* sample (from which I have excluded the overwhelmingly self-reproduced miners) consisted of about seventy sons of tradesmen who took up trades, in about half the cases their father's. And we know that in Crossick's *Kentish London* (1873–5) 43 per cent of engineering craftsmen were sons of men in these crafts, and 64 per cent came from skilled fathers in general; 64 per cent and 76 per cent of shipbuilding craftsmen came from shipbuilding and skilled families respectively; as did 46 per cent and 69 per cent respectively of building tradesmen. I leave open the question whether, as Crossick suggests, the links binding artisans together and separating them from the unskilled, actually tightened during the mid-Victorian period.[57]

This does not mean that entry into the trades was closed. It could hardly be, considering the rate of growth in the labour force, not to mention powerful enterprises like the railways, which deliberately saw to the training and promotion of unskilled labour, and provided a significant road for its upgrading; in the *Dictionary* sample this is very noticeable. What it does suggest is the relative advantage the stratum of tradesmen had in reproducing itself, and the significance within the skilled labour force of this block of self-reproducing artisans; and not least their capacity to assimilate the non-artisans who succeeded in joining their ranks, so long as artisan status meant a special and lengthy education in skill, essentially conducted by artisans in the workshop. And in 1906, according to an estimate, about 18 per cent of occupied males between the ages of fifteen and nineteen were still classified as apprentices and learners.[58] In industries and regions dominated by artisans – the North-east coast immediately comes to mind – their ability to assimilate new entrants was clearly enormous. One recalls that even in 1914, in spite of considerable efforts, 60 per cent of the workforce of the Engineering Employers' Federation were still classified as skilled.[59] Under these circumstances the artisans, or the bulk of them, were both privileged and relatively secure.

The crux of their position lay in the economy's reliance on *manual* skills, that is, skills exercised by blue-collar workers. The real crisis of the artisan set in as soon as tradesmen became replaceable by semi-skilled machine operators or by some other division of labour into specialized and rapidly learned tasks – broadly speaking in the last two decades of the nineteenth century. This phase of artisan history has been fairly intensively investigated, at least for some industries,[60] and it is at this point that the main attack on the concept of an 'aristocracy of labour' has concentrated. Apart from a diminishing minority, the craftsman's position was no longer protected by the length of training and practice, by skill and the willing toleration of employers. It was protected primarily by job monopoly secured by trade unions and by workshop control. Yet the jobs now monopolized and protected were no longer skilled jobs in the old sense, though those who were best at protecting them were usually formerly skilled trades, like compositors and boilermakers, which insisted on their members' monopolizing the new de-skilled jobs. But even this undermined the special position of the artisan. For, as we all now know from the Fleet Street printing trade, when skill and privilege or high wages are no longer correlated, artisans are merely one set of workers among many others who might, given the right circumstances – generally the occupation of a strategic bottleneck – establish such strong bargaining positions.

Speaking generally, at the end of the nineteenth century the trades found themselves, for the first time since the 1830s and 1840s, threatened by industrial capitalism as such but without the hope of bypassing it. Their existence as a privileged stratum was at stake. Moreover the employers' main attack was now against their craft privileges. Hence, for the first time, their key sectors turned against capitalism. Thus unlike some of the traditional trades, the new metalworking crafts of the industrial economy had not been given to breeding political activists. There are few if any engineers and metal shipbuilders among the nationally prominent Lib–Lab politicians before the 1890s. Yet almost from the start, engineers were prominent among the socialists. At the ASE's Delegate Meeting in 1912 more than half the delegates present appear to have been advocates of 'collectivism' to be achieved by class war.[61] The small argumentative Marxist sects like the SLP (Socialist Labour Party) were full of them. Engineering shop stewards and revolutionary radicalism in the First World War went together like cheese and pickles, and metalworkers – generally highly skilled men – later came proverbially to dominate the proletarian component of the Communist Party, to be followed a long way after by builders and miners.[62] The left attracted them for two reasons. In the first place a class-struggle analysis made sense to men engaged in battle with organized employers on what seemed to be the crucial sector of the front of class conflict; and by the same token the belief that capitalism wanted 'a just balance of all interests' was plainly no longer tenable. In the second place, the radical left in the unions, ever since the 1880s, specialized in devising strategies and tactics designed to meet precisely those situations which appeared to find traditional craft methods wanting.

I do not wish to underestimate this shift to the left, which now gave to the British labour movement a political outlook fundamentally different from that of Chartist democracy, which still prevailed amid the sober suits of liberal radicalism – a new political outlook which, some might argue, was *de facto* more radical than many continental socialist movements. At the same time this shift should not be identified with the various brands of socialist ideology which now sprang up, and, naturally, attracted young artisans conscious of their new predicament: in the 1880s men in their mid- to late twenties, from Edwardian times perhaps men in their late teens. For most tradesmen the shift to anti-capitalism simply began as an extension of their trade experience. It meant doing what they had always done: defending their rights, their wages and their now threatened conditions, stopping management from telling the lads how to do their job, and relying on the democracy of the workplace rank and file and against the world, which, if need be, included their unions' leaders. Only now they had to fight management all the time, because management was permanently threatening to reduce them to 'labourers', and now had the technical means to do so.

They were far from revolutionaries, but how did this constant confrontation differ from the class struggle which the revolutionaries preached? If the masters no longer recognized the interests of the skilled men, why should the men recognize those of the masters? I do not believe that many tradesmen were as yet affected by the drastic renunciation of old craft assumptions suggested by some of the ultra-left, who recommended fighting capitalism with its own market principles, by working as little or even as badly as possible for as much money as the traffic would bear. Such ideas were put forward in the syndicalist period. However, at this stage there is no evidence that tradesmen – still often suspicious of payment by results, though increasingly pushed into it – thought in such terms which, as the Webbs pointed out, undermined their basic principle of pride in work, rewarded by a wage which recognized their standing.

Yet the period from 1889 to 1914 introduces us to an artisan predicament which is similar to that of the British economy as a whole, because it is one aspect of it. Just as there were men in business who recognized that fundamental modernization was needed in the British productive system, but failed to mobilize sufficient support to achieve it, so also in the field of labour. The left, including the artisan left, knew that craft unionism of the high Victorian kind was doomed. It was the target of all critics. The mass of proposals for trade-union reform between 1889 and 1927, ranging from federation and amalgamation to a complete restyling of the union movement along industrial lines,[63] were all directed against a position which was barely defended in theory even among the leaders of old-style craft unions. Yet no systematic general union reform was achieved, though craft unions recognized some need to expand, federate and amalgamate, and also accepted that elite organization must henceforth be part of the mass unionization of all workers, and that in such mass unionism the craft societies would inevitably be less dominant, either numerically or strategically. Yet attempts at general reform failed so clearly that after 1926 they were *de facto* abandoned.

Railways and engineering are obvious examples of this failure. The new National Union of Railwaymen, designed as the model of a comprehensive industrial union, never succeeded in integrating most of the skilled footplate men, and the engineers did not even try, though their left-wing leadership time and again committed them to broaden their recruitment: in 1892, in 1901 and again in 1926. But as late as 1931 the Amalgamated Engineering Union told the Transport and General Workers:

> With regard to the organizing activities of the AEU, whilst it was true that the constitution of the union was amended to permit of all grades of workers being organized within the union, this had not been operated, the AEU confining its organizing activities strictly to those sections of the industry which it had always organized. It was not the intention of the AEU to depart from this policy.[64]

For, just as the British industrial economy appeared to enjoy its Edwardian Indian summer, so did the artisans. Did they need to reform themselves out of existence? Sheer bloody-minded shop-floor resistance reversed the total victory won by the Engineering Employers' Federation in the 1897–8 lock-out, incidentally driving the union's socialist general secretary George Barnes into the wilderness.[65] It had so far restored the position that buying off the craftsmen became the major task of the 1914 war economy. Their position had actually been strengthened, because the system of payment by results, which employers preferred to Taylorist and Fordist strategies, laid the base for endless shop-floor conflicts and, in consequence, shop-steward power. Moreover, during the war the industry was flooded, not with promotable semi-skilled machine men, but with 650,000 women, virtually all of whom rapidly disappeared from the labour market after 1919. The union had to be defeated once again in frontal battle in 1922. After that unions were virtually driven out of such new sectors of the industry as motors and electrical goods, even though once again employers in general found the costs of systematic plant rationalization too high, and the foreseeable profits insufficiently attractive to justify such heavy outlays.

Once again the artisans therefore had their chance in the 1930s, as recovery, rearmament and war made times more propitious for labour organization. This was the last triumph of the Victorian trades. The men who brought the waters of unionism back into the desert of non-union shops were largely, perhaps mainly, craftsmen, like the toolmakers and the men who built the aircraft of the 1930s and 1940s, and whose role in the growth of mass metals unionism was crucial. They were the first nucleus of the revived shop-stewards' movement. These men were craftsmen, or at least, even when engaged on what was in effect semi-skilled work, craftsmen by background and training. They were now also largely communists, or became communists.[66]

Yet, whether they wanted to or not, they were initiating their own liquidation as a special stratum of the working class. This was largely because the mechanized engineering industries they organized no longer rested on artisan skill, though they still needed it. But it was also partly because the left no longer had a coherent union policy. Given the failure of general union reform, it lacked a practicable 'new model' of union organization. It benefited from a government policy, particularly from 1940 when Ernest Bevin took over the Ministry of Labour, which favoured unionism; but it neither controlled nor often understood or usually even approved it. Its major weapon (leaving aside the production-oriented unionism of the communists in 1941–5) was much the same as in 1889–1921: sheer blinkered, dour, stubborn defence of 'the custom of the trade' in the shops. It is irrelevant that some of the left may have identified this in some way with the road to revolution or at least to political radicalization. *De facto*, the left had no specific union strategy, but merely pursued the old tactics with intelligence, dynamism and efficiency – in a situation quite unlike that of 1889–1921.

What they achieved was the generalization of the old craft-monopoly methods to all sectors of the trade-union movement, and in industries where tradesmen formed a diminishing minority among the mass of semi-skilled operatives. And in doing so the artisans became merely one set of workers among many others who were in a position to apply such methods, and not necessarily the ones who could strike the best bargains. In the Fleet Street of the 1970s, not only had the qualitative difference between compositors and 'printers' labourers' disappeared, but the chapel of the National Graphical Association was not necessarily a more powerful bargainer than that of SOGAT '82. There was no longer anything special about being a tradesman.

Some are clearly on the way out, like the locomotive drivers of the old craft union ASLEF. Some survive, but in a world they no longer quite understand. It works for as much money as it can get, and nothing more.[67] This is a fundamental break in craft tradition, which, as has been argued, aimed at an income corresponding to the craftsman's status as a group, as professors still do.[68] Hence the persistent historical distrust of piece-rates. A communist engineer, interviewed by a researcher, recalls his amazement when he discovered during the war in Coventry that workers not merely could, but were expected to push their earnings into what seemed the stratosphere. And, indeed, the famous Coventry Toolroom Agreement of 1941 reflected this curious intermingling of old and new principles, until its breakdown in the 1970s. Whereas in the past the toolmakers' earnings had provided the measuring-rod of their 'differential' over and above less favoured groups, this differential was henceforth fixed against the entirely undetermined level of what non-toolmakers on piece-work could earn. Craftsmanship, good work, was no longer the essential foundation of good earnings. If anything, it was now a liability, since it stood in the way of the sky-high wages which could be earned by the men who deliberately and consciously put speed and skimping before sound work. Financially, the 'cowboy' – the term is of uncertain origin, but seems to emerge in the building trade during the heyday of the 'lump' in the 1960s – could do better than the good tradesman.

Finally, the possibility of training as a craftsman grew less. In 1966 the number of apprentices was only about three-quarters of what it had been sixty years earlier, or indeed in 1925, and by 1973 it had plummeted to 25 per cent of the 1966 figure.[69] And so did the incentive to follow one's father into a proper trade. Book education and not skill is now the road to status and, with diminishing exceptions, even skill has moved into the world of diplomas. And, of course, the road into that world has broadened. There was a time when miners might want their sons out of the pit at all costs, but engineers were content to offer their sons a presumably improving version of their own prospects. How many of the sons of toolmakers today are content to become toolmakers?

The artisans no longer reproduce themselves or their kind. The generation of men who grew up with artisan experience and artisan values in the 1930s and 1940s still survives, but is growing old. When the last men who have driven and cared for steam locomotives retire – it will not be long now – and when engine-drivers will be little different from tram-drivers, and sometimes quite superfluous, what will happen? What will our society be like without that large body of men who, in one way or another, had a sense of the dignity and the self-respect of difficult, good and socially useful manual work, which is also a sense of a society not governed by market-pricing and money: a society other than ours and potentially better? What will a country be like without the road to self-respect which skill with hand, eye and brain provide for men – and, one might add women – who happen not to be good at passing examinations? Tawney would have asked such questions and I can do no better than to conclude by leaving them with you.

CHAPTER 7

Man and Woman:
Images on the Left

The importance of iconography for the study of labour was discovered in the 1970s. The present excursion into it, largely made possible by the help of art-historical friends and the eccentric riches of the Warburg Institute library, was first published in History Workshop Journal *in 1978. It was criticised at the time by some feminists and, less passionately, on possibly misconceived iconographical grounds. It asks two questions, one light-hearted, the other more serious. How does it come about that, in the course of a century of labour history, the female figure is increasingly dressed, the male increasingly topless? What can the evidence of images, whether realistic or even symbolic, tell us about the actual relations between men and women in labour movements?*

Women have often pointed out that male historians in the past, including Marxists, have grossly neglected the female half of the human race. The criticism is just; the present writer accepts that it applies to his own work. Yet, if this deficiency is to be remedied, it cannot be simply by developing a specialized branch of history which deals exclusively with women, for in human society the two sexes are inseparable.[1] What we need also to study is the changing forms of the relations between the sexes, both in social reality and in the image which both sexes have of one another. The present paper is a preliminary attempt to do this for the revolutionary and socialist movements of the nineteenth and early twentieth centuries by means of the ideology expressed in the images and emblems associated with these movements. Since these were overwhelmingly designed by men, it is of course impossible to assume that the sex-roles they represent express the views of most women. However, it is possible to compare these images of roles and relationships with the social realities of the period, and with the more specifically formulated ideologies of revolutionary and socialist movements.

That such a comparison is possible is the assumption which underlies this paper. It is not suggested that the images here analysed directly reflect social realities, except where they were specifically designed to do so, as in pictures intended to have documentary value, and even then they clearly did not only reflect reality. My assumption is merely that in images designed to be seen by and to have an impact upon a wide public, for example of workers, the public's experience of reality sets limits to the degree to which they may diverge from that experience. If the capitalist in socialist cartoons of the Belle Epoque were to have been *habitually* presented not as a fat man smoking a cigar and in a top hat, but as a fat woman, these permissible limits would have been exceeded, and the caricatures would have been less effective; for most bosses were not only conceived as males but were males. It does not follow that all capitalists were fat with top hats and cigars, though these attributes were readily understood as indicating wealth in a bourgeois society, and had to be understood as specifying one particular form of wealth and privilege as distinct from others, for example the nobleman's. Such a correspondence with reality was evidently less necessary in purely symbolic and allegorical images, and yet even here they were not completely absent; if the deity of war had been presented as a woman, it would have been with the intention to shock. To interpret iconography in this manner is naturally not to make a serious analysis of image and symbol. My purpose is more modest.

Let us begin with perhaps the most famous of revolutionary paintings, though one not created by a revolutionary: Delacroix's *Liberty on the Barricades* in 1830. The picture will be familiar to many: a bare-breasted girl in Phrygian bonnet with a banner, stepping over the fallen, followed by armed men in characteristic costumes. The sources of the picture have been much investigated.[2] Whatever they are, its contemporary interpretation is not in doubt. Liberty was seen not as an allegorical figure, but as a real woman (inspired no doubt by the heroic Marie Deschamps, whose feats suggested the picture). She was seen as a woman of the people, belonging to the people, at ease among the people:

> C'est une forte femme aux puissantes mamelles,
> à la voix rauque, aux durs appas
> qui...
> Agile et marchant à grands pas

Se plaît aux cris du peuple...
Barbier, *La Curée*

(A strong woman, stout bosom'd,
With raucous voice and rough charm...
She strides forward with confidence,
Rejoicing in the clamour of the people...
The Bandwagon)

She was, for Balzac, of peasant stock: 'dark-skinned and ardent, the very image of the people'.[3] She was proud, even insolent (Balzac's words), and thus the very opposite of the public image of women in bourgeois society. And, as the contemporaries stress, she was sexually emancipated. Barbier, whose *La Curée* is certainly one of Delacroix's sources, invents an entire history of sexual emancipation and initiative for her:

qui ne prend ses amours que dans la populace,
qui ne prête son large flanc
qu'à des gens forts comme elle

(who takes her lovers only from among the masses,
who gives her sturdy body only to men as strong as herself)

after having, *enfant de la Bastille* ('child of the Bastille'), spread universal sexual excitement around her, tired of her early lovers and followed Napoleon's banners and a *capitaine de vingt ans* ('twenty-year-old captain'). Now she returned,

toujours belle et *nue* [italics added]
avec l'écharpe aux trois couleurs

(still beautiful and *naked* with the tricolour sash)

to win the 'Trois Glorieuses' (the July Revolution) for her people.[4]

Heine, who comments on the picture itself, pushes the image even further towards another ambiguous stereotype of the independent and sexually emancipated woman, the courtesan: 'a strange mixture of Phryne, fishwife and goddess of freedom'.[5] The theme is recognizable: Flaubert in *Education sentimentale* returns to it in the context of 1848, with his image of Liberty as a common prostitute in the ransacked Tuileries (though operating the habitual bourgeois transition from the equation liberty = good to that of licence = bad): 'In the ante-chamber, bolt upright on a pile of clothes, stood a woman of the streets posing as a statue of liberty.' The same note is hinted at by the reactionary Félicien Rops, who had actually represented 'the Commune personified by a naked woman, a soldier's cap on her head and sword at her side',[6] an image which came not only to his own mind. His powerful *Peuple* is a naked young woman, in the posture of a whore dressed only in stockings and a night cap, possibly hinting at the Phrygian bonnet, her legs opening on her sex.[7]

The novelty of Delacroix's *Liberty* therefore lies in the identification of the nude female figure with a real woman of the people, an emancipated woman, and one playing an active – indeed a leading – role in the movement of men. How far back this revolutionary image can be traced is a question which must be left to art historians to answer.[8]Here we can only note two things. First, its concreteness removes it from the usual allegorical role of females, though she maintains the nakedness of such figures, and this nudity is indeed stressed by painter and observers. She does not inspire or represent: she acts. Second, she seems clearly distinct from the traditional iconographic image of woman as an active freedom-fighter, notably Judith, who, with David, so often represents the successful struggle of the weak against the strong. Unlike David and Judith, Delacroix's *Liberty* is not alone, nor does she represent weakness. On the contrary, she represents the concentrated force of the invincible people. Since 'the people' consists of a collection of different classes and occupations, and is presented as such, a general symbol not identified with any of them is desirable. For traditional iconographic reasons this was likely to be female. But the woman chosen represents 'the people'.

The Revolution of 1830 seems to represent the high point of this image of Liberty as an active, emancipated girl accepted as leader by men, though the theme continues to be popular in 1848, doubtless because of Delacroix's influence on other painters. She remains naked in Phrygian cap in Millet's *Liberty on the Barricades*, but her context is now vague. She remains a leader-figure in Daumier's draft of *The Uprising* but, once again, her context is shadowy. On the other hand, though there are not many representations of the Commune and of Liberty in 1871, they tended to be naked (as in the design of Rops mentioned above) or bare-breasted.[9] Perhaps the notably active part played by women in the Commune also accounts for the symbolization of this revolution by a non-allegorical (that is, clothed) and obviously militant woman in at least one foreign illustration.[10]

The revolutionary concept of republic or liberty thus still tended to be a naked, or more likely bare-breasted, female. The Communard Dalou's celebrated statue of the Republic on the Place de la Nation still has at least one breast bared. Only research could show how far the revelation of the breast retains this rebellious or at least polemical association, as perhaps in the cartoon from the Dreyfus period

(January 1898) in which a young and virginal Marianne, one breast exposed, is protected against a monster by a matronly and armed Justice over the line: 'Justice: Have no fear of the monster! I am here.'[11] On the other hand the institutionalized Republic, Marianne, in spite of her revolutionary origins, is now normally though lightly, clothed. The reign of decency has been re-established. Perhaps also the reign of lies, since it is characteristic of the allegorical female figure of Truth – she still appears frequently, notably in the caricatures of the Dreyfus period – that she should be naked.[12] And indeed, even in the iconography of the respectable British labour movement of Victorian England, she remains naked, as on the emblem of the Amalgamated Society of Carpenters and Joiners, 1860,[13] until late-Victorian morality prevails.

Generally, the role of the female figure, naked or clothed, diminishes sharply with the transition from the democratic–plebeian revolutions of the nineteenth century to the proletarian and socialist movements of the twentieth. In a sense, the main problem of this paper consists in this masculinization of the imagery of the labour and socialist movement.

For obvious reasons the working woman proletarian is not much represented by artists, outside the few industries which were predominantly female. This was certainly not due to prejudice. Constantin Meunier, the Belgian who pioneered the typical idealization of the male worker, painted – and to a lesser extent sculpted – women wage-workers as readily as men; sometimes, as in his *Le Retour des mines* (Coming back from the mines) (1905) working together with men – as women still did in Belgian mines.[14] However, it is probable that the image of woman as a wage-worker and an active participant together with males in political activity[15] was largely due to socialist influence. In Britain it does not become noticeable in the trade-union iconography until this influence is felt.[16] In the emblems of pre-socialist British trade unions, uninfluenced by intellectuals, real women appear mainly in those small images by which unions advertised their fraternal help to members in distress: sickness, accident and funeral benefit. They stand by the bedside of the sick husband as his mates come to visit him adorned with the sash of their union. Surrounded by children, they shake hands with the union representative who hands them money after the death of the breadwinner.

Of course women are still present in the form of symbol and allegory, though towards the end of the century in Britain union emblems are to be found without any female figures, especially in such purely masculine industries as coalmining, steel-smelting and the like.[17] Still, the allegories of liberal self-help continue to be largely female, because they had always been. Prudence, Industry (= diligence), Fortitude, Temperance, Truth and Justice presided over the Stone Masons' Friendly Society in 1868; Art, Industry, Truth and Justice over the Amalgamated Society of Carpenters and Joiners. From the 1880s on one has the impression that only Justice and Truth, possibly supplemented by Faith and Hope, survive among these traditional figures. However as socialism advances, other female persons enter the iconography of the left, though they are in no sense supposed to represent real women. They are goddesses or muses.

Thus on a banner of the (left-wing) Workers' Union, 1898–1929, a sweet young lady in white drapery and sandals points to a rising sun labelled 'A better life' for the benefit of a number of realistically painted workers in working dress. She is Faith, as the text below the picture makes clear. A militant figure, also in white draperies and sandals, but with sword and buckler marked 'Justice & Equality', not a hair out of place on her well-styled head, stands before a muscular worker in an open shirt who has evidently just defeated a beast labelled 'Capitalism' which lies dead on the ground before him. The banner is labelled 'The Triumph of Labour', and represents the Southend-on-Sea branch of the National Union of General Workers, another socialist union. The Tottenham branch of the same union has the same young lady, this time with flowing hair, her dress marked 'Light, Education, Industrial Organisation, Political Action and Real International', pointing out the promised land in the shape of a children's playground to the usual group of workers. The promised land is labelled 'gain the Cooperative Commonwealth', and the entire banner illustrates the slogan 'Producers of the Nation's Wealth, Unite! And have your share of the world.'[18]

These images are all the more significant because they are obviously linked to the new socialist movement, which develops its own iconography, and because (unlike the old allegorical vocabulary) this new iconography is in part inspired by the tradition of French revolutionary imagery, from which Delacroix's *Liberty* is also derived. Stylistically, in Britain at least, it belongs to the progressive arts-and-crafts movement and its offshoot, art nouveau, which provided British socialism with its chief artists and illustrators, William Morris and Walter Crane. Yet Walter Crane's widely popular image of humanity advancing to socialism – a couple in loose summery clothes, the man carrying a child on his shoulder – like so many of his designs still reflects the debt to 1789 in the presence of the Phrygian bonnet.[19] The earliest of the First-of-May badges of the Austrian social democrats make the connection even more obvious. They represent a female figure with the motto: Fraternity, Equality, Liberty and the Eight-Hour Day.[20]

Yet what is the role of the women in this new socialist iconography? They inspire. The emblem of the *Labour Annual*,[21] published from 1895, is T. A. West's *Light and Life*. A lady in flowing robes, half-visible behind an escutcheon, blows a ritual trumpet for the benefit of a handsome boy with open-necked shirt and sleeves rolled up beyond the elbow, carrying a basket from which he sows the seed of, presumably, socialist propaganda; rays, stars and waves form the background to the design. Insofar as human women appear in this iconography, they are part of an idealized couple, with or without children. Insofar as each is symbolically identified with some activity, it is the man who represents industrial labour. In Crane's couple he has beside him a pick and a shovel, while she, carrying a basket of corn, and with a rake by her side, represents nature or at most agriculture. Curiously enough, the same division occurs in Mukhina's famous sculpture of the (male) worker and the (female) *kolkhoz* peasant on the Soviet Pavilion at the Paris International Exposition of 1937: he the hammer, she the sickle.

Of course actual women of the working classes also occur in the new socialist iconography, and embody a symbolic meaning, at least by implication. Yet they are quite different from the militant girls of the Paris Commune. They are figures of suffering and endurance. Meunier, that great pioneer of proletarian art and socialist realism – both as realism and as idealization – anticipates them, as usual. His *Femme du peuple* (Woman of the People) (1893) is old, thin, her hair drawn back so tightly as to suggest little more than a naked skull, her withered flat chest suggested by the very (and untypical) nakedness of her shoulders.[22] His even better-known *Le Grisou* (Firedamp) has the female figure, swathed in shawls, grieving over the corpse of the dead miner. These are the suffering proletarian mothers best known from Gorki's novel or Kaethe Kollwitz's tragic drawings.[23] And it perhaps not insignificant that their bodies become invisible under shawls and headcloths. The typical image of the proletarian woman has been desexualized and hides behind the clothes of poverty. She is spirit, not body. (In real life this image of the suffering wife and mother turned militant is perhaps exemplified by the blackclad eloquence of *La Pasionaria* in the days of the Spanish Civil War.)

Yet while the female body in socialist iconography is increasingly dressed, if not concealed, a curious thing is happening to the male body. It is increasingly revealed for symbolic purposes. The image which increasingly symbolizes the working class is the exact counter-part to Delacroix's *Liberty*, namely a topless young man: the powerful figure of a masculine labourer, swinging hammer or pick and naked to the waist.[24] This image is unrealistic in two ways. In the first place, it was by no means easy to find many nineteenth-century male workers in the countries with strong labour movements labouring with a naked torso. This, as Van Gogh recognized, was one of the difficulties of an era of artistic realism. He would have liked to paint the naked bodies of peasants, but in real life they did not go naked.[25] The numerous pictures representing industrial labour, even under conditions when it would today seem reasonable to take off one's shirt, as in the heat and glow of ironworks or gasworks, almost universally show them clothed, however lightly. This includes not merely what might be called broad evocations of the world of labour such as Madox Brown's *Work*, or Alfred Roll's *Le Travail* (1881) – a scene of open-air building work – but realistic paintings or graphic reporting.[26] Naturally bare-torsoed workers could be seen – for instance among some, but by no means all, British coalface workers. In such cases workers could be realistically presented as semi-nudes, as in G. Caillebotte's *Raboteurs de parquet* (Floor-polishers),[27] or in the figure of a coal-hewer on the emblem of the Ironfounders' Union (1857).[28] In real life, however, these were all special cases. In the second place, the image of nakedness is unrealistic because it almost certainly excluded the vast body of skilled and factory workers, who would not have dreamed of working without their shirts at any time, and who, incidentally, in general formed the bulk of the organized labour movement.

When the bare-torsoed worker first appears in art is uncertain. Certainly what must be one of the earliest sculptured proletarians, Westmacott's slate-worker on the Penrhyn monument, Bangor (1821),[29] is dressed, while the peasant girl near him is, perhaps semi-allegorically, rather décolletée. At all events from the 1880s on he was familiar in sculpture in the work of the Belgian Constantin Meunier, perhaps the first artist to devote himself wholeheartedly to the presentation of the manual worker; possibly also of the Communard Dalou, whose unfinished monument to labour contains similar motifs. Obviously he was much more prominent in sculpture, which had, by long tradition, a much stronger tendency to present the human figure nude than painting. In fact, Meunier's drawings and paintings are much more often realistically clothed, and, as has been shown for at least one of his themes, dockers unloading a ship, were only undressed in the three-dimensional design for a monument of labour.[30] Perhaps this is one reason why the semi-nude figure is less prominent in the period of the Second International, when the socialist movement was not in a position to commission many public monuments as yet, and comes into his own after 1917 in Soviet Russia, where it was. Yet, though a direct comparison between painted and sculptured image is therefore misleading, the bare male torso may already be found here and there on two-dimensional emblems, banners and other pictures of the labour movement even in the nineteenth century. Still, in sculpture he triumphed after 1917 in Soviet Russia, under such titles as *Worker*, *The Weapons of the Proletariat* and *Memorial of Bloody Sunday 1905*.[31] The theme is not yet exhausted, since a statue called *Friendship of the Peoples* of the 1970s still presents the familiar topless Hercules swinging a hammer.[32]

Painting and graphics still found it harder to break the links with realism. It is not easy to find any bare-torsoed workers in the heroic age of the Russian revolutionary poster. Even the symbolic painting *Trud* (Toil) presents a design of an idealized young man in working clothes, surrounded by the tools of a skilled artisan,[33] rather than the heavy-muscled and basically unskilled titan of the more familiar kind. The powerful hammer-swinger engaged in breaking the chains binding the globe, who symbolized the *Communist International* on the covers of its periodical from 1920, wore clothes on his torso, though only sketchy ones. The symbolic decorations of this review in its early numbers were non-human: five pointed stars, rays, hammers, sickles, ears of grain, beehives, cornucopias, roses, thorns, crossed torches and chains. While there were more modern images such as stylizations of smoking factory chimneys in the art-nouveau fashion* and driving bands or transmission-belts, there were no bare-chested workers. Propaganda photographs of such men do not become common, if they occur at all, before the first Five-Year Plan.[34] Nevertheless, though the progress of the two-dimensional bare torso was slower than might be thought, the image was familiar. Thus it is the symbol decorating the cover of the French edition of the *Compte rendu analytique* of the 5th Congress of Comintern (Paris, 1924).

Why the bare body? The question can only be briefly discussed, but takes us back both to the language of idealized and symbolic presentation and to the need to develop such a language for the socialist revolutionary movement. There is no doubt that eighteenth-century aesthetic theory linked the naked body and the idealization of the human being, often quite consciously as in Winckelmann. An idealized person (as distinct from an allegorical figure) could not be clothed in the garments of real life, and – as in the nude statues of Napoleon – should if possible be presented without garments. Realism

---

* In Russia this motif occurs as early as 1905–7.

had no place in such a presentation. When Stendhal criticized the painter David, because it would have been suicidal for his warriors of antiquity to go into battle naked, armed only with helmet, sword and shield, he was simply drawing attention, in his usual role as provocator, to the incompatibility of symbolic and realistic statement in art. But the socialist movement, in spite of its profound attachment in principle to realism in art – an attachment which goes back to the Saint-Simonians – required a language of symbolic statement, in which to state its ideals. As we have seen, the emblems and banners of the British trade unions – rightly described by Klingender as 'the true folk-art of nineteenth century Britain'[35] – are a combination of realism, allegory and symbol. They are probably the last flourishing form of the allegorical and symbolic language outside public monumental sculpture. An idealized presentation of the subject of the movement, the struggling working class itself, must sooner or later involve the use of the nude – as on the banner of the Export Branch of the Dockers' Union in the 1890s, where a naked muscular figure, his loins lightly draped, kneels on a rock wrestling with a large green serpent, surrounded by suitable mottoes.[36] In short, though the tension between realism and symbolism remained, it was still difficult to devise a complete vocabulary of symbol and ideal without the nude. On the other hand, it may be suggested that the total nude was no longer acceptable. It cannot have been easy to overlook the absurdity of the 1927 *Group: October*[37] which consists of three muscular men, naked except for the Red Army cap worn by one of them, with hammers and other suitable paraphernalia. Let us conjecture that the bare-torsoed image expressed a compromise between symbolism and realism. There were after all *real* workers who could be so presented.

We are left with a final, but crucial question. Why is the struggling working class symbolized exclusively by a *male* torso? Here we can only speculate. Two lines of speculation may be suggested.

The first concerns the changes in the actual sexual division of labour in the capitalist period, both productive and political. It is a paradox of nineteenth-century industrialization that it tended to increase and sharpen the sexual division of labour between (unpaid) household work and (paid) work outside, by depriving the producer of control over the means of production. In the pre-industrial or proto-industrial economy (peasant farming, artisanal production, small shopkeeping, cottage industry, putting-out and so on) household and production were generally a single or combined unit, and though this normally meant that women were grossly overworked – since they did most of the housework and shared in the rest of the work –

they were not confined to one type of work. Indeed, in the great expansion of 'proto-industrialism' (cottage industry) which has recently been investigated the actual productive processes attenuated or even abolished the differences in work between men and women, with far-reaching effects on the social and sexual roles and conventions of the sexes.[38]

On the other hand in the increasingly common situation of the worker who laboured for an employer in a workplace belonging to the employer, home and work were separate. Typically it was the male who had to leave home every day to work for wages and the woman who did not. Typically women worked outside the home (where they did so at all) only before or, if widowed or separated, after marriage, or where the husband was unable to earn sufficient to maintain wife and family, and very likely only so long as he was unable to do so. Conversely, an occupation in which an adult man was normally unable to earn a family wage was – very understandably – regarded as underpaid. Hence, the labour movement quite logically developed the tendency to calculate the desirable minimum wage in terms of the earnings of a single (that is, in practice male) breadwinner, and to regard a wage-working wife as a symptom of an undesirable economic situation. In fact the situation was often undesirable, and the number of married women obliged to work for wages or their equivalent was substantial, though a very large proportion of them did so at home – that is, outside the effective range of labour movements.[39] Moreover, even in industries in which the work of married women was traditionally well established – as in the Lancashire textile region – its scope can be exaggerated. 38 per cent of married and widowed women in Blackburn were employed for wages in 1938, but only 15 per cent of those in Bolton.[40]

In short, conventionally women aimed to stop working for wages outside the house once they got married. Britain, where in 1911 only 11 per cent of wage-working women had husbands and only 10 per cent of married women worked, was perhaps an extreme case; but even in Germany (1907) where 30 per cent of wage-working women had husbands the sex-difference was striking. For every wife at wage-work in the age-groups from twenty-five to forty years, there were four wage-working husbands.[41] The situation of the married woman was not substantially changed as yet by the tendency – rather marked after 1900 – for women to enter industry in larger numbers, and by the growing variety of occupations and leisure activities open to unmarried girls.[42] 'The trend towards a larger number of married women having a specified occupation had not been firmly established at the turn of the century.'[43] The point is worth stressing, since some feminist historians, for reasons difficult to understand, have attempted to deny it. Nineteenth-century industrialization (unlike twentieth-century industrialization) tended to make marriage and the family the major career of the working-class woman who was not obliged by sheer poverty to take other work.[44] Insofar as she worked for wages before marriage, she saw wage-work as a temporary, though no doubt desirable, phase in her life. Once married, she belonged to the proletariat not as a worker, but as the wife, mother and housekeeper of workers.

Politically the pre-industrial struggle of the poor not only produced ample room for women to take part beside men – neither sex had such political rights as the right to vote – but in some respects a specific and leading role for them. The commonest form of struggle was that to assert social justice, that is the maintenance of what E. P. Thompson has called 'the moral economy of the crowd', through direct action to control prices.[45] In the form of action, which could be politically decisive – we recall the march of the women on Versailles in 1789 – women not only took the lead, but were conventionally expected to. As Luisa Accati rightly states: 'in a large number of cases (I would almost say in practically all cases) women have the decisive role, whether because it is they who take the initiative, or because they form a very large part of the crowd'.[46] We need not here consider the well-known pre-industrial practice in which rebellious men take action disguised as women, as in the so-called Rebecca Riots of Wales (1843).

Furthermore, the characteristic urban revolution of the pre-industrial period was not proletarian but plebeian. Within the *menu peuple*, a socially heterogeneous coalition of elements, united by common 'littleness' and poverty rather than by occupational or class criteria, women could play a political role, provided only they could come out on the streets. They could and did help to build barricades. They could assist those who fought behind them. They could even fight or bear arms themselves. Even the image of the modern 'people's revolution' in a large non-industrial metropolis contains them, as anyone who recalls the street scenes of Havana after the triumph of Fidel Castro will testify.

On the other hand the specific form of struggle of the proletariat, the trade union and the strike, largely excluded the women, or greatly reduced their visible role as active participants, except in the few industries in which they were heavily concentrated. Thus in 1896 the total number of women in British trade unions (excluding teachers) was 142,000 or something like 8 per cent; but 60 per cent of these were in the extremely strongly organized cotton industry. By

1910 it was above 10 per cent but though there had been some growth in trade unionism among white-collar and shopworkers, the great bulk of the expansion in industry was still in textiles.[47] Elsewhere their role was indeed crucial, but distinct, even in small industrial and mining centres where place and work and community were inseparable. Yet, if in such places their role in strikes was public, visible and essential, it was nevertheless not that of strikers themselves.

Moreover, where men's work and women's work were not so separate and distinct that no question of intermixture could arise, the normal attitude of male trade unionists towards women seeking to enter their occupation was, in the words of S. and B. Webb, 'resentment and abhorrence'.[48] The reason was simple: since their wages were so much lower, they represented a threat to the rates and conditions of men. They were – to quote the Webbs again – 'as a class, the most dangerous enemies of the artisan's Standard of Life', though the men's attitude was also, in spite of the growing influence on the left, strongly influenced by what would today be called 'sexism':[49] 'the respectable artisan has an instinctive distaste for the promiscuous mixing of men and women in daily intercourse, whether this be in the workshop or in a social club'.[50] Consequently the policy of all unions capable of doing so was to exclude women from their work, and the policy even of those unions incapable of doing so (for example, the cotton weavers) was to segregate the sexes or at least to avoid women and girls working 'in conjunction with men, especially if [they are] removed from constant association with other female workers'.[51] Thus both the fear of the economic competition of women workers and the maintenance of 'morality' combined to keep women outside or on the margins of the labour movement – except in the conventional role of family members.

The paradox of the labour movement was thus that it encouraged an ideology of sexual equality and emancipation, while in practice discouraging the actual joint participation of men and women in the process of labour as workers. For the minority of emancipated women of all classes, including workers, it provided the best opportunities to develop as human beings, indeed as leaders and public figures. Probably it provided the only environment in the nineteenth century which gave them such opportunities. Nor should we underestimate the effect on the ordinary, even the married, working-class women of a movement passionately committed to female emancipation. Unlike the petty-bourgeois 'progressive' movement which, as among the French Radical Socialists, virtually flaunted its male chauvinism, the socialist labour movement tried to overcome the tendencies within the proletariat and elsewhere to maintain sexual inequality, even if it failed to achieve as much as it would have wished.[52] It is not insignificant that the major work by the charismatic leader of the German socialists, August Bebel – and by far the most popular work of socialist propaganda in Germany at that period – was his *Woman and Socialism*.[53] Yet at the same time the labour movement unconsciously tightened the bonds which kept the majority of (non-wage-earning) married women of the working class in their assigned and subordinate social role. The more powerful it became as a mass movement, the more effective these brakes on its own emancipatory theory and practice became, at least until the economic transformations destroyed the nineteenth-century industrial phase of the sexual division of labour. In a sense the iconography of the movement reflects this unconscious reinforcement of the sexual division of labour. In spite of and against the movement's conscious intentions, its image expressed the essential 'maleness' of the proletarian struggle in its elementary form before 1914, the trade-union struggle.

It should now be clear why, paradoxically, the historical change from an era of plebeian and democratic to one of proletarian–socialist movements should have led, iconographically, to a decline in the role of the female. However, there may be another factor which reinforced this masculinization of the movement: the decline of classical pre-industrial millennialism. This is an even more speculative question, and I touch on it with caution and hesitation.

As has already been suggested, in the iconography of the left the female figure maintained herself best as an image of utopia: the goddess of freedom, the symbol of victory, the figure who pointed towards the perfect society of the future. And indeed the imagery of the socialist utopia was essentially one of nature, of fertility and growth, of blossoming, for which the female metaphor came naturally:

> Les générations écloses
> Verront fleurir leurs bébés roses
> Comme églantiers en Floréal
> Ce sera la saison des roses...
> Voilà l'avenir social.
>   (E. Pottier)[54]

> (The budding generations
> Will see their rosy babies flower
> Like briars in the spring.
> It will be the season of roses...
> That's the people's future.)

Eugène Pottier, the Fourierist author of the Internationale, is full of such images of femaleness, even in its literal sense of the maternal breast:

> pour tes enfants longtemps sevrés
> reprends le rôle du mamelle
> ('L'Age d'Or')

> Ah, chassons-la. Dans l'or des blés
> Mère apparais, les seins gonflées
> à nos phalanges collectives
> ('La Fille du Thermidor')

> Du sein de la nourrice, il coule ce beau jour
> Une inondation d'existence et d'amour.
> Tout est fécondité, tout pullule et foisonne
> ('Abondance')

> Nature ...
> Toi qui gonfles ton sein
> Pour ta famille entière
> ('La Cremaillère')

> (To your children, though weaned long ago,
> Give once again your breast.
> *The Golden Age*

> In the golden meadows come to us Mother,
> Your breasts full for the collective hosts.
> *Daughter of Thermidor*

> This beautiful day flows from the nurse's breast,
> A flood of life and love.
> All is fruitfulness, everything swarms and abounds.
> *Abundance*

> Nature – you whose breast has swell'd
> To feed your entire family...
> *Celebration*)

So, in a less explicitly physical way, is Walter Crane who, as we have seen, was largely responsible for the themes of socialist imagery in Britain from the 1880s on. It was an imagery of spring and flowers, of harvest (as in the well-known *The Triumph of Labour* designed for the 1891 May Day demonstration), of girls in light flowing dresses and Phrygian bonnets.[55] Ceres was the goddess of communism.[56]

It is not surprising that the period of socialist ideology most deeply imbued with feminism, and most inclined to assign a crucial, indeed sometimes a dominant, role to women was the romantic-utopian era before 1848. Of course at this period we can hardly speak of a socialist 'movement' at all, but only of small and atypical groups. Moreover, the actual number and prominence of women in leading positions in such groups was far smaller than in the years of the non-utopian Second International. There is nothing to compare in the Britain of Owenism and Chartism with the role of women as writers, public speakers and leaders in the 1880s and 1890s, not only in the middle-class ambience of the Fabian Society, but in the much more working-class atmosphere of the Independent Labour Party, not to mention such figures as Eleanor Marx in the trade-union movement. Moreover, the women who then became prominent, like Beatrice Webb or Rosa Luxemburg, did not make their reputation because they were women, but because they were outstanding irrespective of sex. Nevertheless, the role of women's emancipation in socialist ideology has never been more obvious and central than in the period of 'utopian socialism'.

This was partly due to the crucial role assigned to the destruction of the traditional family in the socialism of that period,[57] a role which is still very clear in *The Communist Manifesto*. The family was seen as the prison-house not only of the women, who were not on the whole very active in politics, or indeed as a mass very enthusiastic about the abolition of marriage, but also of young people, who were much more attracted to revolutionary ideologies. Moreover, as J. F. C. Harrison has rightly pointed out, even on empirical grounds the new proletarians might well conclude that 'their rude little homes were a restrictive and circumscribing influence, and that in community they would have a means of breaking out of this: "we can afford to live in palaces as well as the rich ... were we only to adopt the principle of combination, the patriarchal principle of large families, such as that of Abraham" '.[58] It has been the consumer society, combined – paradoxically – with the replacement of mutual aid by state welfare, which has weakened this argument against the privatized nuclear-family household.

Yet utopian socialism also assigned another role to women, which was basically similar to the female role in the chiliastic religious movements with which the utopians had much in common. Here women were not only – perhaps not even primarily – equal, but superior. Their specific role was that of prophets, like Joanna Southcott, founder of an influential millennial movement in early nineteenth-century England, or the 'femme–mère–messie' (woman–mother–messiah) of the Saint-Simonian religion.[59] This role incidentally provided opportunities for a public career in a masculine world for a small number of women. The foundresses of Christian Science and Theosophy come to mind. However, the tendency of the socialist and labour movements to move away from chiliasm towards rationalist theory and organization ('scientific socialism') made this social role for women in the movement increasingly marginal. Able women, whose talents lay in filling it, were pushed out of the centre of the movement into fringe religions which provided more scope for them. Thus Annie Besant, secularist and socialist, found fulfilment and her major political role after 1890 as high priestess of Theosophy and – through Theosophy – an inspirer of the Indian national liberation movement.

All that remained of the utopian/messianic role of women in socialism was the image of the female as inspiration and symbol of the better world. But paradoxically this image by itself was hardly distinguishable from Goethe's 'das ewig weibliche zieht uns hinan' ('the eternal feminine raises us to the heavens'). In actuality it could be no different from the bourgeois–masculine idealization of the female in theory, which was only too readily compatible with her inferiority in practice. At most the female image of the inspirer became the image of a Joan of Arc, easily recognizable in Walter Crane's designs. Joan of Arc was indeed an icon of women's militancy, but she did not represent either political or personal emancipation, or indeed activism, in any sense that could become a model for real women. Even if we forget that she excluded the majority of women who were no longer virgins – that is, women as sexual beings – there was, by historic definition, room for only a very few Joans of Arc in the world at any given moment. And, incidentally, as the increasingly enthusiastic adoption of Joan of Arc by the French right-wing demonstrates, her image was ideologically and politically undetermined. She might or might not represent Liberty. She might be on the barricades, but she did not – unlike Delacroix's girl – necessarily belong there.

Unfortunately it is at present impossible to continue the iconographic analysis of the socialist movement beyond a point of history which is already fairly remote. The traditional language of symbol and allegory is no longer much spoken or understood, and with its decline women as goddesses and muses, as personifications of virtue and ideals, even as Joans of Arc, have lost their specific place in political imagery. Even the famous international symbol of peace in the 1950s was no longer a woman, as it would almost certainly have been in the nineteenth century, but Picasso's dove. The same is probably true of masculine images, though the hammer-wielding

Promethean man survived longer as the personification of movement and struggle. The iconography of the movement since, say, the Second World War, is non-traditional. We do not at present have the analytical tools to interpret it, for example to make symbolic readings of the main modern iconographic medium, which is ostensibly naturalistic, the photograph or film.

Iconography can therefore not throw significant light at present on the relations between men and women in the mid-twentieth-century socialist movement, as it can for the nineteenth century. Still, it can make one final suggestion about the masculine image. This, as has already been suggested, is in some senses paradoxical, since it typifies not so much the worker as sheer muscular effort; not intelligence, skill and experience, but brute strength – even, as in Meunier's famous Iron-puddler, physical effort which virtually excludes and exhausts the mind. One can see artistic reasons for this. As Brandt points out, in Meunier 'the proletariat is transformed into a Greek athlete',[60] and for this form of idealization the expression of intelligence is irrelevant. One can also see historical reasons for it. The period 1870–1914 was above all the period in which industry relied on a massive influx of inexperienced but physically strong labour to perform the very large proportion of labour-intensive and relatively unskilled tasks, and when the dramatic environment of darkness, flame and smoke typified the revolution in man's capacity to produce by steampowered industry.

And yet, as we know, the bulk of the militants of organized labour in this period consisted, if we leave aside the admittedly important contingent of miners, essentially of skilled men. How is it that an image which omits all the characteristics of their kind of labour, established itself as the expression of the working class? Three explanations may be suggested. The first, and perhaps psychologically the most convincing, is that for most workers, whatever their skill, the criterion of belonging to their class was precisely the performance of manual, physical labour. The instincts of genuine labour movements were *ouvriériste*: a distrust of those who did not get their hands dirty. This the image represented. The second is that the movement wished to stress precisely its inclusive character. It comprised all proletarians, not merely printers, skilled mechanics and their like. The third, which probably prevailed in the period of the Third International, was that in some sense the relatively unskilled, purely manual labourer, the miner or docker, was considered more revolutionary, since he did not belong to the labour aristocracy with its penchant for reformism and social democracy. He represented 'the masses' to whom revolutionaries appealed over the heads of the social democrats. The image was reality, insofar as it represented the fundamental distinction between manual and non-manual work; aspiration insofar as it implied a programme or a strategy. How realistic it was in the second respect is a question which does not belong to the present paper. But it is nevertheless not insignificant that, as an image, it omitted much that was most characteristic about the working class and its labour movement.

CHAPTER 8

Birth of a Holiday:
The First of May

This paper was originally given, to mark the centenary of the socialist May Day, in 1990 in Queen Mary and Westfield College of the University of London as the first S. T. Bindoff Lecture, in memory of an eminent member of the college history department. It was published separately by the College, and again, modified, as a contribution to Chris Wrigley and John Shepherd (eds), On the Move: Essays in Labour and Transport History Presented to Philip Bagwell *(London and Rio Grande, 1994).*

In 1990 Michael Ignatieff, writing about Easter in the *Observer*,[1] observed that 'secular societies have never succeeded in providing alternatives to religious rituals'. And he pointed out that the French Revolution 'may have turned subjects into citizens, may have put *liberté, égalité* and *fraternité* on the lintel of every school and put the monasteries to the sack, but apart from the Fourteenth of July it never made a dent on the old Christian calendar'. My present subject is perhaps the only unquestionable dent made by a secular movement in the Christian or any other official calendar, a holiday established not in one or two countries, but in 1990 officially in 107 states. What is more, it is an occasion established not by the power of governments or conquerors, but by an entirely unofficial movement of poor men and women. I am speaking of May Day, or more precisely of the First of May, the international festival of the working-class movement, whose centenary ought to have been celebrated in 1990, for it was inaugurated in 1890.

'Ought to be' is the correct phrase, for, apart from the historians, few have shown much interest in this occasion, not even in those socialist parties which are the lineal descendants of those which, at the inaugural congresses of what became the Second International, in 1889 called for a simultaneous international workers' demonstration in favour of a law to limit the working day to eight hours to be held on 1 May 1890. This is true even of those parties actually represented at the 1889 congresses, and which are still in existence. These parties of the Second International or their descendants today provide the governments or the main oppositions or alternative governments almost everywhere in Europe west of what until recently was the self-described region of 'really existing socialism'. One might have expected them to show greater pride, or even merely greater interest in their past.

The strongest political reaction in Britain to the centenary of May Day came from Sir John Hackett, a former general and, I am sorry to say, former head of a college of the University of London, who called for the abolition of May Day, which he appeared to regard as some sort of Soviet invention. It ought not, he felt, to survive the fall of international communism. However, the origin of the European Community's spring May Day holiday is the opposite of Bolshevik or even social democratic. It goes back to the anti-socialist politicians who, recognizing how deeply the roots of May Day reached into the soil of the western working classes, wanted to counter the appeal of labour and socialist movements by co-opting their festival and turning it into something else. To cite a French parliamentary proposal of April 1920, supported by forty-one deputies united by nothing except *not* being socialists:

> This holiday should not contain any element of jealousy and hatred [the code word for class struggle]. All classes, if classes can still be said to exist, and all productive energies of the nation should fraternize, inspired by the same idea and the same ideal.[2]

Those who, before the European Community, went furthest in co-opting May Day were on the extreme right, not the left. Hitler's government was the first after the USSR to make the First of May into an official National Day of Labour.[3] Marshal Pétain's Vichy government declared the First of May a Festival of Labour and Concord and is said to have been inspired to do so by the Phalangist May Day of Franco's Spain, where the Marshal had been an admiring ambassador.[4] Indeed, the European Economic Community which made May Day into a public holiday was a body composed not, in spite of Mrs Thatcher's views on the subject, of socialist but of predominantly anti-socialist governments. Western official May Days were recognitions of the need to come to terms with the tradition of the unofficial May Days and to detach it from labour movements, class consciousness and class struggle. But how did it come about that this tradition was so strong that even its enemies thought they had to take it over, even when, like Hitler, Franco and Pétain, they destroyed the socialist labour movement?

The extraordinary thing about the evolution of this institution is that it was unintended and unplanned. To this extent it was not so much an 'invented tradition' as a suddenly erupting one. The immediate origin of May Day is not in dispute. It was a resolution passed by one of the two rival founding congresses of the International – the Marxist one – in Paris in July 1889, centenary year of the French Revolution. This called for an international demonstration by workers on the same day, when they would put the demand for a Legal Eight-Hour Day to their respective public and other authorities. And since the American Federation of Labor had already decided to hold such a demonstration on 1 May 1890, this day was to be chosen for the international demonstration. Ironically, in the USA itself May Day was never to establish itself as it did elsewhere, if only because an increasingly official public holiday of labour, Labor Day, the first Monday in September, was already in existence.

Scholars have naturally investigated the origins of this resolution, and how it related to the earlier history of the struggle for the Legal Eight-Hour Day in the USA and elsewhere, but these matters do not concern us here. What is relevant to the present argument is how what the resolution envisaged differed from what actually came about. Let us note three facts about the original proposal. First, the call was simply for a single, one-off, international manifestation. There is no suggestion that it should be repeated, let alone become a regular annual event. Second, there was no suggestion that it should be a particularly festive or ritual occasion, although the labour movements of all countries were authorized to 'realize this demonstration in such ways as are made necessary by the situation in their country'. This, of course, was an emergency exit left for the sake of the German Social Democratic Party, which was still at this time illegal under Bismarck's anti-socialist law. Third, there is no sign that this resolution was seen as particularly important at the time. On the contrary, the contemporary press reports barely mention it, if at all, and, with one exception (curiously enough a bourgeois paper), without the proposed date.[5] Even the official Congress Report, published by the German Social Democratic Party, merely mentions the proposers of the resolution and prints its text without any comment or apparent sense that this was a matter of significance. In short, as Edouard Vaillant, one of the more eminent and politically sensitive delegates to the Congress, recalled a few years later: 'Who could have predicted ... the rapid rise of May Day?'[6]

Its rapid rise and institutionalization were certainly due to the extraordinary success of the first May Day demonstrations in 1890, at least in Europe west of the Russian Empire and the Balkans.[7] The socialists had chosen the right moment to found or, if we prefer, reconstitute an International. The first May Day coincided with a triumphant advance of labour strength and confidence in numerous countries. To cite merely two familiar examples: the outburst of the New Unionism in Britain which followed the Dock Strike of 1889, and the socialist victory in Germany, where the Reichstag refused to continue Bismarck's anti-socialist law in January 1890, with the result that a month later the Social Democratic Party doubled its vote at the general election and emerged with just under 20 per cent of the total vote. To make a success of mass demonstrations at such a moment was not difficult, for both activists and militants put their hearts into them, while masses of ordinary workers joined them to celebrate a sense of victory, power, recognition and hope.

And yet the *extent* to which the workers took part in these meetings amazed those who had called upon them to do so, notably the 300,000 who filled Hyde Park in London, which thus, for the first and last time, provided the largest demonstration of the day. For, while all socialist parties and organizations had naturally organized meets, only some had recognized the full potential of the occasion and put their all into it from the start. The Austrian Social Democratic Party was exceptional in its immediate sense of the mass mood, with the result that, as Frederick Engels observed a few weeks later, 'on the continent it was Austria, and in Austria Vienna, which celebrated this festival in the most splendid and appropriate manner'.[8]

Indeed, in several countries, so far from throwing themselves wholeheartedly into the preparation of May Day, local parties and movements were, as usual in the politics of the left, handicapped by ideological arguments and divisions about the legitimate form or forms of such demonstrations – we shall return to them below – or by sheer caution. In the face of a highly nervous, even on occasion hysterical, reaction to the prospect of the day by governments, middle-class opinion and employers who threatened police repression and victimization, responsible socialist leaders often preferred to avoid excessively provocative forms of confrontation. This was notably the case in Germany, where the ban on the party had only just been revoked after eleven years of illegality. 'We have every reason to keep the masses under control at the First of May demonstration,' wrote the party leader August Bebel to Engels. 'We must avoid conflicts.' And Engels agreed.[9]

The crucial matter at issue was whether the workers should be asked to demonstrate in working time, that is to go on strike, for in

1890 the First of May fell on a Thursday. Basically, cautious parties and strong established trade unions – unless they deliberately wanted to be or found themselves engaged in industrial action, as was the plan of the American Federation of Labor – did not see why they should stick their own and their members' necks out for the sake of a symbolic gesture. They therefore tended to opt for a demonstration on the first *Sunday* in May and not on the first day of the month. This was and remained the British option, which was why the first great May Day took place on 4 May. However, it was also the preference of the German party, although there, unlike Britain, in practice it was the First of May that prevailed. In fact, the question was to be formally discussed at the Brussels International Socialist Congress of 1891, with the British and Germans opposing the French and Austrians on this point, and being outvoted.[10] Once again this issue, like so many other aspects of May Day, was the accidental by-product of the international choice of the date. The original resolution made no reference at all to stopping work. The problem arose simply because the first May Day fell on a weekday, as everybody planning the demonstration immediately and necessarily discovered.

Caution dictated otherwise. But what actually *made* May Day was precisely the choice of symbol over practical reason. It was the act of symbolically stopping work which turned May Day into more than just another demonstration, or even another commemorative occasion. It was in the countries or cities where parties, even against hesitant unions, insisted on the symbolic strike that May Day really became a central part of working-class life and of labour identity, as it never really did in Britain, in spite of its brilliant start. For refraining from work on a working day was both an assertion of working-class power – in fact, the quintessential assertion of this power – and the essence of freedom, namely not being forced to labour in the sweat of one's brow, but choosing what to do in the company of family and friends. It was thus both a gesture of class assertion and class struggle and a holiday: a sort of trailer for the good life to come after the emancipation of labour. And, of course, in the circumstances of 1890 it was also a celebration of victory, a winner's lap of honour round the stadium. Seen in this light May Day carried with it a rich cargo of emotion and hope.

This is what Victor Adler realized when, against advice from the German Social Democratic Party, he insisted that the Austrian party must provoke precisely the confrontation which Bebel wanted to avoid. Like Bebel he recognized the mood of euphoria, of mass conversion, almost of messianic expectation which swept through so many working classes at this time. 'The elections have turned the heads of the less politically educated [*geschult*] masses. They believe they have only to want something and everything can be achieved,' as Bebel put it.[11] Unlike Bebel, Adler still needed to mobilize these sentiments to build a mass party out of a combination of activists and rising mass sympathy. Moreover, unlike the Germans, Austrian workers did not yet have the vote. The movement's strength could not therefore be demonstrated electorally as yet. Again, the Scandinavians understood the mobilizing potential of direct action when, after the first May Day, they voted in favour of a repetition of the demonstration in 1891, 'especially if combined with a cessation of work, and not merely simple expressions of opinion'.[12] The International itself took the same view when in 1891 it voted (against the British and German delegates as we have seen) to hold the demonstration on the First of May and 'to cease work wherever it is not impossible to do so'.[13]

This did not mean that the international movement called for a general strike as such, for, with all the boundless expectations of the moment, organized workers were in practice aware both of their strength and of their weakness. Whether people should strike on May Day, or could be expected to give up a day's pay for the demonstration, were questions widely discussed in the pubs and bars of proletarian Hamburg, according to the plain-clothes policemen sent by the Senate to listen to workers' conversations in that massively 'red' city.[14] It was understood that many workers would be unable to come out, even if they wanted to. Thus the railwaymen sent a cable to the first Copenhagen May Day which was read out and cheered: 'Since we cannot be present at the meeting because of the pressure exerted by those in power, we will not omit fully supporting the demand for the eight-hour working day.'[15] However, where employers knew that workers were strong and solidly committed, they would often tacitly accept that the day could be taken off. This was often the case in Austria. Thus, in spite of the clear instruction from the Ministry of the Interior that processions were banned and taking time off was not to be permitted; and in spite of the formal decision by employers *not* to consider the First of May a holiday – and sometimes even to substitute the day *before* the First of May as a works holiday – the State Armaments Factory in Steyr, Upper Austria, shut down on the First of May 1890 and every year thereafter.[16] In any case, enough workers came out in enough countries to make the stop-work movement plausible. After all, in Copenhagen about 40 per cent of the city's workers were actually present at the demonstration in 1890.[17]

Given this remarkable and often unexpected success of the first May Day it was natural that a repeat performance should be demanded. As we have already seen, the united Scandinavian movements asked for it in the summer of 1890, as did the Spaniards. By the end of the year the bulk of the European parties had followed suit. That the occasion should become a regular annual event may or may not have been suggested first by the militants of Toulouse who passed a resolution to this effect in 1890,[18] but to no one's surprise the Brussels congress of the International in 1891 committed the movement to a regular annual May Day. However, it also did two other things, while insisting, as we have seen, that May Day must be celebrated by a single demonstration on the first day of the month, whatever that day might be, in order to emphasize 'its true character as an economic demand for the eight-hour day and an assertion of class struggle'.[19] It added at least two other demands to the eight-hour day: labour legislation and the fight against war. Although it was henceforth an official part of May Day, in itself the peace slogan was not really integrated into the popular May Day tradition, except as something that reinforced the international character of the occasion. However, in addition to expanding the programmatic content of the demonstration, the resolution included another innovation. It spoke of 'celebrating' May Day. The movement had come officially to recognize it not only as a political activity but as a festival.

Once again, this was not part of the original plan. On the contrary, the militant wing of the movement and, it need hardly be added, the anarchists opposed the idea of festivities passionately on ideological grounds. May Day was a day of struggle. The anarchists would have preferred it to broaden out from a single day's leisure extorted from the capitalists into the great general strike which would overthrow the entire system. As so often, the most militant revolutionaries took a sombre view of the class struggle, as the iconography of black and grey masses lightened by no more than the occasional red flag so often confirms.[20] The anarchists preferred to see May Day as a commemoration of martyrs – the Chicago martyrs of 1886, 'a day of grief rather than a day of celebration',[21] and where they were influential, as in Spain, South America and Italy, the martyrological aspect of May Day actually became part of the occasion. Cakes and ale were not part of the revolutionary game-plan. In fact, as a recent study of the anarchist May Day in Barcelona brings out, refusing to treat it or even to call it a 'Festa del Traball', a labour festival, was one of its chief characteristics before the Republic.[22] To hell with symbolic actions: either the world revolution or nothing. Some anarchists even refused to encourage the May Day strike, on the ground that anything that did not actually initiate the revolution could be no more than yet another reformist diversion. The revolutionary syndicalist French Confédération Générale du Travail (CGT) did not resign itself to May Day festivity until after the First World War.[23]

The leaders of the Second International may well have encouraged the transformation of May Day into a festival, since they certainly wanted to avoid anarchist confrontational tactics and naturally also favoured the broadest possible basis for the demonstrations. But the idea of a class holiday, both struggle and a good time, was definitely not in their minds originally. Where did it come from?

Initially the choice of date almost certainly played a crucial role. Spring holidays are profoundly rooted in the ritual cycle of the year in the temperate northern hemisphere, and indeed the month of May itself symbolizes the renewal of nature. In Sweden, for instance, the First of May was already by long tradition almost a public holiday.[24] This, incidentally, was one of the problems about celebrating wintry May Days in otherwise militant Australia. From the abundant iconographical and literary material at our disposal, which has been made available in recent years,[25] it is quite evident that nature, plants and above all flowers were automatically and universally held to symbolize the occasion. The simplest of rural gatherings, like the 1890 meeting in a Styrian village, shows not banners but garlanded boards with slogans, as well as musicians.[26] A charming photograph of a later provincial May Day, also in Austria, shows the social democratic worker–cyclists, male and female, parading with wheels and handlebars wreathed in flowers, and a small flower-decked May child in a sort of baby-seat slung between two bicycles.[27]

Flowers appear unselfconsciously round the stern portraits of the seven Austrian delegates to the 1889 International Congress, distributed for the first Vienna May Day. Flowers even infiltrate the militant myths. In France the *fusillade de Fourmies* of 1891, with its ten dead, is symbolized in the new tradition by Maria Blondeau, eighteen years old, who danced at the head of 200 young people of both sexes, swinging a branch of flowering hawthorn which her fiancé had given her, until the troops shot her dead. Two May traditions patently merge in this image. What flowers? Initially, as the hawthorn branch suggests, colours suggestive of spring rather than politics, even though the movement soon comes to settle on blossoms of its own colour: roses, poppies and above all red carnations. However, national styles vary. Nevertheless, flowers and those other symbols of burgeoning growth, youth, renewal and hope, namely young women, are central. It is no accident that the most universal icons for the occasion, reproduced time and again in a variety of languages, come from Walter Crane – especially the famous young woman in a Phrygian bonnet surrounded by garlands. The British socialist movement was small and unimportant and its May Days, after the first few years, were marginal. However, through William Morris, Crane and the arts-and-crafts movement, inspirers of the most influential 'new art' or art nouveau of the period, it found the exact expression for the spirit of the times. The British iconographic influence is not the least evidence for the internationalism of May Day.

In fact, the idea of a public festival or holiday of labour arose, once again, spontaneously and almost immediately – no doubt helped along by the fact that in German the word *feiern* can mean both 'not working' and 'formally celebrating'. (The use of 'playing' as a synonym for 'striking', common in England in the first part of the century, no longer seems common by its end.) In any case it seemed logical on a day when people stayed away from work to supplement the morning's political meetings and marches with sociability and entertainment later, all the more so as the role of inns and restaurants as meeting-places for the movement was so important. Publicans and *cabaretiers* formed a significant section of socialist activists in more than one country.[28]

One major consequence of this must be immediately mentioned. Unlike politics, which was in those days 'men's business', holidays included women and children. Both the visual and the literary sources demonstrate the presence and participation of women in May Day from the start.[29] What made it a genuine class display, and incidentally, as in Spain, increasingly attracted workers who were not politically with the socialists,[30] was precisely that it was not confined to men but belonged to families. And in turn, through May Day, women who were not themselves directly in the labour market as wage-workers, that is to say the bulk of married working-class women in a number of countries, were publicly identified with movement and class. If a working life of wage-labour belonged chiefly to men, refusing to work for a day united age and sex in the working class.

Practically all regular holidays before this time had been religious holidays, at all events in Europe, except in Britain where, typically, the European Community's May Day has been assimilated to a Bank Holiday. May Day shared with Christian holidays the aspiration to universality, or, in labour terms, *internationalism*. This universality deeply impressed participants and added to the day's appeal. The numerous May Day broadsheets, often locally produced, which are so valuable a source for the iconography and cultural history of the occasion – 308 different numbers of such ephemera have been preserved for pre-fascist Italy alone – constantly dwell on this. The first May Day journal from Bologna in 1891 contains no fewer than four items specifically on the universality of the day.[31] And, of course, the analogy with Easter or Whitsun seemed as obvious as that with the spring celebrations of folk custom.

Italian socialists, keenly aware of the spontaneous appeal of the new *festa del lavoro* to a largely Catholic and illiterate population, used the term 'the workers' Easter' from, at the latest, 1892, and such analogies became internationally current in the second half of the 1890s.[32] One can readily see why. The similarity of the new socialist movement to a religious movement, even, in the first heady years of May Day, to a religious revival movement with messianic expectations was patent. So, in some ways, was the similarity of the body of early leaders, activists and propagandists to a priesthood, or at least to a body of lay preachers. We have an extraordinary leaflet from Charleroi, Belgium in 1898, which reproduces what can only be described as a May Day sermon: no other word will do. It was drawn up by, or in the name of, ten deputies and senators of the Parti Ouvrier Belge, undoubtedly atheists to a man, under the joint epigraphs 'Workers of all lands unite (Karl Marx)' and 'Love One Another (Jesus)'. A few samples will suggest its mood:

This [it began] is the hour of spring and festivity when the perpetual Evolution of nature shines forth in its glory. Like nature, fill yourselves with hope and prepare for The New Life.

After some passages of moral instruction ('Show self-respect: Beware of the liquids that make you drunk and the passions that degrade' and so on) and socialist encouragement, it concluded with a passage of millennial hope:

Soon frontiers will fade away! Soon there will be an end to wars and armies! Every time that you practise the socialist virtues of Solidarity and Love, you will bring this future closer. And then, in peace and joy, a world will come into being in which Socialism will triumph, once the social duty of all is properly understood as bringing about the all-round development of each.[33]

Yet the point about the new labour movement was not that it was a Faith, and one which often echoed the tone and style of religious discourse, but that it was so little influenced by the religious model, even in countries where the masses were deeply religious and steeped in church ways.[34] Moreover, there was little convergence between the old and the new Faith except sometimes (but not always) where Protestantism took the form of unofficial and implicitly oppositionist sects rather than Churches, as in England. Socialist labour was a militantly secular, anti-religious movement which converted pious or formerly pious populations *en masse*.

We can also understand why this was so. Socialism and the labour movement appealed to men and women for whom, as a novel class conscious of itself as such, there was no proper place in the community of which established Churches, and notably the Catholic Church, were the traditional expression. There were indeed settlements of 'outsiders', by occupation as in mining or proto-industrial or factory villages, by origin like the Albanians of what became the quint-essentially 'red' village of Piana dei Greci in Sicily (now Piana degli Albanesi), or united by some other criterion that separated them collectively from the wider society. There 'the movement' might function as *the* community, and in doing so take over many of the old village practices hitherto monopolized by religion. However, this was unusual. In fact a major reason for the massive success of May Day was that it was seen as the *only* holiday associated exclusively with the working class as such, not shared with anyone else, and moreover one extorted by the workers' own action. More than this: it was a day on which those who were usually invisible went on public display and, at least for one day, captured the official space of rulers and society.[35] In this respect the galas of British miners, of which the Durham miners' gala is the longest survivor, anticipated May Day, but on the basis of one industry and not the working class as a whole.[36] In this sense the only relation between May Day and traditional religion was the claim to equal rights. 'The priests have their festivals,' announced the 1891 May Day broadsheet of Voghera in the Po valley, 'the Moderates have their festivals. So have the Democrats. The First of May is the Festival of the workers of the entire world.'[37]

But there was another thing that distanced the movement from religion. Its key word was 'new', as in *Die Neue Zeit* (New Times), title of Kautsky's Marxist theoretical review, and as in the Austrian labour song still associated with May Day, and whose refrain runs: 'Mit uns zieht die neue Zeit' ('The new times are advancing with us'). As both Scandinavian and Austrian experience shows, socialism often came into the countryside and provincial towns literally with the railways, with those who built and manned them, and with the new ideas and new times they brought.[38] Unlike other public holidays, including most of the ritual occasions of the labour movement up till then, May Day did not commemorate anything – at all events outside the range of anarchist influence which, as we have seen, liked to link it with the Chicago anarchists of 1886. It was about nothing but the future, which, unlike a past that had nothing to give to the proletariat except bad memories ('Du passé faisons table rase,' sang the Internationale, not by accident), offered emancipation. Unlike traditional religion, 'the movement' offered not rewards after death but the new Jerusalem on this earth.

The iconography of May Day, which developed its own imagery and symbolism very quickly, is entirely future-oriented.[39] What the future would bring was not at all clear, only that it would be good and that it would inevitably come. Fortunately for the success of May Day, at least one way forward to the future turned the occasion into something more than a demonstration and a festival. In 1890 electoral democracy was still extremely uncommon in Europe, and the demand for universal suffrage was readily added to that for the eight-hour day and the other May Day slogans. Curiously enough, the demand for the vote, although it became an integral part of May Day in Austria, Belgium, Scandinavia, Italy and elsewhere until it was achieved, never formed an *ex officio* international part of its political content like the eight-hour day and, later, peace. Nevertheless, where applicable, it became an integral part of the occasion and greatly added to its significance.

In fact, the practice of organizing or threatening general strikes for universal suffrage, which developed with some success in Belgium, Sweden and Austria, and helped to hold party and unions together, grew out of the symbolic work stoppages of May Day. The first such strike was started by the Belgian miners on 1 May 1891.[40] On the other hand trade unions were far more concerned with the Swedish May Day slogan 'shorter hours and higher wages' than with any other aspect of the great day.[41] There were times, as in Italy, when they concentrated on this and left even democracy to others. The great advances of the movement, including its effective championship of democracy, were not based on narrow economic self-interest.

Democracy was, of course, central to the socialist labour movements. It was not only essential for its progress but inseparable from it. The first May Day in Germany was commemorated by a plaque which showed Karl Marx on one side and the Statue of Liberty on the other.[42] An Austrian May Day print of 1891 shows Marx, holding *Das Kapital*, pointing across the sea to one of those romantic islands familiar to contemporaries from paintings of a Mediterranean character, behind which there rises the May Day sun, which was to be the most lasting and potent symbol of the future. Its rays carried the slogans of the French Revolution: Liberty, Equality, Fraternity, which are found on so many of the early May Day badges and mementoes.[43] Marx is surrounded by workers, presumably ready to man the fleet of ships due to sail to the island, whatever it might be, their sails inscribed: Universal and Direct Suffrage, Eight-Hour Day and Protection for the Workers. This was the original tradition of May Day.

That tradition arose with extraordinary rapidity – within two or three years – by means of a curious symbiosis between the slogans of the socialist leaders and their often spontaneous interpretation by militants and rank-and-file workers.[44] It took shape in those first few marvellous years of the sudden flowering of mass labour movements and parties, when every day brought visible growth, when the very existence of such movements, the very assertion of *class*, seemed a guarantee of future triumph. More than this: it seemed a sign of imminent triumph as the gates of the new world swung open before the working class.

However, the millennium did not come and May Day, with so much else in the labour movement, had to be regularized and institutionalized, even though something of the old flowering of hope and triumph returned to it in later years after great struggles and victories. We can see it in the mad futurist May Days of the early Russian Revolution, and almost everywhere in Europe in 1919–20, when the original May Day demand of the Eight Hours was actually achieved in many countries. We can see it in the May Days of the early Popular Front in France in 1935 and 1936, and in the countries of the continent liberated from occupation, after the defeat of fascism. Still, in most countries of mass socialist labour movements, May Day was routinized some time before 1914.

Curiously, it was during this period of routinization that it acquired its ritualistic side. As an Italian historian has put it, when it ceased to be seen as the immediate antechamber of the great transformation, it became 'a collective rite which requires its own liturgies and divinities',[45] the divinities being usually identifiable as those young women in flowing hair and loose costumes showing the way towards the rising sun to increasingly imprecise crowds or processions of men and women. Was she Liberty, or Spring, or Youth, or Hope, or rosy-fingered Dawn or a bit of all of these? Who can tell? Iconographically she has no universal characteristic except youth, for even the Phrygian bonnet, which is extremely common, or the traditional attributes of Liberty, are not always found. We can trace this ritualization of the day through the flowers which, as we have seen, are present from the beginning, but become, as it were, officialized towards the end of the century. Thus the red carnation acquired its official status in the Habsburg lands and in Italy from about 1900, when its symbolism was specially explicated in the lively and talented broadsheet from Florence named after it. (*Il Garofano Rosso* appeared on

May Days until the First World War.) The red rose became official in Sweden in 1911–12.[46] And, to the grief of incorruptible revolutionaries, the entirely unpolitical lily-of-the-valley began to infiltrate the French workers' May Day in the early 1900s, until it became one of the regular symbols of the day.[47]

Nevertheless, the great era of May Days was not over while they remained both legal – that is, capable of bringing large masses on to the street – and unofficial. Once they became a holiday given or, still worse, enforced from above, their character was necessarily different. And, since public mass mobilization was of their essence, they could not resist illegality, even though the socialists (later communists) of Piana degli Albanesi took pride, even in the black days of fascism, in sending some comrades every First of May without fail to the mountain pass where, from what is still known as Dr Barbato's rock, the local apostle of socialism had addressed them in 1893. It was in this same location that the bandit Giuliano massacred the revived May Day community demonstration and family picnic after the end of fascism in 1947.[48] Since 1914, and especially since 1945, May Day has increasingly become either illegal or, more likely, official. Only in those comparatively rare parts of the third world where massive and unofficial socialist labour movements developed in conditions that allowed May Day to flourish is there a real continuity with the older tradition.

May Day has not, of course, lost its old characteristics everywhere. Nevertheless, even where it is not associated with the fall of old regimes which were once new, as in the USSR and eastern Europe, it is not too much to claim that for most people even in labour movements the word May Day evokes the past more than the present. The society which gave rise to May Day has changed. How important, today, are those small proletarian village communities which old Italians remember? 'We marched round the village. Then there was a public meal. All the party members were there and anyone else who wanted to come.'[49] What has happened in the industrialized world to those who in the 1890s could still recognize themselves in the Internationale's 'Arise ye starvelings from your slumbers'? As an old Italian lady put it in 1980, remembering the May Day of 1920 when she carried the flag as a twelve-year-old textile worker, just started at the mill: 'Nowadays those who go to work are all ladies and gentlemen, they get everything they ask for.'[50] What has happened to the spirit of those May Day sermons of confidence in the future, of faith in the march of reason and progress? 'Educate yourselves! Schools and courses, books and newspapers are instruments of liberty! Drink at the fountain of Science and Art: you will then become strong enough to bring about justice.'[51] What has happened to the collective dream of building Jerusalem in our green and pleasant land?

And yet, if May Day has become no more than just another holiday, a day – I am quoting a French advertisement – when one need not take a certain tranquillizer, because one does not have to work, it remains a holiday of a special kind. It may no longer be, in the proud phrase, 'a holiday outside all calendars',[52] for in Europe it has entered all calendars. It is, in fact, more universally taken off work than any other days except 25 December and 1 January,[53] having far outdistanced its other religious rivals. But it came from below. It was shaped by anonymous working people themselves who, through it, recognized themselves, across lines of occupation, language, even nationality as a single *class* by deciding, once a year, deliberately not to work: to flout the moral, political and economic compulsion to labour. As Victor Adler put it in 1893: 'This is the sense of the May holiday, of the rest from work, which our adversaries fear. This is what they feel to be revolutionary.'[54]

The historian is interested in this centenary for a number of reasons. In one way it is significant because it helps to explain why Marx became so influential in labour movements composed of men and women who had not heard of him before, but recognized his call to become conscious of themselves as a class and to organize as such. In another, it is important, because it demonstrates the historic power of grassroots thought and feeling, and illuminates the way men and women who, as individuals, are inarticulate, powerless and count for nothing can nevertheless leave their mark on history. But above all this is for many of us, historians or not, a deeply moving centenary, because it represents what the German philosopher Ernst Bloch called (and treated at length in two bulky volumes) *The Principle of Hope*: the hope of a better future in a better world. If nobody else remembered it in 1990, it was incumbent on historians to do so.

CHAPTER 9

Socialism and the
Avant-Garde, 1880–1914

If chapter 8 deals with the impact of the rise of the socialist movement on the workers, this chapter deals with its more complex impact on intellectuals and artists and, incidentally, with the relations of political ideologists and artists in these movements. The avant-gardes of politics and the arts converged in the late nineteenth century, diverged quite sharply in the first phase of radical 'modernism', but found each other again – at least for a few passionate years – under the impact of the Great War and the October Revolution. This paper, originally written for the second volume of the Storia del Marxismo *of the Italian publishing house of Giulio Einaudi (Turin, 1978–82) was first published in* Mouvement Social, 111, *April–June 1980.*

Both socialism as a mass movement and the cultural and artistic avant-garde as a widely recognized, self-conscious and sometimes separately organized representative of 'modernity' and 'progress' within the arts are, as European phenomena, children of the last decades of the nineteenth century. In this paper I propose to consider their relationship.

There is no necessary or logical connection between the two phenomena, since the assumption that what is revolutionary in the arts must also be revolutionary in politics (or the other way round) is based on a semantic confusion of the various senses of the term 'revolutionary', or of analogous terms. On the other hand there is or was frequently an existential connection, since socialists (Marxist, anarchist or other kinds) and the artistic and cultural avant-garde were both outsiders, opposed to and by bourgeois orthodoxy. We may also mention the youth, and quite often relative poverty, of many members of the avant-garde and bohème. The poverty may be exaggerated, but the economic insecurity of young or heterodox artists and writers, petty producers of commodities for which no established market existed, is not to be underestimated, even though for many avant-gardists of bourgeois origins the choice of insecurity over a secure bourgeois existence was deliberate.

Both groups of outsiders were to some extent pressed into a not unfriendly coexistence with each other and with other dissidents from the morals and value systems of bourgeois society. Politically revolutionary or 'progressive' minority movements attracted not only the usual fringe of cultural heterodoxy and alternative lifestyles – vegetarians, spiritualists, Theosophists and so on – but independent and emancipated women, challengers of sexual orthodoxy and young people of both sexes who had not yet made their way into bourgeois society, or rebelled against it in whatever way they thought most demonstrative, or felt excluded from it. Heterodoxies overlapped. Such milieus are familiar to every cultural historian. The small British movement of the 1880s provides several examples. Eleanor Marx was not only a Marxian militant but a free professional woman who rejected official marriage, a translator of Ibsen and an amateur actress. Bernard Shaw was a Marxist-influenced socialist activist, a self-made literary man, a hammer of conventional orthodoxy as a critic of music and drama, and a champion of the avant-garde in arts and thought (Wagner, Ibsen). The avant-garde arts-and-crafts movement (William Morris, Walter Crane) was drawn into (Marxian) socialism, while the avant-garde of sexual liberation – the homosexual Edward Carpenter and the champion of general sexual liberation, Havelock Ellis, operated in the same milieu. Oscar Wilde, though political action was hardly his field, was much attracted to socialism and wrote a book on the subject.

Fortunately for the co-existence of the avant-garde and Marxism, Marx and Engels had written very little specifically about the arts, and had published even less. The early social democrats were therefore not seriously constrained in their tastes by classical doctrine. In fact Marx and Engels had shown no fondness for any contemporary avant-garde after the 1840s. How important and influential other socialist theories about the arts (for example the Saint-Simonian) remained in the 1880s is a question which requires further research. However, it is unlikely that they were considered authoritative in the new socialist movements. The absence of a body of authoritative aesthetic analysis obliged social democrats to evolve one. The most obvious criterion of contemporary arts acceptable to socialist labour movements – there was never any doubt about their admiration for the classics of national and international art and literature – was that they should present the realities of capitalist society frankly and critically, preferably with special emphasis on the workers, and ideally with a commitment to their struggles. This did not in itself imply a preference for the avant-garde. Traditional and established painters and writers could just as easily extend their subject-matter and their social sympathies, and in the 1870s–1890s many painters turned to the depiction of industrial scenes, workers and peasants, and sometimes even labour struggles (for example, Sir Hubert Herkomer's *Strike*).[1] While, by official 'salon' standards many of these artists might be regarded as moderately 'progressive' (for instance, Liebermann), they neither were nor saw themselves as artistic revolutionaries.

This kind of socialist aesthetics raised no special problems for the relations between Marxism and the avant-gardes in the 1880s and 1890s, an era dominated, at least in prose literature, by realistic writers with strong social and political interests, or those which could be interpreted in this way. Some were increasingly influenced by the rise of labour to take a specific interest in the workers. Marxists had no difficulty in welcoming, on these grounds, the great Russian novelists whose discovery in the West was largely due to the 'progressives', the drama of Ibsen as well as other Scandinavian literature (Hamsun and, for modern eyes more surprisingly, Strindberg), but above all the writers of schools described as 'naturalist', who were so patently preoccupied with those aspects of capitalist reality from which conventional artists turned aside (Zola and Maupassant in France, Hauptmann and Sudermann in Germany). That so many naturalists were political and social campaigners or even, like Hauptmann, attracted to social democracy,[2] made naturalism even more acceptable. Of course the ideologists were careful to distinguish between socialist consciousness and mere muck-raking. Mehring, surveying naturalism in 1892–3 welcomed it as a sign that 'art begins to feel capitalism in its own body', drawing a parallel, then less unexpected than it would be today, between it and impressionism:

> Indeed in this manner we can easily explain the otherwise inexplicable pleasure which the Impressionists ... and the Naturalists ... take in all the unclean refuse of capitalist society; they live and work amid such rubbish, and moved by obscure instinct, can find no more tormenting protest to throw at the faces of those who torment them.[3]

But, he argued, this was at best a step toward a 'true' art. Nevertheless *Neue Zeit*, which opened its columns to 'modernists',[4] reviewed or published Hauptmann, Maupassant, Korolenko, Dostoyevski, Strindberg, Hamsun, Zola, Ibsen, Björnson, Tolstoi and Gorki. And Mehring himself did not deny that German naturalism was drawn to social democracy, even if he believed that 'bourgeois naturalists are socialist-minded, as feudal socialists were bourgeois-minded, no more and no less'.[5]

A second significant point of contact between Marxism and the arts was visual. On the one hand a number of socially conscious visual artists discovered the working class as a subject and were therefore drawn towards the labour movement. Here as elsewhere in the avant-garde culture, the role of the Low Countries, situated at the intersection of French, British and to some extent German influences, and with a particularly exploited and brutalized labouring population (in Belgium), is to be noted. Indeed the international cultural role of these countries – especially Belgium – was, at this period, more central than for some centuries past: neither symbolism nor art nouveau and later modernist architecture and avant-garde painting after the impressionists can be understood without their contribution. Specifically, in the 1880s the Belgian Constantin Meunier, one of a group of artists close to the Belgian Labour Party, pioneered what later became the standard socialist iconography of the 'worker' – the muscular, bare-chested labouring man, the emaciated and suffering proletarian wife and mother. (Van Gogh's explorations in the world of the poor became known only later.) Marxist critics like Plekhanov treated this extension of the subject-matter of painting into the world of capitalism's victims with the usual reticence, even when it went beyond mere documentation or the expression of social pity. Nevertheless, for those artists primarily interested in their subject-matter, it built a bridge between their world and the milieu in which Marxism was debated.

A more powerful and direct link with socialism came through the applied and decorative arts. The link was direct and conscious, especially in the British arts-and-crafts movement, whose great master William Morris (1834–96) became a sort of Marxist and made both a powerful theoretical as well as an outstanding practical contribution to the social transformation of the arts. These branches of the arts took as their point of departure not the individual and isolated artist but the artisan. They protested against the reduction of the creative worker–craftsman into a mere 'operative' by capitalist industry, and their main object was to create not individual works of art, ideally designed to be contemplated in isolation, but the framework of human daily life, such as villages and towns, houses and their interior furnishings. As it happened, for economic reasons the main market for their products was found among the culturally adventurous bourgeoisie and the professional middle classes – a fate also familiar to champions of a 'people's theatre' then and later.[6] Indeed, the arts-and-crafts movement and its development, art nouveau, pioneered the first genuinely comfortable bourgeois lifestyle of the nineteenth century – the suburban or semi-rural 'cottage' or 'villa', and the style, in various versions, also found a particular welcome in young or provincial bourgeois communities anxious to express their cultural identity – in Brussels and Barcelona, Glasgow, Helsinki and Prague. Nevertheless, the social ambitions of the artist–craftsmen and architects of this avant-garde were not confined to supplying middle-class needs. They pioneered modern architecture and town-planning, in which the social-utopian element is evident – and these 'pioneers of the modern movement' often, as in the case of W. R. Lethaby (1857–1931, Patrick Geddes and the champions of garden cities came from the British progressive–socialist milieu. On the continent its champions were closely associated with social democracy. Victor Horta (1861–1947), the great architect of the Belgian art nouveau, designed the Maison du Peuple of Brussels (1897), at whose 'art section' H. Van de Velde, later a key figure in the development of the modern movement in Germany, gave lectures on William Morris. The socialist pioneer of Dutch modern architecture, H. P. Berlage (1856–1934), designed the offices of the Amsterdam Diamond Workers' Union (1899).

The crucial fact is that the new politics and the new arts converged at this point. Even more significantly, the nucleus of the original (mainly British) artists who pioneered this revolution in the applied arts were not merely directly influenced by Marxism, like Morris, but also – with Walter Crane – provided much of the internationally current iconographical vocabulary of the social democratic movement. Indeed, William Morris developed a powerful analysis of the relations between art and society, which he would certainly have considered Marxist (since he was a Marxist), even though we can also detect the earlier influences of the Pre-Raphaelites and Ruskin. Curiously enough, orthodox Marxist thinking about the arts remained almost completely unaffected by these developments. William Morris' writings have not, to this day, made their way into the mainstream of Marxist aesthetic debates, though in recent years they have become much better known and have found powerful Marxist champions.[7]

No equally obvious links brought together the Marxists and the other main group of avant-gardists of the 1880s and 1890s, whom we may roughly call the symbolists. Yet it remains a fact that most symbolist poets had revolutionary or socialist sympathies. In France, like most of the newer painters of the period – the older impressionists were, with odd exceptions like Pissarro, rather a-political – they were chiefly attracted to anarchism in the early 1890s. Presumably this was not because they had any objection in principle to Marx – 'the majority of young poets' who were converted 'to the doctrines of revolt, whether those of Bakunin or Karl Marx',[8] probably would have welcomed any suitably rebellious banner – but because the French socialist leaders (until the rise of Jaurès) did not inspire them. The schoolmasterly philistinism of the Guesdists in particular would hardly attract them, while the anarchists not only took a much greater interest in the arts, but certainly contained significant painters and critics among their early militants – for example, Félix Fénéon.[9] Conversely in Belgium it was the Parti Ouvrier Belge which attracted symbolists, not only because it included the anarchizing rebels, but also because the group of its leaders or spokesmen who came from the cultured middle class were visibly and actively interested in the arts. Jules Destrée wrote extensively about socialism and art and published a catalogue of Odilon Redon's lithographs, Vandervelde frequented poets. Maeterlinck remained associated with the party until almost 1914, Verhaeren almost became its official poet, the painters Eeckhout and Khnopff were active in the Maison du Peuple. It is true that symbolism flourished in countries where Marxist theorists keen to condemn it (like Plekhanov) were hardly present. Relations between artistic and political revolt were thus amicable enough.

Hence, until the end of the century, a good deal of common ground existed between the cultural avant-gardes and the arts admired by discriminating minorities on the one hand, and the increasingly Marxist-influenced social democracy on the other. The socialist intellectuals who became leaders in the new parties – characteristically born around 1860 – were still young enough not to have lost contact with the tastes of the 'advanced'; even the oldest, Victor Adler (1852) and Kautsky (1854), were still well below forty in 1890. Victor Adler, a frequenter of the Café Griensteidl, main centre of Viennese artists and intellectuals, was thus not only deeply impregnated with classical literature and music, but also a passionate Wagnerian (like Plekhanov and Shaw he stressed the revolutionary and 'socialist' implications of Wagner more than is usual today), an enthusiast for his friend Gustav Mahler, an early champion of Bruckner, an admirer, in common with almost all socialists of this generation, of Ibsen and Dostoyevski, and profoundly moved by Verhaeren, whose poems he translated.[10] Conversely, as we have seen, a large part of the naturalists, symbolists and other 'advanced' schools of the time were drawn towards the labour movement and (outside France) social democracy. The attraction was not always lasting: the Austrian littérateur Hermann Bahr, who fancied himself as a spokesman of the 'moderns', veered away from Marxism at the end of the 1880s, and the great naturalist

Hauptmann moved in a symbolist direction which confirmed the theoretical reservations of Marxist commentators. The split between socialists and anarchists also had its effects, since it is clear that some (particularly in the visual arts) had always been attracted by the pure rebellion of the latter. Still, the 'moderns' felt at home in the neighbourhood of the labour movements, and the Marxists, at least the cultured intellectuals among them, with the 'moderns'.

For reasons which have not been adequately investigated, these links were broken for a time. Some reasons may be suggested. In the first place, as the 'crisis in Marxism' demonstrated in the late 1890s, the belief that capitalism was on the verge of breakdown, the socialist movement on the verge of revolutionary triumph, could no longer be maintained in western Europe. Intellectuals and artists who had been drawn to a broad, vaguely defined movement of workers by the general air of hope, confidence, even utopian expectation which it generated round itself now faced a movement uncertain of its future prospects and riven by internal and increasingly sectarian debates. This ideological fragmentation was also present in eastern Europe: it was one thing to sympathize with a movement all of whose currents appeared to converge in a generally Marxist direction, as in the early 1890s, or with Polish socialism before the split between nationalists and anti-nationalists, and quite another to make a selection between rival and mutually hostile bodies of revolutionaries and ex-revolutionaries.

In the West, however, there was the additional fact that the new movements became increasingly institutionalized, involved in the daily politics which were unlikely to excite artists and writers, while they became in practice reformist, leaving the future revolution to some version of historical inevitability. Moreover, institutionalized mass parties, often developing their own cultural world, were less likely to favour arts which a working-class public would not readily understand or approve. It is true that the subscribers to German workers' libraries increasingly abandoned political books for fiction – while also reading less poetry and classical literature; but their most popular writer, almost certainly Friedrich Gerstaecker, an author of adventure tales, would not inspire the avant-garde.[11] It is hardly surprising that in Vienna Karl Kraus, though initially much drawn towards the social democrats by his own cultural and political dissidence, moved away from them in the 1900s. He blamed them for not fostering a sufficiently serious cultural level among the workers, and was not inspired by the party's major – and eventually victorious – campaign for universal suffrage.[12]

The revolutionary left of social democracy, initially somewhat marginal in the West, and the revolutionary syndicalist or anarchist tendencies were more likely to attract avant-garde culture of a radical turn of mind. After 1900 the anarchists in particular increasingly found their social base, outside some Latin countries, in a milieu composed of bohemians and some self-educated workers, shading over into the lumpenproletariat – in the various Montmartres of the Western world – and settled down into a general subculture of those who rejected, or were not assimilable by, 'bourgeois' lifestyles or organized mass movements.[13] This essentially individualist and anti-nomian rebellion was not opposed to social revolution. It often merely waited for a suitable movement of revolt and revolution to which it could attach itself, and was once again mobilized *en masse* against the war and for the Russian Revolution. The Munich soviet of 1919 gave it perhaps its major moment of political assertion. Yet both in reality and in theory it turned away from Marxism. Nietzsche, a thinker who was for fairly obvious reasons deeply unattractive to Marxists or other social democrats, in spite of his hatred of the 'bourgeois', became a characteristic guru of anarchist and anarchizing rebels, as of non-political middle-class cultural dissidence.

Conversely, the very cultural radicalism of avant-garde developments in the new century cut them off from workers' movements whose members remained traditional in their tastes, inasmuch as they (and the movement) remained attached to the understood languages and symbolic codes of communication which expressed the contents of works of art. The avant-gardes of the last quarter of the century had not yet broken with these languages, though they had stretched them. With a little adjustment it was perfectly possible to discern what Wagner and the impressionists, or even a good many of the symbolists, 'were about'. From the early twentieth century – perhaps the Paris Salon d'Automne of 1905 marks the break in the visual arts – this was no longer so.

Moreover, the socialist leaders – even the younger generation born after 1870 – were no longer 'in touch'. Rosa Luxemburg had to defend herself against the charge of not liking the 'modern writers'; but though she had been much moved by the avant-garde of the 1890s, such as the German naturalist poets, she admitted that she did not understand Hofmannsthal and had never heard of Stefan George.[14] And even Trotsky, who prided himself on much closer contact with new cultural fashions – he wrote a lengthy analysis of Frank Wedekind for *Neue Zeit* in 1908 and reviewed art exhibitions – does not appear to show any specific familiarity with what the adventurous young in 1905–14 would have regarded as the avant-garde – except, of course, in Russian literature. Like Rosa Luxemburg he noted and disapproved its extreme subjectivism – its capacity, in Luxemburg's words, to express 'a state of mind' – but nothing else ('but one cannot make human beings with states of mind').[15] Unlike her, he attempted a Marxist interpretation of the new trends of subjectivist rebellion and the 'purely aesthetic logic' which 'naturally transformed the revolt against academicism into a revolt of self-sufficient artistic form against content, considered as an indifferent fact'.[16] He ascribed it to the novelty of life in the environment of the modern giant city, and more specifically to the expression of this experience by the intellectuals who lived in these modern Babylons. No doubt both Luxemburg and Trotsky echoed the particularly strong social preconceptions of Russian aesthetic theory, but at bottom they reflected a very general attitude of Marxists, Eastern or Western. Someone particularly interested in the arts and anxious to maintain contact with the latest trends might develop a taste for some of these innovations as private individual, but how exactly was such an interest to be linked to his or her socialist activities and convictions?

It was not simply a matter of age, though few of the established names in the International were below thirty in 1910, and most were well into middle age. What Marxists understandably failed to appreciate was what they saw as a retreat (rather than, as the avant-garde saw it, an advance) into formal virtuosity and experiment, an abandonment of the content of the arts, including their overt and recognizable social and political content. What they could not accept was their choice of a pure subjectivism, almost solipsism, such as Plekhanov detected in the cubists.[17] It was already regrettable, if explicable, that 'among the bourgeois ideologists who go over to the side of the proletariat there are very few practitioners of the arts' (Künstler); and in the years before 1914 there seemed to be even fewer who were drawn towards the workers' movement than before 1900. The avant-garde of French painters was 'à l'écart de toute agitation intellectuelle et sociale, confinés dans les conflits de technique'.[18] But there was more to it than this. In 1912–13 Plekhanov could state as something evident that 'the majority of today's artists occupy the bourgeois standpoint and are totally impervious to the great ideas of freedom of our time'.[19] It was not easy, among the mass of artists who claimed to be 'anti-bourgeois', to find more than a few who were close to the organized socialist movements – even the anarchists found fewer devoted enthusiasts among the painters than they had done in the 1890s – but it was a good deal easier to discover those who complained about the philistinism of the workers, frank elitists like the Stefan George circle in Germany or the Russian acmeists, searchers for (preferably female) aristocratic company, and even – especially in literature – potential and actual reactionaries. Moreover, it must not be forgotten that the new experimental avant-gardes rebelled not so much against academicism as against precisely those avant-gardes of the 1880s and 1890s which had been relatively close to the labour and socialist movements of the time.

In short, what could Marxists see in these new avant-gardes except yet another symptom of the crisis of bourgeois culture, and the avant-gardes in Marxism except yet another proof that the past could not understand the future? No doubt there were some among the few dozen individuals on whose patronage (as collectors or dealers) the new painters depended who were also Marxist sympathizers. The amateurs of rebellious art were unlikely to be politically conservative at this time. The occasional Marxist theorist – Lunacharski, Bogdanov – might even rationalize his sympathy for the innovators, but was likely to meet with resistance. Yet the cultural world of the socialist and labour movements had no obvious place for the new avant-gardes, and the orthodox aesthetic theorists of Marxism (*de facto* a central and east European species) condemned them.

However, if some of the new avant-gardes certainly remained remote from socialism or any other politics, and some were to become frankly reactionary or even fascist, a great part of the rebels in the arts were merely waiting for a historic conjuncture when artistic and political revolt could once again merge. They found it after 1914 in the movement against the war and the Russian Revolution. After 1917 the junction between Marxism (in the shape of Lenin's bolshevism) and the avant-garde was once again made, initially mainly in Russia and Germany. The era of what the Nazis called (not incorrectly) *Kulturbolschewismus* does not belong to the history of Marxism in the period of the Second International. Nevertheless the post-1917 developments must be mentioned, because they led to bifurcation of Marxist aesthetic theory between the 'realists' and the 'avant-gardists' – the conflicts between Lukacs and Brecht, the admirers of Tolstoi and those of James Joyce. And as we have seen this division had its roots in the period before 1914.

If we look back on the period of the Second International as a whole, we must conclude that the relation between Marxism and the arts was never comfortable, even though after 1900 it became very much more difficult. Marxist theorists had never felt completely happy about any of the 'modern' movements of the 1880s and 1890s, leaving their enthusiastic championship to intellectuals on the fringes of Marxism (as in Belgium) or to non-Marxist revolutionaries and socialists. The leading orthodox Marxist critics saw themselves as commentators or referees rather than supporters or players in the football match of culture. This did no harm to their historical analysis of artistic developments as symptoms of the decay of bourgeois society: an impressive analysis. And yet we cannot but be struck by the externality of their observations. Every Marxist intellectual saw himself or herself as a participant in the labours of philosophy and the sciences, however amateur; hardly any saw themselves as participants in the creative arts. They analysed the relation of art to society and the movement and gave good or bad marks to schools, artists and works. At most they cherished such few artists as actually joined their movements, and made allowances for their personal and ideological vagaries, as bourgeois society also did. The influence of Marxism on the arts was therefore likely to be peripheral. Even naturalism and symbolism, which were close to the socialist movements of their time, would have evolved very much in the way they did if Marxists had taken no interest at all in them. In fact, Marxists found it difficult to see any role for the artist under capitalism except as a propagandist, a sociological symptom or a 'classic'. One is tempted to say that the Marxism of the Second International really had no adequate theory of the arts and, unlike in the case of the 'national question', was not obliged by political urgency to discover its theoretical inadequacy.

But within the Marxism of the Second International there was a genuine theory of the arts in society, though the official corpus of Marxist doctrine was not aware of it: the theory most fully developed by William Morris. If there was a major and lasting Marxist influence on the arts, it came through this current of thought, which looked beyond the structure of the arts in the bourgeois era (the individual 'artist') to the element of artistic creation in all labour and the (traditional) arts of popular life, and beyond the equivalent of commodity production in art (the individual 'work of art') to the environment of everyday life. Characteristically, it was the only branch of Marxist aesthetic theory which paid attention to architecture, and indeed regarded it as the key to and crown of the arts.[20] If Marxist criticism was the fly on the wheel of naturalism or 'realism', it was the engine of the arts-and-crafts movement, whose historic impact on modern architecture and design was and remains fundamental.

It was neglected both because Morris, who was one of the earliest British Marxists,[21] was seen merely as a famous artist but a political lightweight and no doubt because the British tradition of theorizing about art and society (neo-romantic medievalism, Ruskin), which he merged with Marxism, had little contact with the mainstream of Marxist thought. Yet it came from within the arts, it was Marxist – at least Morris declared that it was – and it converted and influenced

138

practitioners in the arts, designers, architects and town-planners and not least the organizers of museums and art schools, over a large part of Europe. Nor was it accidental that this major Marxist influence on the arts came from Britain, though in that country Marxism was of negligible importance. For at this period Britain was the only European country sufficiently transformed by capitalism for industrial production to have transformed artisan production. On reflection it is not surprising that Marx's 'classic' country of capitalist development produced the only major critique of what capitalism did to the arts. Nor is it surprising that the Marxist element in this significant movement within the arts has been forgotten. Morris himself was sufficiently realistic to know that, while capitalism lasted, art could not become socialist.[22] As capitalism emerged from its crisis to flourish and expand, it appropriated and absorbed the arts of the revolutionaries. The comfortable and cultured middle class, the industrial designers, took it over. The greatest work of H. P. Berlage, the Dutch socialist architect, is not the building of the Diamond Workers' Union but the Amsterdam Stock Exchange. The nearest that Morrisian town-planners got to their people's cities were 'garden suburbs', eventually occupied by the middle class, and 'garden cities' remote from industry. In this manner the arts reflect the hopes and the tragedy of the socialism of the Second International.

CHAPTER 10

The Left's Megaphone

This reflection on the role of Harold Laski in the Labour politics of the 1930s and 1940s was originally published in the London Review of Books, *8 July 1993. It is also an exploration of a political mood on the left in the days of slump and fascism, which made the Labour government of 1945 the greatest reforming administration of the century.*

'It would not be too much to say', wrote the otherwise unsympathetic Max (now Lord) Beloff after Harold Laski's death in 1950, 'that ... the future historian may talk of the period between 1920 and 1950 as the "The Age of Laski".' Thirty-seven years later a leading historian of the Labour Party observed that 'Laski's time and reputation have gone into almost total eclipse.' How did a thinker, writer and political figure of such prominence come to disappear from sight so completely? It is a problem of both biography and intellectual history, for Laski's impact is inseparable from his personality and style of public appearance. Curiously, after forty years in the shadows he now emerges, almost simultaneously, in two new biographies totalling 1,100 pages, a fact which would have undoubtedly pleased their subject.

Both Michael Newman's *Political Biography* and Isaac Kramnick and Barry Sheerman's *A Life on the Left* rightly insist on their man's public face. But even his political life was peculiar, if only because this profoundly political man never became a politician, or exerted serious influence on the leading people in his party. The Labour victory of 1945 made his fellow rebels from the 1930s, Cripps, Strauss and Bevan, into architects of the new Britain (all four had been threatened with expulsion from the party for advocating unity with the Communist Party; the other three were expelled for a while), but it marginalized Laski completely. It was not that he objected to being an insider. On the contrary, he wanted to be insider and outsider at the same time, not only in the leadership of the Labour Party but in the general pattern of his life: a sincere revolutionary 'delighting in playing the political insider influencing a marginal change here and an incremental policy development there'. Or, as Kramnick and Sheerman put it, unkindly: 'Almost as important as attacking the privileged was dining with them.' Even more obviously, his public life, his academic career and his personal development were all a series of confrontations and controversies, the life 'a moving narrative of rebellion, recognition and repudiation'.

Harold Laski is undoubtedly a rewarding subject for psychological analysis, not least because of his notorious and, one would have thought, quite unnecessary mythomania. For he had no need to invent all those intimate contacts with the eminent and the powerful, from Woodrow Wilson to Stalin, about which his friends and enemies joked. He really did know such people: indeed, he had taken care to know them from the start. President Roosevelt asked to see him whenever he came to the US, and used his arguments in cabinet meetings.

Kramnick/Sheerman's is much the more perceptive of the two biographies because it is keenly aware both that Laski's 'Jewishness and his attitude to it were central issues in his life' and that this made him an anomaly in the Britain of his time, as it would not have done in the US. He was anomalous not only as 'one of the few Jews among the labour movement's earnest Christians', but as an unquestioned upper-middle-class Jew, of neither Sephardic nor German origin, who was as reluctant as older Jewry to identify with what (speaking of the Zionist mathematician Selig Brodetsky, hero of poor immigrant boys in public libraries) he considered 'the worst type of East End Jew'.

It is difficult to recall how uncertain the position of such a person was. Laski's rebellion against father and faith at the age of sixteen – dramatized by his marriage, at eighteen, to the ideologically radical but Christian Frida, six years his senior – left him outside the one community which had no trouble accepting an intellectual *Wunderkind* who suffered lifelong bad health and held advanced ideas: that of the prosperous Anglo-Jews who combined Orthodox religion and communal service with enthusiastic cultural assimilation to the English. He probably never fully appreciated the anti-semitism which surrounded him, and which led British officials to refer to him as a 'snivelling Hebrew', Hugh Dalton to call him 'an undersized Semite' and a Conservative obituary 'an alien mind imbued and impregnated with an alien philosophy'. Yet the effort to make himself look, all his life, like 'an *enfant terrible* among admiring onlookers' (Lionel Robbins) suggests an insecurity which his American Jewish intellectual friends – a Frankfurter, a Lippman or a Brandeis – did not need to have, because there were more of them.

How far this explains the persistent punctuation of Laski's career by public controversy it is impossible to tell. The pattern itself is plain. He got on the wrong side of the authorities on political grounds in his first teaching job at McGill in Montreal. His exit from Harvard in 1920 was drowned in political uproar. After a calm beginning, his career at the London School of Economics (where he was given the Chair in Political Science in 1927) was stormy. The crisis came to a head in the early 1930s when the then Director (Beveridge of the Beveridge Report) suggested that his subversive views and behaviour were incompatible with his position. His career in the Labour Party was the opposite of tranquil and his moment of greatest triumph, as chairman of the party's National Executive in the year of the 1945 electoral triumph, was also his year of disaster. He burned his boats with the Labour leadership by asking Attlee to resign, became Churchill's bogeyman in the election campaign, and lost an ill-judged libel case against an insignificant reactionary who accused him of advocating violent revolution. The problem was not the views which Laski was accused of holding, rightly or not, but his apparent disposition to provoke such public reactions on both sides of the Atlantic. Ironically, for much of his career Laski was not a particularly radical figure. His tragedy was that he remained the *enfant terrible* all his life.

Oddly enough, one of the few who not only recognized this but forgave him for it was his great antagonist in the glory days of the LSE, Lionel Robbins, the economist who, with his colleague Friedrich von Hayek, represented all that Laski abhorred. Robbins, a genuinely first-rate intellect who settled down to a career among the greatest and best of the Great and the Good, was one of Laski's few friends among his colleagues – and his constant defender. Indeed, after Laski's death Robbins and some others were so outraged at the hatchet job the *Times* obituarist did on him that they prepared a second obituary which set out 'to convey the personal qualities of the late Professor Laski which endeared him to his many friends' as well as 'those qualities which gave him such a remarkable influence in the labour movement'. Robbins recognized not only Laski's 'almost juvenile personality – a lack of emotional balance that is nearly painful', and his loneliness, but his 'quick apprehension and sense of fun', his sense of the absurd – and not least his generosity and goodness. (That *The Times* published the second obituary was, incidentally, unprecedented.)

What did Laski actually achieve? A glance at the Citations Indexes for both Social Sciences and Humanities shows that his twenty-five books have not survived. Yet he was a man of many gifts. Leonard Woolf, who knew what Keynes and Russell could do, recalled a meeting of Labour sympathizers with Gandhi in London, where he had been bowled over by 'one of the most brilliant intellectual pyrotechnic displays I have ever listened to':

> Harold ... gave the most lucid, faultless summary of the complicated, diverse expositions of ten or fifteen people to which he had been listening in the previous hour and a half. He spoke for about twenty minutes; he gave a perfect sketch of the pattern into which the various statements and opinions logically composed themselves; he never hesitated for a word or a thought, and, as far I could see, never missed a point. There was a kind of beauty in his exposition, a flawless certainty and simplicity which one feels in some works of art.

He was an unparalleled performer in the lecture theatre, as anyone who ever heard him will confirm. 'One knew he was lecturing when every few minutes or so a great burst of laughter could be heard through the rest of the building ... Postgraduate students of other subjects ... used to go to Laski's lectures "when we wished to relax, almost as we might go to a cinema or theatre".' He was a teacher of genius, and I cannot think of anyone better at inspiring students, especially those from America and what was not yet called the third world; no one has inspired more of them. Thanks exclusively to Laski, the LSE became, in the words of Senator Daniel Moynihan, 'the most important institution of higher education in Asia and Africa'. For most overseas students – and when he came there 300 out of the School's 2,500 students were 'foreign and colonial' – he *was* the LSE. An elderly historian in Bogotá once told me that it was Laski who inspired him in his life's work, to write the history of the Indians' oppression since the Conquest. He had gone to the LSE in the 1920s. 'What has happened to that institution?' he asked. 'Is it still in existence?'

However, the good fairy who had showered the infant Laski with so many mental gifts had withheld two. He was neither an original thinker nor a natural writer, and he never became a good writer, since he wrote too much, too fast, on too many subjects, and without self-criticism and revision. Even at the time of his greatest influence, he was not taken very seriously as a theorist on the intellectual left, though he was, with Shaw, Wells, Marx, G. D. H. Cole and Tawney, among the authors who had had most influence on the Labour MPs of 1962. Unlike Tawney, he produced no text which shaped the vision of socialism; unlike Cole (politically less prominent but far more influential), he produced no histories of the movements which everyone saw as the natural successors to those of the Webbs. Academics paid polite compliments to the early pluralist writings, which were relics of his youthful syndicalism, without actually recommending them. (They may make a modest comeback as part of the post-1989 fashion for anti-state rhetoric.) His magnum opus, *A Grammar of Politics* (1925), barely floated and has sunk from sight.

Yet none of this stood in the way of his extraordinary prominence from 1931 to 1945. In a way, as John Strachey observed perceptively, 'the unresolved themes that ran through his books, articles and speeches ... [were] his main strength. It was just this that gave him his hold over the minds of a whole generation of the British Labour Movement. After all, the contradictions were in our minds too – in a sense they were in the objective situation itself.' He was 'at bottom a mass preacher and public teacher', though Kramnick/Sheerman are surely wrong to argue that he was prepared to sacrifice his political and scholarly reputation to 'his interest in teaching people about and ushering in socialism'. What he preached and taught on the public scene was what most people who turned to the left in Britain in the years between 1931 and 1945 felt about their own times.

This is what makes Laski interesting as a public figure in Britain, as distinct from the US and India, where he operated essentially on and among the decision-making minority. He belongs to the era of the Great Slump and the fight against fascism, and behind the puzzled evolution of his opinions lie the traumas of the period: the failures of the Labour government of 1929–31, the profound shock of Mac-Donald's 'betrayal' and the setting up of the national government, the victory of National Socialism in Germany, the despairing retreat before international aggression and conquest. The history of the 1920s could be written without reference to Laski, for then he represented nothing except himself. It was after 1931 that he became a symptomatic figure, a sort of barometer of the British left inside and outside the Labour Party (but not in the Communist Party). In 1931 he was a major vote-getter in elections for the Labour Party Executive Committee, which remained his 'power-base' (if that is not a question-begging term) thereafter.

The key to his position and that of the 1930s left was the left's isolation. Outside Scandinavia, it had no answer to the Great Slump, except to point to the one economy that seemed immune to it, the USSR, and consequently to call for 100 per cent socialism. Economic policies to overcome the slump came from the Liberal Keynes, against whom Laski, in an American debate of 1934, argued that only public ownership of the means of production could save the US. (Nowhere was he more typical of the British 1930s than in combining a genuine admiration for Roosevelt with admiration and support for the USSR.) Politically the left had an unanswerable policy: anti-fascist unity at home and abroad.

Nevertheless, nobody would listen except those who were already convinced, and not even all of them. Except in Scandinavia and the US there was no significant public shift to the left; in large parts of Europe there was a marked shift to the right – in countries where elections could still be held. The victory of the French Popular Front merely demonstrated the necessity of unity. It polled barely 1 per cent more than the combined votes for the left in 1932. The Labour Party, scarcely recovered from losing a quarter of its electorate in 1931, had no serious prospects of winning an election. Anti-fascism did not extend its popular base until after Munich, and the radicalization of opinion which prepared the Labour victory of 1945 was not visible before 1941–2.

The voices of the left were crying, not exactly in the wilderness, but in despair: against the refusal to unite against Hitler in the 1930s, against the refusal to recognize the potential for social change in the people's war of 1940–5. Laski was the megaphone through which they spoke. He became a force when he stopped making behind-the-scenes suggestions to decision-makers and spoke for the perennial opposition: as the Tony Benn of the 1940s (but, it must be said, in worse prose).

Here lay Laski's strength, but also his limits. Once the left had achieved its triumph, which was to push the party into breaking with Churchill and to fight the 1945 election on a, by our standards today, inconceivably radical programme, he had no more to say. Or rather, the time for lectures and denunciations, especially from a man who showed a spectacular lack of political judgment, was past. Clement Attlee's famous put-down ('a period of silence on your part would be welcome') was appropriate. There was plenty of scope for a left-wing critique of the Labour government, but it assumed a recognition of the constraints as well as the potentialities of power which Laski did not have.

His last years, shadowed by the Cold War, of which he became a posthumous victim, were sad. He died in his mid-fifties of overwork and disillusion. For the new men of 1945, he was (in Denis Healey's words) 'a mousy little man with a small moustache and big sorrowful brown eyes' and 'more than a touch of Charlie Chaplin'. Except by his former students, he was soon forgotten. His was a personal tragedy but also the tragedy of a certain kind of British left-wing thinker. And yet, would the greatest and most humane reforming administration of the century have come about without him?

CHAPTER 11

Peasants and Politics

The three following chapters discuss, essentially, the political relations of 'traditional' peasants to groups and institutions outside their local community: their force and their limitations. They deal, in particular, with the situations in which peasants encounter the political movements and problems of the twentieth century. They continue the study of the main themes in Primitive Rebels *(1959), but, especially in chapters 11 and 12, on the basis of some first-hand work in various countries of Latin America. The present chapter was originally published in the first issue of the* Journal of Peasant Studies *(I, 1, 1973).*

The subject of this paper is vast, and moreover implies some definition of both peasants and politics. A good deal of the effort of definition is, of course, significant for theoretical rather than practical purposes. It may well be a very complex matter for a zoologist to define a horse, but this does not normally mean that there is any real difficulty about recognizing one. I shall therefore assume that most of us most of the time know what the words 'peasants' and 'politics' refer to.

Nevertheless, a few initial clarifications are useful. The politics with which we are concerned in this paper are those in which peasants are involved with the larger societies of which they form part. That is to say the relations of peasants with other social groups, both those which are their economic, social and political 'superiors' or exploiters and those which are not, workers, for instance, or for that matter other sections of the peasantry, and with more comprehensive institutions or social units – the government, the national state. I shall not be concerned with the kind of micro-politics which fill so much of the horizon of villagers, as they do of students, professors and other inhabitants of closed or partly closed little worlds. The distinction between micro-politics and macro-politics in peasant communities is not easy to draw in practice, for the two overlap very considerably, but may nevertheless be properly made.

As for peasants, I merely wish to suggest – or rather to recall – two points: first, that there are profound differences between various forms of family-based agrarian production which any generalization risks underestimating – for example between pastoral and tillage economies – and second, that beyond a certain point in the socio-economic differentiation of the agrarian population the term 'peasantry' is no longer applicable. That point itself is often difficult to establish, but it is evident that, for instance, neither the commercial farmers of nineteenth-century England nor the rural proletarians of some large-scale plantation economies in the tropics belong to the 'peasant problem', though they do constitute part of the 'agrarian problem'.

I would, however, like to insist on one distinction which applies in different ways both to peasants and to politics and which divides life before and after the 'Great Transformation' which, in Europe, occurs with the triumph of bourgeois society and industrial capitalism. I wish to make it clear that this does not imply accepting the crude and non-historical dichotomy between 'traditional' and 'modern' society. History does not consist of a single step. 'Traditional' societies are not static and unchanging, exempt from historic change and evolution, nor is there a single model of 'modernization' which determines their transformation. But to reject the crudities of some social sciences should not lead us to underestimate the profundity, and the qualitative difference from earlier developments, of the transformation which, for most countries, resulted from the triumph of industrial capitalism. The mere fact that the peasantry has ceased to constitute the actual majority of the population in many parts of the world, that it has for practical purposes disappeared in some, starting with capitalist England, and that its disappearance as a class is today quite conceivable in many developed countries, separates the period since the eighteenth century from all previous history since the development of agriculture.

I

We may place peasants somewhere on a continuum between two extreme ideal types, the first represented by something like the mid-nineteenth-century communal peasantry of central Russia, leading the sort of life well described by Dobrowolski for Poland,[1] the second represented by something like the mid-nineteenth-century model of the French peasantry of Marx's *Eighteenth Brumaire*,[2] who operate in a framework of bourgeois institutions and law, especially property law, most likely as individual commodity producers, possibly shading over into commercial farmers, thus forming an aggregate of small individual enterprises without any strong interrelationships – Marx's 'sack of potatoes'. By and large the characteristic of traditional peasants is a much higher degree of formal or informal (mostly localized) collectivity, which both tends to inhibit permanent social differentiation within the peasantry and to facilitate, or even impose, communal action.[3] We need not here consider whether this collectivity is due to economic factors – perhaps the need for co-operation in the process of labour or the management of resources for common use – or to other factors. It does not imply egalitarianism, though probably (perhaps in conjunction with such institutions as those of feudal lordship) it implies some mechanism inhibiting the unrestricted accumulation of resources by individual peasant families. The strength of the 'community' may vary enormously. Nevertheless it is difficult to conceive of a 'traditional' peasantry, outside certain very special situations, without this collective element. Insofar as there may be regions where it is absent, the following discussion evidently does not apply to them. It will deal primarily with 'traditional' peasants or those in the process of transformation, that is of social and economic class differentiation.

Broadly speaking the 'Great Transformation' also transforms politics, including the politics of the popular masses, inasmuch as the sovereign territorial 'national state', with specific institutions including, with growing frequency, nationwide elections, becomes the standard framework for political action, insofar as new forms of political organization and movement with specific, and increasingly secular, ideologies develop, and so on. It should be stressed that the difference is not one between 'traditional' societies 'without politics' and 'modern' ones with politics. There is politics in both. Nor is it a difference between an era when politics is the preserve of the superior classes and one in which the common people, including the peasantry, become permanently active factors in politics. Nevertheless in Europe the politics of the period before and after the French Revolution are distinct in their procedures and their setting. Most of history is that of traditional peasants in traditional politics, but what this paper is chiefly concerned with is what happens when traditional peasants get involved in modern politics: a transitional situation, but one which for many parts of the world is of practical and not merely of historical interest.

Let us next turn to the question which is basic to the problem of peasants in politics: how far can we speak of the peasantry as a class?

Of course objectively it can be defined as a class 'in itself' in the classical sense, namely a body of people who have the same kind of relation to the means of production as well as other common economic and social characteristics. But as Shanin has rightly observed, among such classes the peasantry is 'a class of low classness'[4] compared, say, to the industrial working class, a class of very high 'classness', in the sense that a great deal of its politics can be directly derived from its specific relations to the means of production.

But how far is it a 'class for itself' – a class conscious of itself as such? In traditional societies, hence for the greater part of history, peasants regarded themselves, and indeed were, the basic type of humanity, being of course the great majority of all the people living in the world they knew, or for that matter anywhere in the world. In a sense people or human beings were then typically peasants, the rest being untypical minorities. Secondly, peasants were enormously aware of their distinction from, and almost always their subalternity to, their oppression by, the minorities of non-peasants, whom they did not like or trust. This applies not only to the gentry or lords (where there is lordship), but to traders and townsmen, except perhaps to the peasants' kinsmen who briefly visit towns without actually becoming townsmen themselves. Of course in the twentieth century this situation has changed, and the sharp distinction between town and country can no longer be maintained, given the mass *Landflucht* of the peasantry. Still, traditionally peasants tended to distrust and dislike all who were not peasants, because most other people appeared to belong to a conspiracy to rob and oppress them, and stood above them in whatever social hierarchy was established.

Leonardo Sciascia, the Sicilian writer, has published a harvest song discovered in some obscure local journal of 1876, in which the peasants, while harvesting, go through a litany of hate against anyone who is not a peasant holding a sickle, a song of hate – but also of self-hate and hopelessness, because the peasant is chained to the social order of which his exploiters are part.[5] It is the voice of those of whom La Bruyère wrote in the France of Louis XIV:

Scattered across the countryside one may observe certain wild animals, male and female, dark, livid and burnt by the sun, attached to the earth which they dig and turn over with invincible stubbornness. However, they have something like an articulated voice and when they stand up they reveal a human face. Indeed, they are human beings ... Thanks to them the other human beings need not sow, labour and harvest in order to live. That is why they ought not to lack the bread which they have sown.[6]

Such explosions of hatred may be rare – though they are not surprising in nineteenth-century Sicily – but the underlying sense of separation and rancour of those who feed the others but are regarded by them as subhuman, is not unique. Countrymen, indeed, are often physically different from townsmen, even when there is no difference of race, colour, language or religion. Their behaviour, their costumes are different. In Sicily the 'caps' (the wearers of the old stocking cap or Phrygian bonnet of the French Revolution) are the class enemies of the 'hats'. In Bolivia, on the few occasions when the peasants asserted themselves collectively against the townsmen, as in the rising of 1899,[7] they attacked all those 'wearing trousers' and imposed the costume of the peasants (that is, Indian dress) on the townsmen.

The sense of a common separation from non-peasants may have produced a vague 'peasant consciousness' enabling even peasants from different regions, with different dialects, costumes and customs, to recognize each other as 'peasants' at least in personal relations. Just as among the 'labouring poor' in general a sense of 'they are poor bastards like us' or 'it's the poor who help the poor' is found, so among traditional peasants. The Communist Party guerrillas of Marquetalia (Colombia), a pure peasant movement, roving after their expulsion from their bases in 1964–5, enjoyed this sort of spontaneous recognition and support among other countrymen in a way in which student guerrilleros would not automatically do:

> Their leaders had great prestige among the peasants, even in Conservative areas ... The peasants believed that they had magic powers which made them invulnerable, but in no case did they seem to see them as a means of taking power, not even to occupy the land. They appeared rather as other poor peasants, persecuted unjustly by the powerful, by the urban interests, and to whom it was necessary to give the solidarity of the helpless.[8]

This vague consciousness of 'peasantness' as a special subvariety of subalternity, poverty, exploitation and oppression has no specific geographical limits, since it rests on the mutual recognition by peasants of the similarity of their relation to nature, to production and to non-peasants. Ideally humanity is the limit of this consciousness, and the political action which corresponds to it is the brief but vast millennial sweep or surge which, in theory at least, embraces the whole world. But such sweeps are necessarily as brief as they are ecumenical in scope, precisely because they are based on a recognition of similarity or identity, rather than on the firmer base of a concrete system of economic or social interrelations. The unit of such interrelations among traditional peasants is much smaller and more restricted – the 'community' or more generally the 'little world' within which transactions between people are systematic. Where millennial surges are genuinely spontaneous, they therefore spread characteristically by 'contagion' from one community to the next, and the curve of their spread is similar to that of epidemics.

The 'little world' may indeed vary considerably in size, population and complexity. The basic unit of traditional peasant life, the community, forms only one part of it. Within this area – large or small, more or less complex – people know of one another and the social division of labour, the system of exploitation and stratification, is visible. A full peasant 'class consciousness' is conceivable here, insofar as differentiation within the peasantry is secondary to the common characteristics of all peasants, and their common interests against other groups, and insofar as the distinction between them and other groups is sufficiently clear. And this may indeed happen: the solidarity of all peasants against third parties may outweigh the internal conflicts among them.[9] In the valleys of La Convención and Lares (Peru) during the early 1960s a unified peasant movement against the neo-feudal lords developed, though its participants included peasant groups which exploited one another.[10] On the other hand both the lateral divisions within such an area – for example, between peasant communities – and the personalization of social relations – for example, through clientelism and artificial kinship (*compadrazgo*) – inhibit a permanent class consciousness. The trader or labour recruiter is not merely a type but a person, kin or *compadre* of those with whom he deals, and whom he exploits. The community may be in dispute not only with the estate which has taken its common land, but with other communities over its boundaries, and it may at times be politically expedient to ally with the estate against its neighbours.

Nevertheless, whatever the size and complexity of the 'little world' it is always known not only to abut on or overlap with other analogous 'little worlds', but to form part of a much wider world. A crucial problem for the politics of traditional peasants is the relation between the microcosm and the macrocosm. By themselves they cannot solve this problem, since their unit of political action is either (in practice) the region or (conceptually) the human race: the parish pump or the universe. But in fact the area of major developments and decisions lies somewhere in between, and neither its boundaries nor its structures are determined by the economy or society of the peasant microcosm.

Nor, indeed, are they actually known except, as it were, by hearsay. This is obvious for the ecumene. Journalists who asked Peruvian peasants organized under Castroite slogans where Cuba was were told 'in another department of Peru'. A peasant recently arrived in Cuautla (Mexico) from a village in his native Oaxaca, who interrogated me about my country, found it impossible to situate 'Britain' in any geographical sense. It was in Europe – but what and where was Europe? It was across the ocean. But what was the ocean and what did the distance mean? He could only conceive of it as being 'near Russia' – a country of which he *had* heard. It is less evident, but equally true, that the peasant's knowledge of the nation or state under which he lives is likely to be almost as uncertain and patchy: a matter of personal enquiries and acquaintances. Knowledge of the country itself:

> Here on this course I've learned to talk to the fellows from the coast and those from the hills. Well, up to now those from the coast haven't told me anything. On the other hand those from Cañar have talked to me and told me what their problems are, and that's a comradely thing to do, and those from Chimborazo, they've also talked. But the fellows from the coast, they've told me nothing about their country ... You come out of the church in Quito, and those from the coast stick with each other, and so do those from Cañar with others from Cañar ... none of them said to me 'let's go somewhere together'. So I had to ask them to explain things to me. I asked a fellow from Cañar to tell me what was gong on in their country, and he did. But now the technicians have explained things, and I'm content, because that way I can follow what this course is about better.[11]

Knowledge of the country institutions:

> Me and another comrade, we decided to find out and went to the province of Chimborazo to ask the communities belonging to the Parish of San Juan, El Guabo and Chogol, because I believe they have problems also ... So then we went to Riobamba to the CEDOC and we told them what the people had told us in Guabo, and asked them whether they could deal with our problem. They said, well, they were also talking to Senator Chamara. They called him by telephone and the young lady secretary answered and said he wasn't there, he'd gone to Guayaquil. He'd be back very late tomorrow, maybe tomorrow he'd answer. So I stayed there in Riobamba in an inn...[12]

The above quotations come from a smallish country of perhaps 5 million inhabitants and from 1969. *A fortiori*, the element of sheer ignorance and helplessness of peasants outside the confines of their region is even more important to an understanding of their politics in earlier periods of history and larger states.

II

Bearing this in mind, let us consider whether there can be such a thing as a national peasant movement or a national peasant revolt or uprising. I very much doubt it. Local and regional action, which is the norm, turns into wider action only by external force – natural, economic, political or ideological – and only when a very large number of communities or villages are simultaneously moved in much the same direction. But even when such widespread general action occurs, it rarely coincides with the area of the state (as seen from above), even in quite small states, and it will be less a single general movement than a conglomerate of local and regional movements whose unity is momentary and fragile. The men from the coast and the men from the mountain may be too different from each other to meet more than briefly on the same ground.

The greatest peasant movements all appear to be regional, or coalitions of regional movements. Alternatively, if peasant movements develop all over a state's territory, unless sponsored or organized by the state authorities, they are unlikely to be simultaneous or to have the same political characteristics or demands. In the worst case this composition of large peasant movements from a mosaic of small ones may create merely a series of scattered enclaves which do not affect the rest of the country. Thus in Colombia quite powerful agrarian movements, mostly organized by the Communist Party, developed in the 1920s and 1930s in certain types of zones – in the coffee-growing tracts, in Indian areas, which had their specific problems, in frontier or new settlement areas among squatters and colonists, and so on. Even the national co-ordination of the Communist Party produced not a single peasant movement, but a scattering of 'red' peasant areas often far distant from each other; nor has a nationwide movement developed from these scattered areas, though some have proved capable of spreading their influence regionally. Of course national political or guerrilla cadres may emerge from these isolated and often enduring little nuclei, but that is another matter.

In the best case, such peasant movements may occur in one or two strategically placed regions where their effect on national politics is crucial, or in areas capable of producing powerful mobile military forces. This was very much the case in the Mexican Revolution. The bulk of the peasantry in that country was not much involved in the Revolution of 1910–20, though as a result of the Revolution's victory

153

several areas became organized. Still, the largest mobilization of the Mexican peasantry connected with the Revolution was almost certainly, as it were, the wrong way round – the movement of the Cristeros in the 1920s which rose for Christ the King *against* the secular Agraristas. Subjectively, theirs was undoubtedly a peasant revolution, though both its timing and its ideology made it objectively counter-revolutionary.[13] Nevertheless between 1910 and 1920 two regions happened to exercise enormous political effect. One was the frontier region of the north, with its footloose armed men – cowboys, prospectors, bandits and so on – which produced Pancho Villa's army with its mobility and capacity to range widely: a Mexican equivalent to the Cossacks. The other was the much more solidly based communal revolution of Emiliano Zapata in Morelos, which had purely local horizons but the enormous advantage of being situated next door to the capital city of Mexico. The political influence of Zapata's agrarian programme derives from the fact that his peasant levies were close enough to occupy the capital. Governments in large and loosely administered states such as early-twentieth-century Latin American republics are resigned to losing control of outlying provinces from time to time to local dissidents or insurrectionaries. What really worries them is insurrection in or in the backyard of the capital.

Where peasant revolutions do not have this advantage, their limitations are much more obvious. The great peasant movement in Peru in the early 1960s is a good example, being probably the biggest spontaneous mobilization of this kind in Latin America during that decade. There was at this period nationwide unrest, including unrest among the workers and the students. The agrarian movement was active both in the coastal plantations – which cannot be classified as belonging to the peasant economy but are better called by the local name of 'agro-industrial complexes' – and in the peasant highlands. Within the highlands, again, there were very extensive movements in both the southern and the central highlands and patchier outbreaks of land occupation, strikes, the organization of peasant unions and so on elsewhere. No adequate account of this movement has yet been written. However, two characteristics may be noted. First, though more or less simultaneous – the movement was at its height in 1962–4 and reached its peak in late 1963 in the centre and a little later in the south – the regional movements were not really linked with each other, or effectively with the non-peasant movements. Second, there were curious gaps. Thus the traditional area of 'native risings' in the south, the Department of Puno, was notably inactive. The traditional type of movement was no longer central or relevant, though as recently as 1910–21 it had been very active indeed. In Puno the peasant movement took the form of the establishment of a political machine by local kulaks and traders, which soon after showed remarkable political strength.[14] Meanwhile, immediately to the north, in the Department of Cuzco the direct action of peasants organizing unions and occupying the land, inspired by the success of the frontier peasantry in La Convención, was proceeding on a massive scale, though the men of La Convención themselves, having already achieved their main objectives, were militant chiefly in defence of their conquests. The widespread Peruvian peasant movement in 1962–4 produced unrest rather than revolution.

I am therefore inclined to think that the idea of a *general* peasant movement, unless inspired from outside or, even better, from above, is quite unrealistic.[15] It is a myth, both revolutionary and counter-revolutionary. For conservatives also have this myth, as witness the fear of a new 'Pugachevshchina' – a general peasant insurrection on the model of the Pugachev rising of the 1770s – which played so large a part in the thinking of governments and reactionaries in Russia before the emancipation of the serfs. Perhaps there was more basis for such fears in Russia, for certainly in 1905–7 the Russian peasant movement was extremely widespread, affecting between 80 and 100 per cent of all districts in six Russian regions. Even so the inter-regional variations were substantial in the remaining six regions (omitting the Baltic provinces and Transcaucasia); disturbances ranged between 38 per cent (Urals) and 74 per cent (Lithuania).[16] Incidentally, the original Pugachev movement itself was regionally based rather than national, its power consisting more in the potential threat to Moscow than in its geographical extent.

This is not to underestimate the strength of such conglomerate movements. If unified by some outside force – a national crisis and breakdown, a sympathetic reformist or revolutionary government, or a single nationally structured and effective party or organization, they may make the difference between success and failure for major revolutions. Even by themselves they may make an agrarian system or the structure of rule in the countryside unviable, as the 'Great Fear' of 1789 did in France[17] and the Peruvian wave of land-occupations did in 1962–4. There is good evidence that some time between June 1963 and February or March 1964 the bulk of the estate owners and lords in the central and southern highlands decided to cut their losses, faced with a general peasant mobilization, and began to liquidate their assets and think in terms of compensation for expropriation under some sort of agrarian reform. This did not make agrarian reform automatic. It took another five years and a military coup to impose it; but it merely buried the corpse of a highland landlord economy which had already been effectively killed by the peasant movement.

The potential power of a traditional peasantry is enormous, but its actual power and influence are much more limited. The first major reason for this is its constant, and in general quite realistic, sense of its weakness and inferiority. The inferiority is social and cultural, for instance as illiterates against the 'educated': hence the importance to peasant movements of locally resident and friendly intellectuals, especially the most formidable of village intellectuals, the primary schoolteacher. Their weakness is based not only on social inferiority, on the lack of effective armed force, but on the nature of the peasant economy. For instance, peasant agitations must stop for the harvest. However militant peasants are, the cycle of their labours shackles them to their fate. It is worth speculating about the role of the potato-economy of Ireland – a crop which requires little regular labour – in making possible the notorious frequency of 'agrarian outrage' in that country of the nineteenth century. But, at bottom, peasants are and feel themselves to be subaltern. With rare exceptions they envisage an adjustment in the social pyramid not its destruction, though its destruction is easy to conceive. Anarchism, that is, the dismantling of the superstructure of rule and exploitation, leaves the traditional village as a viable economy and society. But the times when this utopia can be conceived, let alone realized, are few.

In practice, of course, it may not make a great deal of difference whether the peasants are fighting for an entirely different and new society or for adjustment of the old, which normally means either the defence of the traditional society against some threat or the restoration of the old ways which, if sufficiently far in the past, may merely amount to a traditionalist formulation of revolutionary aspirations. Revolutions may be made *de facto* by peasants who do not deny the legitimacy of the existing power structure, law, the state and even the landlords. We have examples of peasantries which appear to deny totally the legitimacy of landlord property, in Tsarist Russia for example, though hardly ever the legitimacy of the supreme ruler's rights over all property. We do not, of course, know what precisely this denial implies in theory or meant in practice. What difference is there between the Russian serfs who held that they belonged to the lords but that the land was theirs and not the gentry's, and the Andean Indians who believed labour service to Inca rulers and Spaniards to be legitimate but resented payment of rent in money or kind[18] and whose descendants appear not to have challenged the existence of large landed estates as such? We can only speculate. A movement which only claims to 'recuperate' communal lands illegally alienated may be as revolutionary in practice as it may be legalist in theory. Nor is the line between legalist and revolutionary an easy one to draw. The Zapatista movement in Morelos began by opposing not *all* haciendas, but merely the new ones which had been introduced in Porfirio Diaz' time, since the benchmark years used to define the good and legitimate old days, which included the fact that gentry were superior to peasants. It did not remain within these limits.

The major difference lies not in the theoretical aspirations of the peasantry, but in the practical political conjuncture in which they operate. It is the difference between suspicion and hope. For the normal strategy of the traditional peasantry is passivity. It is not an ineffective strategy, for it exploits the major assets of the peasantry, its numbers and the impossibility of making it do some things by force for any length of time, and it also utilizes a favourable tactical situation, which rests on the fact that no change is what suits a traditional peasantry best. A communally organized traditional peasantry, reinforced by a functionally useful slowness, imperviousness and stupidity – apparent or real – is a formidable force. The refusal to understand is a form of class struggle, and both nineteenth-century Russian and twentieth-century Peruvian observers have described it in similar ways.[19] To be subaltern is not to be powerless. The most submissive peasantry is capable not only of 'working the system' to its advantage – or rather to its minimum disadvantage – but also of resisting and, where appropriate, of counterattack. The stereotype of the Russian *mujik* in the minds of educated Russians, which is very similar to the stereotype of 'the Indian' in the minds of Andean whites, is largely a reformulation of something which the upper classes cannot understand because they cannot control it: 'credulous, devoted to the tsar and prone (though naturally submissive) to unreasoning violence'.[20] In fact there is a system in such behaviour.

Passivity is not, of course, universal. In areas where there are no lords or laws, or in frontier zones where all men go armed, the attitude of the peasantry may well be very different. So indeed it may be on the fringe of the unsubmissive. However, for most of the soil-bound peasants the problem is not whether to be normally passive or active, but when to pass from one state to the other. This depends on an assessment of the political situation. Broadly speaking, passivity is advisable when the structure of power – local or national – is firm, stable and 'closed', activity when it appears to be in some sense changing, shifting or 'open'.

Peasants are perfectly well able to judge the local political situation, but their real difficulty lies in discerning the wider movements of politics which may determine it. What do they know of these? They are normally aware of belonging to some wider polity – a kingdom, an empire, a republic. Indeed the familiar peasant myth of the remote king or emperor who, if only he knew, would put matters right and establish or re-establish justice both reflects and to some extent creates a wider framework of political action. At the same time it reflects the normal remoteness of the national government from the local political structure which, whatever it may be in theory, in practice consists of state power and law exercised by and identified with the local men of power, their kin, clients or those whom they can bribe and overawe. What else they may know varies widely with the actual political system. Thus if national courts exist, which is by no means always the case, litigation may well bring even remote communities into some relation to the national centre, doubtless via a chain of intermediary urban lawyers. The Peruvian community of Hua-sicancha, some 4,000 metres up in the mountains, could hardly be physically more remote – but, since it obtained its first judgment in the viceregal court at Lima against a usurping Spaniard in 1607, it has never ceased to be aware of at least some dimensions of the wider polity of which it is a distant part.

As we approach the present, the details of national politics become increasingly important and known – for instance, when elections and parties enter the scene, or when the direct intervention of the state in the affairs of localities and individuals requires some knowledge of its institutions and their operation. Moreover, with mass emigration the village is likely to possess direct links with the centre in the form of colonies of its own people settled in the capital or elsewhere, who know city ways. But long before this happens peasants are aware of changes within the system, even if unable to describe or understand them precisely. War, civil war, defeat and conquest may involve the peasants directly and open new possibilities when they put the national rulers at risk and change the local ones. Even lesser events in the politics of the ruling class such as elections and *coups d'état*, which hardly affect them directly, may be rightly read as encouraging or discouraging. They may not know exactly what is happening in the capital, but if family A ceases to provide the local senator while its rival family B appears to be riding high, there will be considerable local reappraisals, doubtless first among the townsmen, but also eventually in the villages. The Mexican Revolution – even in Zapata's

Morelos – began not so much as a revolution but as a breakdown of the long-established local political balance which in turn depended on the smooth operation and permanence of Don Porfirio's system of national government.

If any major national change may open new local possibilities or close old ones, then *a fortiori* news of reform or otherwise favourable change mobilizes peasants. Thus when a reformist government supported by the APRA (Alianza Popular Revolocionaria Americana) party came into office in Lima in 1945, communities which had operated on the assumption of stability promptly changed their tactics. Santa Rosa, which had been negotiating boundary treaties with the neighbouring estates, announced that 'now with the new government we can do what we want and we denounce the existing treaties with Ganadera' (Sociedad Ganadera del Centro).[21] Marc Ferro points out that the resolutions sent by the peasantry immediately after the February Revolution in Russia, doubtless drafted by the village intelligentsia, unlike those of the workers, 'demand' very much more frequently than they 'complain' or 'petition', and also that they 'express more frequently than the workers the desire to punish the masters of the old regime'.[22] It is as though the villages, always conscious of potential strength even within their subalternity, required only the assurance of goodwill or even mere toleration from the highest authorities to straighten their backs. Conversely, of course, any hint that power will once again stamp on them encourages them to retreat into their shells. As the 1945 reformist government led to a wave of agrarian unrest and organization, so the imposition of the military government in 1948 brought land invasions and peasant unions to a brusque stop – until under a new government after 1956 the peasants gradually become aware that the situation is once again rather more open.

This sense of constant potential or actual confrontation of force may perhaps derive from the very exclusion of the traditional peasantry from the official mechanism of politics or even law. Relations of force – either real trials of strength or ritualized ones – replace institutionalized relations. Señor Fernandini's reluctance to expel an encroaching Indian community adjoining his hacienda is interpreted by the peasants as fear: 'There is no Indian around this region who does not say that they can take any advantage they wish from *taita* Eulogio, because *taita* Eulogio is afraid of them.'[23] On the other hand, as Daniel Field rightly recognizes,[24] if the peasants wanted to attract the notice of the authorities they had no effective way of doing so except by challenging authority through direct action, since there was no political machinery for making themselves heard. This was risky, since punishment was normally sure – but certainly peasants, and probably even lords and government, would calculate the dose of violence offered. In the invasions of 1947 it was the inexperienced communities who stayed and were massacred when the soldiers came. Huasicancha, with centuries of experience of alternating litigation and direct action, evacuated the occupied ground quietly when the troops came, and temporarily made the best of what law could achieve.

Confrontation could thus be quite non-revolutionary: it is an error to think of every incident of peasant challenge by force as a 'rising' or an 'insurrection'. But it could also, because of the very nakedness of the typical relation of force which it implied, lend itself to revolution. For what if it looked as though the definitive end of the rule of the gentry was at hand? At this point we are on the border between the territories of hard political assessment and apocalyptic hope. Few peasants would hope that their own region or village alone could achieve permanent liberation. They knew too much about it. But if the entire kingdom, indeed the entire world, was changing? The vast movement of the *trienio bolchevista* in Spain (1918–20) was due to the double impact of the news of the successive collapse of empires – the Russian, followed by the central European ones – and of an actual *peasant* revolution. 'But how', asked Diaz del Moral, 'can you possibly believe that you will triumph? What about the Spanish government and army?' and was answered: 'But, señorito, when Germany has collapsed, what can the bourgeois hope for from this Spanish government, which is not worth much anyway?'[25] And yet the further the centres of decision were from the known and understood local power structure, the hazier the line between actual judgment, hope and myth (in both the colloquial and the Sorelian sense). The signs by means of which men foretold the coming of the millennium were, in one sense, empirical – like those by which they foretold the weather; but in another they were expressions of their feeling. Who could tell whether there was really 'a new law' or a rider carrying the Tsar's manifesto in letters of gold giving the land to the tillers, or whether there simply ought to be?

One might push hypothesis a stage further and suppose that, conversely, the disappointment of hope within a concretely assessable situation would be less lasting than that of global or apocalyptic hopes. When the troops came and expelled the community from the lands it occupied, it would not be demoralized, but wait for the next suitable moment for action. But when the expected revolution failed, it would take much more to restore the peasants' morale. Thus Malefakis[26] has suggested that part of the tragedy of the second Spanish Republic of 1931–9 lies in the fact that the grassroots peasant movement did not become aware that a new era of possibilities was opening until 1933 – by which time the best moments for pushing the republican government into agrarian reform had been missed. After the failure of the *trienio bolchevista* it took more than the fall of a king to revive their confidence.

IV

We have so far considered the wider political structure simply as something which affects peasant action favourably or unfavourably. And yet, especially during the transition to modern politics, the peasants' own effects upon it must also be briefly observed. In pre-eighteenth-century Europe – perhaps in most of the world – they are normally negligible, except at periods of general revolution, when they may become decisive, either for the triumph of revolution or for its defeat. Peasants appear to belong in economic or social history, but rarely in political history, since rulers rarely have to bother for more than a moment about what happens in the villages. China may be the great exception, for in the traditional politics of that country peasant risings play an accepted and expected part in the end of one dynasty and the substitution of another. But in the transition to modern politics in Europe the countryside becomes significant, if only because of the frequency of revolutions or revolutionary threats, and with the development of systems of mass politics, electoral or other-wise, their attitude forms parts of the permanent calculations of politicians.

The traditional peasants are integrated into the prevailing political system by means of three major ideological devices: the 'king', the 'church' (or other religious structures) and what must, with hesitation and consciousness of the danger of anachronism, be called 'proto-nationalism'. All three are politically ambiguous. The 'king' is both the keystone of the stable social structure which rests on the backs of a loyal and uncomplaining peasantry and the remote fount of justice who may be called upon against the real rulers, the gentry. The 'church' has a similar duality, though perhaps a more sharply distinct one: in Christian regions the bishop may belong to 'them', but the saints always to 'us'. Proto-nationalism, often indistinct from religion (as may still be verified in the Irish national movement, where Catholicism is at least as crucial a criterion of nationality as ethnicity), is less regularly identified with political integration, but where it coincides with king or church or both, the combination is powerful, as Napoleon discovered in both Russia and Spain. On the other hand, where it does not, it rarely has political implications on

161

a national scale, at least in Europe before the nineteenth century.

During the transition to modern European politics initially (with the partial exception of proto-nationalism) this ideology mobilizes the peasantry on the political right, or fails to mobilize them on the political left, even when their aspirations are by our standards revolutionary. Modern politics (for example, liberalism) belonged to the cities and the rich, and were either irrelevant or hostile to the peasants, and the defence of the old ways against the new implied the sort of revolutionary traditionalism which the Bourbons utilized to good effect in southern Italy, though not in Sicily where they themselves were 'foreigners'. The interesting question is: when, how and under what circumstances do peasant movements come under the leadership of the left or, more generally, come to be expressed in a new political language? Thus it is evident that in the 1870s the Russian peasants, to the grief of the Narodniks, were still quite inaccessible both to them as non-peasants and to their idiom, but by the early twentieth century they were far more receptive to new ideas and methods. Economic changes, urbanization, migration and so on are obviously very largely responsible for such changes. As a 1908 survey in Russian put it:

> The 'ferment' or 'brain' in the movement ... were the peasants on side-earnings in the factories, in the mines and in the towns. As more developed persons they naturally became the leaders of the movement; in some cases they brought into the countryside – along with the newspapers – news about the agrarian and the workers' movement in other places and unconsciously propagandized the idea of the agrarian movement.[27]

Still, we evidently have examples of traditional peasants who accepted the leadership of the political left (in Sicily and southern Italy of Garibaldi, for instance) long before industrialization and urbanization had seriously affected them. About this question we remain very much in the dark, and further research is needed. It must not, of course, be confused with the ready appeal which heterodoxy, including that of secular political revolutionaries, may have from an early stage to discontented minority groups, such as the Albanian settlers in southern Italy or the tribals in modern India.

One thing may however be suggested. Contrary to what might be supposed, straightforward modern nationalist agitation is likely to capture the peasants rather later than social agitation, unless in the form of simple xenophobia which may be just as easily turned against outgroups belonging to the same 'nation'. Thus the men of Tipperary in the first part of the nineteenth century exercised their notorious 'agrarian terrorism' not only against the Protestant English land-owners, but against the Connaughtmen and Kerrymen who competed with them for land and work. And the clearest example of a popularly based national movement in the nineteenth century, the Irish Fenians, did not acquire a really solid peasant base, overcoming the powerful hostility of the Church, until the agrarian depression and the Land League had given them a social as well as a national programme.

This paper has overwhelmingly dealt with the politics of traditional peasants in traditional or transitional situations. It may be concluded with three brief propositions about peasants in modern political situations. I omit the role of peasants in socialist countries, for in these (with the possible exception of China) peasants once again become a recessive and relatively passive force, though the effectiveness of their refusal to do certain things demonstrates that modern states and economies may be, if anything, more sensitive to the traditional kind of feet-dragging in which peasants are so experienced.

The first proposition is that at some point of economic differentiation 'the peasantry' as a political concept disappears, because conflicts within the rural sector now outweigh what all peasants have in common against outsiders. This development has sometimes been hoped for by revolutionaries (for example, the Russian bolsheviks), but when it happens, at least before revolutions, is normally to their disadvantage. The difficulty encountered by Indian communists in their peasant work today is that they can effectively appeal to some but not all rural strata, and in appealing to one group automatically tend to antagonize others. However, the political disintegration of the peasantry is postponed or concealed by the persistence of the traditional differences between town and countryside, of specific political interests which a very large range of people occupied in agriculture may have in common, for instance a state policy of high and guaranteed prices for farm products, and of traditional institutions and practices. Thus the 'peasant community' of the 1970s may in fact represent the interests of a group of kulaks or rural middle class within it rather than those of all its members, who in turn may now form only a small percentage of the local inhabitants. But it will nevertheless function as a community and be to some extent represented by its members as such. The village poor or the landless may continue to defer to their richer brethren, though modern politics and organization may make them more effective as a group than they once were. Insofar as this is true, it suggests that 'peasant' politics is more likely than not rich farmers' politics.

The second proposition is that democratic electoral politics do not work for peasants as a class. Unlike the 'working-class party', the 'peasant party' is not the regular projection of class consciousness into politics, but a historical freak phenomenon, for practical purposes confined to parts of eastern, south-eastern and central Europe between the world wars. And even these 'peasant parties' were not necessarily very different from other parties with a largely peasant clientele, but which did not base their appeal officially on class. Of the 2,836 Radical rural mayors in France no fewer than 2,600 were peasant cultivators in the early 1950s.[28] There are countries which never developed specific peasant parties, and indeed countries in which there is 'no global correlation between the percentage of the active population engaged in agriculture and the political behaviour of the area'.[29] Thus the five most rural departments of France in 1951 gave their largest blocks of votes respectively to the communists, to an alliance of Christian Democrats and Radicals, to an alliance of Socialists and Radicals, to the Gaullists and to the Christian Democrats. Moreover, even when particular parties gain majority support among peasants, their cadres are hardly of peasant origin. The Italian Demochristian legislators of 1963, though elected by 44 per cent of the peasantry, were overwhelmingly non-peasant in origin. Only 4.5 per cent of their fathers had been peasant proprietors – curiously enough almost twice this percentage had been workers.[30] (For comparison, almost one-third of Italian communist deputies had working-class parents in 1963, whereas 40 per cent of the French communist deputies in the early 1950s had actually begun life as manual workers themselves.) In terms of the national politics of bourgeois–democratic states, peasants tend to be election fodder, except when they demand or inhibit certain specialized political measures. In terms of local politics they are, of course, much more significant. However, the sheer numbers of peasant electors, or the persistent over-representation of the rural electorate, are not to be neglected.

The third proposition is the one that Marx put forward in the *Eighteenth Brumaire*.[31] He argues that because of their peculiarities as a class peasants are:

> incapable of enforcing their class interest in their own name ... They cannot represent themselves; they must be represented. The representative must at the same time appear as their master, or as an authority over them, as an unlimited governmental power that protects them against other classes and sends them rain and sunshine from above. The political influence of the smallholding peasant, therefore, finds its final expression in the executive powers subordinating society to itself.

Whether this argument applies only to peasants or also to other

164

classes and strata incapable of organizing themselves as a class (for example, the lower-middle classes in the European sense of the word) need not be discussed here. It may also be argued that in many cases the apparently passive attitude of peasants to the central government conceals complex hierarchies of clientelist relationships, based on tacit or overt bargaining, which stretch from the localities to the apex of state power.[32] It may also be held that the enormous *de facto* 'veto power' of peasant refusal to act makes this relationship less passive than it seems at first sight. Nevertheless, Marx's argument probably explains more than the nature of mid-nineteenth-century Bonapartism. It need not lead to a right-wing dictatorship, though in a sense the rise of the Nazi Party in Germany between 1928 and 1933 was the last genuine mass movement of peasants at least in the Protestant parts of Germany. Nevertheless, the importance of the political father- or mother-figure, or the patron-state in the politics of peasant countries today, is worth investigating with Marx's observation in mind.

However, the fundamental fact of peasant politics today is the decline of the traditional peasantry, and indeed increasingly the relative numerical decline of any kind of peasantry. Much of what has been discussed in this paper is already of historical rather than current interest. Nevertheless, since the mass of migrants into the cities in many parts of the world consists of men and women from traditional peasant backgrounds, who bring into their new world the modes of action and thought of their old world, history remains a current political force. It would be unwise to neglect it.

CHAPTER 12

Peasant Land Occupations

*Like the stories told about bandits, the procedures of peasant land occupations –
the most fundamental form of collective, but not necessarily revolutionary,
action in traditional peasantries – are remarkably uniform across a wide
range of cultures. This chapter is an attempt to analyse them, more
particularly in one region – the Peruvian Andes – and at a historic moment
of peasant mobilization, when it is possible to discover what they wanted to,
could, and failed to, achieve. The paper was originally published in* Past &
Present, *62, 1974.*

Whoever studies peasant movements is familiar with the phenomenon
of the mass invasion or occupation of land. The present paper attempts
to analyse this form of collective peasant militancy, mainly in the
light of evidence from Peru, though also with some references to
other countries.[1] Its object, however, is not to study a specifically
Peruvian phenomenon but to penetrate behind the actions of peasants
to the social and political assumptions and the strategic thinking
which underlie them. The purpose of this paper is to throw light on
the question of peasant revolutionary activity. The extent to which
the specific historic situation of Peru and of comparable countries
determines the nature and shape of its land invasions will be considered incidentally.

I

There are three possible types of land occupation in Peru, as elsewhere,
depending on the legal situation of the land to be occupied, both in
terms of the prevailing official legal system and the legal norms
actually accepted by the peasantry. The two do not necessarily
coincide. The land to be occupied may belong to the peasants, but
have been alienated, legally or otherwise, in a manner which they

166

do not recognize as valid. Land invasion therefore equals the recuperation of their own land. Thus the peasants of Oyon (in the Andes, north-east of Lima) denied that they had invaded the lands of the Sociedad Agricola y Ganadera Algolan in August 1963, since the land in dispute – some pastures at about 5,000 metres altitude – was and had always been theirs.[2] Second, the land occupied may belong to nobody, or in legal terms to the government as public land. In this case the process of peasant colonization or squatting turns into an 'invasion' only when there is some dispute about legal title. The most usual case is one in which such land is simultaneously claimed by peasants and landlords, neither of whom may, or indeed in most cases will, have a valid property right under official law. This situation is common in the unsettled frontier regions of several South American states, though not particularly so in Peru, except on the subtropical Amazonian slopes of the Andes and sometimes in odd corners of the vast uncultivated stretches of land belonging to some large hacienda which tend to be regarded, understandably, as no-man's land by the peasants.

The legal argument here is different, since there can be no appeal to title, or even custom and prescription. It is rather that the land belongs to him who cultivates it by means of his labour. This argument was accepted in Spanish colonial law, which adjudicated empty lands (*tierras baldías*) to those who cleared, sowed or otherwise cultivated them within a given time-limit, fixing the size of the holding according to the ability of the holder to cultivate it.[3] The Civil Code of, for example, Colombia recognized this mode of possession among others, and Law 200 of 1936, passed in consequence of large-scale agrarian agitation, made this the primary criterion of the ownership of empty lands. The appeal here is not to a legal title or its equivalent (for example prescriptive right), but to a general principle. Thus in 1963, 350 squatters organized in an Asociación de Nuevos Colonos occupied two estates in the subtropical zone of Tingo María on the ground that 'they are unproductive, so we have a right to them'.[4]

Thirdly, the land may unquestionably belong to someone other than the invaders, even by the legal doctrines and documents which they themselves accept, as when peasants expropriate landlords from their demesne holdings. This situation must be sharply distinguished from that in which peasant tenants, paying rent either in labour, money or kind, assert property rights as freeholders in the land they actually occupy and cultivate, for this does not in itself challenge the right of the landlord to the land he cultivates directly or with hired labour. Nor does it constitute an 'invasion', since the peasants are already on the holdings whose legal title they wish to change. Clearly expropriation is the most consciously revolutionary form of land occupation. In Peru, and more generally in Latin America, it is also the rarest (except, of course, in the historically common form of the expropriation of the weak by the strong). To be precise, it seems to occur rarely if at all among peasant movements which are not directly influenced by modern political ideologies.

The present paper will deal primarily with land invasions of the first type, which form the overwhelming bulk of recorded invasions in twentieth-century Peru.[5] The characteristic movement of this sort is the recuperation of lost common lands by peasant communities. The basis of such claims, so far as we can follow the reasoning of peasant jurisprudence, is threefold, though we cannot tell (except in the case of no-man's land) whether two of the three elements in the claim to possession are essential, and what importance each has in the minds of the claimants. As Dr Saturnino Paredes put it, arguing against some deviationist members of the small (Maoist) Peruvian Communist Party of which he was then general secretary:

> In Peru the fact is that the peasantry living in communities ... is convinced that the lands now in possession of the latifundists belong to the peasants, because they have worked them, and because they hold title to them in some cases and because of the right of immemorial possession in others.[6]

The right by labour is clearly implicit in all the other claims to possession, though (except in the case of newly settled land) it is not distinct from the right by immemorial possession, since this merely means that uncounted generations of peasants have tilled a particular piece of land or grazed their animals on it. Hence perhaps the fact that I have not come across any land invasion justified purely by the slogan 'the land to the tiller' except where modern political ideologies enter into the affair. This does not mean that it is insignificant. In the Cilento (southern Italy) before the 1848 Revolution 'every Christmas the peasants went onto the lands to which they laid claim in order to carry out agricultural labours, thus seeking to maintain the ideal principle of possession of their rights'.[7] During the 1848 Revolution, in the same region, 800 peasants, having torn down the walls and fences on usurped former common lands, marched out again the next day 'most of them provided with spades, picks and sticks, only five or six being armed, demonstrating to the cry of "Long Live the King and the Constitution! We want to dig. We are dying of hunger. We want to get back our ancient lost rights".' In the Calabrian Sila 400 men with drum and national flag, partly armed, were seen digging, and, when asked why, some of them replied: 'They intended to acquire their ancient rights, that is by preparing their common lands for the fallow and paying one *tomolo* local measure for each *tomolata* of land.'[8] In Pozoblanco and neighbouring townships in Andalusia in 1873 the peasants demanded the return and division of some common lands on the ground that those who laboured had more rights to them than those who paid men a miserable wage with ill-gotten money.[9] The importance of the 'labour principle' in Russian peasant theory is well known. In short, for peasants, possession without labour is unthinkable, since what land they have must be used.

But if immemorial possession is title enough, such possession validated by actual documents is even better. Given the nature of the Spanish colonial system, there are plenty of Indian communities with such documents, and these are typically adduced to legitimize land invasions. Thus the Comunidad of Tusi cited titles going back to 1716, these being 'expedited in Rome and Egypt' according to its spokesman;[10] the invaders of five estates in the department of Huancavelica claimed by titles of the same date; the community of Huaylacucho (Huancavelica) exhibited titles going back to 1746; and so on.[11] The young sectarians of the Maoist Communist Party regarded this as a petty-bourgeois aberration, arguing that the only thing to do with land titles of the feudal or bourgeois period, whoever they favoured, was to burn them; but, as Dr Paredes pointed out justifiably, and speaking from ample experience: 'All this reveals that the opportunist left liquidators have no experience of the peasant movement and have never had anything to do with any [peasant] community.'[12] The entrenched legalism of peasant land invasions is a fact which both the student and the agitator neglect at their peril. To possess *papelitos* ('little pieces of paper') is very important for a Latin American peasant community. Whether real or forged they are cherished, preserved, hidden from possible robbers, because to lose them would in some way affect their rights, though one can hardly say that it would weaken their sense that they exist. John Womack has given a moving account of the preservation of the land titles of Anenecuilco, the *pueblo* of the great Emiliano Zapata, from the days of his fathers to the present.[13] There are even, I am told, cases of Bolivian villages which, having been given land by the agrarian reform, went to the former owner asking for a document of transfer to make it all legal. As we shall see, this legalism does not prevent such peasants from making revolutions. For one thing, they are inclined to reject as morally invalid and 'unnatural' laws, however constitutionally correct, which take away common lands.

At this point the peculiarities of the Latin American situation must be mentioned, since they turn legalism in the strictest sense into a potent, if also limited, social force among the peasantry. The Spanish conquest guaranteed legal recognition and communal lands to the Indian communities, under the control of the royal bureaucracy, while simultaneously attempting strict control of the conquistador settlers, though with little success. The hacienda, the large estate whose owners became the *de facto* holders of power, therefore developed side by side with the peasant communities, its territorial expansion legally limited by the rights both of the crown and of the Indians – legal limits which were not entirely abolished, though for practical purposes made inoperative, in the period of independence. Consequently their expansion took place largely by naked appropriation, especially in the late nineteenth and twentieth centuries, when large tracts of land formerly without much economic value became both potentially profitable and accessible to markets. The typical large hacienda of Latin America is therefore based not on legal ownership (by virtue of a 'new law' as against an 'old law'), but simply on the fact that the power of the large landowner was greater than that of the state, where the two did not actually coincide in his person. An old lawyer and ex-politician in the Peruvian central highlands has gone so far as to argue that land reform had been unnecessary, since all that was required to secure an effective redistribution of the land was to ask landowners – *any* landowner – to show title to their estates, and return the land held without good title to the peasants from whom it had originally been taken.[14] One need not take forensic flights too seriously, but this one rests on a good basis of fact.

Thus in Colombia, following an agrarian agitation, the titles of three latifundia belonging to J. Otero Torres and covering something like 300,000 hectares were officially investigated. The original title to the property in 1823 referred to 426 hectares.[15] In the Peruvian central highlands, the Hacienda Tucle in 1887 held title to some 12,000 hectares, though even this was not undisputed. By 1915 it had somehow acquired 103,000 hectares.[16] How? Some examples may illustrate the shamelessness of the procedure. In 1870 the state auctioned off waste lands in the pampa of Chimbote (Peru), some of which belonged to a community. On these lands the Hacienda Tambo Real was established 'which has not ceased for a single day to expand at the expense of communal land'.[17] In 1926 the Hacienda Tucle acquired the estate of Rio de la Virgen (claimed in its entirety by a neighbouring community) from the Church, the parish of Huancayo claiming possession from time immemorial. Unfortunately, the Church admitted, in the course of time immemorial all actual titles had been lost. Nor had it surveyed the area it was selling and so did not know how large it actually was or what its boundaries were.[18] Since the owners who thus acquired stolen property did so in proper legal form, they expected, and normally got, the protection of the courts; and if they had no title at all, their ability to overawe the Indians and their political influence over local judges and policemen was normally quite sufficient to fend off challenges.

This is, of course, to oversimplify a complex situation. Haciendas might have legal titles to enormous territories, but actually use only a small part of them, leaving the rest to nobody or to the *de facto* occupation of the peasantry, which would naturally assume that actually working the land gave it right of possession or property, at any rate better right than the inactive landlords. Communities might strengthen their moral claim to the land by forging or extending ancient titles. Moreover, as we shall see, rival legal claims to land opposed not only peasants to haciendas but also communities to other communities, especially when – as happened in the course of time – groups of peasants left the original settlement to establish themselves elsewhere in communal territory (normally, in Peru, by moving into another ecological niche higher or lower on the Andean slopes which stretch from the tundra at the top to the subtropics and. tropics at the bottom). They would then attempt to form separate communities carving out their own communal lands, whose boundaries were in dispute with the mother-settlement.

Nevertheless, Latin America in general and the areas of solid Indian settlement in particular provide an unusually large number of peasant communities with legal documents of communal ownership of land alienated by naked or barely disguised robbery. To this extent the problem of legitimizing peasant rights is unusually simple in theory. On the other hand, very frequently the demand for land, however objectively revolutionary, requires no ideological challenge to existing legality.

II

Let us now turn to some actual invasions of land. A land invasion is normally a rather standardized affair, decided and carried out by the entire community as a collective entity. This means that it is normally discussed in advance. Thus in the Cuzco region most such invasions 'are announced beforehand', often in detail. Before the invasions 'the peasants held meetings addressed in Quechua'.[19] The intention to invade is therefore normally known to the landlords and the authorities, who are in a position to take countermeasures, if police, troops or their own armed men can be got to the disputed frontier, which may of course be rather remote and inaccessible.[20] The politically sophisticated organizers of Cuzco in 1960–4 used this to play a cat-and-mouse game with the authorities, whose limited forces were made to dash from one threatened hacienda to another in the generally disaffected zone of the Pampa de Anta; but this is not characteristic of the traditional grassroots invasions, whose strategic and tactical thinking is less complex.

The invasion itself is a major ceremonial occasion. Such events 'take place amid great clamour. The leaders appear on horseback blowing horns' (Cuzco, 1964), 'to the sounds of horns and drums' (Cuzco), 'to the accompaniment of huzzas and horns' (Anta, Cuzco), 'singing and dancing to the tunes of regional music' (Paruro, Cuzco), 'sounding horns and firing off rockets' (Potaca, Junin).[21] In recent years they seem to have been accompanied by large numbers of flags. Indeed, the absence of flags normally indicates that the invasion is not in full swing: 'A significant detail: in an invasion there are many banners, but this crowd [a reconnaissance?] had only one'.[22] Peruvian flags were universal in the 1960s, but in the politically radicalized Cuzco department they were accompanied by Castroite slogans – 'Tierra o Muerte', 'Venceremos' and so on. Red flags are hardly mentioned during this period, though an invasion with red flags is recorded during the first phase of politically conscious agrarian agitation in 1930–2.[23] The national flag undoubtedly became a symbol of agrarian ambitions: in the northern department of Piura 'many peasants in the region are making Peruvian flags for the purpose of invasions'. In Junin (Yantac, Q'ero, San Pedro de Cajas), Mocquegua (Mauca Llacta), Cuzco (Chumbivilcas), Ancash (Recuay) and elsewhere, the carrying of the red-and-white colours is specifically reported.[24] There is no evidence of this practice for the invasions of the 1946–8 period or earlier, at least in the central highlands. As in all great collective ceremonials it is also far from unlikely that the participants are often rather drunk, though the evidence – which comes overwhelmingly from landlords or officials – is inclined to overstress this point.

The mobilization for an invasion normally takes place in the evening, the actual operation, on sound military principles, at dawn, though this is not invariable. A more or less large mass of men, women and children – to the number of hundreds or even thousands – accompanied by livestock, implements and building materials, occupies the disputed territory, tearing down fences, walls and other boundary marks, and immediately proceeds to build simple huts or other structures, generally along the line of the boundary claimed as legitimate. The families immediately establish themselves there, start to pasture their flocks (where necessary expelling the landlords' animals), and to plough up and sow the land.[25] In some instances a more cautious line is followed, a reconnaissance party being infiltrated which, if there is no sign of massive opposition, is followed by mass occupation. We may note in passing that (in Peru at least) that characteristic phenomenon of the past few years, the urban land invasion (or mass squatting), proceeds on exactly similar lines. A mass of families invade a plot of empty land, immediately construct a host of small hutments – generally a rudimentary frame with matting as walls and roof – in which they settle down, preparatory to building more permanent quarters with the aid of the neighbours, defying the authorities to expel them. As in several other respects, such shanty-towns are urban adaptations of village communal ways.[26]

An important distinction between the classical communal land invasion and land occupations organized by more modern political movements must, however, be pointed out. The strategy and tactics of modern occupations, whether of land or workplace ('sit-ins' or 'work-ins') envisage them as demonstrations or means of bringing pressure to bear on the authorities, that is to say as a means to an end. Thus – to take an example from an organized peasant movement – the movement led by Jacinto Lopez in the state of Sinaloa (Mexico) in the 1950s used land invasions in this limited way. The peasant congress of Los Mochis, Sinaloa, in 1957 threatened invasions if the promises to provide a legal solution for the problems of the petitioners were not soon kept. When nothing happened, land occupations took place in early 1958, but the invasion of 20,000 hectares of irrigated land by 3,000 peasants was symbolical. 'In the cultivated parts it consisted of the planting of the national banner in the middle of those lands, while the main bulk of the peasantry stood or sat on the roads along those fields ... When army units came to dissolve the sit-ins, the intentionally unarmed peasants left peacefully.'[27] The mass land occupations organized in the spring of 1971 by the Asociación de Usuarios in Colombia were also deliberately short-lived. In brief, unless part of an actual agrarian revolution or insurrection, land occupation in modern politically organized peasant movements is an incident in a long-term campaign. But for the classical communal movement it is campaign, battle and, with luck, final victory. It is not the means but the end itself. So far as the invaders are concerned, all would be well if the landlords, the state or other outside forces withdrew and left the community to live and work on the land they had now justly recuperated. As realists, the peasants may know that this is unlikely though (as we shall see) land invasions tend to be undertaken only when the situation looks favourable. However, even if they are expelled yet again by lord or government, they have at least reasserted both their right to possession by labour and their capacity to work the land they claim as their own – an important point, since their capacity to do so may be challenged.[28] But the object of the operation is not tactical. It is to take the land back and stay there.

It will already have been observed that the classical land invasion is not specifically Peruvian, or even Indian. There are indeed plenty of exact equivalents elsewhere in Latin America. In Chile *all* the land invasions (*tomas de fundos*) by small cultivators up to 1968 were recuperations of alienated common lands by Mapuche Indians,[29] though elsewhere they were undertaken by non-Indian peasants, as in Venezuela, where there were an estimated 500 cases of invasions of expropriable lands at the beginning of the agrarian reform process in the late 1950s and early 1960s. The lands invaded were frequently those taken away from the peasants earlier.[30] But European parallels are also to be found. The Calabrian peasants marched out in 1848 to occupy lands with banners and bands.[31] The Salernitan peasants of the nineteenth century showed the familiar combination of claims for land held by what they considered valid legal title and land invasions 'conducted by masses of people in an absolutely orderly manner. "They bore banners, they went from house to house to mobilize all the people and gathered to the sound of horns, advancing on the lands to be occupied" when dawn began to lighten the mountain tops.'[32] Flags, drums and horns were the normal ceremonial accompaniment of the invasions of 1848. As one observer noted perceptively, the landless labourers 'abandoned their slums and cottages as soon as they *heard* the wild sound of the *tofa*, which in peaceful times had been the music lightening the labour of the field and accompanying the joys of the grape-harvest, but which in 1848 became the call to union and revolt'.[33] The Italian land occupations after the First World War, largely independent of socialist organization, continued along the old lines. Thus the movement in Latium, which set off a nationwide wave of land invasions in 1919, claimed 'to defend the land to which they asserted legal rights against the usurpers'. The *Osservatore Romano* described the simultaneous invasions in forty municipalities as follows: 'At dawn ... improvised caravans of peasants, to the sound of music and with banners, marched upon the latifundia of the region and decreed their occupation, indicating the boundaries of the areas they occupied with special marks.'[34] And the great land occupations of March 1936 in Spain, which followed upon the victory of the Popular Front, began as recuperations of lost lands, and, incidentally also, as might be expected, were launched at dawn.[35] These scattered examples are at least sufficient to show that something very like the classical communal land invasion can be found in circumstances very different from those of the Peruvian highlands. They belong to the history not of Peruvian Indians or Latin America, but of peasant communities.

III

To understand the nature of such invasions and the role they play in peasant action, it may be convenient to follow one particular such movement through at least some of its ramifications: that of the community of Huasicancha, a small and overwhelmingly pastoral Indian settlement in the central highlands of Peru, roughly near the point where the departments of Junin, Lima and Huancavelica meet. We are fortunately in a position to trace the struggle of this community for a particular area of common pasturelands back to the sixteenth century, a fairly rare example of continuous documentation.[36] Peruvian statistical data being what they are, all we can really say about Huasicancha, in spite of a variety of censuses and other nominally quantitative inquiries, is that it became large or noticeable enough by 1930 to be formed into a 'district' – the smallest administrative unit of rural Peru – that it has consisted of not more than a few hundred souls in the past century, and that it seems to have, and probably to have had, a relatively large amount of livestock. In 1970 it ranked fifth out of thirty-two communities for sheep and total livestock, second for cattle.

Somewhere on the high *puna* – at and above 4,000 metres – Huasicancha had always possessed a large tract of communal pastures 'belonging to the Inca king', which were apparently usurped by one Juan Iparraguirre, against whom they obtained an *expediente* in the year 1607 from an authority described by the representatives of the community in the 1960s as 'el Virrey de la Republica residente en Lima', from which we may infer that litigation had begun some decades earlier. The boundaries of this tract are defined in this document, and remained those which the community claimed in the 1960s, being verified at that date by ocular inspection, toponymy and other suitable methods by an inspecting judge. The dispute, which dragged along the centuries, settled down into a conflict with the Hacienda Tucle, which appears to have been formed towards the end of the sixteenth century and to have expanded over the centuries into a vast livestock ranch. Like most such haciendas, Tucle lived in a relation of conflict and symbiosis with its surrounding communities, whose lands it had taken[37] and whose members supplied it with labour. The typical highland situation in this part of Peru was one in which a block of haciendas was thus surrounded by marginal communities. By the 1960s Tucle formed such a block with Laive and Antapongo, each, in spite of rivalries, attempting to concert their policy towards the peasantry, the first two having absorbed other haciendas (Rio de la Virgen and Ingahuasi respectively). They bordered on thirty-three communities, of which three bordered on more than one hacienda. These in turn, in spite of their own rivalries, had some interest in concerting their strategy towards the estates.

During the colonial period Huasicancha obtained judgments against Tucle in the seventeenth and eighteenth centuries, presumably with little practical effect. The Republic put an end to the protective legislation of the colony and, until 1920, to the recognition of Indian communities as such, but not to the determination of Huasicancha to claim its pastures. The War of the Pacific (1879–84), gave the community its chance. At this stage Tucle was owned by a formidable lady, Bernarda Piélago, whose testament, dated 1887, observes with some bitterness that the hacienda had been reduced to 3,000 sheep, since 40,000 and more had been carried off in that year by the neighbouring *pueblos* under the pretext of national war. 'For this usurpation and robbery I have initiated legal proceedings before the supreme government.'[38] What had happened was that in this part of Peru, as elsewhere, the Indians had been armed as guerrillas against the victorious Chileans, and had immediately entered upon the only war that made sense to them, occupying their alienated lands. Professor Henri Favre informs me that the leader of this local *montonera* or armed band was a man from Huasicancha, who eventually fell into an ambush and was killed. Local legend, in the usual syncretic fashion, confuses him with the great Indian rebel Tupac Amaru and claims that he was drawn and quartered in Huancayo.

Huasicancha soon appears to have lost its lands again. No period was less favourable to Indian communities than the Civilista decades after the 1880s, though the community managed yet again to confirm some of its rights in 1889 and in 1902. From 1919 on, however, the situation became somewhat more favourable. The era of President Leguía (1919–30) improved the situation of the Indians, at least theoretically, both by providing legal recognition for communities and perhaps even more by setting up a Department of Native Affairs. Henceforth landowners tended to blame trouble not so much on the natural cussedness of Indians, or even on the machinations of the *tinterillos* – the provincial lawyers who, whatever their politics, could hardly fail to compete for so potentially lucrative a plum as peasant (including of course communal) land litigation – as on the encouragement given to the peasants by the Department of Native Affairs. The accusation was hardly fair. But for the simultaneous emergence of political agitation which reached into the countryside, first by philanthropic *indigenistas*[39] and later by the more formidable political movements of the Peruvian Communist Party (1930) and above all the APRA (Alianza Popular Revolucionaria Americana, officially founded 1924), Native Affairs would hardly have been on less good terms with the estate owners (supposing these to be on the 'right' political side) than other parts of the Peruvian civil service. There are complaints of communist agitation, and reports (almost certainly wrong) of a demonstration of three communities with red flags in 1931, the headman of one being accused of 'frankly communist speeches'.[40] But if there was a communist presence in this region it was clearly much more shadowy than APRA's, for that party, whose subsequent General Secretary Sr Ramiro Prialé came from Huancayo, established a strong base in the central highlands. And the mood of the peasantry was in turn affected not only by the increased opening of communications with Leguía's modernizing policies fostered, but by economic developments.

Since these have not yet been adequately investigated, they can only be sketched in a provisional and tentative way. Two major developments appear to have taken place. On the highland pastures the expansion of the market for wool (and, for more local purposes, meat) had favoured the establishment of a large ranching economy, both by the expansion of old and the formation of new haciendas (such as the Sociedad Ganadera del Centro complex, formed originally in 1910). At the same time it probably introduced an economy of cash sales to the market in the livestock-raising highland communities, which supplemented or replaced the barter-trade with the communities in the different climatic/ecological zones lower down the slopes. In the broad Mantaro valley meanwhile (where, incidentally, trading along the new railways and roads replaced the former 'vertical' system of exchanges), the older mixed-crop economy of the non-Indian landlords declined, and a fairly substantial process of sale by them (and also by the Church) seems to have taken place – mainly to the wealthier Indian villagers – in the 1920s and 1930s. An increasing polarization between the upland latifundia and the peasant economy and minifundia of the valley therefore developed, the upland communities occupying the sensitive position between both. The post-war fall in the price of wool (1921) and a few years later the world crisis made the position of the livestock zone even more sensitive.

At this time Huasicancha, much reduced, seems to have been less militant in the matter of its lost pastures than one or two other communities, notably Yanacancha and Chongos Bajo (with whose offspring Chongos Alto it was to form an offensive alliance in 1945). The Yanacancha situation was complex.[41] This community up the mountain, which made itself independent of Ahuac in 1928, was as much concerned with the threat from Ahuac as with the pastures disputed with the hacienda, and indeed disposed to accept, for the time being, the support of Laive against the rival community, which in turn pressed Yanacancha to push the various communities' claims against the estate. Its militancy was thus reluctant, and it preferred (with the goodwill of the Ganadera del Centro, whose diplomacy towards the communities was always intelligent and sophisticated) to make a compromise settlement, its leader getting into trouble as a result, as we will see below. Chongos was less biddable. It was the people of this community 'who have taken possession of a large area of pasture land' belonging to Hacienda Laive in the 1920s. ('The Society has energetically prevented them from usurping further territory, and has offered to negotiate a boundary settlement.')[42] Both continued to preoccupy the estates into the early 1930s, by their reluctance to sign settlements, in spite of considerable pressure.[43] Chongos seems to have remained the most militant community for the rest of the decade. About halfway through the 1930s, however, the communities in the area – somewhat later than those on the other side of the Mantaro river valley – awoke to the possible advantages of registering officially as 'recognized communities', and here Huasicancha, perhaps because of its long experience of litigation, appears to have been quicker off the mark than most, registering in 1936, quickly followed by Chongos in 1937.[44] Between 1935 and 1939 sixteen out of the twenty-five recognized communities acquired their new legal status.

The decision to acquire legal recognition evidently marks a stage in the development of communal political consciousness, those in the more advanced regions of northern and central Peru being in general quicker to do so than those in the south. In the central highlands the years 1935–45 clearly form the crucial phase of this process. Recognition affected communal agitation in three ways. It gave a more formal standing to the elected officers of the *de facto* community – until 1963 the *comunidad indigena* was the only official administrative unit of government in which the local election of officers was sanctioned and permitted[45] – but, what is more important, it also implied the formulation of the community's specific claims to its collective patrimony, and hence its definition. Asking for registration thus often grew out of communal land claims. In extreme cases it could amount to a declaration of independence of a collective of peasants against estates or, for that matter, against larger communities of which they were regarded merely as 'annexes' (*anexos*). Finally, the process of registering was complex and expensive, and therefore helped the political organization of the community since it necessitated both the formation of a cadre of campaigning leadership (drawn from both resident and emigrant *comuneros*) and a mechanism for collecting funds.

Huasicancha, always quick to use the law for what it was worth, had beaten the Hacienda Tucle by a short head to register its most indisputable titles in the Public Registers at the start of the new period (20 November 1919). As soon as it was 'recognized' it began the process of formally reclaiming all its lost heritage, asking for what amounted to half of Tucle, all of Rio de la Virgen, a large part of Antapongo, possibly even some of Laive, as well as the hamlet (*caserío*) of Palaco and some of Chongos Alto, a project described by the correspondent of Laive as 'baseless and absurd',[46] but which Native Affairs took sufficiently seriously to arrange for a private boundary settlement shortly afterwards between Huasicancha and Palaco.[47] If ever the claim against the estates were to become more than academic, the consequences would be dramatic.

They became so in the years from 1945 to 1948, when a reforming administration under President Bustamente was in office with the support of APRA. Peasant life is a drama played out on a purely local or regional stage, a small area of light beyond which all seems dark and unknown. But Peruvian experience shows, as experience elsewhere confirms, that if peasants do not have much concrete knowledge about the wider framework which encloses their little worlds, they are acutely conscious of the changes in that wider framework which appear to affect its indestructibility. If the power structure is firm and closed, they retreat into their usual posture of waiting. If it begins to open or shake, they prepare for action. This is what happened in 1945 to 1948, until the triumph of the military dictatorship under General Odría (1948–56) once again dropped the habitual weight of coercive power on the countryside for a few years. But not for good. The great rural awakening of 1945–8, no less significant for being virtually unrecorded by historians,[48] was merely interrupted by the dictatorship and resumed a few years later, to produce the even greater wave of land invasions of the early 1960s.

Three things characterized the new period, which was to prove the beginning of the end of latifundism in the central highlands. First, by this time the process of mass emigration to the cities – a function both of demographic pressure and of modernization – had become noticeable. By 1963 the Sociedad Ganadera del Centro noted in a memorandum, 'the restlessness in this zone [is] chiefly due to demographic pressure'.[49] At the same time it had already produced communities of emigrant *comuneros* in Lima with organized nuclei, political know-how and, above all, available cash. It was among these exiles, a notoriously enterprising and successful group, that the money for the legal claim of Huasicancha seems first to have been raised.[50]

Secondly, both political activists and political backing were now available. The most eminent militant from Huasicancha was Elias Tacunan Cahuana (a Cahuana appears as *personero* or legal spokesman of the community in 1940 and again in 1967), a member of APRA from 1930, later an organizer in the mines, but after 1958 the founder and leader of the powerful Fedecoj (Federación Departmental de Comunidades de Junin), which he built, initially on the basis of Huasicancha, Chongos and a few other neighbouring communities, from 1958.[51] It is significant that after Tacunan and his movement broke with APRA in 1959, disappointed with its betrayal of the peasant movement, to found an unsuccessful 'Communal Party', the secretary of the APRA peasant federation (FENCAP) was also a man from Huasicancha – Elías Yaurivilca – thus confirming the reputation of our community as a nursery of active militancy.

The higher officials and politicos of the 'people's party' were indeed already accessible to the temptations and arguments of the men of power, as the confidential correspondence of the estates makes abundantly clear. As early as October 1945 the administrator of Laive noted that the (APRA) prefect of the department 'is a perfect gentleman and has offered all support within his power', though:

> with characteristic tact he has not wished to tackle the situation directly, but has allowed the communities to believe that the purpose of his visit was to hear complaints, appoint local authorities etc. Meanwhile Dr Campos [the APRA Provincial Alcalde of Huancayo], in his capacity as political delegate, has held meetings pointing out to the people the need to maintain order for their own benefit, since neither the government nor the Party of the People would support any movement of the communities to the detriment of the haciendas.[52]

From where the communal activists stood, the Party of the People still looked different. They believed its revolutionary rhetoric and they knew that the situation was favourable to them beyond any recent precedent.

Chongos and Huasicancha, the two activist centres, appear to have got together about this time to reclaim lands – or, in the words of a confidential memorandum, 'to assault the haciendas of Tucle and Antapongo, seize them and force a revision of land titles', instigated, it need hardly be said, 'by two or three Aprista agitators'.[53] They were merely acting on the assumptions expressed simultaneously by the *comuneros* of Santa Rosa, who sent word to the Hacienda Laive, with which they had a long-standing dispute, that 'now with the new government we can do what we want, and we denounce the existing treaties with the Ganadera'.[54] The estates avoided a confrontation in 1945, meanwhile preparing for armed resistance, but could not escape it at the end of 1946. On Christmas Day of that year a mass of men, women and children from Huasicancha invaded Tucle with all their livestock, destroyed boundary walls and refused to evacuate part of the land. The rest of the communities soon followed, until on 23 January a number of peasants were massacred by the 43rd Infantry Battalion, after which the invasions subsided.[55]

Huasicancha, which incidentally seems to have avoided massacre by a timely withdrawal, gained a large part of the Pampa de Tucle by this invasion, for the owners sold it to the community under the mistaken impression that by doing so the community forwent its other claims, the sale-price consisting of the construction of a boundary ditch.[56] Tucle as its neighbouring estates were frequently forced to note, was somewhat deficient in diplomacy, legal acumen and good management, deficiencies not, in the long run, compensated for by the fact that Señor Piélago was a senator, with a senator's influence.

The dictatorship of General Odría (1948–56) postponed the next stage of the campaign – the communities knew when it was wise to keep their heads down – but when the great wave of agrarian unrest which began in the late 1950s reached the central highlands in 1963, Huasicancha was again ready. The invasions in this area began in the summer of that year and reached a climax in early November, when even the careful Ganadera del Centro, which had congratulated itself on its immunity while all around it the peasants were marching in, finally saw its elaborate set of negotiated boundary settlements collapse under the weight of communal incursions.[57] Huasicancha still preferred the law and that month once again lodged a claim against Tucle. When the law appeared to fail them yet again, they invaded some 3,000 hectares with 4,000 beasts, eventually occupying some 15,000 hectares. This time the shaky political power of the estates was insufficient to dislodge them, and in spite of judgments against them they stayed there until the Agrarian Reform was declared in 1969.[58] They finally received a judgment in favour of their historic claims in 1970 from the new Agrarian Tribunal.[59] It is perhaps worth adding that they have since refused to enter the giant agrarian co-operative (SAIS Cahuide) which was formed out of the estates of the Ganadera del Centro, Tucle and Antapongo and twenty-nine adjoining communities. Indeed in the summer of 1971 they were still invading, this time the lands of the new co-operative.

Several points of interest emerge from this history of four centuries of struggle for Huasicancha's pastures. How did a community of illiterates maintain the exact memory of the lands it claimed, so precise that the 'ocular inspection' of 1963 confirmed in every particular the titles of 1607? For, though they had documents, for most of their history they obviously could not read them; indeed even the white lawyers whose business it was had sometimes to employ palaeographers for this purpose. In the 1960s an illiterate witness for the community, one Julian Paucarchuco Samaniego, fifty-nine years old, answered this question by saying that he had known the boundaries since 1922 because 'when he was a boy his father took him up and showed him the boundaries, and that is the reason he knows them'.[60] Presumably in every generation since the sixteenth century fathers had taken sons up to the high pastures to keep alive the memory of the lost lands in the same way.

Secondly, and perhaps more important, the Huasicancha story shows how misleading is the stereotype of the passive and subject Indian. For four centuries Huasicancha, small, remote, isolated and stubborn, never ceased to struggle for its rights. Not being either Western liberals or student insurrectionaries, the peasants quite failed to make a choice in principle between peaceful and violent, legal and non-legal methods, 'physical' and 'moral' force, using either or both as occasion appeared to demand. But they never abandoned their claims.

Thirdly, it is clear that the belief that the peasant horizon is entirely circumscribed by local factors is mistaken. Huasicancha may have known little about Lima and nothing about Madrid, Rome or Egypt, but it was sensitive enough to changes in the wider world which seemed to shake the foundations of the local power structure. Nevertheless, the horizon was local, insofar as the unit of their action was the community, its setting the interlocking system of estates and communities in their part of the highlands. They were, as we have seen, politically mobilized in national terms and produced cadres for national movements. And yet it seems that for the community this was either ancillary to its own struggles or a by-product of its development in a particular historical context. (Thus in Yanacancha, which mobilized in the 1920s, before the APRA became important, the political links if any were with the Leguiist Asociacíon Pro-

Indigena). As far as Huasicancha was concerned, APRA came and went, but did not commit the community. Doubtless they took pride in sons like Elías Tacunan but (except during periods when his activities were focused on their affairs) his career and their struggle were not the same. Their ambition was not to change the system so much as to make the best of it when it was strong, to push it back when it looked liked yielding.

IV

Nevertheless, peasant action and political change interacted in complex ways. Who organized and led land invasions? Since they were affairs of the community as a whole we must assume that in the classical form they were led by its leaders and officials, whose leadership so often (as in the Russian *obshchina*) required the ability to identify and express the consensus of 'the people', though conversely the readiness of the people to listen to men of wisdom and judgment, perhaps coming from families with a record of leadership in the community, was a powerful element in formulating such a consensus. We must remember that communal democracy proceeds by 'the sense of the meeting' rather than by majority vote. But, in the period in which our documentation is best, community decision was a more complex affair than in the example described in the prologue of John Womack's brilliant book on Zapata.

In the first place, the 'community' itself cannot always be regarded as ancient and traditional. As often as not it was new in two senses: because it had broken away from an older community for demographic or other reasons, and because it utilized a specific juridical device which might itself be novel, and which happened to be advantageous, for example from the 1920s the procedure of 'recognition'.[61] No doubt the ways in which bodies of new settlers organized and took collective decisions were the traditional ways of peasants with the age-old experience of communal action, but the element of novelty is not to be overlooked.

In the second place, each Peruvian community was itself being transformed by a process of internal class differentiation, and increasingly also by what may be called external differentiation, namely the formation of a (relatively more prosperous) emigrant group in the city or cities, a group from which the men whose opinions carry weight – not least because of their presumed political know-how – are today often chosen. Paradoxically, the emigration of the kind of local notable whose family used to monopolize village offices may well leave the road to village political leadership open to others, even to newcomers.[62] The uneven progress of education also introduced a new element into village politics. In brief, modernization brought with it broader contacts with the outside world, initially for some, increasingly for many.

A good example of this is the case of Yanacancha, already mentioned in the course of this discussion.[63] Here, in the early 1920s, when the community was engaged in its double conflict with the parent community of Ahuac and the Hacienda Laive, one of the wealthiest *comuneros* convinced one Yauri to take the leadership of the campaign, since he, though from a poor family, had some (incomplete) secondary education and was a schoolmaster in a nearby village, as well as possessing a brother already in Lima. Yauri (who was joined by a former schoolfellow, one Camayo) did indeed become very active in the campaign. This brought him into much closer contact with Lima, to which he had to travel frequently in the next few years – so much so that by 1930–1 he was aware of the student agitations in San Marcos university. His new role may also have helped him to marry into a richer family (in 1931) and to develop into a middleman and subcontractor on road work, labour supply and so on, that is a member of the new village bourgeoisie who, being possessors of substantial quantities of livestock, drew a disproportionate benefit from the extension of communal lands.

We therefore have several elements among the activists. There is the communal middle class. There are those who, according to a hostile but realistic account, ' are recruited from the elements who retain family and social ties with the native mass, but who, by circumstances independent of their will, have left the community and its atmosphere'.[64] In time there are also the immigrant outsiders who take on a political role, notably the student or ex-student. Manuel Grijalba, leader of the movement on the Hacienda Tingo (Jauja, department Junin) combines all these characteristics: of peasant stock, he migrated to the mines at La Oroya, saved money, registered as a medical student at the University of San Marcos in Lima, failed to graduate (possibly because he was active in APRA), and came to the village in 1945, where he already had friends and subsequently married, becoming the founder of its local school and political leader.[65]

Both the new village elite and the wider and more miscellaneous body of linkmen between the community and the outside world play their part in the new structure of village politics. Initially the second group may have consisted of returned seasonal or visiting permanent migrants, of ex-servicemen, apparently significant in the more traditional and less migratory areas,[66] and in the central highlands particularly of miners, an occupation recruited almost exclusively from the communities and which paradoxically breeds both men with confidence and experience of organized labour struggles and, because of the possibility it gives of accumulating cash, potential members of the rural middle class. Eventually the number of men whose very village jobs maintain them in regular contact with the outside world, for example as truck drivers and transport contractors, multiplies. The new group of the village elite probably made its initial impact through the emigrant communities, forming home-town associations in the big city. Among the emigrants from Huasicancha these became the first financiers of the campaign for land recuperation. But here again the situation gradually became more complex. We have cases of local leaders like Abel Quiroz of Oyon who may have been immigrants (Quiroz was a mining entrepreneur in a small way), certainly did not live regularly in the community, but 'are backed by three or four of the richest *comuneros*'.[67] There was a growing body of local kulak modernizers, literate, enthusiastic about education, generally making their money by local transport undertakings or the like while their wives engaged in petty trade, and (as in Pucará) 'very conscious of themselves as a group', but with good relations with the more traditional *comuneros*.[68] Their sons would be the Maoist students of the 1960s, returning home in the vacations with new political ideas, which in some areas such as Ayacucho – but we do not know how many – affected local politics.

Obviously the political movements of the nation operated through such men, whether or not they had official positions in the community; and, conversely, modernization brought closer contacts with such movements. Its most obvious form was the help provided by union and political organization in the local cities (such as Cuzco) or politically committed local intellectuals – students and lawyers – whether on their own initiative or on that of the peasants, aware that such help was available. Too little is known of the political micro-history of communities to generalize, and even the more readily documented spread of peasant unions and federations of communities, such as were powerful for a time in the central highlands, is only known in a rather fragmentary way. However, the role of the political movements – APRA until its transformation, and later the various Marxist movements – is plainly important, as mobilizers of local cadres, as catalysts of peasant activity and perhaps above all as forces turning separate local agitations into a wider movement.

Less obvious, but equally important, is the collapse of the belief in the permanence of the prevailing power structure, which liberated activist peasants who had previously chosen to serve the lords for new positions as popular leaders. As a hostile observer noted in

1963 – and there is similar evidence for the period after 1945 – the new militants were often the old 'estate foremen [*mandones y capataces*] who yesterday followed the *hacendado* and exploited their own race'.[69] Their conversions are probably quite genuine. Communal headmen may, in a period of stable landlord power, support the hacienda not only because they are secretly subsidized by the lord (of which there is good evidence) but also because, when no alternative is available, the most advantageous course for the community might well be to accept the modest help which the hacienda can provide, and is prepared to provide as the price for keeping the discontent of the peasantry down. But whether or not the old authorities change their minds, they must in the new situation change their actions. Thus in 1931 three communities attacked the community of Yanacancha, maltreating and taking prisoner its *alcalde*, whom they accused – apparently with much local support – of being a traitor who had sold pasture-land to the estate.[70] In 1945 the *alcalde* of Chongos Alto, one Orihuela, opposed the plans of the communities for an invasion, whereupon he was attacked, beaten and removed from his post.[71]

The typical land invasion of recent years was therefore a rather complex affair. The official representatives of the community were almost always present, as they had to be; but by their side as often as not were 'instigators' or 'agitators'.[72] Old and new social and power structures in the village intermingle, roles are transformed. This mixed character of the leadership may be illustrated from one of the rare detailed studies of village activism. In Marcantuna (Mantaro Valley) the fourteen men singled out as communal leaders in the mid-1960s included two in their twenties (a student and a book-keeper), one in his thirties (a farmer-cum-trader), four in their forties (white-collar worker, farmer-cum-truckdriver, farmer/labourer, farmer), five in their fifties (three farmers-cum-artisans, two farmers), and two over sixty (both farmers). Seven of these men had incomplete or terminated primary education, five partial secondary education, one higher education, while the educational status of one is unknown.[73] We can unfortunately not rely on the indications of their politics, since press reports tend to present all activists uniformly as bolsheviks.[74]

V

Finally, what light do the invasions throw on the question of peasant revolutionism? It seems evident that *objectively* a mass process of land invasion can have revolutionary consequences independent of the subjective intentions of the invaders, if the proportion of usurped land in estates is large enough, and the population in the communities recuperating their ancient lands sufficiently numerous. Something like this occurred in large parts of Peru in the early 1960s. The nature of Peruvian statistics makes figures little more than figures of speech, indicating general orders of magnitude. But it seems not improbable that there were in 1961 (according to the Census) something like 4,500 'comunidades parcializadas o ayllus', that is peasant communities, of which 2,337 had by 1969 got themselves officially 'recognized'. Their total membership in 1961 may have consisted of say 400,000 heads of families or say two million individuals out of a total rural population in highland Peru of about four million.[75] This figure may be used for preference, being more modest than the guesses of between 2.5 and 4 million in the CIDA Report.[76] In certain areas such as the central highlands the bulk of the rural population is communally organized. Thus the Mantaro Valley with about 150,000 inhabitants in 1969 had thirty-six haciendas and 234 legally recognized or probably 400 or so de facto communities.[77]

Of these communities at least half have disputes about boundaries – a figure based on a series of samples and regional surveys[78] – and pretty certainly this figure is an absolute minimum. Thus 73.3 per cent of the answers to the questionnaire of the Instituto Indigenista Peruano report 'controversy' over boundaries with neighbouring private proprietors.[79] For the area of the central-highland sheep-ranches with which we have been concerned the figures are even more conclusive. Of the fifteen comunidades which eventually merged with the Ranching division of the Cerro de Pasco Corporation to form the SAIS Tupac Amaru I (Sociedad Agricola de Interes Social, a form of agricultural co-operative), no fewer than thirteen had claims against the ranch by virtue of 'immemorial possession' (six) or colonial land titles (seven).[80] We have record of twenty-three communities which at one time or another since the 1920s had boundary disputes with the Hacienda Laive, and only one which may possibly not have done.[81] It is obvious that, when all or most of such communities simultaneously claimed their rights, the structure of local latifundism automatically collapsed (unless restored by military force). That is what happened, broadly speaking, in the central highlands in the second half of 1963. Humpty Dumpty fell off the wall: after 1963 nobody could put him together again and the managements of the great estates – the Ganadera del Centro, the Division Ganadera of the Cerro de Pasco Corporation, Algolan, Corpacancha and the rest were perfectly aware of it. Just so, a year earlier, the structure of latifundism in the valleys of La Convención and Lares had collapsed under the mass refusal – which turned out to be permanent – of the serf-tenants to perform their labour services. For this time – for reasons which would take us beyond the scope of this paper – military force was not used to restore the old order.

At the same time we must ask ourselves whether *subjectively* this process amounts to a peasant revolution. This is very much less certain. Broadly speaking, in primitive rebellions the 'revolutionary' and the 'reformist' movements can normally be distinguished, though not necessarily by the amount of violence involved in either. The former have subjectively much greater ambitions, expressed either in millennial terms or perhaps in the attempt to restore some lost golden age of the past, that is in Peru the Inca Empire.[82] Henri Favre perceptively distinguishes – apropos the Maya of the Chiapas highlands in Mexico – between the two types of what he calls 'rebellion' and 'insurrection': the former both localized and limited in its objectives, to the restoration of the customary balance, temporarily disturbed, the latter an attempt at the total restructuring of the colonial situation.[83] The former implies no ideological innovation. The latter – at least in Chiapas, as in 1712 and 1869 – 'appears at first as a religious reform which then gradually brings about the complete reorganization of social relations, both internal and external'.[84] There is, of course, no reason why in the twentieth century such ideological innovation should not take a modern secular form. The basic point is the complete negation of the prevailing structure of class (or racial) domination.

There are peasant movements which quite evidently challenge not only the abuse of lordship, but the fact of lordship itself, for example the Sicilian jacqueries of the nineteenth century, the Russian peasant movement of the early twentieth and perhaps also of the nineteenth century: we recall the peasants of the Kharkov area who believed the Tsar had ordered the division of all the lands. The lords 'may keep a little bit of land to feed their families, but no more', though the peasants would of course help them if they couldn't manage to plough it themselves. Or those of Nadezhdino (Saratov) who argued that 'the commune does not object to the lord keeping his big house, but whether he can keep his garden needs to be discussed'.[85] On the other hand there is little evidence (apart from cases of known communist or Trotskyite leadership) of Peruvian peasants challenging lordship as such, for example the ownership of demesne lands, though there was a growing and effective reaction against labour services.[86] The traditional patron–client relationship between lords who 'consider themselves protectors of the Indians whom they call their children (*hijitos*)' still remained valid in many parts, the lords being probably more aware of impending changes than the peasants.[87] The classical burning of big houses, murder of landlords and so on are virtually absent from the agitations of 1958–64, which are notably peaceful. What we have here is not the traditional *sublevación indigena* on a large scale, but a spontaneous mass assertion of legal rights, stimulated by, but not apparently – except in a few areas – imbued with, a modern, or for that matter an ancient, revolutionary ideology. There are no signs of any mass conversions to some form of communism, even in Cuzco. Marxism remained the ideology of cadres, though increasingly of peasant cadres, as APRA was, at any rate outside the 'solid North' where that party established itself as a mass movement.[88]

As has been pointed out, this is not incompatible with making what amounts to a social revolution, or even with a vague if growing sense that the old era is coming to and must come to an end. Nor is it in theory incompatible with the evolution of such peasant movements into conscious peasant revolution in a nationally revolutionary situation. On the other hand it must be pointed out that in several regions of Latin America the estate system itself is a fluctuating entity. In the course of post-colonial history haciendas have been formed, expanded, split up and reformed depending on political change and economic conjuncture.[89] The communities probably never benefited permanently from these fluctuations, but their permanent pressure, becoming relatively more effective in periods of recession for the large estates, need not imply the belief that any one such recession marks the final extinction of all haciendas. In brief, we must bear in mind both the strength and the limitations of traditional peasant movements.

These turn into peasant revolutions when the aggregate of the 'little worlds' is simultaneously set into motion, almost invariably by some event or development in the 'big world' over which the peasants have no control, but which moves them into action. (What factors were responsible for this mobilization in the Peru of 1958–64 cannot be discussed here.) They become *effective* peasant revolutions either when unified and mobilized in a sufficiently large number of politically crucial areas by modern organization and leadership, probably revolutionary, or when the national structure and crisis is such that strategically placed regional peasant movements can play a decisive part in its affairs. This happened in Mexico 1910–20 with Pancho Villa's northerners, because of their armed mobility, and with the followers of Zapata, the 'cock of the South', in Morelos, because that state is next door to the capital. Neither of these things happened in Peru, except faintly in the 1880s when Caceres, who sought the support of the Indians whom he had organized into anti-Chilean guerrillas during the War of the Pacific, marched his men from the central highlands into the capital, but hardly as a revolutionary leader and certainly without social-revolutionary consequences. In the early 1960s the land invasions were indeed sufficiently overwhelming in the central highlands and in Cuzco, sufficiently serious in other parts of the highlands, to cause the highland hacienda system to collapse.[90] But, unlike Marx's proletariat, the spontaneous force of the peasantry, though capable of killing landlordism, was unable to dig its grave. It made Agrarian Reform inevitable. But it took an army coup, after several years of shilly-shallying, to bury the corpse of the highland haciendas.

CHAPTER 13

The Bandit Giuliano

This paper, originally published as a book review in the New York Review
of Books, *14 February 1985, returns to the themes discussed in greater
detail in a chapter of* Primitive Rebels *and in* Bandits *(revised edition, New
York 1981) and other writings on banditry as a social phenomenon. The
rise and fall of the bandit Giuliano is seen as part of a larger history of
national and international politics, which, unlike the mafia, figures such as
he could neither understand nor come to terms with.*

With the publication of Mario Puzo's *The Godfather* in 1969, the long-
lasting passion of the American public for the Mafia finally came out
of the closet. In practice it had long been an accepted but minor part
of American city life and business about which nobody got very
excited, but in theory it represented organized crime, sin and the
man-eating shark, and therefore had to be publicly execrated. J. Edgar
Hoover, with his habitual nose for the real sentiments of middle
America, carefully avoided choosing it as a target, and indeed refused
to admit its existence until its involvement in the heroin traffic made
it, at least for a time, genuinely unpopular. Hoover's 'public enemies'
usually challenged the values of business society, at least symbolically.
The Mafia, so far from challenging the values of 'Americanism',
embodied them.

What, after all, could be more American than the success stories
of penniless immigrant boys clawing their way to wealth and respect-
ability by private enterprise? What legitimate American business
tycoon ever objected to being called 'ruthless', to being credited (like
the good boxer) with the 'killer instinct', or to the principle that 'nice
guys finish last'? Mafiosi were as close-mouthed as US frontier
marshals in Westerns, or as Calvin Coolidge. They were – another
trait that facilitated empathy – by no means intellectually inclined.

Their substitution of private violence for state authority was as American as apple pie.

What is more, *The Godfather* could be seen to represent not only some of the continuing principles of the American way of life, but the ancestral ideals it had somehow inexplicably lost on the way. In Don Corleone's world bosses were respected and loved by their subordinates as surrogate fathers. Men were men and women were glad of it. Morality ruled unchallenged, and crime, for the most part, was kept off the streets. Families stuck together under patriarchal control. Children obeyed fathers, and virtuous wives were not afraid of losing their status to mistresses, nor did they dream of ripping off their spouses for alimony. No wonder *New York* magazine exclaimed (according to the paperback edition's blurb): 'You'll find it hard to stop dreaming about it.'

American readers and moviegoers could therefore enjoy *The Godfather* without bothering their heads about the extraordinary island the Corleones were supposed to have come from, just as the followers of the Kennedy saga (real or mythologized) do not really have to know anything about County Wexford. Both are quintessentially stories about the USA. But what can they make of Mr Puzo's new book *The Sicilian*, whose action takes place entirely in the Sicilian past, and which purports to be a barely fictionalized retelling of the real life-history of the bandit Salvatore Giuliano (1922–50), a distinctly non-American figure? For commercial purposes his story is loosely linked here to the earlier instalments of the Corleone epic.

The literature about Giuliano, to which Mr Puzo's book adds nothing of interest, is probably larger than that about any other real European outlaw in history. There are three reasons for this. First, he became a major issue in Italian politics and therefore the subject of much publicity and documentation. The Italian parliamentary commission on the Mafia in the early 1970s devoted nearly 800 pages or almost a third of its report to his affairs. Second, he was the first European bandit to live in the high noon of the modern mass media, which gratefully gave him both national and global exposure. He made *Life* magazine in 1947.

But third, and not least, he was the last real-life member of an ancient species to whose extinction men and women are not yet reconciled: the 'people's bandit'. In the great soap-opera poor and weak people go on dreaming about human inequality and injustice, and there has always been and still is a part for Robin Hood. Turiddu Giuliano was the last recorded real person to be cast for it.

There is no doubt at all that he saw himself in such a role, insofar as any real brigand has done so, and that a great many poor Sicilians accepted him in it. It is mere Hollywood sentimentality for Puzo to make him vow to give half of his band's profits to the needy, but one of the few honest cops to pursue him, the hard-bitten Lo Bianco, testifies to his distributing thousands of lire 'more than once' to people in trouble. 'For such people Giuliano was a god.'[1] And, one may add, for many other Sicilians who heard of such incidents.

If he had any instinctive politics, they were populist. The communists, whom he massacred from 1 May 1947 on, were amazed when he turned against them, for though he had been allied with feudal politicians since 1945 'throughout the entire period of the acute land agitation', to quote their regional leader, he had 'never interfered with the peasants'.[2] It is even claimed by a serious writer that in his early days – before Mafia power had been fully re-established in the countryside – Giuliano had shown signs of principled opposition to the Mafia.[3] In short, as an American journalist who interviewed him said, he was a Robin Hood – a good kid, a sincere kid, with only one thing wrong with him (which fits poorly into the stereotype of the 'noble brigand'): he liked killing people. Four hundred and thirty of them, to be precise, in the course of his career.

Since we are all familiar with the Robin Hood myth, Mario Puzo has little trouble in concocting a macho version of a Mediterranean romantic novel and costume melodrama, which will surely make a gratifying movie when the right young male lead has been found. The hero is handsome as a Greek god. He has a buddy who will betray him, a mamma who fixes him up with a mature woman whose sorrowful departure leaves him free secretly to marry a breathtakingly lovely long-legged teenager whom he sends to safety in America. (There is actually no evidence of any serious involvement with women by Giuliano, after an early home-town girlfriend who left for the US.) He works in a travel-agent's milieu that was suitably reconstructed by the artist who illustrates the preview of the novel in *Playboy* magazine: sea, sunshine, greenery, hillsides with Greek temple ruins, and tables full of what the Sicilian peasantry no doubt fail to recognize as ethnic gourmet nosh. (The author's style livens up markedly when he comes to describe food.)

There the tragedy of this doomed young man, an outlaw since the age of twenty in 1943, is played out. The real-life godfather of Sicily, Don Calogero Vizzini (1887–1954), in a diaphanous disguise, admires him and, lacking a suitable son, wants him to take over the business. But the noble bandit says (I quote): 'I am now committed to free the poor in Sicily and I do not believe that the Friends have the same aim. They are the servitors of the rich and the politicians in Rome and these are my sworn enemies.' So, 'tis war to the knife between the disappointed father and the rebellious son, and, formidable though the young hero is ('He is cunning beyond his years and perhaps as brave as any of us here'), there can be only one end to this unequal contest. The hero is promised a safe passage to the US, then betrayed and killed in the usual Mafia manner.

All this tushery makes a good enough read for a plane trip and is more fun than the Gideon Bible. But what has it to do with the strange island that even its inhabitants find hard to understand, though, living in it, they think they don't have to? But for the foreigner reading about Sicily making sense of the apparently incomprehensible is essential. Sicilian writers, who are nobody's fools – Verga, Pirandello, Vittorini, Tomasi di Lampedusa, Sciascia – find their island so obsessively central a subject, sometimes their only subject, precisely because they know how vital it is to deal with that strangeness, which in turn reflects – in Lampedusa's famous phrase – 'a terrifying insularity of mind'. If these brilliant and subtle artists have trouble with Sicilianness, what can we expect of Puzo?

Nothing – but for his curious insistence that he writes not just as a storyteller but as a lightly disguised historian. His events, dates and persons are real, their names immediately recognizable. The author plainly cares a great deal about his documentary bona fides and, though he doesn't go for footnotes, anyone familiar with the subject will recognize the research behind the book, and how much of it is verifiable fact. Unfortunately for his status as a historian – but doubtless with an eye on yet another movie triumph – he has chosen to write neither 'faction' nor fiction, but something combining the two, in the manner of the apocryphal film producer whose climax of his biography of Beethoven was the composer's public performance of his latest opus, the Blue Danube waltz. Mr Puzo, perhaps encouraged by theorists who claim that all reality is a mental construct, does not seem quite to appreciate that even one or two otherwise insignificant and dramatically beneficial changes in recorded fact may destroy a person's entire credibility as a reporter, courtroom witness or historian. But that is another question.

Now the historian, and especially the foreigner, *can* make a contribution to the understanding of a Sicilian story, especially since the very uncertainties, lies and confusions of the record provide precious handholds on the blank and crumbling rock faces of Sicilian reality. That is why much the finest treatments of the Giuliano story have come from outsiders pursuing the methods of the baffled investigator: Gavin Maxwell's biography[4] and Francesco Rosi's marvellous film of 1961, *Salvatore Giuliano*. But to do this requires at the very least a knowledge of Sicily, Italy and the world between 1943 and 1950, and of politics, of which Puzo shows no sign. He is thus almost obliged to turn his flesh-and-blood hero into a cliché.

For politics is what even Robin Hoods live by, especially if they hold out for seven years in a modern Western country. The crucial fact about Giuliano's career, unmentioned in *The Sicilian*, is that shortly after the end of the war the landowners' Sicilian Separatist Party, which wanted independence for the island or possibly attachment as a state to the United States, needed an armed force and recruited Giuliano's band to it, giving him a commission as a colonel.

This was crucial in two ways. It gave Giuliano, for the first time, real prestige, influential support, publicity and muscle.[5] It made him more than a purely local figure. But above all it turned the head of an ignorant country boy with vague, if sincere, ideals. In the words of the unsentimental Lo Bianco: 'The Separatists appointed him as a leader and Giuliano got drunk on the idea that he really was one. He thought he had really become a big shot and went crazy. I called him "a madman" because that's all he was.'[6] Well, he may not have been clinically insane, though even Puzo hints at an element of mental imbalance. But for hard-nosed Sicilians it was lunacy enough to take oneself seriously as a liberator of Sicily or a political force in the island, or indeed to imagine that an outlaw could survive against the Mafia. They knew that in politics it is not enough to have a bandoleer, be photogenic and command a few score home-town toughs.

In fact Giuliano's tragedy was that the very situation which permitted a brave, sincerely rebellious and perhaps charismatic young local killer to act out, among other things, his fantasy as the poor Sicilians' liberator ('How could a Giuliano, loving the poor and hating the rich, ever turn against the masses of the workers?')[7] had to make him into the rich Sicilians' gunman, and eventual victim. He emerged in the political vacuum left by the Allied invasion in 1943, which swept away the fascists. Nobody knew how things would turn out. Anything seemed possible. He died when everybody knew what the shape of the future would be: Sicilian regional autonomy in an Italy run by the Christian Democrats.

Giuliano's story is that of the interim, during which the only people other than the communists who had a clear idea of what they wanted in politics were the Mafiosi, who simply wanted to back the winning side, since their business is business and their profits are only where power is. Except that after 1943 it was far from clear who would win; the Mafia even tried a few halfhearted side bets on the communists. Nor should we forget, though Puzo seems to, having fallen for his own myth of Don Corleone's power, that in 1943, fifteen years after having been broken by Mussolini, the Mafia was weak and needed to rebuild. American support was no doubt an enormous and probably decisive asset, and military occupation a vast bonanza, but the Mafia was only just entering the big city thanks to the Americans and, thanks to peasant agitation and bandits, was not fully re-established in its old countryside bases. Its top men were still ageing rural racketeers from the remoter corners of the inland corn belt.

Between 1943 and 1946 the Sicilian ruling classes, or significant sections of them, put their money on political separatism or monarchy and lost. Separatism never got off the ground electorally, except when backed by muscle: Giuliano's home-town candidate and personal lawyer won Montelepre easily until the bandit dropped him, after which he got precisely twenty-six votes. Regional autonomy made independence unnecessary. Monarchy had plenty of Sicilian votes – two-thirds – but the national referendum instituted the Republic. In 1946 the causes of both independence and monarchy were dead.

Lacking a clear perspective, conservative Sicilians variously backed monarchists, Separatists, neo-fascists or the old pre-fascist Liberal Party as the tradition and calculation of local bosses suggested. Increasingly they were also drawn, for obvious reasons, to the party with government patronage in Rome, the Demochristians, initially somewhat distrusted because of their populist origins. The real Don of Corleone, the blood-stained Dr Navarra, started among the Separatists, shifted to the Liberals and finally offered his support to the Demo-christians. In this situation of uncertainty the united left had room for manoeuvre. Carried by a major peasant land movement it scored an enormous and unexpected triumph against a divided right in the first regional elections of 1947. It polled almost 40 per cent.

Giuliano had been left badly exposed by the collapse of separatism. For any other Sicilian or Italian regime he was simply an outlaw with a few dozen men. He stayed free because the political situation was confused, because he had the support of the Mafia, and because, in the classic understatement of the Anti-Mafia Commission's report, 'The police organs operating in the period of the Giuliano band behaved in a manner which was not always plausible.'[8] The most he could possibly hope for was to be permitted to return to civilian life, that is impunity, or to take his band to some refuge abroad. (He had offers.) But even for this he badly needed to demonstrate his political indispensability, or at least usefulness, to people in a position to return favours.

Giuliano, or his advisers, had sense enough to know that the best way for a brigand to win friends and influence people in the year 1947 was anti-communism, of which he had not previously shown signs. And the triumph of the Sicilian left in the April elections provided him with an obvious chance to play this card.

The band thus became an anti-red hit squad out of self-preservation. Whether he actually meant to kill and wound forty demonstrators from red villages on 1 May 1947 – the 'massacre of the Portella della Ginestra' is wonderfully reconstructed in Rosi's film – and who actually suggested this act of terror, are still open questions. But there is no doubt at all that the bandit announced himself as a hammer of the reds (not least in a letter to President Truman) and attacked labour halls and party offices in his area. Who put him up to it? We shall never know for certain and it does not matter. What we do know is that in the few days between the elections, when he had still backed the Separatists, and 1 May, Giuliano was desperately negotiating with other backers on the basis of doing favours in return for immunity.

The strategy backfired. Nobody was against terrorizing the voters back into line, and in fact this was done within the year (498 people were murdered in 1948). In 1948 the Demochristians triumphed, doubling their vote, and without serious debts to Giuliano, a locally useful, but regionally embarrassing bloodhound. (For dramatic reasons Puzo concentrates the two elections and the massacre into a few weeks of 1948.) Nobody wanted any part of the killer of Portella della Ginestra, for this massacre became a major national scandal, magnified by the understandable clamour of the Communist Party in Rome. The hands of the government were forced. Within months half the men later tried for the crime were under arrest, and defections from the band began.

Giuliano had to go. He had always been troublesome – too inclined, for one thing, to kill *carabinieri* for the tastes of the Mafia, which still preferred to bypass rather than to defy the structures of power and law. He now became a triple liability: because his demands could not possibly be granted, because in despair he actually began to kill politicians and Mafiosi who 'had not kept their promises', not to mention policemen in large numbers, and because his survival itself was a standing reproach to the Rome government and stopped respectable Sicilian citizens from going about their murders quietly.

Why did he nevertheless survive? We need not accept the operatic theory (a version of which is followed by Puzo), according to which he was safe so long as his friends had a written record naming names, notably those behind the massacre, and that he was killed as soon as he lost control of this document. It is a good story, and may even be true, though (in the best sources) it hinges on one Pasquale Sciortino who is supposed to have taken the document to the US, a man so spectacularly untrustworthy that one can hardly imagine Giuliano trusting him with his life. (The bandit had just forced him into a shotgun wedding with his sister.) And documents in murky Italian affairs disappear after as well as before death.

But who needs such melodrama? Giuliano was not some back-country hood, such as the Mafia were now handing over in large numbers, alive or dead, to grateful Demochristian authorities, but a man deep in Sicilian and national high politics since 1945. It took time and care for everyone concerned to disentangle themselves from him. Besides, apart from his local muscle, he had a genuine independent political base as a people's hero. His elimination had to be considered rather carefully. Anyway, the grafting, politicking and feuding within and between the various forces charged with arresting him gave him, even at the end, some time to play with.

That time was borrowed. Once Sicily and Italy were politically stabilized, there was no room for such as him. What he did during his last two years made no relevant difference, though it was certainly not, as in Puzo's novel, to turn himself into a champion of agrarian reform against feudal lords and Mafia. In fact, at this point, as Puzo sees his hero laying low six elderly *pezzi di novanta* riding on horseback like samurai to intimidate peasants, while a prince watches from his castle, the author's vision of the film of the book has clearly got the better of him. At all events Giuliano was killed by the Mafia, though one wonders why Puzo missed an obvious tie-in with the world of Don Corleone, for the man who is said to have been in charge of the operation was an ex-American mobster from Partinico, Frank Coppola.[9]

He was found dead, in the posture photographed at the time and accurately described by Puzo, in a courtyard at Castelvetrano. Practically everybody who could talk has since died suddenly. Even the Anti-Mafia Commission twenty years later has left several corners of his career in darkness.

All Sicilian judgments on the dead man agree that he was an inevitable loser. For Puzo's Godfather this was because he let sentiment get in the way of business calculations. His political enemies and victims on the left were more generous, though correctly predicting his inevitable end.[10] For them it was obvious that social bandits without good political sense, aims or advice inevitably became pawns and victims of the ruling classes, 'even though you are loved by the people and surrounded by sympathy, admiration, respect and fear'. And yet such an end was 'unworthy of an authentic son of the labouring people of Sicily'.

There is a third, and unSicilian, reaction to Giuliano's death:

Michael Corleone's (and perhaps Puzo's). In the novel the son learns the father's lesson that live Mafia bosses are better than the dead heroes they have betrayed, 'but it made him unhappy'. In some ways he 'envies' the dead bandit, as Lewis Carroll's Walrus weeps for the oysters he proposes to eat.[11] Most Sicilians would read this as a normal piece of rhetorical hypocrisy for public consumption, but Puzo means his character to be sincere. He belongs to a culture in which it is conventional to believe, or at least half-believe, one's own lies. Sentimentality, which Mario Puzo has poured over his hero like chocolate sauce, is not a good guide to the world in which Giuliano lived and died. This novel is an unworthy commemoration of a small figure in history, who deserved better. Fortunately there are others, like Francesco Rosi, who have done him and his world more justice.

CHAPTER 14

Vietnam and the Dynamics
of Guerrilla War

This piece was originally published in The Nation *(New York), in 1965, after the USA had decided to escalate its intervention in Vietnam but before it had launched itself into full-scale war. Its arguments remain valid, though the danger of Washington megalomania opening the way to a nuclear war no longer exists. And neither, except in very unusual circumstances, does the possibility of guerrillas winning wars against effective states. However, the asymmetry of power remains, as demonstrated more recently by Iraq. Superpowers and their allies can win all the battles, but they cannot conquer and occupy recalcitrant countries except at disproportionate, and in most cases prohibitive, cost – political if not economic. David can still hold Goliath at bay. Moreover, Goliath still suffers from 'the well-known disease of infant great powers, a touch of omnipotence'.*

Three things have won conventional wars in this century: greater reserves of manpower, greater industrial potential and a reasonably functioning system of civilian administration. The strategy of the United States in the past two decades has been based on the hope that the second of these (in which it is supreme) would offset the first, in which the USSR was believed to have the edge. This theory was based on faulty arithmetic in the days when the only war envisaged was one against Russia, for the Warsaw Pact powers have no greater population than NATO. The West was merely more reluctant to mobilize its manpower in conventional ways. However, at present the argument is probably more valid, for some of the Western states (like France) will almost certainly stay neutral in any world war that is likely, and China alone has more men than all the Western powers likely to fight in concert. At all events, whether the arguments were right or wrong, the United States has since 1945 put its money entirely on the superiority of its industrial power, on its capacity to throw into a war more machinery and more explosives than anyone else.

Consequently, it has been badly shaken to discover that a new method of winning wars has been developed in our time, and that it more than offsets the organization and industrial power of conventional military operations. That is guerrilla war, and the number of Goliaths who have been felled by Davids with slingshots is now very impressive: the Japanese in China, the Germans in wartime Yugoslavia, the British in Israel, the French in Indo-China and Algeria. At present the United States itself is undergoing the same treatment in South Vietnam. Hence the anguished attempts to pit bombs against small men behind trees, or to discover the gimmick (for surely there must be one?) which allows a few thousand ill-armed peasants to hold at bay the greatest military power on earth. Hence also the simple refusal to believe that it can be so. If the United States is baffled it must be due to some other – measurable and bombable – reason: to the aggressive North Vietnamese, who actually sympathize with their southern brothers and smuggle trickles of supplies to them; to the terrible Chinese, who have the nerve to possess a common border with North Vietnam; and no doubt eventually to the Russians. Before common sense flies completely out of the window, it is therefore worth taking a look at the nature of modern guerrilla war.

There is nothing new about operations of a guerrilla type. Every peasant society is familiar with the 'noble' bandit or Robin Hood who 'takes from the rich to give to the poor' and escapes the clumsy traps of soldiers and policemen until he is betrayed. For as long as no peasant will give him away and as long as plenty will tell him about the movements of his enemies, he really is as immune to hostile weapons and as invisible to hostile eyes as the legends and songs about such bandits invariably claim.

Both the reality and the legend are to be found in our age, literally from China to Peru. Like the military resources of the bandit, those of the guerrilla are the obvious ones: elementary armaments reinforced by a detailed knowledge of difficult and inaccessible terrain, mobility, physical endurance superior to that of the pursuers, but above all a refusal to fight on the enemy's terms, in concentrated force and face to face. But the guerrilla's major asset is non-military and without it he is helpless: he must have the sympathy and support, active and passive, of the local population. Any Robin Hood who loses it is dead, and so is any guerrilla. Every textbook of guerrilla warfare begins by pointing this out, and it is the one thing that military instruction in 'counter-insurgency' cannot teach.

The main difference between the ancient, and in most peasant societies endemic, form of bandit operation and the modern guerrilla is that the Robin Hood type of social bandit has extremely modest and limited military objectives (and usually only a very small and localized force). The test of a guerrilla group comes when it sets itself such ambitious tasks as the overthrow of a political regime or the expulsion of a regular force of occupiers, and especially when it sets out to do this not in some remote corner of a country (the 'liberated area') but over an entire national territory. Until the early twentieth century hardly any guerrilla movements faced this test; they operated in extremely inaccessible and marginal regions – mountain country is the commonest example – or opposed relatively primitive and inefficient governments native or foreign. Guerrilla actions have sometimes played an important part in major modern wars, either alone in exceptionally favourable conditions, as with the Tyrolese against the French in 1809, or, more usually, as ancillaries to regular forces – during the Napoleonic Wars, for example, or in our century in Spain and Russia. However, by themselves and for any length of time, they almost certainly had little more than nuisance value, as in southern Italy where Napoleon's French were never seriously inconvenienced by them. That may be one reason why they did not much preoccupy military thinkers until the twentieth century. Another reason, which may explain why even revolutionary soldiers did not think much about them, was that practically all effective guerrillas were ideologically conservative, even if socially rebellious. Few peasants had been converted to left-wing political views or followed left-wing political leaders.

The novelty of modern guerrilla war, therefore, is not so much military. The guerrillas of today may have at their disposal much better equipment than did their predecessors, but they are still invariably much worse armed than their opponents (they derive a large part of their armament – in the early stages, probably most of it – from what they can capture, buy or steal from the other side, and not, as Pentagon folklore holds, from foreign supplies). Until the ultimate phase of guerrilla war, when the guerrilla force becomes an army, and may actually face and defeat its adversaries in open battle, as Dienbienphu, there is nothing in the purely military pages of Mao, Vo Nguyen Giap, Che Guevara or other manuals of guerrilla warfare which a traditional *guerrillero* or band leader would regard as other than simple common sense.

The novelty is political, and it is of two kinds. First, situations are now more common when the guerrilla force can rely on mass support in widely different areas of its country. It does so in part by appealing to the common interest of the poor against the rich, the oppressed against the government; and in part by exploiting nationalism or the hatred of foreign occupiers (often of another colour). It is, once again, only the folklore of military experts that 'peasants want only to be left alone'. They don't. When they have no food, they want food; when they have no land, they want land; when they are cheated by the officials of a remote capital, they want to get rid of them. But above all they want rights as men and, when ruled by foreigners, to get rid of the foreigners. One ought to add that an effective guerrilla war is possible only in countries in which such appeals can be successfully made to a high percentage of the rural population in a high proportion of the country's territory. One of the major reasons for the defeat of guerrilla war in Malaya and Kenya was that these conditions did not obtain: the guerrillas were drawn almost entirely from among the Chinese or Kikuyu, whereas the Malays (the rural majority) and the rest of Kenya remained largely outside the movement.

The second political novelty is the nationalization not only of support for the guerrillas but of the guerrilla force itself, by means of parties and movements of national and sometimes international scope. The partisan unit is no longer a purely local growth; it is a body of permanent and mobile cadres around whom the local force is formed. They link it with other units into a 'guerrilla army' capable of nationwide strategy and of being transformed into a 'real' army. They also link it with the non-combatant national movement in general, and the politically decisive cities in particular. This implies a fundamental change in the character of such forces: it does *not* mean that guerrilla armies are now composed of hard-core revolutionaries infiltrated from outside. However numerous and enthusiastic the volunteers, the outside recruitment of guerrillas is limited partly by technical considerations, partly because many potential recruits, especially from among city intellectuals and workers, are simply not qualified; they lack the sort of experience which only guerrilla action or peasant life can give. Guerrillas may be started by a nucleus of cadres, but even a totally infiltrated force such as the communist units which maintained themselves for some years after 1945 in Aragon (Spain) soon had to begin systematically recruiting among the local population. The bulk of any successful guerrilla force is always likely to consist of local men, or of professional fighters who were once recruited as local men, and the military advantages of this are immense, as Che Guevara has pointed out, for the local man 'has his friends, to whom he can make a personal appeal for help: he knows the terrain and all the things that are likely to happen in the region; and he will also have the extra enthusiasm of the man who is defending his own home'.

But if the guerrilla force is an amalgam of outside cadres and local recruits, it will nevertheless have been entirely transformed. It will not only have unprecedented cohesion, discipline and morale, developed by systematic education (in literacy as well as military techniques) and political training but unprecedented long-range mobility. The 'Long March' transferred Mao's Red Army from one end of China to the other, and Tito's partisans achieved similar migrations after similar defeats. And wherever the guerrilla army goes, it will apply the essential principles of guerrilla war which are, almost by definition, inapplicable by orthodox forces: (a) to pay for everything supplied by the local population; (b) not to rape the local women; (c) to bring land, justice and schools wherever they go; and (d) never to live better than, or otherwise than, the local inhabitants.

Such forces, operating as part of a nationwide political movement and under conditions of popular support, have proved themselves extraordinarily formidable. At their best they simply cannot be defeated by orthodox military operations. Even when less successful, they can be defeated, according to the calculations of British counter-insurgency experts in Malaya and elsewhere, only by a *minimum* of ten men on the ground for every single guerrilla; that is to say, in South Vietnam by a minimum of something like a million Americans and puppet Vietnamese. (In fact, the 8,000 Malayan guerrillas immo-bilized 140,000 soldiers and policemen.) As the United States is now discovering, orthodox military methods are quite beside the point; bombs don't work unless there is something other than paddies to make craters in. The 'official' or foreign forces soon realize that the only way to fight guerrillas is by attacking their base, that is the civilian population. Various ways of doing this have been proposed, from the old-fashioned Nazi method of treating all civilians as potential guerrillas, through more selective massacre and torture, to the presently popular device of kidnapping entire populations and con-centrating them in fortified village compounds, in the hope of depriv-ing the guerrillas of their indispensable source of supplies and intelligence. The American forces, with their usual taste for solving social problems by technological means, appear to have a preference for destroying everything over large areas, presumably in the hope either that all guerrillas in the area will be killed along with the rest of the human, animal and vegetable life, or that somehow all those trees and underbrush will be vaporized, leaving the guerrillas standing up and visible, where they can be bombed like real soldiers. Barry Goldwater's plan to defoliate the Vietnamese forests by nuclear bombs was no more grotesque than what is actually being attempted along these lines.

The difficulty with such methods is that they merely confirm the local population in their support of the guerrillas, and provide the latter with a constant supply of recruits. Hence the anti-guerrillas devise plans to cut the ground from under the enemy's feet by improving the economic and social conditions of the local population, rather in the manner of King Frederick William I of Prussia, who is reported to have run after his subjects in Berlin, beating them with his stick and shouting: 'I want you to love me.' But it is not easy to convince people that their conditions are being improved while their wives and children are being drenched in burning oil, especially when the people doing the drenching live (by Vietnamese standards) like princes.

Anti-guerrilla governments are more likely to talk about, say, giving peasants the land than actually doing it, but even when they carry out a series of such reforms they do not necessarily gain the gratitude of the peasants. Oppressed peoples do not want economic improvement alone. The most formidable insurrectionary movements (including very notably the Vietnamese) are those that combine national and social elements. A people who want bread and *also* independence cannot be conciliated merely by a more generous distribution of bread. The British met the revolutionary agitation of the Irish under Parnell and Davitt in the 1880s by a combination of coercion and economic reform, and not without success – but this did not forestall the Irish revolutionary movement which threw them out in 1916–22.

Nevertheless, there are limitations to a guerrilla army's ability to win a war, though it usually has effective means to avoid losing one. In the first place, guerrilla strategy is by no means applicable everywhere on a national scale, and that is why it has failed, or partly failed, in a number of countries, for example Malaya and Burma. Internal divisions and hostilities – racial, religious and so on – within a country or a region may limit the guerrilla base to one part of the people, while automatically providing a potential base for anti-guerrilla action in another. To take an obvious case; the Irish revolution of 1916–22, essentially a guerrilla operation, succeeded in the twenty-six counties but not in Northern Ireland, despite a common frontier and active or passive help from the south. (The British government, by the way, never made this sympathy an excuse to drop bombs on the Shannon barrage in order to force the Dublin government to cease its aggression against the free world.)

Again, there may be peoples so inexperienced or so lacking in effective cadres as to allow large-scale and wide-based guerrilla insurrections to be suppressed, at least for some time. That is perhaps the case in Angola. Or the geography of a country may facilitate local guerrilla action, but make co-ordinated guerrilla warfare remarkably difficult (as perhaps in some Latin American countries). Or a people may be simply too small to win independence by direct action without major outside aid against a combination of occupying countries determined to suppress them. This may be the case with the Kurds, superb and persistent guerrilla fighters of the traditional kind, but who have never achieved their independence.

Beyond these obstacles, which vary from country to country, there is the problem of cities. However great the support for the movement in the cities, however urban the origin of its leaders, cities and especially capital cities are the last place a guerrilla army will capture or, unless very badly advised, tackle. The Chinese communists' road to Shanghai and Canton ran via Yenan. The Italian and French Resistance movements timed their urban insurrections (Paris, 1944; Milan and Turin, 1945) for the very last moments before the arrival of Allied armies, and the Poles who did not (Warsaw, 1943) were wiped out. The power of modern industry, transport and administration can be neutralized for a significant length of time only where it lies thin on the ground. Small-scale harassment, such as the cutting of one or two roads and rail tracks, can disrupt military movement and administration in difficult rural terrain, but not in the big city. Guerrilla action or its equivalent is entirely possible in the city – after all, how many bank robbers are ever caught in London? – and there have been some recent examples of it, for instance in Barcelona in the late 1940s, and various cities in Latin America. But it has little more than nuisance value, and merely serves to create a general atmosphere of lack of confidence in the efficiency of the regime, or to tie down armed forces and police which might be better used elsewhere.

Finally, the most crucial limitation of guerrilla warfare is that it cannot win until it becomes *regular* warfare, in which case it must meet its enemies on their strongest ground. It is comparatively easy for a widely backed guerrilla movement to eliminate official power from the countryside, except for the strongpoints actually physically occupied by armed forces, and to leave in government or occupation control no more than the isolated cities and garrisons, linked by a few main roads or railroads (and that only by daylight), and by air or radio. The real problem is to get beyond that point. Textbooks devote a good deal of attention to this ultimate phase of guerrilla war, which the Chinese and Vietnamese handled with brilliant success against Chiang Kai-shek and the French. However, those successes should not include mistaken generalizations. The real strength of guerrilla armies lies not in their ability to turn themselves into regular armies capable of expelling other conventional forces but in their political strength. The total withdrawal of popular support may produce the collapse of local governments often – as in China and Vietnam – heralded by mass desertions to the guerrillas; a crucial military success by the guerrillas may bring this collapse into the open. Fidel Castro's rebel army did not win Havana; when it had demonstrated that it could not only hold the Sierra Maestra but also take the provincial capital of Santiago, the government apparatus of Batista collapsed.

Foreign occupying forces are likely to be less vulnerable and less inefficient. However, even they may be convinced that they are in a war they cannot win, that even their tenuous hold can be maintained only at quite disproportionate cost. The decision to call off the wasting game is naturally humiliating, and there are always good reasons for postponing it, because it will rarely happen that the foreign forces have been decisively defeated, even in local actions like Dienbienphu. The Americans are still in Saigon, apparently drinking their bourbon peacefully, except perhaps for an occasional bomb in a café. Their columns still criss-cross the country apparently at will, and their losses are not much greater than those from traffic accidents at home. Their aircraft are dropping bombs wherever they like, and there is still somebody who can be called the prime minister of 'free' Vietnam, though it may be hard to forecast from one day to the next who he will be.

Thus, it can always be argued that just one more effort will tip the balance: more troops, more bombs, more massacres and torture, more 'social missions'. The history of the Algerian war anticipates the one in Vietnam in this respect. By the time it was over, half a million Frenchmen were in uniform there (against a total Muslim population of nine million, or one soldier to every eighteen inhabitants, not counting the pro-French local white population), and the army was still asking for more, including the destruction of the French Republic.

It is hard, in such circumstances, to cut one's losses, but there are occasions when no other decision makes sense. Some governments may take it earlier than others. The British evacuated Ireland and Israel well before their military position had become untenable. The French hung on for nine years in Vietnam and for seven years in Algeria, but went in the end. For what is the alternative? The old style of local or marginal guerrilla actions, like border raiding by tribesmen, could be isolated or contained by various relatively cheap devices which did not interfere with the ordinary life of a country or its occupiers. A few squadrons of aircraft could occasionally bomb villages (a favourite British method in the Middle East between the wars), a military frontier zone could be established (as on the old north-west frontier of India), and in extreme cases government tacitly left some remote and disturbed region to its own devices for a while, merely seeing to it that the trouble did not spread. In a situation like that of Vietnam today or of Algeria in the later 1950s, this will simply not work. If a people does not want to be ruled in the old way any more, there is nothing more that can be done. Of course, if elections had been held in South Vietnam in 1956, as was provided by the Geneva agreements, the views of its people might have been discovered at considerably less cost.

Where does this leave the anti-insurrectionaries? It would be foolish to pretend that guerrilla war is an invariable recipe for successful revolution or that its hopes, as of now, are realistic in more than a limited number of relatively underdeveloped countries. The theorists of 'counter-insurgency' can therefore take comfort in the thought that they need not *always* lose. But that is not the point. When, for one reason or another, a guerrilla war has become genuinely national and nationwide, and has expelled the official administration from wide stretches of the countryside, the chances of defeating it are zero. That the Mau Mau were defeated in Kenya is no help to the Americans in Vietnam – all the less help when we remember that Kenya is now independent, and the Mau Mau regarded as pioneers and heroes of the national struggle. That the Burmese government has never been overthrown by guerrillas was no help to the French in Algeria. The problem of President Johnson is Vietnam, not the Philippines, and the situation in Vietnam is lost.

What remain in such a situation are illusions and terror. The rationalizations of today's Washington policy were all anticipated in Algeria. We were told by French official spokesmen that the ordinary Algerian was on the side of France, or that, if he was not actually pro-French, he wanted only peace and quiet but was terrorized by the FLN. We were told, practically once a week, that the situation had improved, that it was now stabilized, that another month should see the forces of order regain the initiative, that all they needed was another few thousand soldiers and another few million francs. We were told that the rebellion would soon die down, once it was deprived of its foreign sanctuary and source of supplies. That sanctuary (Tunisia) was bombed and the border hermetically sealed. We were told that if only the great centre of Muslim subversion in Cairo could be eliminated, everything would be all right. The French therefore made war on Egypt. In the last stages we were told that there might just conceivably be some people who *really* wanted to get rid of the French, but since the FLN obviously did not represent the Algerian people, but only a gang of ideological infiltrators, it would be grossly unfair to the Algerians to negotiate with them. We were told about the minorities which had to be protected against terror. The only thing we were not told was that France would if necessary use nuclear weapons, because the French didn't then have any. What was the result? Algeria is today governed by the FLN.

The means by which the illusions are to come true is terror, mostly – in the nature of things – against non-combatants. There is the old fashioned terror against civilians by frightened soldiers, demoralized by the fact that in this kind of war any civilian may be an enemy fighter, and culminating in the infamous mass reprisals – the razing of villages, such as the Nazis' Lidice and Oradour. Intelligent anti-guerrillas will discourage this, since it is apt to make the local population totally hostile. Still, such terror and reprisals will happen. Furthermore, there will be the more selective torturing of prisoners for information. In the past there may have been some moral limitation on such torture, but not, alas in our time. In fact, we have so far forgotten the elementary reflexes of humanity that in Vietnam we photograph torturers and victims and release the pictures to the press.

A second kind of terror is that which is at the base of all modern warfare, whose targets nowadays are essentially the civilians rather than the combatants. (Nobody would ever have developed nuclear weapons for any other purpose.) In orthodox warfare the purpose of indiscriminate mass destruction is to break the morale of population and government, and to destroy the industrial and administrative base on which any orthodox war effort must rest. Neither task is as easy in guerrilla war, because there are hardly any cities, factories, communications or other installations to destroy, and nothing like the vulnerable central administration machine of an advanced state. On the other hand, more modest success may pay off. If terror convinces even a single area to withhold support from the guerrillas, and thus to drive them elsewhere, this is a net gain for the anti-guerrillas. So the temptation to go on bombing and burning at random is irresistible, especially for countries like the United States which could strip the entire surface of South Vietnam of life without dipping too deeply into its supply of armaments or money.

Lastly, there is that most hopeless and desperate form of terror, which the United States is at present applying: the threat to extend the war to other nations unless they can somehow get the guerrillas to stop. This has no rational justification at all. If the Vietnamese war were really what the State Department pretends, namely an 'indirect' foreign aggression without 'a spontaneous and local rebellion', then no bombing of North Vietnam would be necessary. The Vietcong would be of no more importance in history than the attempts to set up guerrilla warfare in Spain after 1945, which faded away, leaving few traces except some local newspaper stories and a few publications by Spanish policemen. Conversely, if the people of South Vietnam really were on the side of whatever general at present claims to be their government, or merely wanted to be left in peace, there would be no more trouble in that country than in neighbouring Cambodia or Burma, both of which had or still have guerrilla movements.

But it is clear by now, and should always have been clear, that the Vietcong will not go away quietly, and no miracle will transform South Vietnam into a stable anti-communist republic within the foreseeable future. As most governments in the world know (though one or two, like the British, are too dependent on Washington to say so) there can be no military solution in Vietnam without at least a major conventional land war in the Far East, which would probably escalate into a world war when, sooner or later, the United States discovered that it could not win such a conventional war either. And it would be fought by several hundreds of thousands of American troops, because the allies of the United States, though doubtless willing to send a token battalion or ambulance unit, are not fools enough to involve themselves seriously in a conflict of this kind. The pressure to escalate a little further will mount, and so will the Pentagon belief in the most suicidal of all the many Vietnamese illusions – that in the last showdown the North Vietnamese and Chinese can be terrorized by the prospect of nuclear war into defeat or withdrawal.

They cannot, for three reasons. First, because (whatever the computers say) nobody believes that a United States government, which is genuinely interested in a stable and peaceful world, will actually start a nuclear war over Vietnam. South Vietnam is a question of vital importance for Hanoi and Peking, just as Soviet missiles off Florida were regarded as a vital issue in Washington; whereas the Vietcong are merely a matter of saving face for the United States as Cuban missile bases were of marginal urgency for Khrushchev. The Russians backed down over Cuba because to them it was not worth any kind of world war, nuclear or conventional. For the same reason the United States can be expected to back down in South Vietnam, provided it is interested in world peace, and provided, presumably, some sort of face-saving formula can be found.

Second, and on the supposition that the United States really is not prepared for any realistic settlement in South Vietnam, its nuclear threat will not work in the long run because North Vietnam, China and quite a few other countries will conclude that nothing is to be expected from concession except further United States demands. There is so much talk about 'Munich' in Washington these days that it is often forgotten how much like Munich the situation must look to the other side. A government which regards itself as free to bomb a country with which it is not at war can hardly be surprised if China and North Vietnam refuse to believe that this is the last concession they will be asked to make. There are, as the United States government is aware, situations today in which countries are willing to face the risks of world war, even nuclear war. For China and North Vietnam, South Vietnam is one such situation and the Chinese have already made that clear. It is dangerous daydreaming to think otherwise.

Third and last, the threat of nuclear war against China and North Vietnam is relatively ineffective, because it is more appropriately a threat made against *industrialized* belligerents. It assumes that in modern warfare there comes a moment when a country or a people must give up because its back is broken. That is a certain outcome of nuclear war for small and medium-sized industrial states and a probable one for large ones (including the United States), but it is not the necessary outcome for a relatively undeveloped state, especially one as gigantic as China. It is certainly true that China (without the USSR) has no chance of defeating the United States. The strength of its position is that neither can it be defeated in any realistic sense. Its token nuclear bombs can be destroyed, and so can its industries, cities and many millions of its 700 million citizens. But all that would merely put the country back to where it was at the time of the Korean War. There are simply not enough Americans to conquer and occupy the country.

It is important for American generals (and for anyone else cal-culating war on assumptions derived from industrial societies) to realize that a nuclear threat will be regarded by the Chinese either as incredible, or as inevitable but not decisive. It will therefore not work as a threat, though doubtless the Chinese will not rush lightly into a major war, especially a nuclear one, even when they believe it cannot be avoided. As in Korea, they are not likely to enter it until directly attacked or threatened. The dilemma of American policy therefore remains. Having three times as many nuclear bombs as the rest of the world is very impressive, but it will not stop people from making revolutions of which Mr McGeorge Bundy disapproves. Nuclear bombs cannot win guerrilla wars such as the Vietnamese are now fighting, and without such weapons it is improbable that even conventional wars can be won in that region. (The Korean War was at best a draw.) Nuclear bombs cannot be used as a threat to win a little war that is lost, or even a medium-sized war, for though the populace can be massacred, the enemy cannot be brought to surrender. If the United States can come to terms with the realities of south-east Asia, it will find itself very much where it was before – the most formidable power in the world, whose position and influence nobody wants to challenge, if only because nobody can, but which, like all other powers, past and present, must live in a world it does not altogether like. If it cannot come to such terms, sooner or later it will blast off those missiles. The risk is that the United States, suffering from the well-known disease of infant great powers – a touch of omnipotence – will slide into nuclear war rather than face reality.

CHAPTER 15

May 1968

This essay was originally published in the New York Review of Books *in 1969. Millennial moments are rarely observed at close hand. 1968 in Paris was one of them. Like the movements of peasants (see chapters 11 and 12), those of students in 1968 were anonymous and powerful, had spokesmen rather than leaders, and were basically unconcerned with the politics of the states they inhabited and could convulse. Unlike peasants, what they were concerned with and wanted was harder to understand. This chapter shows how far intelligent observers at the time could, and could not, understand these movements. (See also chapter 17.) However, writing in 1968 I underestimated the long-term effects of the 1968 shock on the political systems of France and other countries affected.*

Of all the many unexpected events of the late 1960s, a remarkably bad period for prophets, the movement of May 1968 in France was easily the most surprising, and, for left-wing intellectuals, probably the most exciting. It seemed to demonstrate what practically no radical over the age of twenty-five, including Mao Tse-tung and Fidel Castro, believed, namely that revolution in an advanced industrial country was possible in conditions of peace, prosperity and apparent political stability. The revolution did not succeed and, as we shall see, there is much argument over whether it was ever more than faintly possible that it should succeed. Nevertheless, the proudest and most self-confident political regime of Europe was brought to within half an inch of collapse. There was a day when almost certainly the majority of de Gaulle's cabinet, and quite possibly the general himself, expected defeat. This was achieved by a grassroots popular movement, without the help of anyone within the power structure. And it was the students who initiated, inspired and at crucial moments actually represented that movement.

Probably no other revolutionary movement contained a higher

percentage of people reading and writing books, and it is therefore not surprising that the French publishing industry should have rushed in to supply an apparently unlimited demand. By the end of 1968 at least fifty-two books about the May events had appeared, and the flow continues. All of them are rush jobs, some of them no more than brief articles, padded out with reprints of old papers, press interviews, taped speeches and so on.

There is, however, no reason why hasty inquests should not be valuable when conducted by intelligent people, and the Latin Quarter of Paris probably contains more of them per square yard than any other spot on earth. In any case the revolutions and counter-revolutions of France have in their time stimulated some of the most distinguished rush jobs of history, most notably Karl Marx's *Eighteenth Brumaire of Louis Bonaparte*. Moreover, French intellectuals are not merely numerous and articulate, but used to quick and copious writing, a faculty trained by years of moonlighting on reviews and other work for not very generous publishers. Add up the books, the reviews and the newspaper accounts, headed by those in the majestic and indispensable *Le Monde*, and the typical Parisian revolutionary has probably got through the equivalent of several thousand pages about his or her experiences; or at least talks as though he had.

What can we discover from this mass of literature? By far the greater part tries to explain the movement, to analyse its nature and its possible contributions to social change. A fair proportion tries to fit it into one or another of the analytical categories of its sympathizers – who provide the overwhelming majority of the writers – with more or less originality and special pleading. This is natural enough. However, it does not provide us with another *Eighteenth Brumaire* – that is to say, with a study of the politics of May 1968. No doubt the actual events are so vividly engraved on the minds of most French intellectuals that they think they know all about them already. It is no accident that the nearest thing to a coherent analytical narrative of the crisis comes from two British journalists, Seale and McConville. Though not exceptional, it is competent, sympathetic and invaluable to non-Frenchmen if only because it carefully explains what all the confusing initials of the various ideological groups in the Latin Quarter stand for.

Nevertheless, if May 1968 was a revolution which only just failed to overthrow de Gaulle, the situation which allowed what had been, a few weeks earlier, a squabbling collection of campus sects to make the attempt deserves to be analysed. And so must the reasons for the failure of these sects. So it may be useful to leave aside the nature and novelty of the revolutionary forces and try to clarify the less exciting question of their initial success and comparatively rapid failure.

There were, it is clear, two stages in the mobilization of the revolutionary forces, both totally unexpected by the government, by the official opposition, even by the unofficial but recognized opposition of the important left-wing literary intellectuals in Paris. (The established left-wing intelligentsia played no significant part in the May events; Jean-Paul Sartre, with great tact and intuition, recognized this by effacing himself before Daniel Cohn-Bendit, to whom he acted merely as interviewer.) The first stage, roughly between 3 and 11 May, mobilized the students. Thanks to the government's inattention, complacency and stupidity, a movement of activists in a suburban campus was transformed into a mass movement of virtually all students in Paris, enjoying vast public support – at this stage 61 per cent of Parisians were pro-student and only 16 per cent definitely hostile – and then into a sort of symbolic insurrection of the Latin Quarter. The government retreated before it, and in so doing spread the movement to the provinces and, especially, to the workers.

The second phase of mobilization, from 14 to 27 May, consisted essentially in the extension of a spontaneous general strike, the largest in the history of France or perhaps of any other country, and culminated with the rejection by the strikers of the deal negotiated on their behalf between the official union leaders and the government. Throughout this period, up to 29 May, the popular movement held the initiative: the government, caught on the wrong foot at the start, was unable to recover itself, and grew progressively demoralized. The same is true of conservative and moderate opinion, which was at this time passive, even paralysed. The situation changed rapidly when de Gaulle at last took action on 29 May.

The first thing to observe is that only the second phase created revolutionary possibilities (or, to put it another way, it created the need for the government to take counter-revolutionary action). The student movement by itself was a nuisance, but not a political danger. The authorities grossly underrated it, but this was largely because they were thinking about other things, including other university problems and the bureaucratic infighting between various government departments, which seemed to them more important. Touraine, the author of the most illuminating of the books published in the immediate aftermath of May, rightly says that what was wrong with the French system was not that it was too Napoleonic, but that it was too much like the regime of Louis-Philippe, whose government was caught equally on the wrong foot by the riots of 1848, which consequently turned into a revolution.

Yet, paradoxically, the very lack of importance of the student movement made it a most effective detonator of the workers' mobilization. Having underestimated and neglected it, the government tried to disperse it by force. When the students refused to go home, the only choice was between shooting and a public, humiliating retreat. But how could they have chosen to shoot? Massacre is one of the last resorts of the government in stable industrial societies, since (unless directed against outsiders of one kind or another) it destroys the impression of popular consent on which they rest. Once the velvet glove has been put on the iron fist, it is politically very risky to take it off. Massacring students, the children of the respectable middle class, not to mention ministers, is even less attractive politically than killing workers and peasants. Just because the students were only a bunch of unarmed kids who did not put the regime at risk, the government had little choice but to retreat before them. But in doing so it created the very situation it wished to avoid. It appeared to show its impotence and gave the students a cheap victory. The Paris chief of police, an intelligent man, had more or less told his minister to avoid a bluff which virtually had to be called. That the students did not believe it to be a bluff does not change the reality of the situation.

Conversely, the workers' mobilization did put the regime in a risky position, which is why de Gaulle was finally prepared to use the ultimate weapon, civil war, by calling on the army. This was not because insurrection was the serious object of anyone, for neither the students, who may have wanted it, nor the workers, who certainly did not, thought or acted in such political terms. It was because the progressive crumbling of government authority left a void, and because the only practicable alternative government was a popular front inevitably dominated by the Communist Party. The revolutionary students may not have considered this a particularly significant political change, and most Frenchmen would almost certainly have accepted it more or less willingly.

Indeed, there was a moment when even those two Hobbesian institutions, the French police and the army, long accustomed to assess the moment when old regimes ought to be abandoned and new ones accepted, allowed it to be understood that they would not regard a legally constituted popular front government as an insurrection which they were obliged to combat. It would not in itself have been revolutionary – except in its coming to power – and it would not have been regarded as such. On the other hand, it is hard to think of any other positive political outcome of the crisis which even revolutionaries could have expected.

But the Popular Front was not ready to occupy the vacuum left by the disintegration of Gaullism. The non-communists in the alliance dragged their feet, since the crisis demonstrated that they represented nobody except a few politicians, while the Communist Party, through its control of the strongest union federation, was for the time being the only civilian force of real significance, and would therefore have inevitably dominated the new government. The crisis eliminated the sham politics of electoral calculation and left visible only the real politics of power. But the communists in turn had no means of forcing the date of their shotgun wedding with the other opposition groups. For they had themselves been playing the electoral game. They had not mobilized the masses whose action pushed them to the verge of power, and they had not thought of using that action to force their allies' hand. On the contrary, if Philippe Alexandre is to be believed, they seem to have regarded the strike as something that might stop them from concentrating on the really important job of keeping their allies in line.

De Gaulle, a notoriously brilliant politician, recognized both the moment when his opponents lost their momentum and the chance of regaining his own initiative. With an apparently imminent communist-led popular front, a conservative regime could at last play its trump card: the fear of revolution. It was, tactically speaking, a beautifully judged performance. De Gaulle did not even have to shoot. Indeed, not the least curious aspect of the entire May crisis is that the trial of strength was symbolic throughout, rather like the manoeuvres of the proverbial Chinese generals of ancient times. Nobody seriously tried to kill anybody. Perhaps five people in all actually were killed, though a considerable number were beaten up.

Whatever happened, both Gaullists and revolutionaries united in blaming the French Communist Party, either for planning revolution or for sabotaging it. Neither line of argument is very significant except as an indication of the crucial role of the CP in May. It was clearly the only civilian organization, and certainly the only part of the political opposition, which kept both its influence and its head. This is not really surprising unless we assume that the workers were revolutionary in the same way as the students or that they were as disgusted with the CP.

But though the workers were certainly far more advanced than their leaders, for example in their readiness to raise questions of social control in industry which the General Labour Federation was simply not thinking about, the divergencies between leaders and followers in May were potential rather than actual. The political proposals of the CP almost certainly reflected what most workers wanted, and quite certainly reflected the traditional mode of thinking of the French left ('defence of the republic', 'union of all on the left', 'a popular government', 'down with one-man rule', and so on). As for the general strike, the unions had taken it over almost immediately. Their leaders were negotiating with government and the bosses, and, until they came back with unsatisfactory terms, there was no reason at all to expect a major revolt against them. In brief, while the students started their revolt in a spirit of equal hostility to de Gaulle and the CP (from which most of their leaders had seceded or been expelled), the workers did not.

The Communist Party was therefore in a position to act. Its leadership met daily to assess the situation. It thought it knew what to do. But what was it doing? It was certainly not trying to preserve Gaullism, for reasons of Soviet foreign policy or any other. As soon as the overthrow of de Gaulle began to look possible, that is between three and four days after the spontaneous sit-ins started to spread, it formally staked its own and the Popular Front's immediate claim to power. On the other hand it consistently refused to have anything to do with advocating insurrection, on the ground that this would be playing into de Gaulle's hands.

In this it was correct. The May crisis was not a classical revolutionary situation, though the conditions for such a situation might have developed very rapidly as a result of a sudden, unexpected break in a regime which turned out to be much more fragile than anyone had anticipated. The forces of government and its widespread political support were in no sense divided and disintegrated, but merely disoriented and temporarily paralysed. The forces of revolution were weak, except in holding the initiative. Apart from the students, the organized workers and some sympathizers among the college-educated professional strata, their support consisted not so much in allies as in the readiness of a large mass of uncommitted or even hostile opinion to give up hope in Gaullism and accept quietly the only available alternative. As the crisis advanced, public opinion in Paris became much less favourable to Gaullism, somewhat more favourable to the old left, but no clear preponderance emerges from the public opinion surveys. Had the Popular Front come, it would certainly have won the subsequent election, just as de Gaulle won his – but victory is a great decider of loyalties.

The best chance of overthrowing Gaullism was therefore to let it beat itself. At one point – between 27 and 29 May – its credibility would have crumbled so much that even its officials and followers might have given it up for lost. The worst policy would have been to give Gaullism the chance of rallying its supporters, the state apparatus

and the uncommitted against a clearly defined, and militarily ineffective, minority of workers and students. Unwilling to expel the
striking workers from the factories by force, the army and police were
entirely reliable against an insurrection. They said so. And, indeed,
de Gaulle recovered precisely because he turned the situation into a
defence of 'order' against 'red revolution'. That the CP was not
interested in 'red revolution' is another matter. Its general strategy
was right for anyone, including revolutionaries, who unexpectedly
discovered a chance of overthrowing the regime in a basically non-
revolutionary situation. Assuming, of course, that they wanted to
take power.

The communists' real faults were different. The test of a revolutionary movement is not its willingness to raise barricades at every
opportunity, but its readiness to recognize when the normal conditions
of routine politics cease to operate, and to adapt its behaviour
accordingly. The French CP failed both these tests, and in consequence
failed not only to overthrow capitalism (which it did not want to do
just then) but to install the Popular Front (which it certainly did
want to do). As Touraine has sarcastically observed, its real failure
was not as a revolutionary but even as a reformist party. It consistently trailed behind the masses, failing to recognize the seriousness
of the student movement until the barricades were up, the readiness
of the workers for an unlimited general strike until the spontaneous
sit-ins forced the hands of its union leaders, and was taken by
surprise once again when the workers rejected the terms of the strike
settlement.

Unlike the non-communist left it was not pushed aside, since it
had both organization and mass support from the grassroots. Like
them, it continued to play the game of routine politics and routine
labour unionism. It exploited a situation not of its own making, but
it neither led nor even understood it, except perhaps as a threat to
its own position within the labour movement by the bitterly hostile
ultra-left. Had the CP recognized the existence and scope of the
popular movement and acted accordingly, it might just have gained
sufficient momentum to force its reluctant allies on the old left into
line. One cannot say much more than this, for the chances of
overthrowing Gaullism, though real for a few days, never amounted
to more than a reasonable possibility. As it was it condemned itself,
during those crucial days of 27 to 29 May, to waiting and issuing
appeals. But at such times waiting is fatal. Those who lose the
initiative lose the game.

The chances of overthrowing the regime were diminished not only
by the failure of the communists, but by the character of the mass

movement. It had no political aims itself, though it used political phraseology. Without profound social and cultural discontents, ready to emerge at a relatively slight impetus, there can be no major social revolutions. But without a certain concentration on specific targets, however peripheral to their main purpose, the force of such revolutionary energies is dispersed. A given political or economic crisis, a given situation, may provide such precise enemies and objectives automatically: a war which must be ended, a foreign occupier who must be expelled, a crack in the political structure imposing specific and limited options, such as whether or not to support the Spanish government of 1936 against the generals' insurrection. The French situation provided no such automatic targets of concentration.

On the contrary, the very profundity of the critique of society implied or formulated by the popular movement left it without specific targets. Its enemy was 'the system'. To quote Touraine: 'The enemy is no longer a person of a social category, the monarch or the bourgeoisie. He is the totality of the depersonalized, "rationalized", bureaucratized modes of action of socio-economic power ...' The enemy is by definition faceless, not even a thing or an institution, but a programme of human relations, a process of depersonalization; not exploitation, which implies exploiters, but alienation. It is typical that most of the students themselves (unlike the less revolutionary workers) were not bothered about de Gaulle, except insofar as the real objective, society, was obscured by the purely political phenomenon of Gaullism. The popular movement was therefore either sub-political or anti-political. In the long run this does not diminish its historic importance or influence. In the short run it was fatal. As Touraine says, May 1968 is less important even in the history of revolutions than the Paris Commune. It proved not that revolutions can succeed in Western countries today, but only that they can break out.

Several of the books about the May events may be briefly dismissed. However, Alain Touraine's book is in a class apart.[1] The author is an industrial sociologist of Marxist provenance, the teacher of Daniel Cohn-Bendit at Nanterre, the original flashpoint of the student revolt; he was deeply involved in its early stages. His analysis reflects all this to some extent. Its value lies not so much in its originality – where so much has been written, most ideas have already been suggested and contested somewhere – as in the author's lucidity and historical sense, his lack of illusions, his knowledge of labour movements, as well as the incidental contribution of his having first-hand experience. He has, for instance, written the best analysis of the general strike, a grossly under-reported and under-analysed phenomenon when compared to the quantity of literature about the Latin Quarter. (We know practically nothing of what happened in all those plants and offices, which, after all, produced ten million strikers, most of whom were out of contact with students and reporters.) For foreign readers he has the additional advantage of first-hand acquaintance with other parts of the world, notably the United States and Latin America, which helps to correct the inborn provincialism of the French.

Touraine's argument is elaborate and complex, but a few of the points may be noted. What is happening today is the 'great mutation' from an older bourgeois to a new technocratic society, and this, as the May movement shows, creates conflict and dissidence not only at its margins but at its centre. The dividing line of 'class struggle' it reveals runs down the middle of the 'middle classes', between the 'techno-bureaucrats' on the one side and the 'professionals' on the other side. The latter, though in no sense obvious victims of oppression, represent in the modern technological economy something like the elite of skilled labour in an earlier industrial epoch, and for analogous reasons crystallize the new phase of class consciousness:

The main actor in the May movement was not the working class but the totality of those whom we may call the professionals ... and among them the most active were those most independent of the great organizations for which, directly or indirectly, such people work: students, radio and television people, technicians in planning offices, research workers in both the private and public sector, teachers, etc.

They and not the old working-class collectivities of miners, longshoremen, railwaymen, gave the general strike its specific character. Its core incidentally lay in the new industries: the automotive–electronic–chemical complex.

According to Touraine, a new social movement suited to the new economy is emerging, but it is a curiously contradictory one. In one sense it is a primitive rebellion of men who depend on older experiences to cope with a new situation. It may produce a revival of patterns of militancy or, among the new recruits to the social movement who have no such militant experience, something analogous to populist movements in underdeveloped countries, or more precisely to the labour movement of the early nineteenth century. Such a movement is important not for the fight it is now carrying on along old political lines, but for what it reveals of the future: for its vision rather than its necessarily feeble achievement. For the strength of that vision, the 'utopian communism' which it created in 1968 as the young proletariat created it before 1848, depends upon its practical impotence. On the other hand this social movement also includes or implies an up-to-date kind of reformism, a force which may serve to modify rigid and obsolescent structures of society – the educational system, industrial relations, management, government. The future dilemmas of revolutionaries lie here.

Was this new social movement 'revolutionary' in May – apart from its 'revolutionary' formulation of a 'counter-utopia' of libertarian communism to meet the 'dominant utopia' of the academic sociologists and political scientists? In France, Touraine argues, the new movement produced a genuine revolutionary crisis, though one unlikely to achieve revolution, because, for historical reasons, the social struggle, politics and a 'cultural revolution' against all forms of manipulation and integration of individual behaviour were combined. There can be no social movement today which does not combine these three elements, because of the 'progressive disappearance of the separation between state and civil society'. But at the same time this makes the concentration of the struggle, and the development of effective devices for action, such as parties of the bolshevik type, increasingly difficult.

In the United States, by contrast – perhaps because of the absence of state centralization or a tradition of proletarian revolution to focus it – there has been no such combination of forces. The phenomena of cultural revolt, which are symptomatic rather than operational, are the most visible. 'While in France', Touraine writes, 'the social struggle was at the centre of the movement and the cultural revolt was, one might almost say, a byproduct of a crisis of social change, in the United States cultural revolt is central.' This is a symptom of weakness.

Touraine's purpose is not so much to make judgments or prophecies – and insofar as he does so he will be criticized – as to establish that the May movement was neither an episode nor a simple continuation of older social movements. It demonstrated that 'a new period in social history' is beginning or has begun, but also that the analysis of its character cannot be derived from words of the revolutionaries of May themselves. He is probably right on both counts.

CHAPTER 16

The Rules of Violence

At first sight the present chapter, written in 1969, seems out of date. It is simply no longer true that 'most [people], unless they deliberately seek it out, can pass their adult lives without direct experience' of violence, even if we leave Northern Ireland to one side. The ever-rising flood of violence on page and screen reports reality. Yet my essay anticipated these developments, and for this reason its call for rules and conventions against the descent into barbarism remains relevant. The paper was originally published in New Society *in 1969.*

Of all the vogue words of the late 1960s, 'violence' is very nearly the trendiest and the most meaningless. Everybody talks about it, nobody thinks about it. As the just-published report of the US National Commission of the Causes and Prevention of Violence points out, the *International Encyclopedia of the Social Sciences*, published 1968, contains no entry under this heading.

Both the vogue and the vagueness are significant. For most of the people likely to read books with such titles as *The Age of Violence* (as like as not about symbolist poetry) or *Children of Violence* (which is about physically rather tranquil lives) are aware of the world's violence, but their relation to it is unprecedented and enigmatic. Most of them, unless they deliberately seek it out, can pass their adult lives without direct experience of 'behavior designed to inflict physical injury on people or damage to property' (to use the American commission's definition), or even with 'force' defined as 'the actual or threatened use of violence to compel others to do what they might not otherwise do'.

Physical violence normally impinges on them only in one direct and three indirect ways. Directly, it is omnipresent in the form of the traffic accident – casual, unintended, unpredictable and uncontrollable by most of its victims, and about the only peacetime contingency which is likely to bring most people working in homes and offices into actual contact with bleeding or mangled bodies. Indirectly, it is omnipresent in the mass media and entertainment. Probably no day passes in which most viewers and readers do not encounter the image of a corpse, that rarest of sights in real British life. Even more remotely, we are aware both of the existence in our time of vast, concretely unimaginable mass destruction for which convenient symbols are found ('the bomb', 'Auschwitz' and suchlike), and also of the sectors and situations of society in which physical violence is common and, probably increasing. Tranquillity and violence coexist.

These are curiously unreal experiences, and we therefore find it very difficult to make sense of violence as a historical or social phenomenon, as is shown by the extraordinary devaluation of such terms as 'aggression' in popular psycho-sociological small talk, or of the word 'genocide' in politics. The prevailing ideas of liberalism do not make it any easier, since they assume an entirely unreal dichotomy between 'violence' or 'physical force' (bad and backward) and 'non-violence' or 'moral force' (good and the child of progress). Of course one sympathizes with this, as with other pedagogic simplifications, insofar as it discourages people knocking one another over the head, the avoidance of which all sane and civilized persons approve. Yet as with that other product of liberal morality, the proposition that 'force never solves anything', there comes a point where the encouragement of the good becomes incompatible with understanding reality – that is, with providing the foundations for encouraging the good.

For the point to grasp about violence, as a social phenomenon, is that it exists only in the plural. There are actions of differing degrees of violence which imply different qualities of violence. All peasant movements are manifestations of sheer physical force, but some are unusually chary of spilling blood, while others develop into massacres, because their character and objects differ. The English farm-labourers of the early nineteenth century regarded violence against property as legitimate, moderate violence against persons as justifiable under certain circumstances, but systematically refrained from killing; yet under different circumstances (such as affrays between poachers and gamekeepers) the same men did not hesitate to fight to kill. It is quite useless, except as a legal excuse for repression or a debating point about 'never yielding to force', to treat these various types and degrees of violent action as essentially indistinguishable. Again, actions of the same degree of violence may differ sharply in their legitimacy or justification, at least in the minds of public opinion. The great Calabrian brigand Musolino, when asked to define the word 'bad' or 'evil,' said it meant 'killing Christians without a very deep reason'.

Genuinely violent societies are always and acutely aware of these 'rules', just because private violence is essential to their everyday functioning, though we may not be so aware of them, because the normal amount of bloodshed in such societies may seem to us to be so intolerably high. Where, as in the Philippines, the fatal casualties in every election campaign are counted in hundreds, it seems hardly relevant that, by Filipino standards, some of them are more open to condemnation than others. Yet there *are* rules. In the highlands of Sardinia they constitute an actual code of customary law, which has been formally described in legal terms by outside observers.[1] For instance, the theft of a goat is not an 'offence' unless the goat's milk is used by the family of the thieves, or there is a clear intent to 'offend' or spite the victim. In this case revenge is progressively more serious, up to death.

However binding the obligation to kill, members of feuding families engaged in mutual massacre will be genuinely appalled if by some mischance a bystander or outsider is killed. The situations in which violence occurs and the nature of that violence tend to be clearly denied at least in theory, as in the proverbial Irishman's question: 'Is this a private fight or can anyone join in?' So the actual risk to outsiders, though no doubt higher than in our societies, is calculable. Probably the only uncontrolled applications of force are those of social superiors to social inferiors (who have, almost by definition, no rights against them) and even here there are probably some rules.

As a matter of fact some such rules of violence are still familiar to us. Why for instance do abolitionists, who presumably believe in the undesirability of all executions, base so much of their campaigning on the argument that the death penalty sometimes kills innocent people? Because for most of us, including probably most abolitionists, the killing of the 'innocent' evokes a qualitatively different response from that of the 'guilty'.

One of the major dangers of societies in which direct violence no longer plays much part in regulating the everyday relations between peoples and groups, or in which violence has become depersonalized, is that they lose the sense of such distinctions. In doing so they also dismantle certain social mechanisms for controlling the use of physical force. This did not matter so much in the days when traditional kinds of violence in social relations, or at least the more dangerous among them, were diminishing visibly and fast. But today they may be once more on the increase, while new forms of social violence are becoming more important.

Older forms of violence may be increasing because the established systems of maintaining public order, elaborated in the liberal era, are increasingly strained, and such forms of political violence as direct physical action and terrorism are more common than in the past. The nervousness and disarray of the public authorities, the revival of private-enterprise security guards and neo-vigilante movements, are evidence enough. In one respect they have already led to a certain rediscovery of controlled violence, as in the return by so many police forces to a curious medievalism – helmets, shields, armour and all – and the developments of various temporarily disabling gases, rubber bullets and so on, all of which reflect the sensible view that there are degrees of necessary or desirable violence within a society, a view which the ancient common law of England has never abandoned.[2] On the other hand the public authorities themselves have become accustomed to use certain horrifying forms of violence, notably torture, which were regarded until a few decades ago as barbaric, and entirely unsuitable to civilized societies, while 'respectable' public opinion calls hysterically for indiscriminate terror.

This is part of a new *kind* of violence which is today emerging. Most traditional violence (including the revived types) assumes that physical force must be used insofar as no other methods are available or effective, and consequently that violent actions normally have a specific and identifiable purpose, the use of force being proportionate to that purpose. But a good deal of contemporary private violence can afford to be and is non-operational, and public violence is consequently tempted into indiscriminate action.

Private violence does not have to or cannot achieve very much against the really big and institutionalized wielders of force, whether or not these hold their violence in reserve. Where it occurs it therefore tends to turn from action into a substitute for action. The badges and iron crosses of the Nazi army had a practical purpose, though one of which we do not approve. The same symbols on the Hell's Angels and similar groups merely have a motive: the desire of otherwise weak and helpless young men to compensate for their frustration by acts and symbols of violence. Some nominally political forms of violence (such as 'trashing' or some neo-anarchist bombing) are similarly irrational, since under most circumstances their political effect is either negligible or more usually counter-productive.

Blind lashings-out are not necessarily more dangerous to life and limb (statistically speaking) than the violence of traditionally 'lawless' societies, though probably they do more damage to things, or rather to the companies which insure them. On the other hand such acts are, perhaps rightly, more frightening, because they are both more random and cruel, inasmuch as this kind of violence is its own reward. As the Moors murder case showed, the terrible thing about dreams of Nazi jackboots, which flicker through various Western underworlds and subcultures today, is not simply that they hark back to Himmler and Eichmann, the bureaucrats of an apparatus whose purposes happened to be insane. It is that for the disoriented fringe, for the weak and helpless poor, violence and cruelty – sometimes in the most socially ineffective and personalized sexual form – are the surrogate for private success and social power.

What is scarifying about modern American big cities is the combination of revived old and emerging new violence in situations of social tension and breakdown. And these are the situations with which the conventional wisdom of liberal ideas are quite incapable of coping, even conceptually; hence the tendency to relapse into an instinctive conservative reaction, which is little more than the mirror image of the disorder it seeks to control. To take the simplest example. Liberal toleration and freedom of expression help to saturate the atmosphere with those images of blood and torture which are so incompatible with the liberal ideal of a society based on consent and moral force.[3]

We are probably once again moving into an era of violence within societies, which must not be confused with the growing destructiveness of conflicts between societies. We had therefore better understand the social uses of violence, learn once again to distinguish between different types of violent activity, and above all construct or reconstruct systematic rules for it. Nothing is more difficult for people brought up in a liberal culture, with its belief that all violence is worse than non-violence, other things being equal (which they are not). Of course it is, but unfortunately such an abstract moral generalization gives no guidance to the practical problems of violence in our society. What was once a useful principle of social amelioration ('settle conflicts peacefully rather than by fighting', 'self-respect does not require bloodshed', and so on) turns into mere rhetoric and counter-rhetoric. It leaves the growing area of human life in which violence takes place without any rules and, paradoxically, without even any practically applicable moral principles, as witness the universal renascence of torture by the forces of the state. The abolition of torture was one of the relatively few achievements of liberalism which can be praised without any qualification, yet today it is once again almost universally practised and condoned by governments, and propagated by the mass media.

Those who believe that all violence is bad in principle can make no systematic distinction between different kinds of violence in practice, or recognize their effects both on those who suffer and on those

227

who inflict it. They are merely likely to produce, by reaction, men and women who consider all violence good, whether from a conservative or a revolutionary point of view, that is to say who recognize the subjective psychological relief provided by violence without any reference to its effectiveness. In this respect the reactionaries who call for the return of indiscriminate shooting, flogging and execution are similar to those whose sentiments have been systematized by Fanon and others, and for whom action with gun or bomb is *ipso facto* preferable to non-violent action.[4] Liberalism makes no distinction between the teaching of the milder forms of judo and the potentially more murderous forms of karate, whereas Japanese tradition is perfectly aware that these are intended to be learned only by those who have sufficient judgment and moral training to use their power to kill responsibly.

There are signs that such distinctions are once again being slowly and empirically learned, but in a general atmosphere of disorientation and hysteria which makes the rational and limited use of violence difficult. It is time that we put this process of learning on a more systematic basis by understanding the social uses of violence. We may think that all violence is worse than non-violence, other things being equal. But the worst kind is the violence which gets out of anyone's control.

CHAPTER 17

Revolution and Sex

This chapter on the contemporary western 'cultural revolution' supplements chapter 15, which deals primarily with the politics of 1968. Like chapter 16 it was published in 1969 in New Society under the editorship of Paul Barker, who made this journal into perhaps the most brilliant weekly of its day.

The late Che Guevara would have been very surprised and acutely irritated by the discovery that his picture is now on the cover of *Evergreen Review*, his personality the subject of an article in *Vogue* and his name the ostensible excuse for some homosexual exhibitionism in a New York theatre (see *Observer*, 8 May 1969). We can leave *Vogue* aside. Its business is to tell women what it is fashionable to wear, to know and to talk about; its interest in Che Guevara has no more political implications than that of the editor of *Who's Who*. The other two jokes, however, reflect a widespread belief that there is some sort of connection between social revolutionary movements and permissiveness in public sexual or other personal behaviour. It is about time someone pointed out that there are no good grounds for this belief.

In the first place, it ought now to be evident that conventions about what sexual behaviour is permissible in public have no specific connection with systems of political rule or social and economic exploitation. (An exception is the rule of men over women and the exploitation of women and the exploitation of women by men which, at a guess, imply more or less strict limitations on the public behaviour of the inferior sex.) Sexual 'liberation' has only indirect relations with any other kind of liberation. Systems of class rule and exploitation may impose strict conventions of personal (for example, sexual) behaviour in public or private or they may not. Hindu society was not in any sense more free or egalitarian than the Welsh nonconformist community, because the one used temples to demonstrate a vast variety of sexual activities in the most tempting manner, whereas the other imposed rigid restrictions on its members, at any rate in theory. All we can deduce from this particular cultural difference is that pious Hindus who wanted to vary their sexual routine could learn to do so much more easily than pious Welshmen.

Indeed, if a rough generalization about the relation between class rule and sexual freedom is possible, it is that rulers find it convenient to encourage sexual permissiveness or laxity among their subjects if only to keep their minds off their subjection. Nobody ever imposed sexual puritanism on slaves; quite the contrary. The sort of societies in which the poor are strictly kept in their place are quite familiar with regular institutionalized mass outbursts of free sex, such as carnivals. In fact, since sex is the cheapest form of enjoyment as well as the most intense (as the Neapolitans say, bed is the poor man's grand opera), it is politically very advantageous, other things being equal, to get them to practise it as much as possible.

In other words, there is no necessary connection between social or political censorship and moral censorship, though it is often assumed that there is. To demand the transfer of some kinds of behaviour from the impermissible to the publicly permitted is a political act only if it implies changing political relations. Winning the right for white and black to make love in South Africa would be a political act, not because it widens the range of what is sexually allowed but because it attacks racial subjection. Winning the right to publish *Lady Chatterley* has no such implications, though it may be welcomed on other grounds.

This should be abundantly clear from our own experience. In the 1960s and 1970s the official or conventional prohibitions on what can be said, heard, done and shown about sex in public – or for that matter in private – were virtually abolished in several Western countries. The belief that a narrow sexual morality is an essential bulwark of the capitalist system is no longer tenable. Nor, indeed, is the belief that the fight against such a morality is very urgent. There are still a few outdated crusaders who may think of themselves as storming a puritan fortress, but in fact its walls have been virtually razed.

No doubt there are still things that cannot be printed or shown but they are progressively harder to find and to get indignant about. The abolition of censorship is a one-dimensional activity, like the movement of women's necklines and skirts, and if that movement goes on too long in a single direction, the returns in revolutionary satisfaction of the crusaders diminish sharply. The right of actors to fuck each other on stage is palpably a less important advance even of personal liberation than the right of Victorian girls to ride bicycles was. It is today becoming quite hard even to mobilize those prosecutions of obscenity on which publishers and producers have so long relied for free publicity.

For practical purposes the battle for public sex has been won. Has this brought social revolution any nearer, or indeed any change outside the bed, the printed page and public entertainment (which may or may not be desirable)? There is no sign of it. All it has obviously brought is a lot more public sex in an otherwise unchanged social order.

But though there is no intrinsic connection between sexual permissiveness and social organization, there is, I am bound to note with a little regret, a persistent affinity between revolution and puritanism. I can think of no well-established organized revolutionary movement or regime which has not developed marked puritanical tendencies: including Marxist ones, whose founders' doctrine was quite unpuritanical (or in Engels' case actively anti-puritanical); including those in countries like Cuba, whose native tradition is the opposite of puritan; including the most officially anarchist–libertarian ones. Anyone who believes that the morality of the old anarchist militants was free and easy does not know what he or she is talking about. Free love (in which they believed passionately) meant no drink, no drugs and monogamy without a formal marriage.

The libertarian, or more exactly antinomian, component of revolutionary movements, though sometimes strong and even dominant at the actual moment of liberation, has never been able to resist the puritan. The Robespierres always win out over the Dantons. Those revolutionaries for whom sexual, or for that matter cultural, libertarianism are really central issues of the revolution are sooner or later edged aside by it. Wilhelm Reich, the apostle of the orgasm, did indeed start out, as the new left reminds us, as a revolutionary Marxist-cum-Freudian and a very able one, to judge by his *Mass Psychology of Fascism* (which was subtitled *The Sexual Economy of Political Reaction and Proletarian Sexual Policy*). But can we be really surprised that such a man ended by concentrating his interest on orgasm rather than organization? Neither Stalinists nor Trotskyites felt any enthusiasm for the revolutionary surrealists who hammered at their gates asking to be admitted. Those who survived in politics did not do so as surrealists.

Why this is so is an important and obscure question, which cannot be answered here. Whether it is necessarily so is an even more important question – at all events for revolutionaries who think the official puritanism of revolutionary regimes excessive and often beside the point. But that the great revolutions of our century have not been devoted to sexual permissiveness can hardly be denied. They have advanced sexual freedom (and fundamentally) not by abolishing sexual prohibitions, but by a major act of social emancipation: the liberation of women from their oppression. And that revolutionary movements have found personal libertarianism a nuisance is also beyond question. Among the rebellious young, those closest to the spirit and ambitions of old-fashioned social revolution also tend to be the most hostile to the taking of drugs, advertised indiscriminate sex, or other styles and symbols of personal dissidence: the Maoists, Trotskyites and communists. The reasons given are often that 'the workers' neither understand nor sympathize with such behaviour. Whether or not this is so, it can hardly be denied that it consumes time and energy and is hardly compatible with organization and efficiency.

The whole business is really part of a much wider question: What is the role in revolution or any social change of that cultural rebellion which is today so visible a part of the new left, and in certain countries such as the United States the predominant aspect of it? There is no great social revolution which is not combined, at least peripherally, with such cultural dissidence. Perhaps today in the West, where 'alienation' rather than poverty is the crucial motive force of rebellion, no movement which does not also attack the system of personal relations and private satisfactions can be revolutionary. But, taken by themselves, cultural revolt and cultural dissidence are symptoms, not revolutionary forces. Politically they are not very important.

The Russian Revolution of 1917 reduced the contemporary avant-garde and cultural rebels, many of whom sympathized with it, to their proper social and political proportions. When the French went on general strike in May 1968, the happenings in the Odeon Theatre and those splendid graffiti ('It is forbidden to forbid', 'When I make revolution it makes me feel like making love', and so on) could be seen to be forms of minor literature and theatre, marginal to the main events. The more prominent such phenomena are, the more confident can we be that the big things are not happening. Shocking the bourgeois is, alas, easier than overthrowing him.

CHAPTER 18

Epitaph for a Villain:
Roy Cohn

This footnote to the culture of the Cold War USA was published on 28 October 1989. It was written, in New York, for the series 'Heroes and Villains' published in The Independent Magazine *in the early and hopeful years of that paper.*

Few villains start their career as international jokes, but this happened to my choice, in his days as a young witch-hunter. Well, it was not quite the start. Roy Cohn (1927–86) had already dodged military service, tried to bribe his professor Lionel Trilling, hounded the eminent expert on central Asia, Owen Lattimore, and helped to sentence the Rosenbergs to death as Russian spies, before he and his partner David Schine, two young men in their twenties who sounded like a bad vaudeville act, visited Europe in 1953 to investigate the Communist World Conspiracy for Senator McCarthy. The parts of the Conspiracy that interested them were the failure of US Information Service libraries abroad to eliminate the works of Dashiell Hammett, and also the insufficient anti-communism of the BBC.

Cohn and Schine provided a wonderful excuse for demonstrating European anti-McCarthyism, not to mention cultural snobbery, and were murdered by the press wherever they went. Faced with some sixty reporters at Heathrow, they changed plans and headed for home. After this, most Europeans forgot about them.

However, if Schine did not survive his brief notoriety – he is still alive somewhere – Roy Cohn resurfaced as a well-connected New York shyster lawyer living, in the words of his biographer, 'in a matrix of crime and unethical conduct'. In the 1970s he became a major New York 'in' celebrity, in the 1980s a friend of the Reagans (what else?). Even old liberals became reconciled to a man who could get them into the cocaine paradise of the Studio 54 nightclub, in which he had an interest. He was not just famous for being famous in the Warhol manner, but famous as an influential and, above all, a dangerous politico-criminal fixer, deal-maker and extortionist. When in 1986, dying of Aids (which he denied having), he was finally expelled from the New York bar whose ethics, flexible as they were, he had managed to overstrain, there was no obituary politeness, let alone sympathy. Even Big Apple atheists, as one of them told me, felt that divine justice had caught up with Cohn.

Real villains are hard to find, but Roy Cohn was probably a genuine prince of darkness. He was brought up by a caricature Jewish momma in whose eyes, of course, he could do no wrong. He made his legal and political career in a milieu where money and power override rules and law – indeed where the ability to get, and get away with, what lesser citizens cannot, is what proves membership of an elite. What made Cohn immoral rather than amoral was a certain built-in contrariness, Mephistopheles' 'spirit that always says no'. A life-long Democrat, he bragged about shafting his party's 1972 presidential campaign. A Jew, he ran with the anti-semites; a spectacularly visible cruising gay, he took his boyfriends to meetings where he campaigned against homosexual rights. Even his anti-communism, which, unlike Senator McCarthy's, seems to have been genuine, fits the pattern, since his New York Jewish Roosevelt-liberal milieu abhorred intolerance and witch-hunts.

As a lawyer ('I don't care what the law is, tell me who the judge is') he visibly preferred shady clients and mobsters, and not only found it useful but enjoyed suggesting that he could get people killed. More to the point, because it eventually sank him, he flouted not only routine obligations but the unspoken obligations of professionalism. He bilked not only tradesmen, but the ghostwriter of his books – anyone who could, he thought, do him no harm. He betrayed his clients without hesitation. In the decades when it was child's play for a bright and connected lawyer to make millions legally in the Big Apple, he was a crook because he liked to be.

He had neither convictions nor even ambitions. The great experiences of his life-time passed him by: the War, civil rights, Vietnam, Israel and the cause of minorities. He was tempted neither by office nor by the pure thrill of capital accumulation which moved so many of the men with whom he consorted, one-dimensional Fausts to whom he played Mephisto the facilitator. He owned nothing, collected nothing, looked after nothing.

What did he really want, except getting his own way in all things, avoiding uncomfortable thoughts and enjoying power behind the scenes, the ability to do favours and to carry out threats, recognized by those who counted and in the media by which he always lived? It is too late to know. Apart from a few unrequited personal favours to friends and lovers, and an ability to entertain, he did good to none and brought ruin to many – not only to McCarthy's victims but, by his irresponsibility, to the senator himself. He died as he had lived, jumping the queue over other Aids victims. The best that can be said of him is that, born in any other country, he would not have become what he did. In no other country would he have received a presidential telegram in hospital ('Nancy and I are keeping you in our thoughts and prayers'). But when he died, even Reagan's White House kept shtum.

CHAPTER 19

The Caruso of Jazz

This essay originally appeared in the New York Review of Books *on 12 May 1988 as a review of* Sidney Bechet: The Wizard of Jazz *by John Chilton (New York, 1988) and* Jazz Odyssey: The Autobiography of Joe Darensbourg *as told to Peter Vacher (Baton Rouge, 1988).*

He was the first among the players of the barely baptized 'jazz' to be identified as 'an artist of genius'. Very few jazz musicians are as well known as Sidney Bechet, especially among people not particularly familiar with the music. No one has a voice more easily and immediately recognizable. Within months of his death in 1959 a statue of him was unveiled on the French Riviera and, thanks to the labours of his biographer, we now know that his face is on postage stamps of the republics of Chad and Gabon. The poet Philip Larkin wrote about him:

> On me your voice falls as they say love should
> Like an enormous yes.

Equally to the point, in the 1920s Bechet was admired by other musicians, including men of considerable discernment like Duke Ellington and Benny Carter. And small wonder. He was, after all, one of the first, if not the first, to turn the saxophone into a major jazz instrument.

Why is it, then, that the career of Sidney Joseph Bechet (1897–1959) is, or rather became, peripheral to the mainstream of jazz development? He was strategically placed, and had more than enough originality and talent to become a model and inspiration for other musicians, or a permanent model for those playing an instrument: like Louis Armstrong, Coleman Hawkins, Django Reinhardt, Charlie Parker, Charlie Christian, John Coltrane. Yet, while he had inspired Johnny Hodges of the Ellington band, his impact during his lifetime is otherwise hard to trace except on white Dixieland disciples. When white fans launched the Bechet vogue in the late 1930s, he was not even particularly well known among the musicians themselves.

John Chilton's book, one of those monuments of devoted and scholarly data-collection which jazz has so often inspired among its loyalists, probably provides as much material for understanding Bechet's isolation as we are now likely to get. It certainly replaces the romances that passed as Bechet's autobiography.[1] It will provide the indispensable basis for any subsequent exploration of an extra-ordinary life, which will sooner or later find its way on to film or television. For how many men can claim to have been expelled from both Britain and France (the former after an arrest for rape, the latter after a gunfight in Montmartre), to have had long affairs with both Bessie Smith and Josephine Baker and a long, passionate, if intermittent, relationship with Tallulah Bankhead, to have been the toast of Moscow in the mid-1920s after having taught the clarinet to the man who is supposed to be the original for James Bond's M? He also, later, played a couple of seasons at a communist summer camp in the Berkshires, oblivious to the warnings of Willie 'The Lion' Smith, who could not stand it for more than a week, on the ground that 'it was the most mixed-up camp I ever saw or heard about – the races, the sexes, and the religions were all mixed'.

Unlike most other jazz musicians of his generation, Sidney Bechet was essentially a loner and, in the opinions of those who had business with him, which almost invariably ended in acrimony, a man to handle with great care. At the more egomaniacal end of the entertainment business, where a number of jazz musicians are also to be found, those who have dealings with artists are inclined to regard them (privately) as monsters rather than human beings, but the critical consensus about the difficulties of life with Bechet goes well beyond the complaints of bookers and managers.

'He was *dangerous* if he thought you didn't like him,' observed Sammy Price, the Texan blues pianist, who came from a milieu where mere shortness of temper would not necessarily warrant this adjective. He could be a 'fiend' admits his biographer. 'A very difficult person to work with, self-centred and inconsiderate of others, and never happy to share a spotlight,' observed one of his many bookers. Even his admiring pupil Bob Wilber concedes that 'he could be evil and, it's not too strong a word, paranoic [sic]'. Others were constantly conspiring against him – on at least one occasion, he was convinced, by witchcraft, against which he took appropriate action by setting the Twenty-third Psalm to music. He was so worried that he did so without payment.

In short, as in Cocteau's joke about Victor Hugo, Sidney Bechet was pretty close to being a madman who imagined he was Sidney Bechet. In both cases the illusion was justified by the man's undeniably extraordinary talents. Moreover, in both cases illusion became reality. The French reopened the Pantheon for the dead Hugo and they put up a statue to the dead Bechet. Bechet took this for granted. 'My most durable memory', wrote a musician of a week's gig, 'is of seeing Sidney sitting backstage, as though he were a king on a throne. He received his loyal subjects, and there were quite a few, with imperious acknowledgments. Alfred Lion of Blue Note records came and feted Sidney with champagne, which he accepted with an egocentric but regal bow.'

These characteristics are probably enough to explain his musical isolation. By and large, in the structured and expensive forms of stage and screen entertainment the excesses of solipsism were (until the rise of rock-and-roll) kept under some control. And jazz is a democratic art, shaped by those who play together, which imposes limits on all participants: no skater, however brilliant, has as much scope for personal display in a hockey game as in figure skating.

But Bechet, while naturally recognizing the collective nature of his music, seems to have resented any version of jazz which did not either build the collective round his central and dominant voice, or at least provide him with a regular virtuoso showcase. Indeed, he switched from his original instrument, the clarinet, to the soprano saxophone, in which hardly anyone else specialized in his lifetime, most certainly because of its greater capacity to lead, or to impose itself on, an ensemble. Bechet could not stand trumpeters who took the lead which conventionally belonged to their instrument, especially not those like Louis Armstrong, who might have outshone him, and of whom he was acutely jealous. He worked best with good and even-tempered partners who did not compete for first place, like the trumpeters/cornetists Tommy Ladnier and Muggsy Spanier, with both of whom he produced ravishing records. In such cases he made adequate room for their solos. He was even more at ease with instruments that complemented his, such as the piano, as with Earl Hines in the famous 'Blues in Thirds'.

However, basically he had the instincts, but not the talents, of a commanding officer; or perhaps of the old-fashioned actor–manager who took it for granted that his shows were about *him*. That is why in later years he felt at ease with young, less talented and less experienced French musicians, for whom he was the honoured *sensei* or master, even when he cut out the solos of those who had eyes for the girls he fancied himself.

But Bill Coleman, the delicate expatriate trumpeter, was unfair to accuse Bechet of being 'only happy when he can bark orders at amateurs'. The most one can say is that he needed more control than he liked or usually got. His finest work was done in small groups of players who took each other's talent and, above all, professionalism for granted. He played some marvellous sides in 1949 with the bop drummer Kenny Clarke, though neither had much sympathy or feeling for the other's music. He was even better when he shared the basic ideas on format and procedure with his partners, as a former sideman recalled:

> Bechet and [the bass player Wellman] Braud arrived wearing big old coats and hats; I think Bechet had a beret on. They sat down opposite one another and exchanged pleasantries. It was like an ancient ritual between chieftains. Muggsy [Spanier] joined in whilst he was warming up – same sort of approach. Being used to the razzmatazz [of his swing-band preparations] I wondered what was going to happen: one, two, three, four, and wham! This music explodes all around me.

However, Bechet's isolation was not only personal but also geographical. Jazz is, among other things, diaspora music. Its history is part of the mass migration out of the Old South, and it is, for economic as well as often for psychological reasons, made by footloose people who spend a lot of time on the road. It would certainly not have become a national American music as early as it did if men with horns had not physically brought it into places where it had not previously been known. Joe Darensbourg's autobiography *Jazz Odyssey* illustrates this diffusion of New Orleans jazz excellently, and in doing so it throws light on the pioneer generation to which Bechet belongs. It takes its hero in the 1920s from Baton Rouge, via Los Angeles, Mississippi, Tennessee, St Louis and Harrisburg, Illinois back to the West Coast and up to the Pacific North-west which he helped to open up to jazz. In the history of this music, cities like Seattle, Portland and Spokane have hardly counted for much, but Darensbourg demonstrates that at least social historians of jazz should take the North-west seriously. ('Word spread round among musicians that you could make money in Seattle. It was a money town,' Darensbourg says.)

Nevertheless, most migratory jazzmen stayed in the US, which was, in any case, the place where the action was. Bechet belonged to the minority who from the start looked to the global market for black artists: women like Josephine Baker, who was discovered by Paris, men like the pianist Teddy Weatherford who, from the mid-1920s, operated mainly in the great Asian port cities like Shanghai and Calcutta; or the trumpeter Bill Coleman who lived mainly in

France from the early 1930s. Bechet himself spent only three years of the 1920s in the US (1922–5) and the rest in England, France, Germany, Russia and a number of lesser European countries, which explains both why he recorded much less in that decade than musicians of lesser talents, and why, when he returned to the US in 1931, younger players thought of him as passé, compared to influential sax players like Hawkins and Benny Carter. A great deal had happened to the fast-evolving music in the almost six years since he had left. Probably a lot of the younger musicians of the Swing Era continued to think of him as a strong but old-fashioned player, if they thought about him at all.

Indeed, Bechet's position was so marginal that he and Tommy Ladnier left full-time music to open a clothes-repair and cleaning shop in Harlem in 1933 (unsuccessfully, like all business projects of Bechet, who mistakenly saw himself as an entrepreneur), and as late as 1939 he considered quitting music again to open a hash house in Philadelphia. In short, the man who had been a major figure and influence in the early 1920s, at forty-two seemed an exhausted talent, an impression reinforced by his looking older than his years.

Admittedly he returned to the US at a bad time for jazz. It was not so much that the slump knocked the bottom out of the market for jazz records, which were hardly yet money-spinners for sidemen, as that hot jazz, somehow tied to the mood of the Roaring Twenties, fell victim to the depressed atmosphere as well as the money problems of the slump years. The shift of public taste away from the fast and loud and toward dreamland – it has not been much noted by jazz historians – was international in the early 1930s. German music critics observed it, mainly with satisfaction, between 1931 and 1933. Chilton demonstrates that it was equally marked in Harlem. In 1932 Rudy Vallee pulled in 2,800 customers a night in a leading ballroom, but Ellington only a quarter of that; Guy Lombardo 2,200, but Cab Calloway 500; Ben Bernie 2,000 but Louis Armstrong 350. Bechet was not the only player for whom the times were out of joint in the early 1930s, but it must have been particularly hard for a man so conscious of his gifts to lack both money and reputation among his peers.

What saved him was the strange and unexpected phenomenon of jazz antiquarianism in the form of the search for the true music of New Orleans by impassioned groups of young white fans for whom jazz was not only a music but also a symbol and a cause. The Dixieland revival, which grew out of this search, has been dismissed (in *The New Grove*) as 'the longest-lasting movement in jazz but ... the only one to have produced no music of value'.[2] However, if it had done no more than to recover Bechet for the main jazz tradition, it would have justified its existence.

Bechet had always attracted the musical cognoscenti. Ernest Ansermet wrote his universally quoted panegyric in 1919, when Edward J. Dent, the champion of Mozartian opera, also singled him out favourably from among the rest of the Southern Syncopated Orchestra, which he otherwise considered 'nightmare entertainment'. Ansermet's forgotten praise ('I wish to set down the name of this artist of genius; as for myself, I shall never forget it, it is Sidney Bechet') was given general circulation after 1938 when it was republished in the (French) *Le Jazz Hot* and the (British) *Melody Maker*.[3]

The small but select group of knowledgeable jazz lovers had no trouble in recognizing his quality, but few others listened to fugitive groups like the New Orleans Feetwarmers of 1932–3 and the half-dozen sides they recorded. After a market for jazz developed again in the mid-1930s these aficionados managed to get Bechet a few small-group sessions which for the first time brought him before the main jazz public and made his reputation: the 1937 tracks on the Variety label (initiated by Helen Oakley, supported by Bechet's old admirers Ellington and Hodges), the classic 1938 Bechet–Ladnier records organized by the French pioneer critic Hugues Panassié, and, of course, John Hammond and *New Masses*' famous 1938 Carnegie Hall concert 'From Spirituals to Swing'. These inspired the 1939 recordings of Bechet by a recent refugee jazz enthusiast from Berlin, Alfred Lion, which established the fortunes of his new Blue Note label as well as confirming those of Bechet.

While Bechet's Euro-American rescuers appreciated the New Orleans tradition – how could any jazz lover fail to do so? – and were always anxious to bring back unjustly forgotten artists, they were not New Orleans buffs. Even the Bechet–Ladnier sessions which, it has been claimed, 'had more to do with the Dixieland revival than any others' were distinguished for their artistry more than their authenticity. Yet behind them an obscure tide of nostalgia was rising, especially among young middle-class whites, for the pure, the beautiful, the only *true* music of jazz which had somehow been betrayed when Storyville was shut down and the players moved up the Mississippi, though the survivors of the 1920s doing their own thing in small groups were better than nothing, especially if they were black.

Dixieland or the New Orleans revival was essentially a non-musical phenomenon, though it was to enable vast numbers of amateurs to enjoy themselves playing 'Muskrat Ramble' and similar numbers. It belongs to cultural and intellectual history, which is why it deserves the serious investigation it has not yet received. It was a purely white movement, though naturally welcomed by ageing Creole musicians, especially those down on their luck. 'New Orleans' became a multiple myth and symbol: anti-commercial, anti-racist, proletarian–populist, New Deal radical, or just anti-respectable and anti-parental, depending on taste.

In the US and other English-speaking countries, its ideological centre was unquestionably located on the borders between the New Deal and the Communist Party, though for most of the young fans it was probably just something that spoke straight to even uninformed hearts. The internationally influential book *Jazzmen* of 1939, the first American history of the music based on research, which established the 'up the river from Storyville' version in its purest form, was co-edited by a music critic on the *Daily Worker*. Revivalism linked the cause of the blacks and the (minority) taste for jazz with folk song and folk music, ancient and modern, which were and long remained the central pillars of the left-wing subculture that merged into the New Deal culture.

So Bechet, 'a man of catholic musical tastes', found that he 'had somehow been swept into the dixieland world'. For him Dixieland was in the first instance the key to recognition. The 1940 recordings on which he shared the bill with Louis Armstrong were the proof that he had won it, and (granting his late restart) with remarkable speed. From then on no shortlist of the 'jazz greats' would ever leave him out. In the second instance, the Dixieland movement gave him a licence to go on doing what he had done all along, since he had told Ansermet in 1919 that he followed 'his own way', without taking much notice of others. His age made him an undeniable founding father of New Orleans jazz, and his style was therefore *ipso facto* beyond criticism. In fact, Bechet felt quite at home within the limited Dixieland format, for he was primarily a linear improviser and melodist, and not much interested in harmonic games as such. In any case he was only too pleased that his strong, fluent, looping and pulsating ropes of beautiful sound ('a jugful of golden honey' Armstrong called his tone) were easily accessible even to the non-musical, except for those – they always existed – who found his striking vibrato intolerable. He was not, and did not have to be, a purist, but neither did he have to keep up with the times; this did not stop him from playing superbly with any first-rate musician irrespective of style.

How far did Dixieland provide him with a living, the question that was undoubtedly uppermost in his mind? It is certain that he relied heavily on the public for the rediscovered small-group jazz of the

1920s players, which found a Greenwich Village home at Nick's and its public-relations man in Eddie Condon. He clearly also relied on the left-wing connections for gigs, though it is not clear how far this was purely commercial. (Still, in spite of suggestions of communist sympathies, and his undoubted fond memories of Russia, it is hard to see Bechet as a political figure, still less a red among black jazz players.) As for the New Orleans revival, he recognized its potential for a certified charter member of the Crescent City. Whatever the motives, his 1945 partnership with Bunk Johnson, an ancient trumpeter disinterred by the purists and turned into an icon of authenticity, showed the fans where he stood. Like earlier partnerships, this one also ended in bad feelings.

Yet none of these jobs provided him with an adequate income at the level Bechet thought appropriate to his standing, though by the late 1940s he now had reasonable record royalties. What finally solved his problems was the invitation to France in 1949. In that country, where jazz had enormous intellectual and cultural prestige and Resistance associations, he discovered what he had always dreamed of – a vast public for whom the man with a French name and sponsored by French critics was a certified genius of jazz, and a community of young fan-musicians whose hearts beat faster at the very thought that he would honour them by stepping into their cellars. France became his permanent home. He became a cultural mascot as Josephine Baker had been. It did his music little good, but his finances no harm at all. It removed him from the personal and entrepreneurial frictions that had always complicated his life in the US. He lived out his life as a happy expatriate.

The man who emerges from Chilton's admirable researches was both a typical product of New Orleans and a very odd character. As a member of the Creoles of colour, members of the (Francophone) free mulatto artisan and lower-middle class, pressed back toward the blacks by post-Civil War segregation, he acquired the musical and professional skills of his community. Throughout his life he could do tailoring and cook, although he refused to be apprenticed to a craftsman's trade as most Creole players were. But then he also, and quite uncharacteristically, refused to learn to read music, initially no doubt because it seemed unnecessary for so brilliant a natural musician, later out of rebellion, in the end perhaps out of defensive pride.

He shared the New Orleans Creole social courtesy, their taste for dressing respectably, their justified pride in the city's musical tradition, and perhaps the unusual lack of interest in race relations that seems to have been characteristic of New Orleans musicians. From Joe

Darensbourg's autobiography it is impossible to discover whether he was white or black. Bechet himself frequently said that he was more interested in a man's musical talent than in the colour of his skin and, apropos of Mezz Mezzrow, a white champion of black superiority, that 'race does not matter – it is hitting the notes right that counts'.

And perhaps the intense interest in classical music that he had a chance to develop in Moscow – on free days he would regularly go to symphony concerts before hitting the nightclubs – was based on the pre-1914 musical culture which lower-middle-class Louisiana Creole families shared with James Joyce's Dublin equivalents. Caruso, from whom Bechet claimed to derive his vibrato, was part of both. At all events Bechet, a great man for the *espressivo*, put a quote from *Pagliacci* into a solo as readily as he put Beethoven's picture on his wall.

And yet there can be no denying that he was a man who stood at a fairly acute angle to his universe. Jazz players are more tolerant of the vagaries of human behaviour than any other group of people, but while nobody who played with him failed to admire his marvellous musicianship, the general view about Bechet from the bandstands was distinctly unenthusiastic, whether he was with or without the dog and the knife that often accompanied him. Even his admirer Ellington, who seriously considered bringing him into the band again in 1932, in the end chose not to. He must plainly have been a hard man to get along with for any length of time, although with women he found it easier to maintain his soft-spoken and courteous New Orleans charm.

He remains an extraordinary figure in jazz: a role-player who was not good at choosing his roles, a man often living in a world of fantasy, a wayfaring stranger who rode into and out of town, nowhere at home except on the throne he thought of as his right, loyal to nobody except himself; but he was an astonishing, unforgettable artist, utterly original in spite of remaining firmly within an obsolescent tradition. After his death he acquired a reputation even among the modernists, as shown by the spread of the soprano saxophone among them. It had been virtually Bechet's monopoly. Coltrane took to it from 1961. He became a posthumous classic.

All the same, if it were not for the handful of jazz intellectuals who rescued him, the small jazz labels of the late 1930s, the white kids in basement clubs, the French who made his dreams come true, what would have happened to him? He would not have fitted into the big swing bands. He would have been around, but why should younger musicians have made space for an old man with a voice from the past who seemed to take no interest in new ideas, and had the reputation of being a self-centred, truculent and tightfisted son of a bitch? Perhaps after his death some musicians might, by sheer accident, have discovered the forgotten six sides from 1932 and, listening to that astonishing 'Maple Leaf Rag', have felt what Coltrane said apropos of the same session: 'Did all of those old guys swing like that?' No, but Bechet did.

Thanks to middle-class whites we do not have to recover a handful of old 78s from beyond the grave. We were lucky to recover a classic while he was still alive. There is some justification for the jazz fans after all, even the ones who don't know much about jazz. When they heard it, they had no trouble recognizing the eloquence, the lyrical passion, the swinging joy and the blues that came out of Bechet's horn whenever he blew into it. Fans do not always fall in love with the best in the arts, but this time they did.

CHAPTER 20

Count Basie

This essay originally appeared in the New York Review of Books *on 16 January 1986, as a review of* Good Morning Blues: The Autobiography of Count Basie *as told to Albert Murray (New York, 1986) and* The World of Count Basie *by Stanley Dance New York, 1985).*

Some time in the 1950s American popular music committed parricide. Rock murdered jazz. Count Basie describes a moment of the murder in his autobiography. There was:

> a heck of a thing going on at a theater down on Fourteenth Street somewhere, and we used to get down there at around eleven o'clock and you couldn't get near the place for the crowd ... I remember this and I also remember how things went. The first acts would go on, and the kids would all be jammed in there having a ball and applauding and whistling. Then when it came time for us to go on, just about all of them would get up and go outside and get their popcorn and ice cream and everything, and we just played our act to an almost empty house. Then when we finished our set they would all come back in. No kidding.
>
> So we would just go downstairs and play poker till it was time to go on again. That's the way it actually went. Those kids didn't care anything about jazz. Some of them would stay and come down front and stand and listen and try to hear it as long as they could, and we would try fast and slow, and it made no difference. That was not what they came to hear. To them we were just an intermission act. That's what that was. It didn't mean anything but just that. You had to face it.

If anyone wanted to turn *Good Morning Blues* into a play, this image of the ageing bandleader stoically accepting a deeply resented defeat might make a good curtain. But Basie's career continued for another thirty years, though his memoir rather races through them. He did not quite see the current resuscitation of jazz as the American classical music of the professional middle class and the dinner music of lower Manhattan Yuppie restaurants.

These last decades before he died in 1984 were not the most distinguished in the career of what was not the greatest big band in jazz – Basie himself constantly stresses the supremacy of Ellington – but was, in many ways, the quintessential expression of the populism of jazz; and jazz remains much the most serious musical contribution of the United States to world culture. Basie is a central figure both in the golden age of the music which coincided with the New Deal years and in the discovery of jazz, hitherto a music of unrespectable poor blacks and hipflask-swigging white dancers, as an art to be taken with the utmost seriousness, and a breeding ground of great artists. The discovery was largely the achievement of political radicals who devoted themselves passionately and selflessly to the joint cause of the blacks and their music, without, as Basie underlines, exploiting them.[1] In the debates about the history of the American left in the Roosevelt period that are now raging, this achievement in music of the reds and fellow travellers of the time has not been sufficiently appreciated.

Until it loses itself in the repetitive details of touring and personnel changes, *Good Morning Blues* is therefore of considerable interest to anyone who wishes to understand the evolution of one of the few twentieth-century arts that owe nothing to middle-class culture. And the original Basie band, recognized as the purest expression of big-band swing as soon as it roared out of Kansas City, owed less to the middle class and intellectuals than any other – except, of course, its discovery and training for fame.

It was not much of a 'reading band' at its best. In its heyday it used little except head-arrangements. 'I don't think we had over four or five sheets of music up there at that time,' Basie recalls. It was not a respectable band, even by jazz standards. The arranger Eddie Durham, used to the college men in the Lunceford band, found Basie's group too much for him. They 'didn't believe in going out with steady black people', in the words of Gene Ramey, whose sketch of the Kansas City atmosphere in Stanley Dance's invaluable collection of interviews, now republished, is one of the best:

They'd head straight for the pimps and prostitutes and hang out with them. Those people were like a great advertisement for Basie. They didn't dig Andy Kirk. They said he was too uppity. But Basie was down there, lying in the gutter, getting drunk with them. He'd have patches in his pants and everything. All of his band was like that.

This is not the image stressed in *Good Morning Blues*, a notably reticent work in many ways, though in fact the attraction of the milieu of gambling, good times, women and, not least, whisky constantly shines through the cracks in the autobiographical façade of the elder jazz statesman. His book brings out, perhaps more clearly than any other memoir, both how attractive and how important to the development of the music was that floating, nomadic community of professional black musicians, living on the self-contained and self-sufficient little islands of the popular entertainers and other night people – a street or two where the action was, rooming houses, bars, clubs – which were scattered like a Micronesian archipelago across the US.

For that is where players found a milieu that accepted the overriding importance of professionalism, of getting the music right, of the strange marriage between group co-operation and ferocious competitive testing of individuals, which is analogous to the milieu of that other creation of working-class culture, professional sports. Once again Basie's understatements and exceptional – indeed for the autobiographer excessive – modesty muffle his account. The most he allows himself to say in the way of hype is 'I don't mean to pat myself on the back, but that band was strutting, really strutting.' He is much more likely to record occasions when he suffered or evaded defeat than to exult in public. The band's true sound of locker-room triumph is to be heard elsewhere:

> We were only Count Basie's band, and we got out of a ragged bus, but when we got on that bandstand we started jumping and showering down ... We put a hurting on them that night and washed Lunceford out of the dance hall.
>
> (the trumpeter Harry 'Sweets' Edison, quoted in Stanley Dance's *The World of Count Basie*)

The conviction of the early Basie band lay in this capacity to exult. For the professional musician of Basie's day, as he himself puts it, 'playing music has never really been work'. It was more even than a way of having a good time. It was, as sport is for the athlete, a continuous means of asserting oneself as a human being, as an agent in the world and not the subject of others' actions, as a discipline of the soul, a daily testing, an expression of the value and sense of life, a way to perfection. Athletes cannot use their voices to say this, but musicians can, without having to formulate it in words. So the working-class athlete's conviction produced a great art in the form of jazz, and, thanks to the phonograph, a permanent art.

Basie's strength as a bandleader lay in his capacity to distil the essence of jazz as black players felt it. That is why this inarticulate dropout from New Jersey was doubly lucky to find himself stranded, in the mid-1920s, in Kansas City. First, because it allowed him to recognize his vocation. Till then he had merely been a poor black youngster who liked playing piano and chose the only form of freedom available to his kind, the gypsy life of show business. Liberation and not money was the object ('I don't think I ever came into contact with any rich entertainers when I grew up') and he neither made nor kept money. 'I liked playing music and I liked the life.' *Good Morning Blues* is a superb evocation of the underside of black showbiz in the 1920s – the casts of burlesque shows like *Hippity-Hop* thirsting for some action in the desert of Omaha, Gonzelle White and her Big Jazz Jamboree slowly foundering as she sailed along the TOBA circuit of black vaudeville theatres, finally sinking in KC. After the wreck Basie drifted into full-time jazz 'without quite being aware of the big change I was making'. It was his first stroke of luck.

The second was finding himself in Kansas City, capital of that apparent cultural desert south-west of the Missouri which even blacks bypassed *en route* from the Delta to the bright lights of Chicago and Detroit, and which even the black vaudeville circuit still wrote off. KC was long its westernmost point, which is why shows like Gonzelle White's disbanded there if not turned around, rerouted, or re-formed. Kansas and Oklahoma were not meccas of showbiz. Apart from KC and Texas, the entire South-west had only small and scattered black populations. The first tour of the newly formed Basie band was a row of one-nighters through places like Tulsa, Muskogee, Okmulgee, Oklahoma City and Wichita.

Yet this was the region that produced two major developments in jazz. It fused the down-home blues with popular dance-band music, and the arranged performance with the jam session, to create both the classic swing band and the most powerful experimental laboratory of jazz. Kansas City produced not only Count Basie but also Charlie Parker.

Much has been written about this apparent paradox. Most of it has concentrated on the peculiar character of Kansas City (Missouri), in the wide-open, free-spending days of Boss Pendergast, whose gang-run night-time municipal Keynesianism kept KC in the Depression an oasis where black musicians could at least eat. (It would be too much to call the player's life of hot dogs, plates of beans, jugs of whisky, perhaps with a little subsidy from a girl, prosperity.) But in fact, though *Good Morning Blues* makes little of it, regular work was scarce in Kansas City. As one of Basie's pioneers puts it, 'the work was around, out on the road', though in Kansas City itself there was an enormous amount of ill-paid casual gigging with tips, and even more unpaid jamming.

Most of the talent seems to have come out of the territory, with relatively little direct recruitment from the Deep South and even less from the East. Walter Page's Blue Devils, the foundation and inspiration of Basie's team, was a territory band working in Oklahoma. And the down-home blues that Kansas City integrated into band jazz was not a big-city product; nor, at this stage, were band-accompanied male blues shouters, who became Basie's trademark, of any interest to a white public.

The KC musicians, in short, played what came naturally to Southwestern blacks and largely what a segregated audience wanted. The blues was imposed on them by the ghetto. Independently, Basie and Jimmy Rushing observe of each other that in the mid-1920s Basie 'couldn't play the blues then', and Rushing, who could, 'wasn't really a blues singer in those days'. Ten years later they sang and played little else.

The gems mined in the dance halls of places like Muskogee were cut and polished in the countless nightclubs and after-hours sessions of Kansas City by an unusually large community of professional musicians. But in spite of the KC myth which insists on battles won with visiting stars, and admiration from outsiders, this community thought of itself as in some sense marooned:

> We were really behind the Iron Curtain. There was no chance for us.
> So there was nothing for us to do but play for ourselves.
>
> (the great drummer Jo Jones, quoted in *The World of Count Basie*)

It could have been said about the Kansas City scene as a whole. It was said about its most characteristic product, the Basie band.

Yet at first sight Basie himself had few qualifications for eminence. By jazz standards he was not a top-class pianist, especially when compared to the New York stride-piano giants in whose style he had been formed and against whom he constantly measured himself – to his disadvantage. As one of his arrangers said: 'He knew he couldn't challenge Fats Waller or Earl Hines. He didn't have the same kind of gift from above.'

Nor was he a particularly literate musician, unlike most of the big-band leaders, who tended to come from a schooled black background. He came into the big time with little more than a number of head-arrangements and blues, not only because he did not lead a reading band, but because he himself was not a writer or arranger in the ordinary sense. Even his ideas had short breath: 'He'd only go about four measures,' says his arranger Eddie Durham. His provincial ignorance, even within the limits of commercial dance music, was startling. In 1936 he risked his booking in a great New York ballroom because, he claims, 'I don't believe I even knew what a goddamn tango was.' There was nothing original about the format of his band, except perhaps using two saxophones in contest. And any reader of his memoir will wonder how this easygoing, frequently drunk, tongue-tied man managed the job of holding his team together.

In short, on paper he had no qualifications to be anything except another adequate jazz player. And with the modesty, or honesty, which is his trademark, he says as much in his tribute to John Hammond, who heard his broadcast from the Reno Club on a shortwave car radio in 1935 as he drove through the Middle West, was bowled over by it, and made Basie into a national figure: 'Without him I probably would still be back in Kansas City, if I still happened to be alive. Or back in New York ... trying to be in somebody's band, and then worrying about getting fired.'

But what was it that Hammond, and later the rest of the world, recognized in Basie? Once again, the best descriptions come from others:

He was and is [says Harry 'Sweets' Edison] the greatest for stomping off the tempo. He noodles around on the piano until he gets it just right. Just like you were mixing mash and yeast to make whiskey, and you keep tasting and tasting it ... Freddie Green and Jo Jones would follow him until he hit the right tempo, and when he started it they *kept* it.

That 'tempo' was the clue to Basie, and *Good Morning Blues* begins with his discovery in, of all places, Tulsa, Oklahoma, of what Albert Murray elsewhere calls 'that ever-steady, yet always flexible trans-continental locomotive-like drive of the Kansas City 4/4'[2] in Walter Page's Blue Devils, who are by common consent the pioneers of that lovely, easy, lilting rhythm both driving and relaxed. They were to form the core of his early band.

Having set the tempo, Basie would next:

set a rhythm for the saxes first ... then he'd set one for the bones and we'd pick that up. Now it's our rhythm against theirs. The third rhythm would be for the trumpets ... The solos would fall in between the ensembles, but that's how the piece would begin, and that's how Basie put his tunes together.

(Dicky Wells, trombonist, quoted in *The World of Count Basie*)

The great waves of ensemble riffs, hitting the audience like Atlantic rollers, were therefore – initially at least – not stylistic tricks or ends in themselves. They were the essential groundswell of the music, the setting for what the musicians themselves, in the great days, saw not as an ensemble band, but (apart from the self-effacing members of the stupendous rhythm section) as a company of creative soloists. Alas, it eventually declined into an ensemble band in response to the public. Self-effacement was also the secret of Basie's minimalist arrangements and his increasingly sparse piano interventions, whose purpose was entirely to keep the music moving.

Whatever the origin of an arrangement, it was whittled down into the Basie version by ruthless selection and cutting. Basie, who 'never wrote down anything on paper', composed by editing, in other words by fitting his numbers to his musicians. But unlike Ellington, who had precise musical ideas and picked his players to fit them – even if some had originally been suggested by listening to other musicians – the less articulate Basie was fundamentally a selector. What he heard in his head was the shapes and patterns of numbers, the rhythm and dynamics, the stage mechanics and effects rather than the plot or words of the play. ('I have my own little ideas about how to get certain guys into certain numbers and how to get them out. I had my own way of opening the door for them to let them come in and sit around awhile. Then I would exit them.') But none of this became real until he heard musicians play and recognized in the sound what he had in mind. Listening was his essential talent. That is how the Basie band in its prime – between 1936 and 1950 – came to be built up and shaped by apparently haphazard recruitment and playing.

The only time during this period that Basie groped and showed uncertainty was when he came into the big time and his booking agent, the devoted Willard Alexander, told him that for commercial reasons he had to double the size of his band. He floundered, and almost failed. Fortunately both his backers and other musicians (Fletcher Henderson generously gave him his own arrangements) were so convinced of the band's merits that he had time to adjust.

Consequently the Basie band was a marvellous combination of solo creation and collective exhilaration. It attracted and held a remarkable collection of individual talent. The intense joy of being in the early Basie band, a band of brothers, shines through the reminiscences of hardbitten and jealous pros. Some of that joy was owing to the temperament and tact of the leader who led, as it were, like the headman of a traditional Russian village commune, by articulating and crystallizing consensus. Even more was owed to the players' sense of equality, fraternity and above all liberty to create, controlled only by their own collective sense of what sounded 'right'. And to the end of his days Basie liked to present himself not as leader or driver, but as the fulcrum of his band, the small still centre: 'keep your eye on the fellow at the piano. The sparrow. He don't know nothing, but you just keep your eyes on him and we'll all know what's going down.' It was not entirely an affectation.

Those who were young in the 1930s and first heard the unanswerable sound of the early Basie band rolling across continent and oceans are tempted, like Yeats with the Easter Rising, to call the muster roll of heroes: Basie, Page, Jones and Green, Herschel Evans and Lester Young, Buck Clayton and Harry Edison, Benny Morton, Dicky Wells and Jimmy Rushing singing the blues. But in retrospect these were men who not only produced remarkable music and helped to create what is in fact the classic music of the US, but who did so in an extraordinary and unprecedented way. *Good Morning Blues* and *The World of Count Basie* are not works of cultural sociology. (Perhaps luckily: Adorno wrote some of the most stupid pages ever written about jazz.) Nevertheless, they should be read by all who want to explore the obscure zone that links society with the creation of art.

Stanley Dance's book is a collection of interviews by one of the oldest and most knowledgeable jazz lovers in the world. *Good Morning Blues* is more than a ghosted autobiography. Albert Murray, a distinguished black writer who worked with Basie on the book for years and backed it – as all good oral history should be backed – by research far more extensive than the actual interviewing, deserves credit for a remarkable achievement. He has, like his subject, effaced himself to let someone else speak as he would have wanted to, but, without his help, could not have done. He has respected Basie's reticence, and neither concealed nor disguised the limitations of a man of great gifts, but with all the reluctance to commit himself publicly that one would expect of a black entertainer who grew up in the days when they were still called 'sepia'. The man who emerges is a man to respect. Basie was always good at finding others to voice his ideas. *Good Morning Blues* is his last success in doing so.

CHAPTER 21

The Duke

This essay originally appeared in the New York Review of Books *on 19 November 1987 as a review of* Duke Ellington *by James Lincoln Collier (New York, 1987).*

Of the great figures in twentieth-century culture, Edward Kennedy Ellington is one of the most mysterious. On the evidence of James Lincoln Collier's excellent book, he must also be one of the least likeable – cold to his son, ruthless in his dealings with women, and unscrupulous in his use of the work of other musicians. But there can be no denying the extraordinary fascination he plainly exercised over the people he mistreated and was loyal to at the same time, including those who allowed him to establish power over them, that is most of his colleagues and lovers.

There was nothing blatant about what must strike impartial observers as his appalling behaviour. He was the opposite of the short-fused brawlers who briefly joined so many bands of his time, including his own, though his habit of stealing his musicians' tunes and, occasionally, their women must have put a strain on even the more placid among them. However, the only people who actually took a knife or a gun to him, so far as the record shows, were legal or *de facto* wives, who had more than adequate provocation.

In fact, nothing was obvious about Duke Ellington the man, except the mask he invariably wore in public and behind which his personality became invisible: that of a handsome, debonair and seductive man about town, whose verbal communications with his public, and very likely with the startlingly large numbers of his female conquests, consisted of vapid phrases of flattery and endearment ('I love you madly'). The autobiography he wrote shortly before his death, *Music Is My Mistress*[1] is a singularly uninformative document as well as a mistitled one. For while he probably despised and tried to subjugate his lovers, indeed all women except his mother and sister, both of whom he idealized and regarded as asexual – at least this is the view of his humiliated son[2] – his relationship to music was entirely different. Even so, music was not his mistress in the original sense of someone exercising dominion. Ellington liked to keep control.

Here, in fact, lies the heart of the mystery that James Lincoln Collier has tried to elucidate in his book. For Ellington, who has been called, with Charles Ives, the most important figure in American music,[3] utterly fails to conform to the criteria of the conventional idea of the 'artist', just as his improvised productions fail to conform to the conventional idea of the 'work of art'. As it happens, unlike most of his jazz contemporaries, Ellington saw himself as an 'artist' in this sense and took to composing 'works' for the concert hall, where they were periodically performed. In the black middle-class milieu of the Ellingtons, which Collier rightly insists was important, the conception of the 'great artist' was familiar, whereas it was meaningless to someone like Louis Armstrong, who came from a less self-conscious and entirely unbourgeois world.

When Ellington, on his triumphant visit to England in 1933, discovered that for British intellectuals he was not just a bandleader but an artist like Ravel or Delius, he took to the role of 'composer' as he conceived it. However, hardly anyone claims that his reputation rests on the thirty-odd ill-organized mini-suites of programme music, and still less on the 'sacred concerts' to which he devoted much of his final years. As an orthodox composer, Ellington simply does not rate highly.

And yet there is no doubt that the corpus of his work in jazz, which, in Collier's words, 'includes hundreds of complete compositions, many of them almost flawless', is one of the major accomplishments in music – *any* American music – of his era (1899–1974). And that but for Ellington this music would not exist, even though almost every page of Collier's admiring but demystifying book bears witness to his musical deficiencies. Ellington was a good but not brilliant pianist. He lacked both a technical knowledge of music and the self-discipline to acquire it. He had trouble reading sheet music, let alone more elaborate scores. After 1939 he relied heavily for arrangements and musical advice on Billy Strayhorn, who acted as his *alter ego* in running the band and who became something like an adopted son. The musically trained and immensely sophisticated Strayhorn was better able to judge from a score how the music would sound.

Apart from some informal tips in the 1920s from formally trained black musical professionals like Will Vodery, Ziegfeld's musical director, he learned little except by a process of trying it out in practice.

He was too lazy, and perhaps not sufficiently intellectual, to read much, nor did he listen intently to other people's music. He did not even, if Collier is to be believed, make any special efforts to find the right kind of musicians for his band, but accepted the first vaguely suitable ones to fill vacancies – though this does not account for the majestic brass and reed line-ups of the Ellington band between the later 1920s and early 1940s. He was certainly not a great songwriter, if we follow Collier's demonstration that 'of all the songs on which Ellington's reputation as a songwriter – and his ASCAP royalties as well – is based, only "Solitude" appears to have been entirely his work. For the rest he was at best a collaborator, at worst merely the arranger of a band version of the tune.' And at least one of his sidemen told him, at a characteristic moment of mutual irritation: 'I don't consider you a composer. You are a compiler.'

Last, and perhaps most damaging of all, is Collier's justified observation that he neither had the talent, the 'raw natural gift', of other great jazz musicians nor was 'drawn, indeed driven, to [jazz] by an intense feeling for the music itself'. Unlike many other great jazz musicians, he showed little promise until he was nearly thirty, and he did not start doing his best work until he was forty.

Here lies the chief interest of Collier's book. In broad outline his judgments are not new. It has long been accepted that Ellington was essentially an improvising musician whose 'instrument was a whole band', and that he could not even think about his music except through the particular voices of its members. That he was musically short-winded and therefore incapable of developing a musical idea at length was always obvious, but conversely it was already known in 1933 that no other composer, classical or otherwise, could beat him over the distance of a 78 r.p.m. record – that is, three minutes. He has been called by a critic of both jazz and classical music 'art's major miniaturist'.[4] Collier's comments on particular works and phases of the Ellington *oeuvre* are, as usual, knowledgeable, perceptive and illuminating, but his general judgment could hardly differ from what may be regarded as the general consensus.

Only through jazz could a man of Ellington's evident limitations have produced a significant contribution to twentieth-century music. Only a black American, and probably a black middle-class American of Ellington's generation, would have sought to do so as a bandleader. Only a person of Ellington's unusual character would have actually achieved this result. The merit of Collier's book lies in showing what the music owes to the man, but its novelty is to see the man as formed by his social and musical milieu.

The peculiarities of Ellington's personality have often been described, with varying degrees of indulgence. He saw himself, with total and unforced conviction, as 'uniquely gifted by God, uniquely guided through life by some mysterious light, uniquely directed by the Divine to make certain decisions at certain points in his life', and consequently entitled to total power. The critic Alexander Coleman tried to sum up Ellington's inner thoughts as follows: 'I must be able to give and to take away. I command the world because I am ever lucky, careful beyond compare, the slyest fox among all the foxes of this world.'[5]

This is substantially also Collier's reading of the man, though the present book insists less than it might on the imperatives of street-smart survival and success that the Duke – the name was given to him early in life – acquired as a smooth young black hustler: the deviousness, the refusal to give anything about himself away, the power strategies of manipulation, the godfather-like insistence on 'commanding respect'. In this regard Mercer Ellington's memoir of life with his father may usefully supplement Collier's book.

In short, Ellington, as he himself recognized,[6] was a spoiled child who succeeded in maintaining something of the infant's sense of omnipotence throughout life. In Washington, DC, his father worked his way up from coachman to butler in the service of Dr M. F. Cuthburt, 'reputedly a society doctor who tended Morgenthaus and Du Ponts', according to Collier. From this family background and from the relatively large number of politically sheltered or college-educated blacks he knew in his parents' Washington milieu, he acquired self-respect, self-assurance and strong pride in his race – and a sense of superiority within it. 'I don't know how many castes of Negroes there were in the city at that time,' he once said, 'but I do know that if you decided to mix carelessly with another you would be told that one just did not do that sort of thing.' He preferred not to have a racially mixed band even when this was possible. The charisma that surrounded him derived largely from the consequent, and very striking, air of being a *grand seigneur* who expected to be deferred to, and this impression was reinforced by charm, good looks and an indefinable magnetic quality.

However, the spoiled child began as an idle and ignorant failure at school, looking for a good time, who never acquired the knack of learning, hard work or self-discipline, yet never abandoned his sense of status or his ambition. Music, which he seems to have seen originally merely as an adjunct to having a good time, became an obvious as well as an easy way of earning a living, given the enormous demand of the jazz age and the position of blacks in the dance bands, which was still strong, in spite of the influx of whites.

If educated and college-trained blacks made their way as musicians – often becoming bandleaders or arrangers, as did Fletcher Henderson and Don Redman – it was even more natural for a middle-class ne'er-do-well without qualifications to do so, especially one who had recently been pressured into marriage. In the early 1920s good money was to be made in music, probably more readily than by commercial art, for which the young Ellington seems to have shown some gift.

It was Ellington's good luck that he entered jazz at the moment when the music was discovering itself, and he was able to discover himself as he grew into it. There is no sign that he particularly wanted to compose, until he formed a partnership with Irving Mills, who, as a music publisher, knew the financial pay-off of songs in the world of show business. There is no sign that Ellington wanted to be more than a very successful bandleader.

His band moved from the rough-and-ready syncopated music played by an army of nondescript young groups into 'hot' jazz in the middle 1920s, because that was the general trend. Indeed the typical Ellington style may well have been worked out for commercial reasons by means of the 'jungle music' that fitted in with the expectations of the Cotton Club clientele. 'During one period at the Cotton Club,' Ellington said, 'much attention was paid to acts with an African setting, and to accompany these we developed what was termed a "jungle style" jazz.' This had the advantage both of building on the talents of some valued members of the band and of providing the band with an immediately recognizable 'sound' or trademark.

Collier also argues that the size and instrumentation of the band grew because Ellington's competitors had more brass than he. The models for the big band were white. The arranged music they used was built around what Collier calls a 'saxophone choir', a co-ordinated reed section pioneered by Art Hickman and Ferde Grofé around 1914 and developed by Grofé and the 'King of Jazz' Paul Whiteman in the 1920s. Fletcher Henderson and Don Redman created a black version by means of a complex interplay between soloists and band sections.

Ellington thus became a 'composer' because the future of successful bands in the 1920s lay not with freewheeling small groups of blowers but with larger bands playing arranged music. He was in no position to imitate Henderson, whom he admired and from whom, Collier argues, he took over the 'system of punctuating, answering, supporting everything with something', because he was incapable of writing complex music and his men could not read complex orchestration. On the other hand the combination of jazz rhythms with harmonic devices taken from or similar to those of classical music, which Whiteman had pioneered, was easier to follow and came naturally to a man who lived and breathed the atmosphere of New York show business, and, in fact, did not much like being called a jazz musician. As Collier rightly points out, the real triumph of 'symphonic jazz' is not Gershwin's *Rhapsody in Blue* (commissioned by Whiteman) but the band music of Duke Ellington.

Once Ellington found himself responsible for his own band's repertoire, he was forced to discover himself as a musician. His personal method of creating compositions is well described by Collier:

He would begin by bringing into the recording studio or rehearsal hall a few musical ideas – scraps of melodies, harmonies, and chord sequences usually clothed in the sound of particular instrumentalists in the band. On the spot he would sit down at the piano and quickly rough out a section – four, eight, sixteen bars. The band would play it; Duke would repeat it; the band would play it again until everybody got it. Years later, the pianist Jimmy Jones said: 'What he does is like a chain reaction. Here's a section, here's a section and here's another and, in between, he begins putting in the connecting links – the amazing thing about Ellington is that he can think so fast on the spot and create so quickly.' Along the way, members of the band would make suggestions ... As a piece was developing, it would frequently be up to the men in the sections to work out the harmonies, usually from chords Duke would supply. When the trombonist Lawrence Brown came into the band ... to make a third trombone, he was expected to manufacture for himself a third part to everything. 'I had to compose my own parts ... you just went along and whatever you heard was missing, that's where you were.'

It is obvious that Ellington brought something to this mode of music-making beyond his usual disinclination for planning and preparation. He brought natural and growing fascination for the mixing of different sounds and timbres, a growing taste for pushing harmony to the edge of dissonance, a tendency to break the rules, and a great deal of confidence in his unorthodoxies if they 'sounded right' to him. He also brought a tonal sense that is usually compared – by Collier also – to a painter's colours, but is better thought of as a feeling for show-business effects. Ellington, an unabashed composer of programme music, seems not to have thought in colours, which occur hardly at all in the titles of his records (except for the non-pictorial 'black' and 'blue'), but to have drawn on 'a sensory experience, a physical memory', as in 'Harlem Airshaft' or 'Daybreak Express'; a mood, as in 'Mood Indigo' or 'Solitude'; or sentimental stories, like those preferred by traditional choreographers, as in 'Black and Tan Fantasy' or many of his longer pieces.

None of this would have amounted to much except in and through a group of creative musicians with independent personalities and identifiable voices: in short, except in jazz. Unquestionably every piece of Ellington's music was or is unmistakably the Duke's, whatever the composition of his band at any moment. Indeed he achieved the same, or analogous, effects through very different combinations of players, even though the band benefited from the long presence of certain quintessential Ellington voices: Cootie Williams, Johnny Hodges, Joe Nanton, Barney Bigard, Harry Carney. (But they developed their style because of what the Duke heard in them.) Moreover, it is undeniable that the musical impressionism that reminded classically educated listeners of Debussy, and the consistently brilliant form of the band's three-minute recorded pieces – beyond that length they tended to sag or fall apart – are Ellington's alone.

Nevertheless, his music is important above all because of the way it was made. Duke, the devious manipulator, knew that each musician in the band had to make the music his own. He might do so by being left deliberately without instructions, discovering on his own what Ellington had intended him to – as Cootie Williams was made to see himself as the successor to Bubber Miley's 'growling' trumpet. Or he might be needled by Duke's deliberate insults into showing what he could really do. There was a method behind the apparently chaotic indiscipline of the band.

Conversely, Ellington was nourished by his musicians, not only because he drew on their ideas and tunes but because their voices were what gave him his own. He was, of course, lucky in his time. Being mostly untrained as well as highly competitive, players developed individual voices, which made possible the most exciting and original combinations. Collier and just about everyone else agrees that the discovery of one such voice, Bubber Miley's, began the transformation of the Ellington band, and enabled Duke to form those endlessly varied liaisons between the rough and the smooth, the raw and the cooked, which are among his characteristics. It was lucky that the masters of the new hot jazz so often came from New Orleans – Sidney Bechet himself briefly joined the band before it officially became Ellington's. This almost certainly gave Ellington the taste for mellow and sinuous reeds, the sounds of the saxophonist Johnny Hodges and the clarinettist Barney Bigard.

But Ellington's dependence on his musicians is most convincingly demonstrated by the fact that he kept the band going to the end of his life although it lost money. Whether with better management it could have paid for itself is unclear, but there is no doubt that Duke poured his own royalties into keeping it on the road. It was his voice. Ellington showed no interest in making or keeping scores of his works, not because he did not have their sound and shape in his mind but because his numbers had no meaning for him except as played, and, as in all jazz, they varied with the players, the occasion and the mood. There could be no such thing as a definitive version, only a preferred but provisional one. Constant Lambert, an early classical admirer, was wrong in arguing that the record was Ellington's equivalent to the straight composer's score.[7]

It is evident that works created in this manner do not fit into the conventional category of the 'artist' as the individual creator and only begetter, but of course this conventional pattern has never been applicable to the necessarily co-operative or collective forms of creation that fill our stages and screens, and are more characteristic of the twentieth-century arts than the individual in his studio or at his desk. The problem of situating Ellington as an 'artist' is in principle no different from that of describing great choreographers, directors or others who impress their character as individuals on team products. It is merely rather unusual in musical composition.

But this undoubtedly raises serious questions about the accepted definition or description of art and artistic creation. Patently the term 'composer' fits Ellington as badly as the term 'author' fits the Hollywood directors to whom it was applied by French critics with the national penchant for bourgeois and Cartesian reductionism. But Ellington produced co-operative works of serious art that were also his own, just as film and stage directors can, and unlike the megalomaniacs he knew himself to be engaged in a genuinely collective creation.

Collier asks such questions, but is sidetracked by his conviction that Ellington allowed his talents to be diverted from what he did best into 'music in emulation of models from the past, which in many cases he did not really understand', and which was not very good. Whether this 'drew him away from developing the form he was at home with' is less certain. After all, by this book's estimate, he produced upwards of 120 hours of recorded jazz, which is a large enough corpus for most composers, and he developed and innovated to the end of his life. If he produced fewer masterpieces after the age of fifty, the pull of Carnegie Hall is less to blame than the business troubles afflicting his instrument, the big band.

All the same, Ellington will live through music like 'Ko-Ko' and not through compositions like the 'Liberian Suite'. But Collier is surely wrong to contrast jazz, as a sort of *Gebrauchsmusik* 'to accompany dancing, to support singers or dancers, or to excite and entertain audiences', with 'art as a special practice with its own principles existing in the abstract, apart from an audience', and not 'created out of a wish to act directly and immediately on the real feelings of people'. Whatever the relation of the accepted conventional arts to the public, which has undoubtedly been a difficult one for avant-garde artists since the beginning of this century, this oversimplifies the relation of jazz musicians to their audience, even if we leave aside the musicians who, since the birth of bebop, have defied the audience to follow them.

For, while it is quite true that Ellington's finest work was created for cabarets and ballrooms, for the purposes of much of the audience schlock music would have done just as well or better; and in fact the same audiences were content with third-rate bands. Like most jazz organizations of its generation, the Ellington band earned its living playing dances, but did not play *for* the dancers. The band members played for each other. Undoubtedly their ideal audience accepted their kind of music and was excited by it, but above all it did not get in the way.

The present reviewer, at the age of sixteen, lost his heart for good to the Ellington band at its most imperial, playing what was called a 'breakfast dance' in a suburban London ballroom to an uncomprehending audience entirely irrelevant to it, except that a swaying mass of dancers was what the band was used to seeing in front of them. Those who have never heard Ellington playing a dance or, even better, a supper room of sophisticated night people, where the real applause consisted in the falling silent of table conversations, cannot know what the greatest band in the history of jazz was really like, playing at ease in its own environment.

On the other hand the people who expected Ellington to 'act directly and immediately on the real feelings' did get in the way. In his later years most Americans and all foreigners heard Ellington live only on concert tours. The hushed or applauding halls full of fans waiting for the revelation rarely brought out the best in the band. They brought out the Ellington who knew that enough honking (mostly by Paul Gonsalves) would bring the house down.

Nor is it sufficient to say, as Collier does, 'When jazz becomes confounded with art, passion flies out and pretension flies in.' The reason why jazz is important is not that it is passionate and unpretentious. So is most romantic fiction. It is not that, unlike the art Collier dislikes, 'millions of people care about it'. It is and has always been a minority art, even by the standards of classical music and serious literature, let alone the real public of millions. It is certainly not a mass art in the US, where New York jazz clubs (like British theatre managers) count on the tourist trade as well as the local jazz audience.

Jazz is important in the history of the modern arts because it developed an alternative way of creating art to that of the high-culture avant-garde, whose exhaustion has left so much of the conventional 'serious' arts as adjuncts to university teaching pro-grammes, speculative capital investment or philanthropy. That is why the tendency of jazz to turn itself into yet another avant-garde is to be deplored.

More than any other person, Ellington represented this ability of jazz to turn people who are unconcerned with 'culture', and pursuing their passions, ambitions and interests in their own way, into creators of serious and, on a small scale, of great art. He demonstrated this both through his own evolution into a composer and by the integrated works of art he created with his band, a band containing fewer utterly brilliant individual talents than other bands – until the late 1930s perhaps only one, Hodges – but in which extraordinary individual performance was the foundation of collective achievement. There is no other flow of musical creation by a collective to compare with it. Certainly he, and they, acted directly and immediately on the feelings of listeners, but this itself does not explain why, as Collier notes, their music was so much more complex than that of other jazz groups. In short, the author is at times tempted into populist theory of the arts, by which the artist not only 'rejoices to concur with the common reader' (to use Dr Johnson's phrase) but takes the common reader's preferences as a guide. That the theory is inadequate is shown, among other examples, by comparing the American to the German phases of the careers of both George Grosz and Kurt Weill.

However, Collier is entirely right in the belief that the great achievements of jazz, of which Ellington's music is in some ways the most impressive, grew in a soil quite different from that which produced high art. It was a music of professional entertainers of modest expectations, made in the community of night people with folk roots. It was not supposed to be 'art' like chamber music; it did not benefit by being treated as 'art' and it tended to get as lost as the high arts when its practitioners turned themselves into yet another avant-garde. Its major contribution to music was made in a social setting that no longer exists. It is difficult to imagine that a great musician of the future will be able to say, like one of Ellington's major soloists: 'All I wanted to be was a successful pimp, and then I found I could make it on the horn.'

Today's jazz, played largely by educated musicians, often with classical training, essentially for a listening public, by a generation whose links with the blues are largely mediated through rock and musically impoverished gospel sounds, will have to find another way, if it can, to make a mark as great as the jazz of those who grew up in the first half of this century. But all of its players, without exception, will continue to listen to the records of Ellington, about whom Collier has written the best book we have: spare, lucid, perceptive about the man, good criticism and good history.

CHAPTER 22

Jazz Comes to Europe

This was originally published as 'On the Reception of Jazz in Europe' in Theo Mäusli (ed.), Jazz und Sozialgeschichte *(Zurich, 1994).*

Discussion of jazz must begin, like all historical analyses of society under modern capitalism, with technology and business: in this instance the business of supplying the leisure and entertainment of the increasingly urban masses of the lower and middle classes. Until the First World War, technology, in the form of radio and the phonograph which were to be crucial to the diffusion of Negro music from the 1920s, was not yet significant. However, by the end of the nineteenth century 'show business' and the popular music industry were already sufficiently developed to have generated national and even transatlantic networks – agencies, theatre circuits, even chains and so on – not to mention the publication and distribution of a constantly changing supply of popular musical numbers.

Technically these businesses were antique, unlike the other great art of our century, the film. They remained confined by the need for face-to-face or mouth-to-ear communication. Only in one crucial respect had they been revolutionized. The speed of transatlantic transport was such that ideas, notes and people could already cross the ocean very rapidly indeed. Will Marion Cook's musical revue *Clorindy: The Origin of the Cakewalk* – Cook was later to bring Sidney Bechet to Britain – was performed in 1898 in both New York and London. The foxtrot, the basic dance routine associated with jazz, first appeared in Britain in the summer of 1914, a few months after its first appearance in the USA, and in Belgium in 1915. Jazz had hardly been baptized in the USA when groups under that name already toured Europe. They were there from the middle of 1917. Consequently the obstacles to a rapid diffusion of jazz were not technical but social and cultural.

However, the interesting thing about this diffusion is what was being diffused. It was one of several kinds of novel cultural and artistic creation that emerged, in the late nineteenth century, from the plebeian, mainly urban, milieu of Western industrial society, most probably in the specialized lumpenproletarian environments of the entertainment quarter in the big cities, with their specific subcultures, male and female stereotypes, costumes – and music. The Buenos Aires tango which secured for Latin American music a permanent but minor place on the international dance floor at the same time as jazz did, is one example. Cuban music is another. That jazz was both novel and, in origin, an art belonging to an autonomous subculture is significant for two reasons. First, because the machinery of commercial diffusion caught it, as it were, on the wing, in the middle of its formation and evolution. The reception of jazz was the opposite of phenomena like the 'folk-music revival' which discovered musical fossils in Somerset or Appalachia. At the same time the rapid evolution of the music itself generated just such a taste for nostalgia and musical archaeology among the secondary public for jazz. It was to generate 'traditional' or 'revival' (Dixieland) jazz. Second, and more important, jazz was not simply received as a *Gebrauchsmusik*, another set of sounds to accompany dancing or beer-drinking, but as something symbolic and significant in itself. This is an important element in the European reception of jazz.

This still leaves us with the major question why, of all the contemporary plebeian city arts, taken up by a secondary public, American black music had so much greater a capacity to conquer the Western world than any other. It was by no means the first art of its kind to be taken up by the socially superior and the literate, artists, aristocrats and intellectuals. In fact, given the absence of aristocrats and intellectuals of the European type in the USA, it was one of the last. Before the 1930s, or at best the 1920s, there is no equivalent in jazz history of the *cante hondo* scholarship of Andalusia in the 1880s, of Pinto de Carvalho's 1903 *History of the Fado*, of the Max Beerbohms and the Toulouse-Lautrecs who celebrated music-hall artists in the 1890s, or even of the campaign by devoted aficionados which created the tango vogue in Europe in the 1900s. The first serious books on jazz were written in Europe, or anywhere, in 1926; the first books demonstrating the sort of knowledge of artists and music of the late-nineteenth-century Iberian writers, not until the middle and late 1930s.

The answer to the question must remain open, but I want to contribute one element to it. American Negro music benefited from being American. It was received not merely as the exotic, the primitive, the non-bourgeois, but as the modern. Jazz bands came from the same country as Henry Ford. The intellectuals and artists who took up jazz immediately after the First World War on the European continent almost invariably include modernity among its attractions. Hence the absurd fashion for linking this music in some obscure way to the civilization of the machine, with which (except for railway engines) it showed no affinity whatever. British intellectuals or artists in 1918, by the way, showed none of the interest in jazz so evident among the continental avant-garde – Cocteau, Milhaud and the rest – at the time.

However, a third element in the reception of Negro music is highly relevant. Jazz made its way and triumphed, not as a music for intellectuals but as a music for dancing, and specifically, for a transformed, revolutionized social dance of the British middle and upper classes, but also, and almost simultaneously, the British working-class dance. During the 1900s the upper-crust dance was transformed in two ways. (An expert contemporary witness dates the major change precisely to the season 1910–11.) First, urban dancing had already ceased to be a seasonal occupation linked to special occasions, and was being practised all the year round as a regular social and leisure activity. To some extent it was practised privately, but special dancing clubs developed – there were three in Edwardian Hampstead alone – and it occurred in hotels and what were not yet called 'nightclubs'. The tea-dance and the restaurant-dance appeared on a modest scale. Second, the dance lost its formality and ordered succession. At the same time it became simpler, more easily learned and less demanding and exhausting. The crucial change here was that from the turning dance (for example, the waltz) to the walking dance, such as the Boston, a sort of rectilinear waltz, in the early 1900s. It seems clear that these developments reflected a substantial loosening of aristocratic and middle-class conventions, and they are a striking and neglected symptom of the notable emancipation of women in these classes before 1914. The link between the dance revolution, even specifically between the new primacy of rhythm in social dancing, and the emancipation of women, did not pass unperceived. It is noted in the most intelligent of the early jazz books, Paul Bernhard's *Jazz: Eine musikalische Zeitfrage* (1927). Bernhard stressed that this development came to the continent from the Anglo-Saxon countries.

Little need be said about the chronology of the jazz reception. We may, briefly, distinguish a palaeolithic era before jazz was known under that name. It saw the penetration of American Negro elements into fashionable British dance music, where they became dominant around 1912, when syncopation became an essential element in it. There was a neolithic revolution after 1917, as jazz erupted into the European consciousness, as a loud and raucous noise, as a symbol for whatever journalists, preachers and intellectuals chose to denounce or praise, and as the name and instrumentation of the music which accompanied a new epidemic of mass social dancing. Within this wide area of dance and (American) entertainment music, a small, passionate and knowledgeable public of fans in the 1920s singled out a particular field of 'hot' jazz as an art music to admire. In the 1930s, which form the next period in the history of jazz reception, the specific European public for jazz became both larger and more organized, mainly in jazz clubs, and collectors began to penetrate the new medium of radio. The Europeans even began, in a modest way, to generate native jazz musicians of their own. However, from the late 1930s an essentially white secondary public, both in the USA and in Europe, developed both a flourishing corps of amateur players and a specific conservative or traditionalist reaction against further jazz evolution in the form of the New Orleans revival or Dixieland movement. In Europe, and certainly in Britain, this became 'the basic social music for many young people' (to quote Lincoln Collier) during the Second World War. It remained so until the rise of rock-and-roll.

This emergence of a broadly based popular youth music from among a small, exclusive, highbrow minority of jazz aficionados is significant in two ways. It demonstrates the almost completely secondary character of the naturalization of black music in Europe. This was based overwhelmingly on young men listening to, collecting and discussing records of Americans. The centrality of records and record-inspired performers is indicated by the insignificance of the live visits of American musicians. In Britain, as indeed for other reasons in Germany and the USSR, tours by American groups were actually banned for long periods. Again, the formation of the new public's taste by a minority of impassioned and often esoteric jazz scholars allowed Europe to become familiar with elements in the black tradition which a purely commercial evolution of taste would simply not have brought to their attention. An obvious example is the Negro blues, for which even in the USA the white market was negligible. This was to be crucially important for the naturalization of rock-and-roll in Britain and may explain why rock, in its naturalized British form, became the first Europeanized version of American black music which itself took the USA by storm in the 1960s. The link is quite clear in the case of the Rolling Stones, strongly influenced by one of the tiny group of passionate British blues-scholars, the late Alexis Korner. However, more generally, in the middle 1950s typical teenagers in

Birmingham were more likely to be familiar with Chicago blues-bar performers like Muddy Waters than typical teenagers in Indiana.

After this brief reminder of periodization, let us consider two particular aspects of the reception of jazz: who it appealed to and what the public read into it.

There is a striking difference here between Britain and the rest of Europe, at least in respect of the first question. The reception of the music was far more broadly based in Britain than elsewhere, it was far more readily naturalized and assimilated, since Britain already formed part of a linguistically and musically unified zone of popular culture with the USA. It therefore formed a bridge between the USA and the rest of Europe. Time and again continentals had their first experience of American jazz in London. Ansermet's well-known 1919 tribute to Bechet was inspired in London. In the 1920s not only did British bands tour the continent – one thinks, reluctantly, of the British ladies' jazz orchestra which played the Tabarin in Vienna – but the records of Jack Hylton were probably better known than those of the Americans and virtually represented jazz for many continentals. Hylton, a working-class boy and strong Labour Party supporter, shrewd enough to become a millionaire later, had recognized the potential of ragtime as early as 1913 when working as a dance-band musician at the London Savoy Hotel. By 1921 he was firmly in jazz. Even the British smart set was closer to America than café society elsewhere, again for obvious reasons. Clubs like the Embassy and hotels like the Savoy acted as pace-setters even before 1914, and in 1928 the Savoy actually engaged a genuine indigenous 'hot' band under a young Filipino gentleman of means, Federico or Fred Elizalde, who had plunged into jazz at Cambridge. Again, in the 1960s it was British rock-groups alone among the Europeans who established American reputations.

British jazz had a broad popular base, because its uniquely large working class had developed a, for Europe, uniquely recognizable, urbanized, non-traditional lifestyle. Even before 1914 huge popular dance halls had already been built for the holiday demand of specifically proletarian seaside resorts like Blackpool, Morecambe, Margate and Douglas on the Isle of Man. The post-war mania for dancing was immediately met by the new institution of the so-called Palais de Danse, of which the Hammersmith Palais, the first, immediately became a jazz venue by booking the Original Dixieland Jazz Band in 1919. No doubt the music to which the plebs danced would not always be considered jazz today. Indeed, the central tradition of British mass dancing moved away from jazz towards a curious phenomenon called 'strict tempo' dancing, which was to become a competitive sport on British television. Nevertheless, jazz made its mark as a name, an idea, a novel and demotic sound.

The massive dance mania produced an unusually large body of dance-band musicians, mainly of proletarian origin, or at least raised in the environment of the brass-band movement, much appreciated in the industrial areas. These formed the original core of the jazz public. In the Roaring Twenties the number of musicians rose by 50 per cent; between 1901 and 1911 it had grown by only 10 per cent. In 1931 there were about 30,000 of them, including, it must be admitted, a substantial body of cinema musicians whose interest in jazz was weaker. They had to learn the tricks of the music – much of the jazz literature of the decade was instructional – and were very likely to develop an interest in the real stuff, if only because of boredom with their usual activities. The trade journal of the profession, the *Melody Maker*, founded in 1926, almost immediately became a champion of jazz and was to remain the main European medium for jazz fans.

Socially speaking, dance-band musicians, who did rather better in the 1920s than in the depressed 1930s, were on the borders between the skilled workers and the lower-middle classes. It was in the higher parts of this zone that the bulk of British jazz evangelists were to be found before 1945. They were typically self-made intellectuals. In London we find 'Rhythm Clubs' (ninety-eight of which sprang up in Britain between 1933 and 1935) not in middle-class quarters like Chelsea, Kensington or even Hampstead, but in the outlying districts like Croydon, Forest Gate, Barking or Edmonton. The student component, while not absent, did not become very visible, let alone dominant, until much later. Jazz certainly retained its links with high society, but there is practically no sign of that appeal to culture, culture-snobbery and the avant-garde which is so striking on the continent, except on the fringe of avant-garde ballet, with Frederick Ashton and the composer–conductor Constant Lambert, and among some young camp-followers of the not very significant British surrealist movement. The established, even the up-and-coming, figures in culture and their reviews did not feel obliged to pay their respects to jazz. The writers who were to advertise a taste for it in the 1950s (Amis, Larkin, John Osborne) did so precisely because it was the badge of the provincial and the outsider. The intellectual press did not give it house-room until the middle 1950s. Perhaps this is the reason why the profile of the middle-class British jazz fan of the 1930s – generally someone reaching the age of fifteen or sixteen not earlier than 1933–5 – is comparatively low. The existence of a jazz underground among academics of the late 1930s vintage suggests that, while silent, at least some future intellectuals listened. The war expanded the jazz public enormously in Britain as elsewhere.

The strong popular and demotic component in the British jazz public distinguished it from the continental jazz publics, which were overwhelmingly composed of members of the established middle classes or the college-going classes. This is familiar ground to the students of continental *Kulturgeschichte*. 'Jazz was the music of the decade,' not only in the opinion of the numerous central European modernist musicians, but, as Michael Kater reminds us, for the brilliant young historian Eckart Kehr. The fluctuations of this public have been less noted, although it seems that at the end of the 1920s the passion for jazz as the music of the future diminished somewhat, a situation which opponents both on the right and on the Frankfurt School left welcomed. The fortunes of jazz under the Nazi and Soviet regimes have recently been fully described by Michael Kater and Frederick Starr, but so far no treatment of equivalent weight is known to me for fascist Italy.

Let us finally ask what this music meant to those who received it. To the ordinary public it meant, apart from a music for dancing, a certain kind of rhythm and a loud and unconventional sound ('a noisy and often deafening music created by various instruments of percussion and others', to quote a German dance manual of 1922); possibly also a music performed with wild abandon. Being, in the French phrase, 'a kind of legitimized barbarism' (*une certaine barbarie devenue licite*) it clearly suited rebels against convention and the older generations. In the 1920s, as we have seen, its associations were plainly with being 'modern' or 'contemporary'. *Paris-Midi* in 1925 coupled the jazz band with small motor-cars, Gillette razors and short hair for women. After the 1920s Negro music lost significance as a symbol of modernity, but especially after the Second World War it increasingly became a symbol of generational self-assertion. In the form of rock, it became the major international expression of an age-group's youth culture.

We can leave aside the reaction of high society and its associated intellectuals. In Britain this was of no great importance, though doubtless it pleased Duke Ellington to have the future King Edward VIII sit in on drums at a party for his band in London. Much more important, as has been suggested, was the democratic and populist character of the music, which made the *Melody Maker* state approvingly: 'It appeals not only to the fauteuils but to the gallery also. It considers no class distinction.' In Britain – but only here – we can also neglect the creative avant-garde which elsewhere, convinced of the exhaustion of the old music, looked to circus, music hall, street musicians and jazz to regenerate it, or the central European cultural bolsheviks who went a step further and associated it with the proletariat and revolution. Britain escaped this phase. What it did develop, however, probably in close association with American New Deal radicalism, was a powerful bonding of jazz, blues, folk and the extreme left, mainly communist but also, marginally, anarchist. For such people jazz and blues were essentially 'people's music' in three senses: a music with folk roots and capable of appealing to the masses, a do-it-yourself music which could be practised by ordinary people, as distinct from those with technical training, and lastly a music for protest, demonstration and collective celebration. Revivalist or Dixieland jazz lent itself unusually well to all these purposes. So much so that at its peak in the 1950s it came closer to turning jazz from the art of a coterie into a mass music than has been achieved anywhere else, except perhaps, for a moment, during the swing boom of the later 1930s in the USA. It is no accident that a typical anthem of the 'trad' jazz fans also became the typical song of the football fans on the terraces: 'When the Saints Go Marching In'. However, it should be noticed that, while revivalist jazz became *de facto* the music of an age-group, in which students, and particularly art students, became prominent for the first time, it was neither consciously nor militantly a youth music. In this it differed from its successor, rock-and-roll. The heros of 'trad' jazz were ancients disinterred from blues bars and the back country of the Deep South. Its intellectual guides and organizers, even some of its leaders, were growing middle-aged. Several were old enough to have been through the war. (Of fifteen leaders of British 'trad' groups in the 1950s one was born in 1917, three in 1920–1, two in 1926, nine in 1928–32, six of the latter in 1928–9.) The 'trad' boom prepared the triumph of rock, but only rock turned itself into a conscious manifesto of immaturity.

The overwhelming majority of the jazz public and (privately) of the first-generation jazz evangelists and critics, remained loyal to the 'old' music when the bop revolution penetrated across the Atlantic after the second war. Broadly speaking, until the very late 1950s, when Miles Davis began to make his impact, 'modern' jazz appealed only to a minority of young professional band musicians, now decimated by the decline of the big band, and soon to be even more marginalized by the rise of the disco. It was slow to establish any kind of public. The majority jazz community was small enough. My own calculations, made in the late 1950s, suggest that the British hard-core jazz public in that decade was somewhere between the 25,000 who bought a specialist jazz journal like the *Jazz News* and the 115,000 who bought the traditional weekly of the jazz lover, the *Melody Maker*. The total national public for a major tour by a major American band could then be estimated at about 100,000. Its intellectual sector was much smaller. Jazz books could be expected to sell about 8,000 copies. However, there can be no doubt that between 1945 and 1955 jazz established itself in Britain as an accepted and recognized part of educated culture, as it had not been up to the war. It emerged from the war in France, perhaps in part due to the anti-fascist associations of an anti-racist music, not so much as a main pillar of *la culture française* but rather as something to which even the cultural pillars had to pay their respects: *Le Monde* reviewed it, as *Le Temps* would never have dreamed of doing; Jean-Paul Sartre acknowledged it. However, its position in official music remained somewhat marginal until much later.

The reception of jazz in Europe therefore consists of two quite different phenomena. The reception of the broad jazz-based, jazz-influenced forms of popular music was virtually universal. The reception of jazz as a form of popularly generated high-art music was confined to a minority, and remains so confined, although a certain acquaintance with jazz eventually became an accepted part of educated culture. Small as it is, the European jazz public has long played a significant role in jazz, since it formed a much more stable body of support than the very volatile American public. This was to be important in the 1960s and 1970s, when the wave of rock swept jazz almost from sight in the USA, and American musicians, often actually based in Europe, came to rely largely on the European concert and festival circuit, as indeed many of them still do. This did not, however, necessarily indicate any major expansion of the hard-core European jazz public. However, developments in the post-war era do not belong in this survey. The jazz public was and remains a much smaller minority than the public for classical music, to judge both by record sales and by the amount of time devoted to it on the radio. The reception of jazz (in the narrower sense) is to be judged not by the number of its converts, but by the merits of the music and the extraordinary interest of the very process of transatlantic transfer for the cultural and social historian.

CHAPTER 23

The People's Swing

This essay was originally published as a review of The Duke Ellington Reader *edited by Mark Tucker (Oxford, 1993) and* Swing Changes: Big Band Jazz in New Deal America *by David Stowe, in the* London Review of Books, *24 November 1994.*

In the elite minority arts of the twentieth century, the US component is one of many, and by no means the most important. On the other hand, it penetrates, indeed dominates, the popular culture of the globe with the single exception of sport, which still echoes the British hegemony over the nineteenth-century era of the bourgeoisie and the first industrial revolution, via tennis, golf and, above all, association football. So it is not surprising that what are generally accepted as the major North American contributions to the high culture of our century are rooted in popular and – the US being what it is – commercial entertainment: films and the music shaped by jazz.

There is a notable difference between Hollywood and Forty-Second Street, however. Hollywood, like Henry Ford, conquered the world by mass production: in this instance, of dreams. Its fundamental concern was with the greatest happiness of the greatest number, as measured by box-office returns. The musical analogue of Hollywood has, of course, been profoundly imbued with the influence of black music, and never more so than since the rise of rock-and-roll in the mid-1950s. Indeed, since the days of ragtime the popular music business could not have existed without this continuous infusion. The jazz which was discovered as a heavyweight art in the late 1920s by little groups of impassioned aficionados was to be found only in the medium of commercial musical entertainment.

Its greatest figure, who has been properly honoured in the 536 pages of Mark Tucker's *Duke Ellington Reader*, a 'source-book of writings on Ellington', lived and died as a travelling bandleader. It was not that he had to – in his later years he subsidized his band out of his royalties – but that he could not conceive of creating his music except in this specific ambience. Nevertheless, jazz was a minority art, practised by a minority and appealing to a public much smaller than the public for classical music. In the early days of its reception, the main problem for enthusiasts was to discover the few needles of 'hot' jazz in the enormous haystack of vaguely rhythmic dance music, to find ways of defining what distinguished the real stuff from the surrounding sweet or syncopated dross, and to defend it against philistines who would not see the difference.

The nature of the milieu in which the extraordinary art of blues and jazz was incubated is by now fairly well known, thanks to a large and increasingly scholarly literature. There has even been a little work done on the nature of the public, though (in the USA) it tends to be inflamed by national *amour propre*. For it is harder for North American than for European writers to accept that a cultural glory of the USA was first taken seriously elsewhere. According to Tucker, it was in the early 1930s that Ellington enjoyed 'the beginnings of critical attention (mostly from abroad)'. We can see one of his earliest champions trying in 1933 to make him acceptable to the readers of *Fortune* by citing his recent triumphs in Europe, 'which is more critical and discriminating about all kinds of music than the US' – though, one must add, not more knowledgeable.

For a few years, from the mid-1930s to the mid-1940s, 'hot' jazz, under the trade-name 'swing' and through the medium of the big band, became the main – or at least a main – idiom of commercial popular music. After that it returned to a musically more ambitious but numerically more restricted ghetto. Chronologically, swing more or less coincided with the era of Franklin Roosevelt. Others have hinted at or speculated about the links between the political and cultural histories of the USA during this period, but David Stowe, who teaches American Thought and Language at Michigan State University, is, to my knowledge, the first writer to have attempted a systematic history of the relationship between jazz and New Deal America.

The most immediate impact of Roosevelt's America on jazz came through the political left, ranging from New Deal enthusiasts for a democratic people's culture to the Communist Party, which took jazz to its bosom from 1935 on. (The *trotskisant* intellectuals of New York appear to have shown no interest in the music, though its greatest champion once signed a letter of protest in *New Masses* with Edmund Wilson, Meyer Schapiro and the Trillings, whom it is difficult to envisage tapping their feet to Count Basie.) The contribution of the left was not only to discover talent, though nobody else took a serious interest in obscure – and, more important, non-commercial – Southern blues singers. Music-business bookers like Moe Gale, the (white) owner of the Savoy Ballroom in Harlem, could be as perceptive in judging future talent, when it came their way, as John Hammond, the greatest of the talent scouts of the decade, though they ranged less widely. What the left did was – deliberately and successfully – to bring black music out of the ghetto by mobilizing that curious combination of radical Jews and well-heeled liberal Wasps, the New York establishment.

John Hammond Jr (1910–87), to whom Stowe (rightly) devotes more space than to anyone else with the exception of Ellington, typified this combination. A Vanderbilt, Hammond was an almost absurdly typical Ivy League product and (in his last years) a devoted member of the Century, New York's quintessential establishment club. At the same time he was an impassioned and lifelong militant for the cause of racial equality, and therefore for years close to the communists. Though never in the party – even the FBI satisfied itself of this after years of investigation – he was nevertheless (if I may quote my own memories of him) much more than the generic New Deal 'progressivism' to which Stowe tries to reduce him.

Hammond's record as a discoverer and developer of talent from 1933 to his death was unparalleled. It rested not only on astonishing knowledge and judgment, but on his ability to mobilize the three crucial components of New York – and therefore national – success: personal relations, a metropolitan public priding itself on the *New Yorker* combination of liberalism and sophistication, and a show-business community secure in the exploitation of this market. Hollywood was to collapse before McCarthyism; Broadway swayed, but remained standing. The *New Yorker* has remained steadily loyal to jazz since the 1930s, and *The Duke Ellington Reader* is worth its price simply for Richard Boyer's magnificent profile of the great man ('The Hot Bach'), which first appeared there in 1944. It is safe to say that, at that time, in no American city outside New York would nightclubs like Café Society, militantly devoted to the social mixing and music-making of black and white, managed by the brother of a Comintern agent (and partly financed by Hammond), have become the toast of the town.

The point, however, is that success in New York was more than purely local, since the city was to radio and records, which were the foundations of success in popular music, what Hollywood was to films. Benny Goodman became the 'King of Swing' not only because Hammond talked this gifted man, then a disenchanted studio musician, into forming a band: Goodman took on a top-class black ex-bandleader as his arranger, devised a jazz sound rather than playing routine commercial dance music and, not least, mixed black musicians with white ones. Thanks to Hammond's contacts, he recorded, and got the engagements which implied radio broadcasts syndicated across the country. As every jazz lover knows, when a discouraged band arrived in California after a cross-country tour in 1935 it found itself already famous among the university students who had listened to the late-night Eastern broadcasts of 'Let's Dance', which reached the Pacific in prime time. Through Columbia Records, MCA and the radio networks, the New York left nationalized swing.

This minority initiative was crucial, since there is no evidence that either the public for popular dance music or the jazz musicians changed much – though the hard core of jazz enthusiasts grew substantially. The public (and especially the adolescent or student young, whose economic potential the pop industry discovered through swing) simply found themselves exposed to, and enjoying, a new sound. The multiplying rival bands criss-crossed the country for their own benefit and that of the record industry, whose sales rose with the bands' popularity, largely thanks to the new vogue for juke-boxes which, in 1940, consumed almost half of all the records produced. Record sales soared from 10 million at the bottom of the Depression to 130 million in 1941 – which was the industry's best year since 1921.

As for the musicians, they remained exactly the same horn-blowing, piano-playing or rhythm-generating pros as before. To what extent they were affected by the political convictions of the time, and those of their patrons, is difficult to establish, though we may take it that the black artists shared the mass conversion of their race to FDR's Democratic Party, which was also the home of working-class ethnics and those Jews who did not stand further to the left. Politics was not a subject about which people whose life was music thought very much. For black artists, the savage and pervasive racial discrimination was a deeply resented fact of life, but almost certainly most of them doubted whether politics could do much about it.

Black intellectuals, on the other hand, were markedly politicized, and were attracted by the communists' genuine passion for racial integration and the promotion of black culture. (The Daily Worker issued a three-column apology for the 'errors' of a purist music critic who had written an insufficiently respectful review of a black swing concert at Carnegie Hall.) Even Ellington, who showed no fondness of the white party-liners – there was notorious friction between him and Hammond – supported various red-tinged causes so frequently that he attracted the attention of the FBI, a fact noted by Stowe, who has looked at their files, but unmentioned in Tucker's *Reader*. The trumpeter Rex Stewart claimed to have read Marx and Spengler, but most jazz players at that time did not see themselves as intellectuals.

It is not excluded that musicians who played the dances at Camp Unity, a Communist Party retreat in the red section of the Borscht Belt, may have improvised on an idea or two between sets, although what most of them remembered – it was then virtually unknown – was the public encouragement of interracial sex. (Nevertheless, the tradition of apartheid was so strong that older musicians like Sidney Bechet forbade his sidemen to fraternize with white women even at Camp Unity, for fear that it might cost him his engagement.) 'I think they were trying to prove how equalitarian they were,' thought the admittedly unusual Dizzy Gillespie, who actually took out a party card, probably not only, as he later claimed, because it would get him more gigs. Count Basie was more typical. He recorded a politically charged satire on Southern poverty and racism with reluctance, out of obligation to his discoverer Hammond, who pressed it on him.

What the jazz of the Roosevelt era owed to the left has long been known. While Stowe's account brings much that is unfamiliar, it brings little that is unexpected. His attempt to establish more general relations between swing and the ethos of New Deal America is more novel. It is based partly on a perceptive analysis of the Chicago-based *Downbeat* (founded in 1934), Middle America's rather than New York's take on the swing phenomenon. Into the inconsistent jumble of this journal's contents he reads a 'swing ideology' which 'expressed reverence for such cherished American ideas as liberty, democracy, tolerance and equality, while holding firmly to the conviction that the experience of swing was both sign and engine of a fundamentally rational and ever-improving American society'. Its conviction was anti-racist, or rather a belief that 'there are no colour lines in music'; it expressed doubts about integrated big bands, and did not exclude a self-righteous belief in American superiority, and hostility to 'un-American ideals', pursued by 'groups of unassimilated peoples here ... breeding hates among themselves and disrespect for American institutions' – that is, Nazis and communists. Moreover, as Stowe notes in passing, the 'swing ideology' had little room for women. Whatever its characteristics, Roosevelt was shrewd enough to appeal to it: Eleanor went to a gospel performance at Café Society and invited the singers to the White House, while their son, Franklin Jr, 'listened raptly' to the (integrated) Benny Goodman quartet in Boston.

Perhaps the most interesting part of Stowe's book is what he has to say on swing music in the war. Unlike the First World War, as observers persistently complained, the Second produced no universally popular war songs and certainly no marching songs. Explanations differed but the fact was not disputed. Tin Pan Alley produced patriotic numbers, but nobody took them up. What Stowe suggests is that 'in this war, morale was best protected not by creating the kind of national pride associated with patriotic songs but by appealing to an exclusive and privatised notion of aesthetic experience'. The United States 'was unable to command' unselfish obligation to the state. Private obligations 'to buddies, to family, American womanhood, the American Way of Life' took its place.

There is something in this. One doubts whether the British or Soviet war could have produced a novel like Heller's *Catch-22*. Yet this cannot be the whole explanation, for the songs which appealed to other armies – 'Lili Marlene' is the obvious case in point – also had little to do with patriotism or the public sphere. Could it not be that the enormous success of the great swing bands blanked out what most native white and working-class Americans really wanted to hear – namely, the sentimental and deeply personal songs of what came to be called 'country music' when it emerged as a major sector of the pop industry after 1950? Glenn Miller's band was the public face of popular culture in the war, but swing was not designed for the private face, except perhaps, eventually, through the vocalists generated by the big bands (Frank Sinatra, for example) who were to survive their collapse as they switched to sentiment. Unfortunately, however, Stowe does not enquire into the other branches of pop music until after the war, when swing's dramatic decline began.

The suddenness of that decline in 1946–7 is clear. Attendances dropped sharply, thus causing economic havoc among big bands, always expensive but with costs swollen by years of unbroken expansion and wartime inflation. In the winter of 1946–7, Goodman, Woody Herman, Artie Shaw, Tommy Dorsey, Les Brown, Harry James, Jack Teagarden and Benny Carter dissolved their bands. The big band was never to recover. Even the 'sweet' bands, traditional rivals to swing, suffered from a decline in public dancing.

There is no adequate explanation – at least the book has none – of this sudden collapse, which entailed the return of jazz to its ghetto. The future of pop music, when it took its lasting post-war shape in the 1950s, would rest on the branches hitherto neglected by the national entertainment industry: country music and, above all, rhythm-and-blues (rock-and-roll), which, as it happens, contained an even larger dose of black musical influence than swing. The jazz component which survived swing – bebop – had no interest in winning a large public; was, indeed, designed to antagonize it. Hammond did not like the new avant-garde. After a fallow period, he returned to discovering and promoting talent – Bob Dylan, Aretha Franklin, Bruce Springsteen – but, unlike the history of jazz in the 1930s, that of popular music since rock hardly needs to refer to him. The old lefties, out-of-sorts with bebop, concentrated on what for most of them had always been the music of their heart, folk-singing.

At this point Stowe's attempt to link the fortunes of swing with the New Deal breaks down. It is all very well to draw a parallel with the fragmentation of 'the Roosevelt coalition of workers, urban ethnics, African-Americans, farmers and intellectuals', which broke up in 1948, but whereas a political or quasi-political mechanism for the rise of swing can be proposed, no such mechanism is suggested for its decline. It would be surprising if there were no connection between swing's collapse and the end of the New Deal era, but one needs to show how and why. This is the weakest part of an interesting book. Perhaps the real mystery is not why swing fell, but why, as a writer in *Downbeat* pointed out in 1949, in the 1930s the general public (assisted, it must be said, by the popular music industry) accepted the musical preferences of jazz musicians and their essentially adolescent and student constituency.

Amid the ruins only one monument was left standing – even Count Basie had briefly reduced his band to a small group. Ellington had been there before swing. Though the phrase 'It don't mean a thing if it ain't got that swing' was his, he never belonged to the swing fashion. He even refused to accept the exclusive label of 'jazz' for his music. He was there after swing, almost certainly the greatest figure in twentieth-century American music. All his admirers will want to own *The Duke Ellington Reader*, admirably selected and edited by a professor of music at Columbia University.

CHAPTER 24

Jazz since 1960

This chapter is based on introductions written for new editions of my book
The Jazz Scene *in 1989 and 1992.*

Jazz has always been a minority interest, like classical music, but unlike classical music the taste for it has not been stable. Interest in it has grown by spurts and, conversely, there have been times when it was in the doldrums. The later 1930s and the 1950s were a period when it expanded quite strikingly, the years of the 1929 slump (in the USA at least) when even Harlem preferred soft lights and sweet music to Ellington and Armstrong. The periods when interest in jazz has grown or revived have also, for reasons obvious to publishers, been the times when new generations of fans wanted to know more about it.

The 1950s were such a period. The golden age of the 1950s came to a sudden end, leaving jazz to retreat into rancorous and poverty-stricken isolation for some twenty years. What made this generation of loneliness so melancholy and paradoxical was that the music that almost killed jazz was derived from the same roots that had generated jazz: rock-and-roll was and is very obviously the offspring of American blues. The young, without whom jazz cannot exist – hardly any jazz fan has ever been converted after the age of twenty – abandoned it, and with spectacular suddenness. Three years after 1960, when the golden age was at its peak, in the year of the Beatles' triumph across the world, jazz had been virtually knocked out of the ring. 'Bird Lives' could still be seen painted on lonely walls, but the celebrated New York jazz venue named after him, Birdland, had ceased to exist. To revisit New York in 1963 was a depressing experience for the jazz lover who had last experienced it in 1960.

This did not mean that jazz disappeared, only that both its musicians and its public grew older, and were not reinforced by the young. Of course outside the USA and Britain, which were the main centres and sources of rock, the youthful public for jazz, though probably socially and intellectually select and upmarket, remained substantial and commercially far from negligible. More than one American jazz player found it convenient for this reason to emigrate to Europe in those decades. In France, Italy and Germany, Brazil and Japan, Scandinavia and – commercially less relevant – the USSR and eastern Europe, jazz remained viable. In the USA and Britain its public was confined to middle-aged men and women who had been young in the 1920s, 1930s or, at best, in the 1950s. As an established English saxophone player put it in 1976: 'I don't think I could make a living totally in this country. I don't think anyone could ... There aren't enough people, there isn't enough money ... The band has been to Germany more times in the last couple of years than it's done gigs in this country.'[1]

Such was the reality of jazz in the 1960s and much of the 1970s, at any rate in the Anglo-Saxon world. There was no market for it. According to the *Billboard International Music Industry Directory* of 1972 a mere 1.3 per cent of records and tapes sold in the USA represented jazz, as against 6.1 per cent of classical music and 75 per cent rock and similar music. Jazz clubs went on closing, jazz recitals declined, avant-garde musicians played for each other in private apartments, and the growing recognition of jazz as something which belonged to official American culture, while providing a welcome subsidy to uncommercial musicians through schools, colleges and other institutions, reinforced the youthful conviction that jazz now belonged to the world of the adults. Unlike rock, it was not *their own music*. Only a certain exhaustion of the musical impulse behind rock, which first became obvious in the later 1970s, began to leave room for a revival of interest in jazz, as distinct from rock. (Some jazz musicians had, of course, devised a 'fusion' of jazz and rock, to the horror of purists especially from the avant-garde, and it was probably through this merger that jazz retained a certain public presence in the years of isolation: through Miles Davis, Chick Corea, Herbie Hancock, the British guitarist John McLoughlin and the Austrian–American combination of Joe Zawinul and Wayne Shorter in 'Weather Report'.)

Why should rock have almost killed jazz for twenty years? Both derived from the music of black Americans, and it was through jazz musicians and jazz fans that the black blues first came to the attention of the public outside the Southern states and the Northern ghettos. Since they were among the few whites who were familiar with the artists and repertoire of 'race record' catalogues (diplomatically renamed 'rhythm-and-blues' in the late 1940s), white jazz- and blues-lovers were instrumental in launching rock. Ahmet Ertegun, who founded Atlantic Records, which became a leading rock label, was one of two brothers who had long formed part of the tiny international community of jazz-record collectors and experts. John Hammond, whose crucial role in the development of jazz in the 1930s has been mentioned, also developed the careers of Bob Dylan, Aretha Franklin and, later, Bruce Springsteen. Where would British rock have been without the influence of the handful of local blues enthusiasts like the late Alexis Korner, who inspired the Rolling Stones, or the ('trad') jazz enthusiasts who imported American country and city blues singers like Muddy Waters and made them familiar in Lancashire and Lanark long before more than a handful of Americans outside some black ghettos even knew of their existence?

Initially there seemed to be no hostility or incompatibility between jazz and rock, even though attentive readers of my book *The Jazz Scene* will register the note of gentle contempt with which critics and, above all, the musical professionals of jazz then treated the early triumphs of rock-and-roll, whose public seemed unable to distinguish between a Bill Haley ('Rock Around the Clock') and a Chuck Berry. A crucial distinction between jazz and rock was that rock was never a minority music. Rhythm-and-blues, as it developed after the Second World War, was the folk music of urban blacks in the 1940s, when one and a quarter million blacks left the South for the Northern and Western ghettos. They constituted a new market, which was then supplied chiefly by independent record labels like Chess Records, founded in Chicago in 1949 by two Polish immigrants connected with the club circuit, and specializing in the so-called 'Chicago Blues' style (Muddy Waters, Howlin' Wolf, Sonny Boy Williamson) and recording, among others, Chuck Berry, who was probably – with Elvis Presley – the major influence on 1950s rock-and-roll. White adolescents began to buy black r&b records in the early 1950s, having discovered this music on local and specialized radio stations which multiplied during those years, as the mass of adults transferred its attentions to television. At first sight they seemed to be the habitual tiny and untypical minority which can still be seen on the fringes of black entertainment, like the white visitors to Chicago ghetto blues clubs. Yet, as soon as the music industry became aware of this potential white youth market, it became evident that rock was the opposite of a minority taste. It was the music of an entire age-group.

Almost certainly that was the result of the 'economic miracle' of the 1950s, which not only created a Western world of full employment, but also, probably for the first time, gave the mass of adolescents adequately paid jobs and therefore money in the pocket, or an unprecedented share of middle-class parents' prosperity. It was this children's and adolescents' market that transformed the music industry. From 1955, when rock-and-roll was born, to 1959 American record sales rose by 36 per cent every year. After a brief pause, the British invasion of 1963, led by the Beatles, initiated an even more spectacular surge: US record sales, which had grown from $277 million in 1955 to $600 million in 1959, had passed $2,000 million by 1973 (now including tapes). Seventy-five to 80 per cent of these sales represented rock music and similar sounds. The commercial fortunes of the record industry had never before depended so overwhelmingly on a single musical genre addressed to a single narrow age-band. The correlation of record sales with economic development and income was utterly obvious. In 1973 the highest per-capita expenditure on records occurred in the USA, followed (in rank order) by Sweden, West Germany, the Netherlands and Britain. All these countries spent between $7 and $10. In the same year Italians, Spaniards and Mexicans spent between $1 and $1.4 per head, and Brazilians $0.66.

Almost immediately rock music thus became the all-purpose medium for expressing the desires, instincts, feelings and aspirations of the age-set between puberty and the moments when adults settle down in some conventional social niche, family or career: the voice and idiom of a self-conscious 'youth' and 'youth culture' in modern industrial societies. It could express anything and everything within this age-range, but while rock clearly developed regional, national, class or politico-ideological variants, its basic idiom, like the equally demotic–populist costume associated with youth (notably jeans) crossed national, class and ideological barriers. As in the lives of its age-groups, in rock music the public and the private, feeling and conviction, love, rebellion and art, acting as doing and as stage-behaviour, were not distinguishable from each other. Older observers, for instance, used to keeping revolution and music apart in principle and to judging each by its own criteria, were apt to be perplexed by the apocalyptic rhetoric which could surround rock at the peak of the global youth rebellion, when *Rolling Stone* wrote, apropos of a 1969 rock concert:

An army of peaceful guerrillas established a city larger than Rochester, New York, and showed itself immediately ready to turn back on the already ravaged city and [its] inoperable life-styles, imminently prepared to move onto the mist-covered field and into the cool, still woods. And they will do it again, the threat of youthful dissidence in Paris and

Prague and Fort Lauderdale and Berkeley and Chicago and London criss-crossing ever more closely until the map of the world we live in is viable for and visible to all of those that are part of it and all those buried under it.[2]

Woodstock was obviously a marvellous experience for the participants, but even then its political significance and the strictly musical interest of a lot of its performers were not as obvious as all that.

A universal cultural idiom cannot be judged by the same criteria as a special kind of art-music, and there was and is no point in judging rock by the standards of good jazz. However, rock deprived jazz of most of its potential new listeners, because the young people who flocked to rock found in it, in a simplified and perhaps coarsened version, much, if not everything, that had attracted their elders to jazz: rhythm, an immediately identifiable voice or 'sound', real (or faked) spontaneity and vitality, and a way of directly transferring human emotions into music. Moreover, they discovered all this in a music which was related to jazz. Why would they need jazz? With rare exceptions, the young who would have been converted to jazz now had an alternative.

What made that alternative increasingly attractive, and helped to reduce the space for an embattled and isolated jazz still further, was its own transformation. As the bebop revolutionaries rejoined the mainstream of jazz in the second half of the 1950s, the new avant-garde of 'free jazz', moving towards atonality and breaking down everything that had hitherto given jazz a structure – including the beat round which it was organized – widened the gap between the music and its public, including the jazz public. And it was not surprising that the avant-garde reacted to the desertion of the public by taking an even more extreme and embattled stance. At the start of the new revolution it was perfectly easy to recognize in, say, Ornette Coleman's saxophone the blues feeling of his native Texas, and the tradition of the great horn-players of the past was obvious in Coltrane. Yet those were not the things the innovators wanted the public to notice about them.

But the situation of the new avant-garde in the dark decades was paradoxical. The loosening of the traditional framework of jazz, its increasing shifts towards something like avant-garde classical music developed from a jazz base, opened it to all manner of non-jazz influences, European, African, Islamic, Latin American and especially Indian. In the 1960s it went through a variety of exoticisms. In other words, it became less American than it had been, and far more cosmopolitan than before. Perhaps because the American jazz public became relatively less important in jazz, perhaps for other reasons, after 1962 free jazz became the first style of jazz whose history cannot be written without taking account of important developments in Europe and, one might add, of European musicians.

At the same time – and equally paradoxically – the new avant-garde which broke with jazz tradition was unusually anxious to stress its links with the tradition, even when they had previously taken very little notice of it: as when Coltrane (1926–67) in 1961 took up the soprano saxophone, hitherto virtually monopolized by the recently deceased Sidney Bechet, and was followed by numerous young avant-garde horn-players. Bechet had been little more than a musically irrelevant name to most musicians of Coltrane's generation. This reassertion of tradition was political rather than musical. For – the third aspect of the paradox – the 1960s jazz avant-garde was consciously and politically *black*, as no previous generation of black jazzmen had been, though *The Jazz Scene* already noted the links between jazz experimentation and black consciousness. As Whitney Balliett put it in the 1970s: 'Free jazz is actually the blackest jazz there is.'[3] Black and politically *radical*. Thus *Charlie Haden: Liberation Music Orchestra* (1969) contained four Spanish Civil War songs, a number inspired by the riots at the 1968 Chicago Democratic Convention, a commemoration of Che Guevara and a version of 'We Shall Overcome'. Archie Shepp (tenor and soprano sax), one of the major figures of the avant-garde, created a musical commemoration of Malcolm X and an *Attica Blues* inspired by the well-known black prison riot. Political consciousness continued to link the avant-garde to the mass of the American black people and its musical traditions, and therefore provided a possible way back to the mainstream of jazz. However, in the short run it must have made the isolation of that avant-garde from an uncomprehending black public particularly frustrating.

A rejection of success (except on those uncompromising terms proposed by this artist) is characteristic of avant-gardes, and in jazz, which has always lived by the paying customer, concessions to the box office seemed particularly dangerous to the player who wanted the status of 'artist'. How could they compromise with rock? ('There is a certain political position involved in the choice of those who seldom refer to the more readily assimilated rock-rhythms.')[4] And yet, for three reasons, rock had to influence jazz.

The first is that American (and British) jazz musicians born since the 1940s grew up in an atmosphere drenched in rock, or its ghetto equivalent, and therefore could hardly avoid assimilating some of it.

The second is that rock, an art of amateurs and the musically or even the alphabetically illiterate, required – and because of its limitless wealth could call upon – the technical and musical competence of jazz professionals, and jazz musicians could hardly be blamed for wanting to cut themselves thin slices of so huge and sweet a cake. But third, and most important, rock was musically innovative. As so often in the history of the arts, major artistic revolutions come not from self-described revolutionaries but from those employing innovation for commercial purposes. As the early movies were more effectively revolutionary than cubism, so the rock entrepreneurs have changed the musical scene more profoundly than classical or free jazz avant-gardes.

The major innovation of rock was technological. It secured the mass breakthrough of electronic music. Pedants may point out that in jazz there were pioneers of electrified instruments (Charlie Christian revolutionized the guitar that way and Billie Holiday transformed the use of the human voice by marrying it to the personal microphone) and that revolutionary ways of generating sound, such as syn-thesizers, were pioneered for classical avant-garde music concerts. However, it is undeniable that rock was the first music that sys-tematically substituted electrified instruments for acoustic ones and systematically used electronic technology not for special effects but for the normal repertoire accepted by a mass public. It was the first music to turn the technicians of sound and recording studios into equal partners in the creation of a musical performance, chiefly because the incompetence of the actual rock performers was often such that no adequate records or even performances could have been achieved otherwise. It is evident that such innovations could not but interest musicians of genuine originality and talent.

The second rock innovation concerns the concept of the 'group'. The rock group not only developed an original instrumentation behind the voice or voices (basically, percussion and various kinds of electric guitars, the bass guitar taking the place of the bass), but consisted essentially of a collective rather than a small group of virtuosos who expected to demonstrate their skills.[5] Of course the members of very few rock groups, unlike those of jazz combos, had any individual skills to demonstrate. Moreover, the 'group' was ideally characterized by an unmistakable 'sound', an auditory trademark by means of which it, or rather its studio technicians, attempted to establish its individuality. And, unlike the old 'big band' of jazz, the rock group was small. It produced its 'big sound' (which does not necessarily mean a large volume of sound, though rock preferred ultra-strong amplification) with a minimal number of people. This helped to bring small jazz groups back to something that had commonly been lost sight of in the days of the bebop succession of solos, namely the possibility of collective improvisation and small-group *texture*. Sophisticated rock arrangements like the Beatles' *Sergeant Pepper*, not unreasonably described as 'symphonic rock', could not but give intelligent jazz musicians ideas.

The third interesting element in rock was its insistent and pulsating rhythm. While initially it was plainly much cruder than jazz rhythm, the combination of various rhythm instruments which made up the rock group – for all its keyboards, guitars and percussion would normally have belonged to the rhythm section of a jazz band – produced its own potential complexities, which jazz players could transform into multi-layered and shifting ostinatos and rhythmic counterpoints.

And yet, while, as we have seen, some of the most talented jazz musicians developed a jazz–rock 'fusion' in the 1970s – Miles Davis' *Bitches Brew* of 1969 set the pace – the merged style did not permanently shape the future of jazz, nor did the injection of jazz elements provide a permanent life-giving blood transfusion for rock. What seems to have happened is a growing musical exhaustion of rock in the course of the 1970s which may or may not be connected with the retreat of the great wave of youth rebellion which reached its peak in the late 1960s and early 1970s. Somehow, insensibly, the space for jazz seemed to become a little less cramped. One began to observe that intelligent or fashionable fifth- or sixth-formers once again began to treat parents of their friends who possessed Miles Davis records with a certain interest.

By the late 1970s and early 1980s there were undeniable signs of a modest revival, even though by then much of the classical repertoire of jazz had been frozen into permanent immobility by the death of so many of its great and formative figures, ancient and modern: the jazz life has not favoured longevity. For by 1980 even some of the formative 'new music' stars had disappeared: for example, John Coltrane, Albert Ayler, Eric Dolphy. Much of the jazz which the new fans learned to love was thus incapable of further change and development, because it was a music of the dead, a situation which was to provide scope for a curious form of resurrectionism, by which live musicians reproduced the sounds of the past, as when a team under the direction of Bob Wilber reconstituted the music and sound of the early Ellington band for the film *Cotton Club*. Moreover, initially a very high proportion of the live jazz the new fans could hear came from musicians ranging from the rather middle-aged to the very ancient. Thus at the time I wrote a similar introduction for an Italian reprint of *The Jazz Scene* which appeared in 1982, jazz lovers in

London had the choice of listening to a variety of veterans: to Harry 'Sweets' Edison, Joe Newman, Buddy Tate and Frank Foster, who had been enrolled in the Basie band of long ago; to Nate Pierce, known since the days of Woody Herman; Shelly Manne and Art Pepper, familiar from the 'cool' days of the 1950s; Al Grey, who went back to the swing bands of the 1930s; Trummy Young of 1912 vintage, who had spent long years with Louis Armstrong; and other members of the older generation. Indeed, among the important players performing that week perhaps only the pianist McCoy Tyner (born 1938), known for his work with Coltrane in the 1960s, would not have been immediately familiar to most jazz lovers in 1960.

The jazz revival has continued since then. It has, inevitably, benefited the diminishing band of survivors, some of whom, returning from exile in Europe or in the anonymity of television, film and recording studios, have reconstituted groups dissolved long since, at least for occasional engagements and tours, such as the Modern Jazz Quartet, and the Art Farmer–Benny Golson Jazztet. It has been a particular blessing for the survivors of the first jazz revolution, for it is bebop that emerged or re-emerged as the central style of 1980s and 1990s jazz and the basic model for youthful musicians. Conversely, the new revival has left out the old, the first 'return to tradition' of those who wanted to recapture the music of New Orleans and the 1920s. 'Trad', 'Dixieland' or whatever it may be called, the longest-lasting of jazz styles, the one which, based on the happy nostalgia of white middle-class and increasingly middle-aged amateurs best resisted the cavalry charge of rock, has not felt the new wind in its sails.

The players who have probably benefited most from it are the gifted musicians who soldiered on through the dark days of the avant-garde in the 1960s and 1970s and who are tempted back into the jazz mainstream by the reappearance of a living jazz public. Such players were not young by the standards of the days when an Armstrong won a world reputation in his twenties, a Charlie Parker was dead at thirty-five, and nobody was surprised that the jazz guitar was revolutionized by a player (Charlie Christian) who was scarcely out of his teens. Thus the members of the influential World Saxophone Quartet, which made its reputation in the 1980s (Hamiett Bluiett, Julius Hemphill, Oliver Lake, David Murray) were born, respectively, in 1938, 1940, 1942 and 1955 – that is to say all except one were, at the time of writing (1988), in their late forties. Where we find new American jazz stars with a reputation while in their twenties, they are, very likely, second-generation players like the brothers Marsalis (Wynton, classical and jazz trumpet, was born in 1960; Branford, a saxophonist, in 1961).[6] More recently genuinely youthful first-generation musicians of major achievement have emerged. Yet there was something strange about this revival, even though that strangeness made it more familiar to such ancient jazz lovers as the present author. The jazz of the early 1990s looked back.

Consider the *Downbeat Critics Poll* of 1991, which lists as its 'Jazz Artists of the Year' Wynton Marsalis, Benny Carter, Sonny Rollins, Jackie McLean, Dizzy Gillespie, Cecil Taylor, Henry Threadgill and David Murray. Five of these eight were household names in 1961, two came up in the hard years of jazz exile and are now middle-aged, and only Wynton Marsalis (a second-generation jazz-man) belongs to the 1980s. The *Readers Poll* (December 1990) is not noticeably future-oriented, though it gives more space to middle-aged talents who paid their dues in the dark years (Jack de Johnette, Marcus Roberts, Phil Woods, Pat Metheny).

Suppose we look at what they play. The basis of what is played today is essentially what was played in the 1940s and 1950s. Every one is a bopper. It is not that nothing has been happening in jazz since then, but rather that the innovations of the past thirty years, from free jazz to fusion, have been silently marginalized. Even the most enthusiastic obituaries of Miles Davis, the key figure in the development of jazz since the early 1950s, grow noticeably more ambiguous about his last twenty years and prefer to keep quiet about his last ten. This suits senior citizens who have no trouble remembering the marvels of the first Quintet, of *Miles Ahead* and *Kind of Blue*, but surely the generation gap should not look quite so narrow? 'Tradition' is the key word now, a term once heard more often among jazz fans deploring the end of Dixieland and their youth than among musicians. And yet here is a twenty-five-year-old sax player ('out of Parker and Adderley') as recently reported: 'Bird is the main influence because he covers so many eras and styles in his playing. He stood for the tradition and I figured if I studied enough Bird I'd get hold of it.' Did Bird think of himself that way when he was twenty-five?

Indeed, the *mode retro* goes back a long way beyond the original boppers. There has been a return to the standard ballads, even if they are now played with avant-garde flourishes by men returned to the mainstream from the more inaccessible frontiers, like Archie Shepp, the terror of the 1960s. There are even signs of the black rediscovery of the original New Orleans tradition, which I predicted in *The Jazz Scene*, admittedly from Wynton Marsalis, who is both from New Orleans and a man in favour of traditions. There has been, above all, an extraordinary return to the blues. Last year's reissue of Robert Johnson is said to have sold 500,000 copies. Benson and Hedges sponsors a Blues Festival in New York. Blues bars are opening right and left in Chicago, to the deserved benefit of old men who could do with a buck or two, and, as I write, they are being imported into a new New York club advertising nothing but Chicago blues.

All this is both comforting and familiar to old-stagers, though it is impossible today to feel, as we did in the later 1950s and in the years from 1936 to 1942, that we are living through a golden age of jazz again. There is just a lot of jazz to listen to, and no shortage (at least in the New York area) of piano-players who are both adventurous and accessible. But it is also a danger sign. Jazz cannot survive like baroque music, as a form of pastiche or archaeology for the cultured public, even among blacks. But this is precisely the danger that threatens it. Black kids do not sing the blues today. They are performed, at best, by elderly artists for elderly neighbourhood audiences and, at worst (as in many of the new Chicago blues rooms), in *white* neighbourhoods, by the same grey-heads, for white students. Black kids do not dream of playing horns (except, paradoxically, among young Caribbeans in Britain, who have no indigenous jazz tradition), but of being in great rap groups, a form of art which, in my opinion, is musically uninteresting and literary doggerel. In fact, it is the opposite of the great and profound art of the blues. There are good reasons for this – what is one sax compared to the ghetto-blaster? – but it cuts off the roots of jazz. The flourishing black media and art scene – what might be called the Spike Lee belt – is impregnated with jazz and so, obviously, are musicians black or white. But jazz has always lived not by the hipness of the public (which has, with the rarest exceptions, always been a minority public), but by what Cornel West calls the 'network of apprenticeship', the 'transmission of skills and sensibilities to new practitioners'. The cords of this network are fraying. Some of them have snapped.

Is jazz then being transformed beyond redemption into another version of classical music: an accepted cultural treasure, consisting of a repertoire of mostly dead styles, performed live by artists – some of them young – for a financially comfortable middle-aged and middle-class public, black and white, and the Japanese tourist? Will it be, once again, accessible to its potential mass constituency basically through radio and recordings, as it was to my European generation half a century ago? To listen to most jazz stations today is to be back in the esoteric world of those who have the true faith, where three days devoted *exclusively* to, say, recordings of Clifford Brown are seen as three days well spent.

Is jazz becoming terminally fossilized? It is not impossible. If this should be the fate of jazz, it will not be much consolation that Clint

Eastwood has buried Bird in a celluloid mausoleum and that every hairdresser and cosmetics store plays tapes of Billie Holiday. However, jazz has shown extraordinary powers of survival and self-renewal inside a society not designed for it and which does not deserve it. It is too early to think that its potential is exhausted. Besides, what is wrong with just listening and letting the future take care of itself?

CHAPTER 25

Billie Holiday

This brief obituary was originally published in 1959 in the column I then wrote (under the name 'Francis Newton') in The New Statesman and Nation. *I reprint it, among other reasons, in memory of my friend John Hammond Jr. (see chapter 23) whom I asked, on his deathbed, of what in his life he was proudest. He said it was to have discovered Billie Holiday.*

Billie Holiday died a few weeks ago. I have been unable until now to write about her, but since she will survive many who receive longer obituaries, a short delay in one small appreciation will not harm her or us. When she died we – the musicians, critics, all who were ever transfixed by the most heart-rending voice of the past generation – grieved bitterly. There was no reason to. Few people pursued self-destruction more wholeheartedly than she, and when the pursuit was at an end, at the age of forty-four, she had turned herself into a physical and artistic wreck. Some of us tried gallantly to pretend otherwise, taking comfort in the occasional moments when she still sounded like a ravaged echo of her greatness. Others had not even the heart to see and listen any more. We preferred to stay home and, if old and lucky enough to own the incomparable records of her heyday from 1937 to 1946, many of which are not even available on British LP, to recreate those coarse-textured, sinuous, sensual and unbearable sad noises which gave her a sure corner of immortality. Her physical death called, if anything, for relief rather than sorrow. What sort of middle age would she have faced without the voice to earn money for her drinks and fixes, without the looks – and in her day she was hauntingly beautiful – to attract the men she needed, without business sense, without anything but the disinterested · worship of ageing men who had heard and seen her in her glory?

And yet, irrational though it is, our grief expressed Billie Holiday's art, that of a woman for whom one must be sorry. The great blues singers, to whom she may be justly compared, played their game from strength. Lionesses, though often wounded or at bay (did not Bessie Smith call herself 'a tiger, ready to jump'?), their tragic equivalents were Cleopatra and Phaedra; Billie's was an embittered Ophelia. She was the Puccini heroine among blues singers, or rather among jazz singers, for though she sang a cabaret version of the blues incomparably, her natural idiom was the pop song. Her unique achievement was to have twisted this into a genuine expression of the major passions by means of a total disregard of its sugary tunes, or indeed of any tune other than her own few delicately crying elongated notes, phrased like Bessie Smith or Louis Armstrong in sackcloth, sung in a thin, gritty, haunting voice whose natural mood was an unresigned and voluptuous welcome for the pains of love. Nobody has sung, or will sing, Bess's songs from *Porgy* as she did. It was this combination of bitterness and physical submission, as of someone lying still while watching his legs being amputated, which gives such a blood-curdling quality to her *Strange Fruit*, the anti-lynching poem which she turned into an unforgettable art song. Suffering was her profession; but she did not accept it.

Little need be said about her horrifying life, which she described with emotional, though hardly with factual, truth in her auto-biography *Lady Sings the Blues*. After an adolescence in which self-respect was measured by a girl's insistence on picking up the coins thrown to her by clients with her hands, she was plainly beyond help. She did not lack it, for she had the flair and scrupulous honesty of John Hammond to launch her, the best musicians of the 1930s to accompany her – notably Teddy Wilson, Frankie Newton and Lester Young – the boundless devotion of all serious connoisseurs, and much public success. It was too late to arrest a career of systematic embittered self-immolation. To be born with both beauty and self-respect in the Negro ghetto of Baltimore in 1915 was too much of a handicap, even without rape at the age of ten and drug-addiction in her teens. But, while she destroyed herself, she sang, unmelodious, profound and heartbreaking. It is impossible not to weep for her, or not to hate the world which made her what she was.

CHAPTER 26

The Old World and the New:
500 Years of Columbus

This chapter, originally given as a lecture at a quincentenary conference in Seville in 1992, is primarily about the impact of the New World on the Old, and argues that it came not through the conquerors but the conquered, not through the rulers but the peoples. It was first published in the London Review of Books, *9 July 1992.*

At the beginning of 1992, in Mexico, I was asked to sign a protest against Christopher Columbus, on behalf of the original native populations of the American continents and islands, or rather, of their descendants. I understood the feelings which inspire such gestures, and have some sympathy with them, but it seemed and seems to me that the only object of protesting against something that happened half a millennium ago is to get a little publicity for a cause of 1992 rather than 1492. The consequences of Columbus' voyages and those of his successors cannot be reversed. The sufferings imposed on indigenous Americans and imported Africans, whether by deliberate human action or as the unintended consequences of conquest and exploitation, are undeniable and cannot be cancelled in retrospect. That the impact of conquest and exploitation on these populations was catastrophic, and not only during the first 150 years of European conquest, must not be denied or overlooked either. Nevertheless, we cannot cancel history, but only remember or forget or invent it. Everyone who lives in the Americas today, whether descended from the Aboriginal population or from voluntary or involuntary settlers, has been shaped by the 500 years that have passed since Columbus sailed. But so has everyone in the Old World, though in ways of which we are rarely conscious.

That both sides were transformed was and is masked, in the first instance, by the very fact of conquest and overwhelmingly superior power. It was only on the periphery of settlement, and usually after the initial assertion of European power, that Europeans and native Americans met one another on anything like equal terms: an equality reinforced, on the northern and southern frontiers, for one or two centuries, by the 'horse revolution' which made the plains Indians of the North American deserts and prairies, and of the southern cone, into formidable cavalry raiders. Here and on the Amazonian jungle frontiers, as well as in a scattering of maroon settlements beyond the slave plantations, we find long-lasting resistance to conquest and colonization – and only here. The settled American civilizations, especially in Central America, succumbed rapidly. Under these circumstances we cannot realistically speak of a 'clash' of cultures, given the virtually total dominance of one side.

This dominance was reinforced by the combination of Christianity and barbarian conquest, which, as Edward Gibbon observed in the case of the Roman Empire, is a very effective destroyer of cultures. With all due respect to Las Casas and to the moral scruples of the Spanish crown, with all admiration for the Jesuits' protection of the Indians, we must never forget that the object of the conquest was the destruction of a heathen culture and the substitution for it of the true faith. As in Córdoba, so in Mexico, we see the conquerors tearing down the fabric of one kind of holy place to build churches on their sites. This initial destruction was so systematic that – in spite of some belated attempts at rescue – only three of the written Maya codices are still extant, and their characters have been only incompletely deciphered. In fact, we can read the records of pre-Columbian civilizations far less than ancient hieroglyphics and cuneiform tablets. The art and artefacts of these civilizations found their way to Europe, admired by experts like Albrecht Dürer for their technical workmanship and beauty, but, so far as we can tell, without becoming the subject of serious artistic interest until the twentieth century. Several of its most important monuments, which have become major centres of global tourism, such as the Maya sites and Machu Picchu, were not even known or recovered until then.

In short, whatever the conquerors and settlers hoped to get from the New World, they did not expect to learn much from its inhabitants that would be of value in the Old. The most interesting and instructive thing about it was its very novelty: the discovery of other human societies, unknown and unmediated by history, literature or oral tradition; the discovery of territories with a geological and climatic structure unlike any in Europe, and with an overwhelmingly strange and rich but quite unfamiliar flora and fauna – in some areas it seemed a paradise before the fall. This confrontation with novelty was for long the American impact on European culture. It has been argued that this is what precipitated the European concept of the ideal society or utopia. I need not remind you that the discoverer of Utopia in Thomas More's book was supposed to have been a Portuguese by birth who had sailed with Amerigo Vespucci to New Castile, but stayed behind when Vespucci returned, to explore the New World further. Equally, and perhaps more important, was the novelty of the Americas as a stimulus to rethinking our scientific world-picture. After all, in the nineteenth century it was the experience of South America which led both Charles Darwin and Russell Wallace to formulate the theory of evolution. Darwin himself said so in the very first sentences of *The Origin of Species*.

In the field of politics, institutions and high culture, it is safe to say, Europeans did not think they had anything to learn from the New World until the age of North American independence. Its institutions were derived from those of the Old World. Its culture and arts were remote provincial versions of metropolitan models. Politically, all this changed dramatically with the revolt of the American colonies, for after that the New World became the model of political innovation in an age of incomplete or unsuccessful metropolitan revolution. It was a continent of republics in a world of monarchies, and the USA was the pioneer political democracy. Still, even in politics the Old World did not quite lose its hegemony. The French Revolution was a more universal model than the revolution of the American colonies, and even in Latin America the tricolour was the dominant model for national flags. However, the New World remained a dependency of the Old, in intellectual life and in the arts, and few wealthy or educated Americans denied this until the end of the nineteenth century.

The mass of the American populations, native, slave or settler, if they knew anything about Europe at all, knew that they were not living in an inferior version of the metropolis. Creoles or settlers were perhaps the first conscious 'Americans', and it is clear to us that, with numerically small exceptions, the indigenous and mestizo populations lived in a syncretic culture that fused European and autochthonous elements. The settler/Creole version of this New World culture combined with the indigenous versions in varying degree. At one extreme we find regions of heavy European settlement – urban or rural – and comparatively thin indigenous population, regions which colonists could treat virtually as empty land, from which the aborigines could simply be eliminated. For practical purposes, the native Americans in the USA were to leave no significant traces on US culture, after their initial contact with the early colonists, except as something which stood outside it. At the other extreme we find small settler or pioneer populations on pioneer frontiers or in indigenous milieus, who might be heavily 'nativized'. In the special case of Paraguay and the adjoining areas of what is now Brazil and Argentina, a native language, Guaranì, actually became the main medium of communication among local white settlers, but this was quite exceptional. Again, as one might suppose, European intellectual and cultural influence rose as one proceeded from the less to the more educated, and was at its lowest among the illiterate. Nevertheless, most inhabitants of the Western hemisphere, before the era of mass emigration from Europe to North and the southern cone of South America, lived in something like a syncretic New World culture which fused elements from both worlds.

The impact the Americas have made on the culture of the Old World has been specifically that of this New World culture. Here we must distinguish between the impact of Latin and Caribbean America and that of North America, especially the USA, for two reasons. That of the USA has been enormously magnified by the transformation of that country into the greatest industrial economy of the twentieth century and the model of wealth and technological progress, and later by its transformation into a superpower. Almost everything that comes from there has had a major 'demonstration effect' and is likely to be imitated. If we want to assess the strength of this effect, we have only to compare US influence with that of Canada in both Britain and France. Canada is, after all, one of the seven most powerful economies in the world. Unlike the USA, or both Britain and France, Canada remains culturally provincial, though interesting things and people occasionally emerge from it. Again, since the late eighteenth century, the USA has been a political model for the rest of the world, though not, as it happens, a model much imitated. Initially there was nothing specifically American about this model, except the fact that ideas common to progressive intellectuals everywhere in Europe first led to political transformation across the Atlantic. Later, once again, the growing strength of the USA reinforced its impact. Roosevelt's New Deal was a phenomenon of world interest, but the contemporary Cardenas era in Mexico was seen as having only regional interest. The situation is similar in the more strictly cultural field. Everyone in the world knows about the cowboys of the old US West. The Mexican *vaqueros* from whom their costumes, their equipment and even their vocabulary are derived are not world-famous. No doubt if Hollywood had been situated in a Mexican rather than a Yankee Los Angeles, the epics of the Wild West would have paid more attention to Latin America.

One might, of course, argue that in some ways the USA represents a civilization, an economy, a polity more completely 'new world' than any other in the Americas, because it made a more complete break with the institutions of the Old World than did any other set of European transatlantic colonies. It is certainly the case that even today visiting Europeans find the USA in many respects a stranger society, and one whose mores are harder to understand, than those of the Latin American countries. In some ways the rise of the USA to its position as the world's super-economy and superpower owes much to its situation in the New World – for instance, to its potential for transcontinental territorial expansion – but I would not wish to exaggerate the importance of such factors. If the rise of the USA is to be explained by its being a new country in a new world, then what about the rise of Japan?

I do not want to speak primarily about the repercussions of the USA on Europe, however, even though when most of us think of American influence in Europe, this is what we have in mind. I want rather to consider those cultural repercussions of America as a whole which owe nothing of significance to the size, wealth and power of their countries of origin. To take the extreme case of Rubén Darío in literature, his importance in the history of modern Spanish poetry is as great as the importance of his country, Nicaragua, in the early twentieth century was negligible.

If we consider the balance of European and New World elements in our culture, an interesting contrast between elite or high culture and popular culture becomes apparent. In the field of high culture, the balance still favoured the Old World until the late twentieth century, in spite of the enormous prestige, resources and creative energy of the USA. The Americas are still net importers of talent and ideas, and nowhere more so than in the USA, even in the area of its greatest intellectual triumph, scientific research. In the rest of the Americas, the continued hegemony of the Old World continues among intellectuals, though particular mother countries have learned that their cultural superiority to their former colonies has disappeared.

Nevertheless, even in the fields of high culture, the Old World has increasingly taken notice of the New, though officially with some delay. The Nobel Prize did not begin to go to North American writers until 1930, or to Latin American ones in any numbers until after the late 1960s. Still, US literature has been accepted as a serious and independent component of world literature for at least 150 years. Latin American writing had difficulty in making an impact outside the Iberian language zone, but it made its major breakthrough in the second half of the present century, and it is today in some ways more

299

influential internationally than that of the USA. No doubt this was due largely to the Cuban Revolution, which, small as it was by international standards, was the first home-grown Latin American event since the execution of Maximilian to be seen as a global event. In its time, the far greater Mexican Revolution was overshadowed by events in Russia, even though it also achieved a significant cultural breakthrough with Mexican revolutionary painting – the first globally recognized modernist image-making originating in the Americas. Revolution has, in fact, been the secret weapon of Latin American high culture abroad, encouraged by the fashion for revolutionary tourism in that part of the world since 1959, particularly among intellectuals who found Spanish and Portuguese a lot easier to learn than Arabic or south-east Asian languages. Moreover, until today, the hopes of revolution have survived better here than in any other part of the world, and so has the positive image of revolution, as in Mexico. Latin America is the last bastion of the left in the world. For this reason its literature has so far escaped the worst consequences of the privatization of the imagination. But for how long?

Compared to the mixed fortunes of American high cultures, however, American popular cultures, from the middle or, at the latest, the end of the nineteenth century, have shown a remarkable power to penetrate the Old World. Once again, this has been the characteristic achievement of a mixed culture – in this instance, a Euro-American culture vitalized by African elements. Both North American, Caribbean and South American dances and popular music conquered Europe from the first years of the twentieth century and have continued their advance from tango, maxixe and ragtime to the present. The mass popular music of industrial society comes essentially from the Western hemisphere today, whereas the transatlantic music of high culture, from the Colon in Buenos Aires to the Lincoln Centre in New York, remains dependent on Europe. Let us not dismiss these cultural repercussions of the New World. Popular culture is the universal culture of our century. It is shared by all of us, including the most uncompromisingly intellectual. High culture belongs to minorities, and sometimes very small ones. In saying this, I am not making a judgment of value. On the other hand, I *am* implying a 'clash of cultures'. And indeed, if there is a genuine clash of cultures between the New World and the Old, it is here: between a New World whose main strength and dynamic force is popular and an Old World whose cultural impact on the New has overwhelmingly been through elites and rulers.

This contrast leads me to my main contention. By far the most significant way in which the discovery of the New World has affected the Old is through an almost entirely anonymous process of mass conquest initiated from the West. The major contribution of the Americas to the Old World has been to distribute across the globe a cornucopia of wild and cultivated products, mainly plants, without which the modern world as we know it would not be conceivable. You may say that this has nothing to do with culture. But what we cultivate and eat, especially if it is a new kind of foodstuff quite unfamiliar to our way of life, or even an entirely new form of consumption, *must* influence, and may even transform, not merely our consumption but the way we live in other respects. Consider only the basic foodstuffs. Four of the seven most important agricultural crops in the world today are of American origin: potatoes, maize, manioc and sweet potato. (The other three are wheat, barley and rice.) The classic work on 'the history and social influence of the potato' was written by Redcliffe Salaman as long ago as 1949. Arturo Warman's *La historia de un bastardo: maiz y capitalismo* was published in 1988. Both these excellent works demonstrate how far beyond mere food the social history of these crops takes us. But what about those products of the New World which were not simply substitutes for things already consumed in the Old World but opened new dimensions, new social styles? Chocolate, tobacco, cocaine? Or which have come to form the crucial elements of such novelties as chewing-gum, or Coca-Cola (even if it has lost its original cocaine component), the tonic in gin and tonic? What about the significant additions to the world's medical pharmacopoeia, such as quinine, for long the only drug capable of controlling malaria? What about the sunflowers which Rembrandt and Van Gogh were to paint, the peanuts without which modern Western sociability is incomplete – not to mention their more practical use as major sources of vegetable oils?

What I am arguing is that the adoption of new products, or even, in traditional peasant societies, the change from one basic food to another, is far more than a mere shift in consumer choice. Potatoes and maize could feed far more people per unit of the cultivated area than earlier crops. We know what happened when rapidly expanding populations became dependent on such a single crop – the history of Ireland is a tragic example. But who will say that the potato-based transformation in Ireland, and the great famine that followed, and the massive haemorrhage of population which that country has suffered ever since, did not entail cultural repercussions, not to mention political ones, on both sides of the Atlantic? Without Pizarro it could not have happened. Everything about the use of tobacco, which was unknown outside the Americas before the conquest, has cultural implications, as I did not need to tell anyone in Seville, where

Carmen met Don José in the celebrated Real Fabrica de Tabacos. Everything about the use of tobacco is linked to human emotions, ideas, hopes and fears: from the last cigarette offered to the condemned man before execution to the smoker automatically reaching for a cigarette after sexual intercourse; even the campaign to eliminate smoking, which is rather more successful in the Anglo-Saxon countries than elsewhere, tells us more about late-twentieth-century beliefs concerning how life should be lived than about the medical effects of nicotine. We are, in short, talking about products of the New World which were unknown and indeed unknowable before the conquest of the Americas, but which have since transformed the Old World profoundly and unpredictably, and still continue to do so. And I may add that in this respect the Old World owes more to the New than the Americas owe to Europe.

The point I wish to stress is that these products were not simply 'discovered' by the Europeans, still less deliberately searched for, in the way that the Conquistadors searched for silver and gold. They were products known, collected and systematically cultivated and processed by the indigenous societies. Conquistadors and settlers learned how to prepare and use them from these local societies. Indeed, if the settlers had not let themselves be taught by the natives, they would have found it difficult, perhaps impossible, to survive. To this day the great symbolic festival of the USA, Thanksgiving, records a debt of the first colonists to the Indians, which subsequent white civilization repaid by driving them out. Thanksgiving is celebrated by a meal that consists essentially of the New World foods which the colonists learned to live on from the Indians: culminating, as we all know, in the turkey.

My argument is that the true nature and significance of the meeting of cultures inaugurated when Columbus landed on his first Caribbean island cannot be understood in terms of conventional history alone. If we ask, what did Europe get from the conquest of the New World? the obvious answer is an expansion of some countries on the western side of that continent, through imperial rule, through wealth extracted from the labour of Indians and Africans; and through the settlement of migrants and colonists from the countries of Europe. The Americas were the first regions outside Europe in which empires were overthrown by European soldiers, and where European colonists established new Castiles, new Portugals and, later, new Englands. For a thousand years before 1492, conquest and settlement had gone the other way: from Asia and Africa into Europe. That is why it is historically significant that the date of Columbus' discovery of America is also the date of the conquest of Granada and the expulsion of the

Jews from Spain: all three are symbols of this reversal. Fourteen-ninety-two marks the beginning of Eurocentric world history, of the conviction that a few western and central European countries were destined to conquer and rule the globe, of Euromegalomania.

Yet all this is past history. Spain, Portugal, Britain, France and the rest have long ceased to rule the Americas. They have themselves declined from world powers, even from 'great powers' in the European context, to states which, by themselves, exercise no particular influence, but are important only collectively through the European Community. At most, Spain and Britain benefit from the fact that their languages have, thanks to their past conquests in the Americas, become world languages. The countries of the Americas have long ceased to be transatlantic extensions of Spain, Portugal and England, even for the local elites. The era of the 'expansion of Europe', a subject on which history students were still proudly examined in my youth, is over.

But other direct consequences of the conquest and settlement of the Americas are still with us. They do not belong to famous men, or governments. And yet they have transformed the fabric of European life for good. And indeed that of other continents also. When the cultural, social and economic history of the modern world is written in realistic terms, the conquest of southern Europe by maize, of northern and eastern Europe by the potato and of both by tobacco and more recently Coca-Cola will appear more prominently than the gold and silver for the sake of which the Americas were subjected.

NOTES

CHAPTER 2: THE MACHINE-BREAKERS

1. J. H. Plumb, *England in the Eighteenth Century* (Harmondsworth, 1950), p. 150; T. S. Ashton, *The Industrial Revolution* (London, 1948), p. 154.
2. L. Dechesne, *L'Avènement du Régime Syndical à Verviers* (Paris, 1908), pp. 51–64 and passim.
3. F. O. Darvall, *Popular Disturbance and Public Order in Regency England* (London, 1934), p. 1.
4. E.g. woollen- and silk-making machines in Wiltshire, paper-making machines in Buckinghamshire, iron-making machines in Berkshire (Public Record Office, Home Office Papers, HO 13/57, pp. 68–9, 107, 177; Assizes 25/21 passim); J. L. and B. Hammond, *The Village Labourer* (various editions) is the most accessible account; see also two unpublished theses: N. Gash, 'The Rural Unrest in England in 1830' (Oxford University), and Alice Colson, 'The Revolt of the Hampshire Agricultural Labourers' (London University).
5. For discussion of high-price rioting, T. S. Ashton and J. Sykes, *The Coal Industry of the Eighteenth Century* (Manchester, 1929), ch. 8; A. P. Wadsworth and J. de L. Mann, *The Cotton Trade and Industrial Lancashire* (Manchester, 1931), pp. 355 ff.
6. Darvall, *Popular Disturbance*, ch. 8 passim.
7. Bonner and Middleton's *Bristol Journal*, 31 July 1802. Some of these were due to ordinary labour disputes, some to opposition to new machines. See J. L. and B. Hammond, *The Skilled Labourer*; for an account of the movement A. Aspinall (ed.), *The Early English Trade Unions* (London, 1949), pp. 41–69, for some of the documents.
8. *House of Commons Journals*, xviii, p. 715 (1718); xx, p. 268 (1724).
9. *House of Commons Journals*, xx, pp. 598–9 (1726); Salisbury Assize Records cited in *Wiltshire Times*, 25 January 1919 (*Wiltshire Notes & Queries*).
10. *Gentleman's Magazine* (1738), p. 658.
11. Public Record Office, State Papers Domestic Geo. 2 (1741), pp. 56, 82–3.
12. E. Welbourne, *The Miners' Unions of Northumberland and Durham* (Cambridge, 1923), p. 21.
13. Ashton and Sykes, *Coal Industry*, pp. 89–91.
14. 10 Geo. 2, c.32, 17 Geo. 2, c.40, 24 Geo. 2, c.57, 31 Geo. 2, c.42 (E. R. Turner, 'The English Coal Industry in the Seventeenth and Eighteenth

Centuries', *American Historical Review* 27, p. 14). Turner seems to have neglected 13 Geo. 2, c.21, 9 Geo. 3, c.29, 39 and 40 Geo. 3, c.77, 56 Geo. 3, c.125 which are also directed against wrecking in mines (*Burn's Justice of the Peace*, ed. Chitty, 1837 edn, vol. 3, pp. 643 ff.).

15. Welbourne, *Miners' Unions*, p. 31.

16. W. Felkin, *A History of the Machine-wrought Hosiery and Lace Manufactures* (London, 1867) is the main authority.

17. For the French mines cf. M. Rouff, *Les Mines de charbon en France au XVIIIe siècle* (Paris 1922).

18. E. M. Saint-Léon, *Le Compagnonnage* (Paris, 1901), vol. 1, ch. 5.

19. Aspinall, *Early English Trade Unions*, p. 175.

20. The men of Bolton were alleged in 1826 to have planned the destruction of all the cotton-yarn ready packed for export, as well as of machines (Public Record Office, Home Office Papers HO 40/19, Fletcher to Hobhouse, 20 April 1826).

21. Cf. the discussion of these problems in E. Pouget, *Le Sabotage* (Paris, n.d.), pp. 45 ff.

22. E.g. the Welsh ironworkers in 1816 (*The Times*, 26 October 1816), the general strike of 1842 (F. Peel, *The Risings of the Luddites, Chartists and Plugdrawers*, Heckmondwike, 1888, pp. 341–7), and the German miners in 1889 (P. Grebe, 'Bismarcks Sturz u.d. Bergarbeiterstreik vom Mai 1889', *Historische Zeitschrift* 157, p. 91).

23. Aspinall, *Early English Trade Unions*, p. 196: 'I cannot help thinking that the morning meetings and roll-callings at present are the *bond* of union.'

24. H. L. Smith and V. Nash, *The Story of the Dockers' Strike* (London, 1889), passim.

25. R. Rigola, *Rinaldo Rigola e il Movimento Operaio nel Biellese* (Bari, 1930), p. 19. Rigola reports no actual wrecking by weavers, only by hatters.

26. See chapter on 'Machinery' in his *Principles*. On this, inserted only into the 3rd edition, see P. Sraffa and M. H. Dobb, *Works and Correspondence of David Ricardo* (Cambridge, 1951), vol. 1, pp. lvii–lx.

27. M. D. George, *London Life in the Eighteenth Century* (London, 1925), pp. 187–8, 180.

28. *Parl. Papers* 1802, Report fr. Committee on Woollen Clothiers' Petition, pp. 247, 249, 254–5. *Rules and Articles of . . . the Woollen-Cloth Weavers' Society . . . 1802* (British Mus. 906.k.14 (1)).

29. E. Howe and H. Waite, *The London Compositor* (London, 1948), pp. 226–33.

30. Wadsworth and Mann, *Cotton Trade*, pp. 499–500.

31. S. and B. Webb, *Industrial Democracy* (London, 1898), ch. 8, 'New Processes and Machinery'.

32. For policy-change of compositors cf. Howe and Waite, *London Compositor*; engineers, J. B. Jefferys, *The Story of the Engineers* (London, 1945), pp. 142–

3, 156–7; tin-plate workers, J. H. Jones, *The Tinplate Industry* (London, 1914), pp. 183–4, ch. 9.

33. J. Lofts, *The Printing Trades* (New York, 1942) for the long fight of American compositors against the technical revolution in the 1940s.

34. Wadsworth and Mann, *Cotton Trade*, p. 412. See also the detailed analysis of the fate of Hargreaves, pp. 476 ff.

35. *Select Committee on Agriculture*, 1833, 64 estimates – doubtless with some exaggeration – that only 1 in 100 of the threshing machines existing before 1830 were now in use in Wiltshire and Berkshire.

36. On foreign shearmen's agitation, F. R. Manuel, 'The Luddite Movement in France', *Journal of Modern History* (1938), pp. 180 ff.; F. R. Manuel, 'L'Introduction des machines en France et les ouvriers', *Revue d'Histoire Moderne*, 18, pp. 212–5. Actual Luddism in France seems to have been virtually confined to shearmen, with less success than in Britain, though Luddite intentions were sometimes expressed by others. See the documents in G. and H. Bourgin, *Le Régime de l'industrie en France de 1830 à 1840* 3 vols. (Paris, 1912–41).

37. Hammond, *Skilled Labourer*, p. 127.

38. Manuel, 'Luddite Movement', p. 187; Darvall, *Popular Disturbance*, passim. See also the note in E. C. Tufnell, *Character, Objects and Effects of Trade Unions* (1834), p. 17, on the reluctance of the men actually working machines to join in the strike against them. But Tufnell admits that they did, threatened or persuaded by their unemployed mates.

39. The shearmen (croppers) raised the nap on the finished cloth and shaved it off with heavy iron shears. They had to be both very strong and very skilful.

40. Darvall, *Popular Disturbance*, p. 207.

41. Aspinall, *Early English Trade Unions*, pp. 57–8.

42. Thomas Helliker, executed as such in 1803, is generally held to have been innocent.

43. G. H. Tupling, *Economic History of Rossendale* (Manchester, 1927), p. 214.

44. MS Correspondence of M. Cobb, clerk to the Justices at Salisbury, in Library of Wiltshire Archaeol. & Nat. Hist. Soc., Devizes: 26 November 1830.

45. Printed Circular, 8 December 1830. This is referred to in Hammond, *Village Labourer* (Guild Books edn), vol. 2, pp. 71–2.

46. See the brilliant analysis of the 'democratic petty-bourgeois' in Marx's Address to the Central Council of the Communist League, in Karl Marx and Frederick Engels, *Collected Works*, vol. 10 (London, 1978), pp. 277–87.

47. The phrase 'threshold of profit' is S. G. Gilfillan's: 'Invention as a Factor in Economic History', *Supp. to Journal of Economic History* (December 1945).

48. They were helped by the cheapness of the new machines. A western clothier installed jennies with 70–90 spindles for £9 apiece in 1804. Hence the possibility of piecemeal mechanization.

49. Tufnell, *Trade Unions*, p. 18.

50. Manuel, 'Luddite Movement', p. 186.
51. E. Lipson, *Economic History of England*, 4th edn, vol. 2, pp. cxxxv–cxxxvi, vol. 3, pp. 300, 313, 324–7. Sir John Clapham, *Concise Economic History of Britain*, p. 301, rightly notes that 'extra streak of hardness that seems to enter public life in the Restoration Age'.
52. See note 45 above.
53. For the 'revolutionary change' in this period, S. and B. Webb, *History of Trade Unionism* (1894), pp. 44 ff. But parliamentary proceedings may give the wrong impression. The normal course of events was that *laissez-faire* progressed quietly, contrary legislation falling into obsolescence, unless a specially active or effective campaign by the workers occurred. Cf. the repeal of the wage-clauses in the Statute of Artificers in 1813 (W. Smart, *Economic Annals of the Nineteenth Century*, 1801–20, p. 368).
54. Philalethes, *The Case as it now stands between the Clothiers, Weavers and other Manufacturers with regard to the late Riot, in the County of Wilts*, London, 1739 (Cambridge Univ. Lib., Acton d. 25.1005), p. 7. At any rate as late as 17 Geo. 3, c.55 the hatters secured an act forbidding any master hatter to sit on the bench in a dispute concerning them – which is more than farm-workers could achieve.
55. Public Record Office, State Papers Domestic Geo. I, 63, pp. 72, 82, 93–4; 64: pp. 1–6, 9–10 (esp. 2–4).
56. *House of Commons Journals*, xx, p. 747.
57. *Burn's Justice of the Peace*, vol. 3, pp. 643 ff., vol. 5, pp. 485 ff., 552 ff., gives a gruesome picture of this mass of uncoordinated piecemeal legislation.
58. W. Sombart, *Der Moderne Kapitalismus*, vol. 1, ii, p. 803 for a bibliography of these; K. Marx, *Capital*, vol. 1 (1938 edn), pp. 259–63; Philalethes, *The Case as it now stands ...* pp. 29, 41, gives typical arguments.
59. E. J. Hamilton, 'The Profit Inflation and the Industrial Revolution, 1751–1800', *Quarterly Journal of Economics* 56 (1942), p. 256.
60. Hammond, *Skilled Labourer*, M. D. George's observation, *London Life*, p. 190 that the rise in weaving prices under the acts was not comparable with that in other trades during the period may be true. More significant is the drastic collapse of prices after the repeal of the acts (ibid., p. 374).
61. Hammond, *Skilled Labourer*, p. 26.
62. William Stark on the reasons why machinery was not adopted in the Norwich worsted trade, and wage-reductions were resisted (Handloom Weavers' Commission, 1838 Ass. Commrs Report II).
63. J. H. Clapham, 'The Spitalfields Acts, 1773–1824', *Economic Journal* 26, pp. 463–4.
64. Hammond, *Skilled Labourer*, p. 142. J. H. Clapham, 'The Transference of the Worsted Industry from Norfolk to the West Riding', *Economic Journal* 20, discusses the question in greater detail.
65. Hammond, *Skilled Labourer*, p. 188.

66. Clutterbuck, *The Agriculture of Berkshire* (London and Oxford, 1861), pp. 41–2.

CHAPTER 3: POLITICAL SHOEMAKERS

1. *A Village Politician: The Life-Story of John Buckley*, ed. J. C. Buckmaster (London, 1897), p. 41.

2. M. Sensfelder, *Histoire de la cordonnerie* (Paris, 1856), quoted in Joseph Barberet, *Le Travail en France: monographies professionnelles*, 7 vols (Paris, 1886–90), vol. 5, pp. 63–4.

3. Rudolf Stadelmann, 'Soziale Ursachen der Revolution von 1848', in Hans-Ulrich Wehler (ed.), *Moderne deutsche Sozialgeschichte* (Berlin, 1970), p. 140; E. J. Hobsbawm and George Rudé, *Captain Swing* (London, 1969), p. 181; Jacques Rougerie, 'Composition d'une population insurgée: l'exemple de la Commune', *Le Mouvement Social*, no. 48 (1964), p. 42; Theodore Zeldin, *France, 1848–1945*, 2 vols (Oxford, 1973), vol. 1, p. 214.

4. Jean-Pierre Aguet, *Les Grèves sous la monarchie de Juillet, 1830–1847* (Geneva, 1954); David Pinkney, 'The Crowd in the French Revolution of 1830', *American Historical Review* 70 (1964), pp. 1–17; David Jones, *Chartism and the Chartists* (London, 1975), pp. 30–2; D. J. Goodway, *London Chartism 1838–1848* (Cambridge 1982), pp. 37–9, shows their proportional participation in London Chartism to be higher than any other large occupation (over 3,000 members) except stonemasons; George Rudé, *The Crowd in the French Revolution* (Oxford, 1959), appendix 4.

5. Georges Duveau, *La Vie ouvrière en France sous le Second Empire*, 7th edn (Paris, 1946), p. 75.

6. Jacques Rougerie, *Paris libre* (Paris, 1971), p. 263.

7. Reinhold Reith, *Zur biographischen Dimension von "Hochverrath und Aufruhr": Versuch einer historischen Protestanalyse am Beispiel des Aprilaufstandes 1848 in Konstanz'* (unpublished master's thesis, University of Konstanz, 1981), pp. 33ff., 44ff.

8. Edgar Rodrigues, *Socialismo e sindicalismo no Brasil, 1675–1913* (Rio de Janeiro, 1969), pp. 73, 223.

9. R. Hoppe and J. Kuczynski, 'Eine Berufs-bzw. auch Klassen-und Schichtenanalyse der Märzgefallenen 1848 in Berlin' *Jahrbuch für Wirtschaftsgesch.* 1964/IV, pp. 200–76.

10. Yves Lequin, *Les Ouvriers de la région lyonnaise, 1848–1914*, 2 vols (Lyon, 1977), vol. 2, p. 281.

11. Karl Obermann, *Zur Geschichte des Bundes der Kommunisten* (East Berlin, 1955), p. 28.

12. Paul Voigt, 'Das deutsche Handwerk nach den Berufszählungen von 1882 und 1895', in *Untersuchungen über die Lage des Handwerks in Deutschland* 9 (Schriften des Vereins für Socialpolitik, lxx, Leipzig, 1897); J. H. Clapham,

Economic History of Modern Britain, 3 vols (Cambridge, 1952), vol. 2, p. 43.

13. Hobsbawm and Rudé, *Captain Swing*, pp. 181–2.

14. Ibid., pp. 218, 246.

15. Keith Brooker, 'The Northampton Shoemakers' Reaction to Industrialisation: Some Thoughts', *Northamptonshire Past and Present* 6 (1980), p. 155.

16. Sample taken from Librairie A. Faure, 15 rue du Val du Grace, catalogue 5, Livres anciens et modernes, items 262–324; checked in Jean Maitron (ed.), *Dictionnaire biographique du mouvement ouvrier français, Pt I, 1789–1864*, 3 vols (Paris, 1964–6).

17. David M. Gordon, 'Merchants and Capitalism: Industrialization and Provincial Politics at Reims and St Etienne under the Second Republic and Second Empire' (unpublished PhD thesis, Brown University, 1978), p. 67.

18. William Sewell Jr, 'The Structure of the Working Class of Marseille in the Middle of the Nineteenth Century' (unpublished PhD thesis, University of California, Berkeley, 1971), p. 299.

19. 'De l'association des ouvriers de tous les corps d'état', repr. in Alain Faure and Jacques Rancière (eds), *La Parole ouvrière, 1830–1851* (Paris, 1976), pp. 159–68.

20. Gian Maria Bravo, *Les Socialistes avant Marx*, 2 vols (Paris, 1970), vol. 2, p. 221.

21. Alfred F. Young, 'George Robert Twelves Hewes, 1742–1840: A Boston Shoemaker and the Memory of the American Revolution', *William and Mary Quarterly*.

22. Maurice Garden, *Lyon et les Lyonnais au XVIIIe siècle* (Paris, 1970), pp. 244 ff. Above-average literacy is noted for rural cordwainers in David Cressy, *Literacy and the Social Order: Reading and Writing in Tudor and Stuart England* (Cambridge, 1981), pp. 130–6, but average or sub-average literacy for the lower classification of 'shoemakers' both in London and the countryside. For various reasons Cressy's London figures are more problematic than his rural ones.

23. Emmanuel Le Roy Ladurie, *Les Paysans du Languedoc*, 2 vols (Paris, 1966), vol. 1, pp. 349–51.

24. Peter Burke, *Popular Culture in Early Modern Europe* (London, 1978), pp. 38–9.

25. Jean Maitron, *Le Mouvement anarchiste en France*, 2 vols (Paris, 1975), vol. 1, p. 131.

26. For example, Anon., *Crispin Anecdotes: Comprising Interesting Notices of Shoemakers, who have been Distinguished for Genius, Enterprise or Eccentricity* (Sheffield and London, 1827); John Prince, *Wreath for St. Crispin: Being Sketches of Eminent Shoemakers* (Boston, Mass., 1848); Anon., *Crispin: The Delightful, Princely and Entertaining History of the Gentle Craft* (London, 1750); William Edward Winks, *Lives of Illustrious Shoemakers* (London,

1883); Thomas Wright, *The Romance of the Shoe* (London, 1922); Anon., *Lives of Distinguished Shoemakers* (Portland, Maine, 1849); Joseph Sparkes Hall, *The Book of the Feet* (New York, 1847).

27. 'Bei leisten, drät und pech der Schumacher sol bleiben und die gelehrten leut lassen die bücher schreiben', 'predigender Schuster macht schlechte Schuhe': *Deutsches Sprichwörter-Lexikon*, 5 vols (Aalen, 1963), vol. 4, cols 398–9. The injustice of such proverbs so outraged the nineteenth-century compilers of this encyclopaedia that they added a footnote citing two highly intellectual shoemakers who also produced excellent shoes (col. 399).

28. Charles Bradlaugh, the champion of atheism, was elected MP for Northampton, a shoemaking constituency. For the 'Schusterkomplott' of Vienna shoemakers accused of atheism in 1794, see E. Wangermann, 'Josephinismus und katholischer Glaube,' in E. Kovacs (ed.), *Katholische Aufklärung und Josephinismus* (Vienna, 1979), pp. 339–40. One of the accused, inspired by the sermons of a Reform Catholic preacher, in typical cobbler style 'bought an old Bible, had it read out to me, compared the ... passages cited in Wiser's sermons ... with the Bible text itself, whereby I became doubtful in my religion'.

29. Karl Flanner, *Die Revolution von 1848 in Wiener Neustadt* (Vienna, 1978), p. 181.

30. Eugenia W. Herbert, *The Artist and Social Reform: France and Belgium, 1885–1898* (New Haven, 1961), pp. 14ff.; for the shoemaker's revenge on Apelles, who originally invited him to stick to his last and abstain from art criticism, cf. the enormous influence (through Grave) of anarchism on post-impressionist painters, see ibid., pp. 184ff.

31. Samuel Smiles, *Men of Invention and Industry* (London, 1884), ch. 12.

32. See Anon., *Crispin Anecdotes*, p. 144; cf. also Hobsbawm and Rudé, *Captain Swing*, pp. 63, 70.

33. Anon., *Crispin Anecdotes*, p. 45; Winks, *Lives of Illustrious Shoemakers*, p. 232.

34. John Brown, *Sixty Years' Gleanings from Life's Harvest: A Genuine Autobiography* (Cambridge, 1858), p. 239, cited in Nicholas Mansfield, 'John Brown: A Shoemaker's Place in London', *History Workshop* 8 (1979), p. 135.

35. Barberet, *Le Travail en France*, vol. 5, pp. 62–3.

36. Wright, *Romance of the Shoe*, p. 218.

37. Ibid., p. 307.

38. Paul Lacroix, Alphonse Duchesne and Ferdinand Seré, *Histoire des cordonniers et des artisans dont la profession se rattache à la cordonnerie* (Paris, 1852), pp. 116–17.

39. Shakespeare, *Julius Caesar*, I, i; Dekker, *The Shoemaker's Holiday*, iv, 48–76. The quotation is from the Cerne Abbas Inquiry of 1594 (Brit. Lib. Harleian

MS 6849, fos 183–90), in *Willobie His Avisa*, ed. G. B. Harrison (London, 1926), appendix 3, p. 264. We are obliged to Michael Hunter for this early example of English radical shoemakers.

40. Anon., *Crispin Anecdotes*, p. 150.

41. Wright, *Romance of the Shoe*, p. 109.

42. Ibid., p. 4.

43. E. P. Thompson, *The Making of the English Working Class* (London, 1963), pp. 183–4.

44. Anon., *Crispin Anecdotes*, p. 126.

45. Lacroix, Duchesne and Seré, *Histoire des cordonniers*, pp. 206–7.

46. Ibid., p. 188.

47. Barberet, *Le Travail en France*, vol. 5, pp. 64–5.

48. Wright, *Romance of the Shoe*, p. 46; Hall, *Book of the Feet*, pp. 196–7. Despite the suggestion of these authors no association between shoemaking and bookbinding has been established. In London sons of shoemakers are probably under-represented in the trade between 1600 and 1815. While bookbinding was not infrequently combined with some other occupation such as merchant-tailor, draper, barber, mason, glazier, weaver, dyer, needle-maker and wheelwright, in *no* case was it combined with shoemaking. Calculated from Ellic Howe, *A List of London Bookbinders, 1648–1815* (London, 1950).

49. Cf. the role of one Hans von Sagan in the traditions of German shoemakers. He gained the emperor's favour and the craft the right to include the imperial eagle in its coat of arms, by intervening in a fourteenth-century battle. The relative scarcity of formalized custom in the trade has been noted in Rudolf Wissell, *Des alten Handwerks Recht und Gewohnheit*, ed. Konrad Hahm, 2 vols (Berlin, 1929), vol. 2, p. 91; Andreas Griessinger, *Das symbolische Kapital der Ehre: Streikbewegungen und kollektives Bewusstsein deutscher Handwerksgesellen im 18. Jahrhundert* (Frankfurt, Berlin and Vienna, 1981). We are very grateful to Andreas Griessinger of the University of Konstanz for making the manuscript of his book available to us prior to its publication.

50. *The Unknown Mayhew*, ed. Eileen Yeo and E. P. Thompson (London, 1971), p. 279. See also 'Mental Character of the Cobblers', cited in *The Man* 9 April 1834 (New York), p. 168: 'Seated all day on a low seat, pressing obdurate last and leather ... or hammering heels and toes with much monotony – the cobbler's mind, regardless of the proverb, wanders into regions metaphysical, political, and theological; and from men thus employed have sprung many founders of sects, religious reformers, gloomy politicians, "bards, sophists, statesmen" and other "unquiet things", including a countless host of hypochondriacs. The dark and pensive aspect of shoemakers in general is a matter of common observation. It is but justice to them, however, to say that their acquisition of knowledge and their

habits of reflection, are often such as to command admiration.'

51. Richard Watteroth, 'Die Erfurter Schuharbeiterschaft', in *Auslese und Anpassung der Arbeiterschaft in der Schuhindustrie und einem oberschleisischen Walzwerke* (Schriften des Vereins für Sozialpolitik, cliii, Munich and Leipzig, 1915), p. 6.

52. Calculated from Joseph Belli, *Die Rote Feldpost unterm Sozialistengesetz* (Bonn, 1978 edn), pp. 54–94. We are obliged to Rainer Wirtz for this reference. Julius Pierstorff, 'Drei Jenaer Handwerke', in *Untersuchungen über die Lage des Handwerks in Deutschland* 9 (Schriften des Vereins für Sozialpolitik, lxx, Leipzig, 1897), p. 36, notes that journeymen stayed a maximum of six months in the same shop.

53. Griessinger, *Das symbolische Kapital der Ehre*, pp. 102–7, describes these rituals excellently for eighteenth-century Germany.

54. Burke, *Popular Culture in Early Modern Europe*, pp. 38–9.

55. Robert Chambers, *The Book of Days*, 2 vols (London and Edinburgh, 1862–4), vol. 2, p. 492; A. R. Wright, *British Calendar Customs: England*, ed. T. E. Lones, 3 vols (Folk-Lore Soc., xcvii, cii, cvi, London and Glasgow, 1936–40), vol. 3, pp. 102–4. In England (but not in Scotland) it may have been aided by the association of St Crispin's Day with nationalism, for this was, as readers of Shakespeare's *Henry V* will recall, the date of the battle of Agincourt against the French.

56. As surveyed in Griessinger, *Das symbolische Kapital der Ehre*, pp. 130–3.

57. Brooker, 'The Northampton Shoemakers' Reaction to Industrialisation', passim, on conflicts arising out of this during industrialization. See also Mansfield, 'John Brown: A Shoemaker's Place in London', passim.

58. *Allgemeine Deutsche Biographie*, vol. 3, entry for Jakob Böhme.

59. *Dictionary of National Biography*, vol. 5.

60. Winks, *Lives of Illustrious Shoemakers*, pp. 81, 180.

61. Brian Dobbs, *The Last Shall Be First: The Colourful Story of John Lobb, the St. James's Bootmaker* (London, 1972), pp. 27–8.

62. B. Aebert, 'Die Schuhmacherei in Loitz', in *Untersuchungen über die Lage des Handwerks in Deutschland* 1 (Schriften des Vereins für Socialpolitik, lxii, Leipzig, 1895), pp. 39, 49; Siegfried Heckscher, 'Über die Lage des Schuhmachergewerbes in Altona, Elmshorn, Heide, Preetz und Barmstedt', in ibid., p. 2.

63. US National Archives RG 217, Fourth Auditor Accounts, Numerical Series, 1141. We owe this reference to Christopher McKee.

64. Bernardino Ramazzini, *Health Preserved, in Two Treatises*, 2nd edn (London, 1750), p. 215.

65. John Thomas Arlidge, *The Hygiene, Diseases and Mortality of Occupations* (London, 1892), p. 216, quoting William Farr's data of 1875 – below-average mortality at all ages except 20–25 as against the very high mortality of tailors – and Ratcliffe, an analyst of the mortality of members

of Friendly Societies, who considered their 'vitality' inferior only to that of farm-labourers and carpenters.

66. Anon., *Crispin Anecdotes*, p. 126.

67. 'The frequency of the development of literary talent among shoemakers has often been remarked. Their occupation, being a sedentary and comparatively noiseless one, may be considered as more favorable than some others to meditation; but perhaps its literary productiveness has arisen quite as much from the circumstance of its being a trade of light labor, and therefore resorted to, in preference to most others, by persons in the humble life who are conscious of more mental talent than bodily strength': Hall, *Book of the Feet*, p. 4. In spite of the fact that the hammering of leather caused shoemaking sometimes to be excluded from certain quarters as a 'noisy craft' (*lärmendes Handwerk*) – cf. W. J. Schröder, *Arbeitergeschichte und Arbeiterbewegung: Industriearbeit und Organisationsverhalten in 19. und frühen 20. Jahrhundert* (Frankfurt and New York, 1978), p. 91 – noise is rarely noted in the literature about shoemaker–intellectuals.

68. Aebert, 'Die Schuhmacherei in Loitz', p. 38.

69. Nicolaus Geissenberger, 'Die Schuhmacherei in Leipzig und Umgegend', in *Untersuchungen über die Lage des Handwerks in Deutschland 2* (Schriften des Vereins für Socialpolitik, lxiii, Leipzig, 1895), p. 169.

70. Pauly-Wissowa, *Real-encyclopädie der classischen Alterthumswissenschaft*, 2nd ser., 4/1, cols 989–94, under 'sutor'. The low status of the trade is demonstrated in the language as well. In France *savetier* was a term of derision; in England a cobbler also meant a 'botcher' or unskilled workman. See Lacroix, Duchesne and Seré, *Histoire des cordonniers*, p. 179.

71. Arlidge, *Hygiene, Diseases and Mortality of Occupations*, p. 216.

72. Schröder, *Arbeitergeschichte*, p. 93.

73. On these references to shoemakers, see Anon., *Crispin Anecdotes*, p. 102; *Deutsches Sprichwörter-Lexikon*, vol. 4, cols 398–401; *English Dialect Dictionary*, vol. 1, under 'cobbler', 'Cobbler's dinner – bread and bread to it'. The popular impression from colonial America to Europe held that, whatever else he was, a shoemaker was rarely prosperous. Poverty and a propensity for philosophizing were not at all contradictory; indeed they may help to explain the long-standing reputation of shoemakers as radicals. Thinking men among the poor were very likely to become political or ideological radicals. John Brown's memory of 'the great orators of the craft' described 'men in ragged habiliments and of squalid looks' who 'pour forth in touching and eloquent language their appeals': Mansfield, 'John Brown: A Shoemaker's Place in London', p. 131.

74. Max von Tayenthal, 'Die Schuhwarenindustrie Österreichs', *Sociale Rundschau* (Arbeitsstatistisches Amt im k. u. k. Handelsministerium), ii, pt I (1901), p. 764.

75. George Unwin, *The Gilds and Companies of London* (London, 1908), p. 82;

Geissenberger, 'Die Schuhmacherei in Leipzig und Umgegend', p. 169; Watteroth, 'Die Erfurter Schuharbeiterschaft', p. 15.

76. In Santiago and Valparaiso provinces in 1854 there were 5,865 of them, compared to 3,720 carpenters, 1,615 tailors, 1,287 masons and bricklayers and 1,088 smiths and farriers: L. A. Romero, *La Sociedad de la Igualdad: los artesanos de Santiago de Chile y sus primeras experiencias politicas, 1820– 1851* (Buenos Aires, 1978), p. 14. See also A. Bernal, A. Collantes de Teran and A. Garcia-Baquero, 'Sevilla: de los gremios a la industrialización', *Estudios de historia social* (Madrid), nos 5–6 (1978), pp. 7–310, esp. Cuadro 8.

77. Griessinger, *Das symbolische Kapital der Ehre*, pp. 87–90.

78. J. A. Faber, *Drie Eeuwen Friesland*, 2 vols (A. A. G. Bijdragen, xvii, Wageningen, 1972), vol. 2, tables 111.8, 111.9, at pp. 444–5, 446–7.

79. Griessinger, *Das symbolische Kapital der Ehre*, pp. 90–5.

80. Thus Winks discusses the problem of the intellectual distinction of shoe-makers under the heading 'A Constellation of Celebrated Cobblers': *Lives of Illustrious Shoemakers*, pp. 229ff. For interchangeability, see also *Scottish National Dictionary*, under 'souter'.

81. C.N.R.S., *Trésor de la langue française* (Paris, 1978), under 'cordonnier'; *Grimms Wörterbuch*, under 'Schuster'.

82. Geissenberger, 'Die Schuhmacherei in Leipzig und Umgegend', p. 175. In the Germany of 1882, 46.5 per cent of all independent shoemakers were in villages of fewer than 2,000 inhabitants (two-thirds of them having another by-employment). Two-thirds of all independent shoemakers were found in centres of fewer than 5,000 inhabitants. (*Statistik des Deutschen Reiches* NF Bd4. 1–2, p. 1194 and NF Bd 111, pp. 104ff.

83. Utz Jaeggle, *Kiebingen: Eine Heimatgeschichte* (Tübingen, 1977), p. 249. Hardly any of the local shoemakers belonged to the upper stratum of the village, and the majority not even to the middle stratum. 'Even today shoemakers count for nothing in the village': ibid. We are obliged to Rainer Wirtz for this reference.

84. Wilhelm Weitling, *Garantien der Harmonie und Freiheit* (Berlin, 1955 edn), p. 289.

85. Flanner, *Die Revolution von 1848 in Wiener Neustadt*, pp. 26–7. Since the city specialized in the metal industries as well as textiles, metal craftsmen (less numerous though they were than shoemakers) are omitted as likely to have been over-represented.

86. Cf. the Calabrian shoemaker cited in E. J. Hobsbawm, *Primitive Rebels* (Manchester, 1959), appendix 9, who prided himself on working even for the *carabinieri*.

87. We owe this point to Dr Mikuláš Teich, who quotes the proverb from his native Czechoslovakia: 'Where there is cutting, weighing or pouring, money is to be made.'

88. Raymond Williams, *Culture and Society* (New York, 1960), p. 16, citing

the *Political Register*, 14 April 1821.

89. Richard Cobb, *Les Armées révolutionnaires*, 2 vols (Paris and The Hague, 1961–3), vol. 2, pp. 486–7.

90. Anon., *Crispin Anecdotes*, pp. 154–5.

91. Dale Tomich and Anson G. Rabinbach, 'Georges Haupt, 1928–1978', *German Critique*, no. 14 (1978), p. 3.

92. Richard Schüller, 'Die Schuhmacherei in Wien', in *Untersuchungen über die Lage des Handwerks in Österreich* (Schriften des Vereins für Socialpolitik, lxxi, Leipzig, 1896), pp. 49–50.

93. J. H. Clapham, *The Economic History of Modern Britain*, 2nd edn (Cambridge, 1930), vol. 1, p. 169.

94. Geissenberger, 'Die Schuhmacherei in Leipzig und Umgegend', p. 190.

95. Tayenthal, 'Die Schuhwarenindustrie Österreichs', pp. 974–5; Heckscher, 'Über die Lage des Schuhmachergewerbes in Altona, Elmshorn, Heide, Preetz und Barmstedt', pp. 4, 6.

96. P. R. Mounfield, 'The Footwear Industry of the East Midlands', *East Midlands Geographer* 22 (1965), pp. 293–306.

97. For the situation in Lynn, Massachusetts, see Alan Dawley, *Class and Community: The Industrial Revolution in Lynn* (Cambridge, Mass., 1976).

98. James Devlin, *The Guide to Trade: The Shoemaker*, 2 vols (London, 1839), is the best manual of shoemaking techniques before mechanization. The author, a radical, activist and minor literary figure (he contributed to Leigh Hunt's *London Journal*) was the best craftsman in the London trade: Goodway, '*London Chartism*', p. 282. For the later nineteenth century, see *John Bedford Leno, The Art of Boot- and Shoe-making ... with a Description of the Most Approved Machinery Employed* (London, 1885). Leno, though a printer by trade and poetaster–reciter by avocation, was long associated with the craft as owner and editor of the journal *St Crispin*; see his *The Aftermath: With Autobiography of the Author* (London, 1892). For a more recent treatment, see R. A. Church, 'Labour Supply and Innovation, 1800–1860: The Boot and Shoe Industry', *Business History* 12 (1970). For Erfurt, see Watteroth, 'Die Erfurter Schuharbeiterschaft', esp. pp. 113–14.

99. Barberet, *Le Travail en France*, vol. 5, pp. 71, 85, 116, 163; Emile Levasseur, *Histoire de classes ouvrières et de l'industrie en France de 1789 à 1870*, 2 vols (Paris, 1940 edn), vol. 2, p. 567; Christopher Johnson, 'Communism and the Working Class before Marx: The Icarian Experience', *American Historical Review* 76 (1971), p. 66; David Landes, *The Unbound Prometheus* (London, 1969), pp. 294–6; Direction du travail, *Les Associations professionelles ouvrières*, 4 vols (Paris, 1894–1904) vol. 2, pp. 11–87; *The Unknown Mayhew*, ed. Yeo and Thompson, pp. 228–79.

100. Sewell, *The Shoemakers of Marseille*, p. 217.

101. Charles Poncy, 'La Chanson du cordonnier', in his *La Chanson de chaque métier* (Paris, 1850), pp. 80–5.

102. Thompson, *Making of the English Working Class*, p. 704.

103. Cited in Faure and Rancière, *La Parole ouvrière, 1830–1851*, p. 161.

104. *James Hawker's Journal: A Victorian Poacher*, ed. Garth Christian (Oxford, 1978), pp. 15, 16. See also Mansfield, 'John Brown: A Shoemaker's Place in London', pp. 130–1, who cites John Brown in 1811: 'So soon as I was settled in a regular seat of work, it became necessary that I should join the trade or shops-meeting, which is a combination for the support of wages.'

105. 'The Reminiscences of Thomas Dunning (1813–1894) and the Nantwich Shoemakers' Case of 1834', ed. W. H. Chaloner, *Trans. Lancs. and Cheshire Antiq. Soc.* 59 (1947), p. 98.

106. Ibid.

107. Based on the biographical data in Hermann Weber, *Die Wandlung des deutschen Kommunismus*, 2 vols (Frankfurt, 1969), vol. 2.

108. Claude Willard, *Le Mouvement socialiste en France, 1893–1905: les Guesdistes* (Paris, 1965), esp. pp. 335–7. See also Tony Judt, *Socialism in Provence, 1871–1914* (Cambridge, 1979), pp. 73, 112.

109. Parti Communiste Français, *Des Français en qui la France peut avoir confiance*, 2nd edn (Paris, 1945); Maurice Duverger (ed.), *Partis politiques et classes sociales en France* (Paris, 1955), pp. 302, 304.

110. Based on data in Jean Maitron and Georges Haupt (eds), *Dictionnaire biographique du mouvement ouvrier international: l'Autriche* (Paris, 1971).

111. Personal information from Hungarian colleagues. M. K. Dziewanowski, 'Social Democrats Versus "Social Patriots": The Origins of the Split in the Marxist Movement in Poland,' *American Slavic and East European Review* 10 (1951), p. 18.

112. Based on Joyce M. Bellamy and John Saville (eds), *Dictionary of Labour Biography*, 9 Vols. (London, 1994).

113. Maitron, *Le Mouvement anarchiste en France*, vol. 1, p. 131.

CHAPTER 4: LABOUR TRADITIONS

1. G. Duveau, *La Vie ouvrière en France sous le Second Empire* (Paris, 1946), p. 543.

2. Ness Edwards, *The History of the South Wales Miners* (London, 1926), p. 39.

3. E. Labrousse, *Le Mouvement ouvrier et les idées sociales en France de 1815 à la fin du XIX siècle* (Les Cours de la Sorbonne 1949: Fasc. III), pp. 83–4.

4. W. Lexis, *Gewerkvereine u. Unternehmerverbaende in Frankreich* (Leipzig, 1879), pp. 123–4.

5. Ibid., pp. 183–4.

6. Duveau, *La Vie ouvrière*, pp. 89–91.

7. Mark Rutherford, *The Revolution in Tanner's Lane* (London, 1887).

8. Reprinted in E. J. Hobsbawm (ed.), *Labour's Turning Point 1880–1900* (London, 1948), p. 89.

9. R. F. Wearmouth, *Some Working-class Movements of the Nineteenth Century* (London, 1948), p. 305.

10. A. Zévaès, *De l'introduction du marxisme en France* (Paris, 1947), pp. 116 ff.

11. For the combination of direct action and extreme moderation in Sheffield, cf. S. Pollard, *A History of Labour in Sheffield* (Liverpool, 1959).

12. A Rossi, *Physiologie du parti communiste français* (Paris, 1948), p. 317.

13. On this crisis in the French CP, cf. L. Trotsky, *The First Five Years of the Comintern*, (New York 1953), vol. 2, almost passim, but esp. pp. 153–5, 281–2, 321.

14. Cf. K. S. Inglis, 'The Labour Church Movement', *International Review of Social History* 3 (1958).

15. For this and the following passages, see the chapter on Labour Sects in my *Primitive Rebels* (Manchester, 1959).

16. Cf. R. Goetz-Girey, *La Pensée syndicale française* (Paris, 1948), pp. 96 ff.

17. Cf. esp. 'Discours prononcé le 12 août 1881 à la réunion électorale du XXe arrondissement', in *Discours ... de Léon Gambetta*, ed. J. Reinach (Paris, 1895).

18. E. Welbourne, *The Miners' Unions of Northumberland and Durham* (Cambridge, 1923), p. 115.

19. E. Halévy, *History of the English People in the Nineteenth Century* (London, 1961), vol 1, pp. 148 ff. For collective bargaining by riot, see above, Chapter 2.

20. W. Gallacher, *Revolt on the Clyde* (London, 1936), ch. 10, for a self-critical account by one of the 'strike leaders, nothing more; we had forgotten we were revolutionary leaders'.

21. Thus in the 1882 London School Board elections the trade-unionist candidates (except for one already sitting member) did extremely poorly; while Helen Taylor and Aveling, whose links were primarily political or ideological, were elected.

22. Conversely in France, Pierre Semard, a pure unionist by origin, was for a time general secretary of the Communist Party, and Léon Mauvais (secretary of the CGTU in 1933) became organizing secretary of the CP in 1947. Charles Tillon, also with a mainly trade-unionist background in Britanny – but combined with municipal politics – became chief military organizer of the communist Resistance and minister in de Gaulle's government; as did Lucien Midol. The list could be prolonged.

23. Cf. F. C. Mather, *Public Order in the Age of the Chartists* (Manchester, 1960).

24. William Carpenter in *The Charter*, 21 July 1839.

25. A. J. Rieber, *Stalin and the French Communist Party, 1941–7* (New York and London, 1962) discusses the matter at length, pp. 142–55.

26. Ibid., pp. 150–1.

27. The most obvious apparent example to the contrary, the Dreyfus affair, proves the point. Its effect within the labour movement was to divide and

not to unite; for against the 'rallying of the Socialist politicians to the cause of the threatened Republic and a *rapprochement* between most of the Socialist groups' there must be set the strengthening of an anti-political syndicalism (G. D. H. Cole, *History of Socialist Thought* (London, 1956) vol. 3, p. 343), not to mention the split caused by the acceptance of cabinet office by Millerand.

CHAPTER 5: THE MAKING OF THE WORKING CLASS, 1870–1914

1. E. P. Thompson, *The Making of the English Working Class* (London, 1963).
2. Martin Jacques and Francis Mulhern (eds), *The Forward March of Labour Halted?* (London, 1982).
3. J. H. Clapham, *The Economic History of Modern Britain*, 2nd edn (Cambridge, 1930), vol. 2, p. 24.
4. Phyllis Deane and Alan Cole, *British Economic Growth, 1688–1959* (Cambridge, 1967), pp. 142–3.
5. H. S. Jevons, *The British Coal Trade* (London, 1915): calculated from data on pp. 65, 117; *Earnings and Hours Enquiry I: Textile Trades* (80/1 of 1909, p. 27); Clapham, *Economic History*, pp. 115, 117.
6. John Marshall, *The Industrial Revolution in Furness* (Barrow, 1958), p. 356; James Hinton, *The First Shop Stewards' Movement* (London, 1973), p. 28; M. C. Reed (ed.), *Railways in the Victorian Economy: Studies in Finance and Economic Growth* (Newton Abbot, 1969), p. 125.
7. E. D. Hunt, *British Labour History, 1815–1914* (1981), p. 17.
8. James E. Cronin, 'Strikes 1870–1914', in C. J. Wrigley (ed.), *A History of British Industrial Relations, 1875–1914* (Brighton, 1982), ch. 4.
9. H. A. Clegg, Alan Fox and A. F. Thompson, *A History of British Trade Unions since 1889* (Oxford, 1964), p. 471.
10. Chris Wrigley, 'The Government and Industrial Relations' and Roger Davidson, 'Government Administration', in Wrigley, *British Industrial Relations*, chs 7, 8.
11. Information about Richardson and Rust is taken from Joyce M. Bellamy and John Saville (eds), *Dictionary of Labour Biography*, 9 Vols. (London, 1994), vol. 2, p. 320, 326.
12. Paul Martinez, 'The French Communard Refugees in Britain, 1871–1880' (unpublished PhD thesis, University of Sussex, 1981), p. 341.
13. Cf. E. J. Hobsbawm and T. Ranger (eds), *The Invention of Tradition* (Cambridge, 1983), p. 295.
14. *Victoria County History of Yorkshire* (London, 1914), vol. 2, pp. 543 ff.
15. E. D. Hunt, *Labour History*, pp. 77–9; D. A. Reid, 'The Decline of Saint Monday, 1766–1876', *Past and Present* 71 (1976), pp. 76–101.
16. T. C. Barker, J. C. McKenzie and J. Yudkin (eds), *Our Changing Fare: Two Hundred Years of British Food Habits* (London, 1966), p. 110; 'Chatchip' (W. Loftas), *The Fish Frier and his Trade: Or How To Establish and Carry On an*

Up-to-date Fish Frying Business (London, n.d.), pp. 15, 23–4. Of the ten firms manufacturing frying ranges mentioned or advertising in this handbook, all but two are in Lancashire and Yorkshire.

17. Tony Mason, *Association Football and English Society, 1863–1915* (Brighton, 1980).

18. C. D. Stuart and A. J. Park, *The Variety Stage* (London, 1895); G. J. Mellor, *The Northern Music Hall* (Newcastle, 1970).

19. J. B. Jefferys, *Retail Trading in Britain, 1850–1950* (Cambridge, 1954); W. Hamish Fraser, *The Coming of the Mass Market, 1850–1914* (London, 1982).

20. Cyril Ehrlich, *The Piano: A History* (London, 1976), pp. 102–3.

21. John Burnett, *Plenty and Want: A Social History of Diet in England from 1815 to the Present* (London, 1966), p. 111.

22. Geoffrey Green, *The History of the Football Association* (London, 1953), p. 125.

23. *Herapath's Railway Journal*, 19 April 1884, p. 441.

24. This was under the General Pier and Harbours Act of 1861. Returns in PP 62, 1863; 55, 1864; 50, 1865; 66, 1866; 63, 1867–8; 54, 1868–9; 59, 1870; 60, 1871; 52, 1872; 58, 1873; 59, 1874; 67, 1875; 65, 1876; 73, 1877; 67, 1878; 64, 1878–9; 66, 1880; 82, 1881; 62, 1882; 62, 1883; 71, 1884; 70, 1884–5; 59, 1886; 74, 1887; 90, 1888; 69, 1889; 66, 1890; 76, 1890–1; 71, 1892; 80, 1893–4; 76, 1894; 87, 1895; 75, 1896; 78, 1897; 83, 1898; 87, 1899. See also: *Return from the Authorities of Harbours ... Giving description of works executed within the last twenty years, distinguishing Piers, Docks ... etc* (P.P. 62 of 1883).

25. Seaside resorts have been assigned their 'social tone' (to use H. J. Perkin's suitably Victorian phrase) in the light of general knowledge (e.g. Torquay or Skegness) and of the researches of numerous researchers, starting with E. W. Gilbert, 'The Growth of Inland and Seaside Health Resorts in England', *Scottish Geographical Magazine* 55 (1939). For a bibliography, see J. Walvin, *Leisure and Society, 1830–1950* (London, 1978); cf. also H. J. Perkin, 'The "Social Tone" of Victorian Seaside Resorts in the Northwest', in his *The Structured Crowd: Essays in English Social History*; J. Lowerson and J. Myerscough, *Time to Spare in Victorian England* (Brighton, 1977), pp. 30–44. In the latter period middle-class investment is probably overstated, partly because several large projects for loans were turned down, partly because in time even middle-class resorts recognized, sometimes reluctantly, the financial potential of the mass market.

26. For an impression of a working-class 'ghetto', see C. F. G. Masterman, *The Heart of the Empire* (London, 1901), pp. 12–13.

27. G. S. Layard, 'Family Budgets II', *Cornhill Magazine*, n.s. 10 (1901), pp. 656 ff.

28. Board of Trade, *Report on Cost of Living* (P.P. 107, 1908), passim. The quotation is from p. 655.

29. Ibid., p. 406.
30. R. Roberts, *The Classic Slum* (Manchester, 1971), p. 13.
31. G. Askwith, *Industrial Problems and Disputes* (London, 1920), p. 10.
32. B. S. Rowntree, *Poverty and Progress: A Second Social Survey of York* (London, 1941), pp. 359–60.
33. Ross McKibbin, 'Working-Class Gambling in Britain, 1880–1939', *Past and Present* 82 (1979), p. 172.
34. Cited in H. Pelling, *Popular Politics and Society in Late Victorian Britain* (London, 1968), p. 147.
35. Fred Reid, 'Keir Hardie's Conversion to Socialism', in Asa Briggs and John Saville (eds), *Essays in Labour History, 1886–1923* (London, 1971), p. 28.
36. Julian Amery, in James L. Garvin, *The Life of Joseph Chamberlain* (London, 1932–69), vol. 6, p. 791.
37. P. Stead, 'The Language of Edwardian Politics', in D. Smith (ed.), *A People and a Proletariat* (London, 1980), p. 150.
38. P. J. Waller, *Democracy and Sectarianism: A Political and Social History of Liverpool, 1868–1920* (Liverpool, 1981), chs 7, 13–15.
39. H. Pelling and F. Bealey, *Labour and Politics, 1900–1906* (London, 1958), p. 158.
40. Ray Gregory, *The Miners and British Politics, 1906–1914* (London, 1968), p. 185.
41. Joseph L. White, *The Limits of Trade Union Militancy* (Westport and London, 1978), pp. 152–5.
42. Cited in David Marquand, *Ramsay MacDonald* (London, 1977), p. 84.
43. Gregory, *Miners*, p. 178.
44. Ibid., p. 188.
45. Beatrice Webb, *Diaries, 1912–1924* (London, 1952), p. 45.
46. Jack Lawson, *The Man in the Cap: The Life of Herbert Smith* (London, 1941).

CHAPTER 6: VICTORIAN VALUES

1. J. Zeitlin, 'The Labour Strategies of British Engineering Employers, 1890–1922', in H. C. Gospel and C. Littler (eds), *Management Strategy and Industrial Relations: An Historical and Comparative Survey* (1983). My reference is to p. 20 of the original paper at the SSRC Conference on Business and Labour History, 23 March 1981.
2. Anon., *Working Men and Women by a Working Man* (London, 1879), p. 102.
3. Waldo R. Browne, *What's What in the Labor Movement: A Dictionary of Labor Affairs and Labor Terminology* (New York, 1921), p. 497.
4. Bob Gilding, *The Journeymen Coopers of East London* (Oxford, 1971), pp. 56–7.
5. N. B. Dearle, *Industrial Training: With Special Reference to the Conditions Prevailing in London* (London, 1914), pp. 31–2.
6. Ibid., p. 31.

7. *Royal Commission on Labour* (P.P. 1892 36/1) Group A, Q. 16064. Evidence of J. Cronin, secretary of the Associated Millmen of Scotland.

8. George Howell, 'Trade Unions, Apprentices and Technical Education', *Contemporary Review* 30 (1877), p. 854.

9. H. A. Clegg, A. J. Killick and Rex Adams, *Trade Union Officers* (Oxford, 1961), p. 50.

10. Cf. Alastair Reid, 'Intelligent Artisans and Aristocrats of Labour: The Essays of Thomas Wright', in Jay Winter (ed.), *The Working Class in Modern British History: Essays in Honour of Henry Pelling* (Cambridge, 1983), pp. 175–6.

11. The Registers of the Institution are preserved in Birkbeck College, University of London, to which I am obliged for access.

12. Dearle, *Industrial Training*, pp. 566–7.

13. 'Report of the Committee on the Petition of the Watchmakers, 1817', cited in A. E. Bland, P. A. Brown and R. H. Tawney (eds), *English Economic History: Select Documents* (London, 1914), pp. 588–90.

14. A. Kidd, *History of the Tin Plate Workers and Sheet Metal Workers and Braziers Societies* (London, 1949), p. 28.

15. Cf. Andreas Griessinger, *Das symbolische Kapital der Ehre: Streikbewegungen und kollektives Bewusstsein deutscher Handwerksgesellen im 18. Jahrhundert* (Berlin, 1981) for an extensive discussion.

16. Iorwerth Prothero, *Artisans and Politics in Early Nineteenth Century London: John Gast and his Times* (Folkestone, 1979), pp. 27–8.

17. Thomas Wright, *Some Habits of the Working Classes* (1867), p. 102. See also the account by F. W. Galton in S. and B. Webb, *History of Trade Unionism* (1894), pp. 431–2, and, for the importance of rituals attached to the workplace, John Dunlop, *Artificial and Compulsory Drinking Usages of the United Kingdom*, 7th edn (1844), passim.

18. See R. Price, *Masters, Unions and Men: Work Control in Building and the Rise of Labour* (Cambridge, 1980), ch. 2, for references.

19. 'It is our duty then to exercise the same control over that in which we have a vested interest, as the physician who holds his diploma, or the author who is protected by his copyright.' Preface to the Rules of the Amalgamated Society of Engineers, 1851, cited in J. B. Jefferys (ed.), *Labour's Formative Years* (London, 1948), p. 30.

20. Cited in G. Stedman Jones, *Languages of Class* (Cambridge, 1983), pp. 136–7.

21. Prothero, *Artisans*, pp. 337–8. For a clear statement, see William H. Sewell Jr, *Work and Revolution in France: The Language of Labour from the Old Regime to 1848* (Cambridge, 1980), p. 283.

22. Amalgamated Society of Carpenters and Joiners (hereafter ASCJ), *Monthly Report* (January 1868), p. 25.

23. See the description of banners in W. A. Moyes, *The Banner Book* (Gateshead, 1974).

24. Price, *Masters, Unions and Men*, p. 62.

25. M. and J. B. Jefferys, 'The Wages, Hours and Trade Customs of the Skilled Engineer in 1861', *Economic History Review* 17 (1947), pp. 29–30; but the inclusion of members of other skilled unions would raise this percentage.

26. LSE Library, Webb Collection, Coll. EA 31, pp. 245–9.

27. Ibid., pp. 311–22.

28. N. B. Dearle, *Problems of Unemployment in the London Building Trade* (London, 1908), p. 93.

29. ASCJ, *Monthly Report*, February 1868, p. 63.

30. Amalgamated Society of Engineers (hereafter ASE), *Monthly Record* (June 1911), cited in M. Holbrook-Jones, *Supremacy and Subordination of Labour* (London, 1982), p. 78.

31. J. B. Goodman (ed.), *Victorian Cabinet Maker: The Memoirs of James Hopkinson, 1819–1894* (London, 1968), p. 24.

32. 'That if the Central Association of Employers carry out their threat of a Masters' strike ... it is the duty of working men to ... begin manufacturing for the public ... That inasmuch as many of our members have lathes and other tools in their possession ... it is to be hoped that they will ... communicate their intention of lending such tools for the benefit of those persons who may be thrown out of employment by the masters' strike.' Announcement by the Council of ASE in *The Operative*, 23 December 1851.

33. Henry Broadhurst, *The Story of his Life from Stone-mason's Bench to the Treasury Bench* (London, 1901), p. 2.

34. Harry Pollitt, *Serving my Time* (London, 1941 edn), p. 14.

35. ASCJ, *Monthly Report* (July 1886), pp. 137–8.

36. The boilermakers appear to have had none: D. C. Cummings, *History of the United Society of Boilermakers and Iron & Steel Ship Builders* (Newcastle, 1905), pp. 36–7, 52. The ASE *Annual Reports* included expenditure for 'loss of tools by fire' in an item of the accounts covering miscellaneous grants, from which its relative insignificance may be inferred.

37. Following branch pressure, lists of tools stolen from members were published in the *Monthly Report* from October 1868 on.

38. Total benefit per member of ASCJ 1860–89 inclusive: Funeral £3 2s 8d, Accident £1 15s 10½d, Tool £1 14s 6½d: G. Howell, *The Conflicts of Capital and Labour historically and economically considered, being a history and review of the trade unions of Great Britain etc.*, 2nd edn (1890), p. 519.

39. Henry Mayhew, *The Morning Chronicle Survey of Labour and the Poor: The Metropolitan Districts* (Horsham, 1982), vol. 5, p. 225.

40. David Dougan, *The Shipwrights: The History of the Shipconstructors and Shipwrights Association, 1882–1963* (1968), pp. 19, 30. See also *Royal Commission on Labour* (P.P. 1893–4, 34) Group A, Q 20, 413, 21,398.

41. Mayhew, *Survey of Labour*, vol. 5, p. 193. For data on tool costs from the

Royal Commission on Labour (Group A), see P.P. 1892 36/2, Q 16,848, 19,466, 19,812–13, 20,367–9.

42. Mayhew, *Survey of Labour*, pp. 94, 96, 155, 167, 214, estimates the weekly cost at between 6d and 2s a week.

43. S. and B. Webb, *Industrial Democracy* (1913 edn), p. 313.

44. Huw Beynon, *Working for Ford* (Harmondsworth, 1973), p. 145: 'On the assembly line one man is as good as the next man ... In a skilled work situation things are slightly different ... by virtue of the fact that [the men] control the tools, or the knowledge, vital to the completion of the job. The foreman *has* to ask *them*.'

45. Zeitlin, 'Labour Strategies', pp. 21, 26.

46. 'The shop foremen will be men who are skilled in the work of their respective shops. Probably as workmen they showed especial ability and skill, which led to their promotion from the ranks': James Clayton, 'The Organization of the Locomotive Department', in John Macauley (ed.), *Modern Railway Working: A Practical Treatise by Engineering Experts* (1912–14), vol. 2, p. 57.

47. Kenneth Hudson, *Working to Rule: Railway Workshop Rules: A Study of Industrial Discipline* (Bath, 1970).

48. Anon., *Working Men and Women*, p. 66; ASE, *Quarterly Report* (December 1893), pp. 48, 59; Dearle, *Industrial Training*, p. 25.

49. Cf. the collection of builders' 'working rules' in the Webb Collection (LSE Library, Coll EB XXXI–XXXVI and Coll EC VI–XVIII); for instance Bridgnorth 1863, Loughborough 1892, Worcester 1891 (Coll EB XXXIV), Shrewsbury (Coll EC VII).

50. Gilding, *Journeymen Coopers*, p. 56.

51. Thomas Wright, *The Great Unwashed* (1868), p. 282: shopmates will lend a long-term tramping artisan 'their best tools'. Charity Organization Society, *Special Committee on Unskilled Labour: Report and Minutes of Evidence, June 1908*, p. 98: 'In the case of mechanics who have been out of work for any time, how far are they short of tools ...? ... There is a lot of freemasonry among them, and they lend each other tools. If you looked into their baskets you would find ten per cent of them deficient in tools.' Note that the witness, a building foreman, claims to be merely guessing. He does not look into the artisans' baskets. For the penalty of losing tools, namely lapsing into unskilled labouring, see Mayhew, *Survey of Labour*, vol. 5, p. 130.

52. J. B. Jefferys, *The Story of the Engineers* (London, 1945), p. 58 on second and third sons, and sons of fathers out of the trade, joining the trade.

53. Coll EB XXXIV: Hull, Redditch, Wakefield; Coll EC VII: Bristol, Dudley, Gornal, Kidderminster, Leicester, Rotherham, Stourbridge, Wigan.

54. Keith McLelland and Alastair Reid, 'The Shipbuilding Workers, 1840–1914' (unpublished paper), p. 18.

55. Dearle, *Industrial Training*, p. 241.

56. Joyce M. Bellamy and John Saville (eds), *Dictionary of Labour Biography*, 9 Vols. (London, 1994), vols 1–6.

57. Geoffrey Crossick, *An Artisan Elite in Victorian Society: Kentish London, 1840–1880* (London, 1978), p. 116.

58. Charles More, *Skill and the English Working Class* (London, 1980), p. 103, table 5.13.

59. M. L. Yates, *Wages and Labour Conditions in British Engineering* (London, 1937), p. 31, table 6.

60. E.g. A. Reid, 'The Division of Labour in the British Shipbuilding Industry, 1880–1920' (unpublished PhD thesis, Cambridge University, 1980); J. Zeitlin, 'Craft Regulation and the Division of Labour: Engineers and Compositors in Britain, 1890–1914' (unpublished PhD thesis, Warwick University, 1981).

61. B. C. M. Weekes, 'The Amalgamated Society of Engineers, 1880–1914: A Study of Trade Union Government, Politics and Industrial Policy' (unpublished PhD thesis, Warwick University, 1970), pp. 318–20, 322. As early as 1895 four ASE members stood as parliamentary candidates under Independent Labour Party auspices: David Howell, *British Workers and the Independent Labour Party 1888–1906* (Manchester, 1983), p. 88.

62. Kenneth Newton, *The Sociology of British Communism* (London, 1969), appendices II, III.

63. Cf. the Resolution of the Hull TUC, 1924, in W. Milne-Bailey (ed.), *Trade Union Documents* (London, 1929), p. 129; for the abandonment of systematic reform, ibid., pp. 133–4.

64. J. Zeitlin, 'The Emergence of Shop Steward Organisation and Job Control in the British Car Industry', *History Workshop Journal* 10 (1980), p. 129.

65. Zeitlin, 'Labour Strategies', pp. 30–2.

66. For this part of the paper I am especially indebted to Nina Fishman *The British Communist Party and the Trade Unions 1933–1945* (Aldershot, 1995). See also R. Croucher, *Engineers at War, 1939–1945* (London, 1982), esp. pp. 168–74, and James Hinton, 'Coventry Communism: A Study of Factory Politics in the Second World War', *History Workshop Journal* 10 (1980).

67. Beynon, *Working for Ford*, p. 145.

68. 'Perhaps the most interesting point about the shipwrights' powers of work control was that they did not use them to maximise their earnings or to create differentials. The shipwrights were willing to accept wages unrelated to the effort or skill of individuals and which tended towards a single rate': David Wilson, 'A Social History of Workers in H.M. Dockyard during the Industrial Revolution, Particularly 1793–1815' (unpublished PhD thesis, Warwick University, 1975), p. 188. For Edwardian skilled builders' insistence on standard rates for standard output, Charity Organisation Society, *Report on Unskilled Labour*, Q 251–272, pp. 104–5). The Webbs argued (*Industrial Democracy*, p. 719), approvingly noting the parallel with middle-

class professional corporatism, that 'the progressive raising of the Common Rule, by constantly promoting the "Selection of the Fittest", causes an increasing specialisation of function, creating a distinct group, having a Standard of Life and corporate traditions of its own which each recruit is glad enough to fall in with.'

69. In absolute numbers – 1906: 343,200 (More, *Skill*, p. 103); 1966: 271,650 (*Ministry of Labour Gazette*, January 1967), 1974: 66,000 (*Ministry of Labour Gazette*, May 1974). The statutory school-leaving age was raised to sixteen as from September 1972. Only male figures are given, in view of the insignificance of female apprenticeship.

CHAPTER 7: MAN AND WOMAN: IMAGES ON THE LEFT

1. This paper grew out of a conversation with Peter Hának of the Hungarian Academy of Sciences, Institute of History, about a paper by Efim Etkind (formerly of Leningrad, now of Nanterre) on '1830 in European Poetry'. On the art-historical side I have since had essential help from Georg Eisler, Francis and Larissa Haskell and Nick Penny. In a sense this is therefore a co-operative work, though the interpretations and errors are all my own.

2. Cf. the catalogue of the exhibition *La Liberté guidant le peuple de Delacroix*, catalogue établi et redigé par Helène Toussaint, Etude au laboratoire de la recherche des musées de France par Lola Faillant-Dumas et Jean-Paul Rioux (Paris, 1982) for a full discussion and bibliography, to which should be added H. Lüdecke, *Eugène Delacroix und die Pariser Julirevolution* (Berlin, 1965), and Efim Etkind, '1830 in der europäischen Dichtung', in R. Urbach (ed.), *Wien und Europa zwischen den Revolutionen (1789–1848)* (Vienna and Munich, 1978).

3. T. J. Clark, *The Absolute Bourgeois* (London, 1973), p. 19.

4. Etkind, '1830', pp. 150–1.

5. Heinrich Heine, *Gesammelte Werke* (Berlin, 1956–7), vol. 4, p. 19.

6. E. Ramiro, *Félicien Rops* (Paris, 1905), pp. 80–1.

7. Eduard Fuchs, *Die Frau in der Karikatur* (Munich, 1906), p. 484. Fuchs described *Peuple* not implausibly as 'Megäre Volk' or 'The People as Virago'; Ramiro, *Félicien Rops*, p. 188. A less explicit version of the same figure, because omitting the lower half of the woman's body, is on an unpaginated plate of Franz Blei, *Félicien Rops* (Berlin, 1921).

8. M. Agulhon, 'Esquisse pour une archéologie de la République: l'allégorie civique féminine', *Annales* 28 (1973), pp. 5–34. A non-revolutionary heroine is almost simultaneously presented in the opposite manner to Delacroix in David Wilkie's *Defence of Saragossa, 1828* (Wilkie Exhibition, Royal Academy, 1958). The real Spanish heroine is shown fully dressed but in allegorical pose, while a male partisan crouches beside her, nude to the waist. (I owe this reference to Dr N. Penny.) Byron, who discusses the role of the Spanish female freedom-fighters and the Maid of Saragossa at length, and admiringly

(*Childe Harold*, 1, 54 ff.) stresses the apparently unfeminine heroism: 'Her lover sinks – she sheds no ill-timed tear; / Her chief is slain – she fills his fatal post; / Her fellows flee – she checks their base career; / The foe retires – she heads the sallying host.' But he also stresses that she remains within the range of what male superiority regards as desirable in women: 'Yet are Spain's maids no race of Amazons, / But formed for all the witching arts of love.' In fact, theirs – unlike Liberty's – is 'the fierceness of the dove'.

9. See Jean Duché, *1760–1960: deux siècles d'histoire de France par la caricature* (Paris, 1961), pp. 142, 143, 145.

10. J. Bruhat, Jean Dautry and Emile Tersen, *La Commune de 1871* (Paris, 1971), p. 190 – an English picture.

11. Jean Grand-Carteret, *L'Affaire Dreyfus et l'image* (Paris, 1898), p. 150.

12. Ibid., pls 61, 67, 106, 251.

13. R. A. Leeson, *United We Stand: An Illustrated Account of Trade Union Emblems* (London, 1971), p. 26.

14. Lucien Christophe, *Constantin Meunier* (Antwerp, 1947), pls 6, 7, 8, 9, 21.

15. Frans Masereel, *Die Stadt* (Munich, 1925).

16. John Gorman, *Banner Bright: An Illustrated History of the Banners of the British Trade Union Movement* (London, 1973), p. 126.

17. Leeson, *United We Stand*, pp. 60–70.

18. Gorman, *Banner Bright*, pp. 122–3.

19. W. Crane, *Cartoons for the Cause: A Souvenir of the International Socialist Workers and Trade Union Congress, 1886–96* (London, 1896).

20. From the collection of Dr Herbert Steiner of Vienna. For the survival of the triple slogan of the French Revolution, see Udo Achten (ed.), *Zum Lichte Empor: Mai-Festzeitungen der Sozialdemokratie, 1891–1914* (Berlin and Bonn 1980), pp. 12–14; D. Fricke, *Kleine Geschichte des Ersten Mai* (Frankfurt, 1980), p. 61.

21. Joseph Edwards (ed.), *Labour Annual 1895* (Manchester).

22. Christophe, *Constantin Meunier*, pl. 12.

23. See E. and M. Dixmier, *L'Assiette au beurre* (Paris, 1974), pl. ix.

24. The replacement of the female allegory by the naked male figure in German socialist iconography round 1900 has been independently noted by Detlev Hoffman and Ursula Schmidt-Linsenhoff, *Unsere Welt trotz alledem* (Frankfurt, 1978), p. 375.

25. 'To draw a peasant's figure in action, I repeat, that's what an essentially modern figure is, the very core of modern art, which neither the Greeks nor the Renaissance nor the old Dutch have done ... People like Daumier – we must respect them for they are among the pioneers. The simple nude but modern figure, as Hennor and Lefèvre have renewed it, ranks high ... But peasants and labourers are not nude, after all, and it is not necessary to imagine them in the nude. The more painters begin to paint workmen's and peasants' figures, the better I shall like it ...' Vincent van Gogh, *The*

Complete Letters of Vincent van Gogh (London, 1958), vol. 2, pp. 400, 402. I owe the reference to Francis Haskell.

26. F. D. Klingender, *Art and the Industrial Revolution* (London, 1947), pls 10, 47, 57, 90, 92, 103; Paul Brandt, *Schaffende Arbeit und bildende Kunst* (Leipzig, 1927–8), vol. 2, pp. 240 ff.

27. Brandt, *Schaffende Arbeit*, p. 243, pl. 314.

28. Leeson, *United We Stand*, p. 23.

29. Nicholas Penny, *Church Monuments in Romantic England* (New Haven and London, 1977), pl. 138.

30. Brandt, *Schaffende Arbeit*, p. 270.

31. I. E. Grabar, V. N. Lazarev and F. S. Kamenov, *Istoriya Russkogo Isskusstva* (Moscow, 1957), vol. 11, pp. 33, 83, 359, 381, 431.

32. Tsigal, Burganov, Svetlov and Chernov (eds), *Sovietskaya Skulptura 74* (Moscow, 1976), p. 52.

33. Grabar et al., *Istoriya Russkogo Isskusstva*, p. 150.

34. In a work celebrating the fifteenth anniversary of the October Revolution, the first photo of this kind ('Socialist man and his enthusiasm are the motor of construction') only occurs in the year 1932. *Fünfzehn Eiserne Schritte. Eine Buch der Tatsachen aus der Sowjetunion* (Berlin, 1932).

35. Klingender, *Art and the Industrial Revolution*, pl. xv.

36. 'An injury to one is an injury to all', 'We will fight and may die, but we will never surrender', 'This is a holy war / and we will not cease / until all destitution / prostitution and exploitation / is swept away.' Gorman, *Banner Bright*, p. 130.

37. Grabar et al., *Istoriya Russkogo Isskusstva*, pl. XI, p. 431.

38. Peter Kriedte, Hans Medick and Jürgen Schlumbohm, *Industrialisierung vor der Industrialiserung* (Göttingen, 1977), chs 2–3.

39. Thus in France 56 per cent of all women employed in industry in 1906 worked in clothing, which also employed 50 per cent of those in Belgian industry (1890), 25 per cent of those in German (1907), and 36 per cent of those in British industry (1891): Peter N. Stearns, *Lives of Labour: Work in a Maturing Industrial Society* (London, 1975), appendix III, p. 365.

40. D. C. Marsh, *The Changing Social Structure of England and Wales, 1871–1961*, rev. edn (London, 1965), p. 129.

41. W. Woytinsky, *Die Welt in Zahlen* (Berlin, 1926), vol. 2, p. 76; Gertraud Wolf, *Der Frauenerwerb in den Hauptkulturstaaten* (Munich, 1916), p. 251.

42. Peter N. Stearns in Martha J. Vicinus (ed.), *Suffer and Be Still: Women in the Victorian Age* (Bloomington and London, 1973), p. 118.

43. Marsh, *Changing Social Structure*, p. 129.

44. The problem here hinted at has been admirably presented in Louise A. Tilly and Joan W. Scott, *Women, Work and Family* (New York, 1978), esp. ch. 8 and pp. 228–9. This excellent discussion confirms the present analysis especially insofar as it situates the rise of that phase of the economy when

'the new organization of manufacturing required an adult male labor force primarily' and when 'during most of her married life a woman served as a specialist in child rearing and consumer activities for her family' precisely in the period when the mass labour movement emerged in the industrially advanced countries.

45. E. P. Thompson, 'The Moral Economy of the English Crowd in the Eighteenth Century', *Past and Present* 50 (1971).
46. L. Levi Accati, 'Vive le roi sans taille et sans gabelle: una discussione sulle rivolte contadine', *Quaderni Storici* (September–December 1972), p. 1078; Heine's comment on Delacroix reflects the role of the market women ('fishwife').
47. H. A. Clegg, Alan Fox and A. F. Thompson, *A History of British Trade Unions since 1889* (Oxford, 1964), vol. 1, pp. 469–70.
48. S. and B. Webb, *Industrial Democracy* (London, 1897), p. 496.
49. Ibid., p. 497.
50. Ibid., pp. 496–7.
51. Ibid., p. 497.
52. See Jean Touchard, *La Gauche en France depuis 1900* (Paris, 1977), p. 113.
53. Bebel's feminism may not be unconnected with his enthusiasm for Fourier, about whom he also wrote a book. Frederick Engels' influential *Origin of the Family* should also be mentioned.
54. Eugène Pottier, *Oeuvres complètes*, ed. Pierre Brochon (Paris, 1966).
55. Gorman, *Banner Bright*, p. 126.
56. The image of utopia increasingly shifted from one based on natural fertility to one based on technological and scientific productivity. Both were clearly present in utopian socialism – see Pottier's poem *L'Age d'Or*, quoted above: 'Oh nations, plus de torpeur. / Mille réseaux vous ont nouées. / L'électricité, la vapeur / sont vos servants dévoués' etc. (Oh nations awake! You are linked to a thousand networks. Electricity and steam are your faithful servants.) However, iconographically nature/fertility prevailed over technology, certainly until 1917.
57. J. F. C. Harrison, *Robert Owen and the Owenites in Britain and America: The Quest for the New Moral World* (London, 1969), pp. 58–62.
58. Ibid., pp. 60–1.
59. Ibid., pp. 98, 102, 121 for frequency of female messiahs in this period.
60. Brandt, *Schaffende Arbeit*, p. 269.

CHAPTER 8: BIRTH OF A HOLIDAY: THE FIRST OF MAY

For a full bibliography, A. Panaccione, 'I 100 anni del 1° maggio nella storiografia', in A. Panaccione (ed.), *I luoghi e i soggetti del 1° maggio* (Venice, 1990).

1. Michael Ignatieff, 'Easter Has Become Chocolate Sunday', *Observer*, 15 April 1990.

2. Maurice Dommanget, *Histoire du Premier Mai* (Paris, 1953), pp. 350–1. Dommanget's book, one of the few to deal with the subject before the late 1970s, remains important, but lacks the strong iconographical orientation of the recent literature.

3. Cf. Helmut Hartwig, 'Plaketten zum 1. Mai 1934–39', *Aesthetik und Kommunikation* 7, no. 26 (1976), pp. 56–9. A. Riosa (ed.), *Le metamorfosi del 1° maggio* (Venice, 1990) contains essays on the Italian, Nazi and Salazarist attempts to co-opt May Day.

4. Dommanget, *Histoire du Premier Mai*, pp. 301 ff.

5. Ibid., pp. 100–1.

6. Ibid., p. 102.

7. The fullest international treatment is Andrea Panaccione (ed.), *The Memory of May Day: An Iconographic History of the Origin and Implanting of a Workers' Holiday* (Venice, 1989). For the first May Day see the same author's *Un giorno perché. Cent'anni di storia internazionale del 1° maggio* (Rome, 1990), ch. 4.

8. Karl Marx and Friedrich Engels, *Werke* (Berlin, 1963), vol. 22, p. 60.

9. Dieter Fricke, *Kleine Geschichte des Ersten Mai* (Frankfurt, 1980), pp. 30–1.

10. Dommanget, *Histoire du Premier Mai*, p. 156.

11. Fricke, *Kleine Geschichte des Ersten Mai*, p. 30.

12. Dommanget, *Histoire du Premier Mai*, p. 136.

13. Ibid., p. 156.

14. R. Evans (ed.), *Kneipengespräche im Kaiserreich. Stimmungsberichte der Hamburger Politischen Polizei, 1892–1914* (Reinbek, 1989), pp. 20, 253–7.

15. Panaccione, *The Memory*, p. 247.

16. Kurt Greussing (ed.), *Die Roten am Land. Arbeitsleben und Arbeiterbewegung im westlichen Österreich* (Steyr, 1989), pp. 58–9.

17. Calculated from Panaccione, *The Memory*, p. 247.

18. Dommanget, *Histoire du Premier Mai*, p. 155.

19. Ibid., p. 156.

20. Cf. the comparison of social democratic and communist May Day iconography in Weimar Germany in W. L. Guttsman, *Workers' Culture in Weimar Germany: Between Tradition and Commitment* (New York, Oxford and Munich, 1990), pp. 1989–99. The finest example of this colour scheme I know is Th. A. Steinlen's undated *La Manifestation* (no. 314 in *Le Bel Heritage: Th. A. Steinlen Retrospective, 1885–1922* (Montreuil, 1987). For comparison: a real workers' May Day demonstration at a time of revolutionary struggle, Kustodiev's 'Demonstration at the Putilovskij Factory for May Day 1906', in Panaccione, *The Memory*, pp. 530–1. While obviously influenced by the black–red convention, the painter clearly reflects the wider range of colours on such occasions in real life. For this artist's other contributions to radical iconography, see David King and Cathy Porter, *Images of Revolution: Graphic Art from 1905 Russia* (New York, 1983).

21. Lucía Rivas Lara, 'El Primer de Maig a Catalunya, 1900–1931', *L'Avenç* (May 1988), p. 9. The substance of this is taken from the same author's *Historia del 1° de mayo en Espana: desde 1900 hasta la 2a Republica* (Madrid, 1987) which is the fullest treatment of the theme for that country.

22. Rivas Lara, 'El Primer de Maig', passim. See also Lucía Rivas Lara, 'Ritualización socialista del 1° de mayo. Fiesta, huelga, manifestación?', *Historia Contemporánea, Revista del Departamento de Historia Contemporánea de la Universidad del Pais Vasco* no. 3 (1990). I owe this reference to Paul Preston.

23. For a (failed) anarchist attempt to turn the demonstration into the revolution, see David Ballester and Manuel Vicente, 'El Primer de Maig a Barcelona. Vuit hores de treball, d'instrucció i de descans', *L'Avenç* (May 1990), pp. 12–17: a study of the 1890 May Day in that city. For the French CGT, see Maxime Leroy, *La Coûtume ouvrière* (Paris, 1913), vol. 1, p. 246, who notes that, once the CGT took over the occasion from the socialists after 1904, 'plus de fête du travail'. Dommanget, *Histoire du Premier Mai*, p. 334.

24. For a most interesting account of a) the transfer (under Peter the Great) of the Western spring festival to Russia, via the German suburb of Moscow, and b) the merger of this *maevka* with the tiny social democratic workers' demonstrations of the 1890s, for which they provided a cover, see Vjaceslav Kolomiez, 'Dalla storia del 1° maggio a Mosca tra la fine del ottocento e gli inizi del novecento: i luoghi delle manifestazioni', in Panaccione, *I luoghi e i soggetti del 1° maggio*, pp. 105–22, N.B. pp. 110–11 for the use of the simile of spring in a political context.

25. Among this literature, the following deserve to be noted: André Rossel, *Premier mai: 90 ans de lutte populaire dans le monde* (Paris, 1977); Udo Achten, *Illustrierte Geschichte des Ersten Mai* (Obserhausen, 1979); Udo Achten, *Zum Lichte Empor: Maifestzeitungen der Sozial-demokratie, 1891–1914* (Berlin and Bonn, 1980); Sven Bodin and Carl-Adam Nycop, *Första Maj, 1890–1980* (Stockholm, 1980); *Upp till kamp: Social-demokratins första majmärken, 1894–1986* (Stockholm, 1986); U. Achten, M. Reichelt and R. Schultz (eds), *Mein Vaterland ist international. Internationale illustrierte Geschichte des ersten Mai von 1886 bis heute* (Oberhausen, 1986); Fondazione Giangiacomo Feltrinelli, *Ogni anno un maggio nuovo: il centenario del Primo Maggio* (Milan, 1988); Comune di Milano, Fondazione Giagiacomo Brodolini, *Per i cent'anni della festa del lavoro* (Milan, 1988); Maurizio Antonioli and Giovanna Ginex, *1° Maggio. Repertorio dei numeri unici dal 1890 al 1924* (Milan, 1988); and, above all, Panaccione, *The Memory*. See also for Switzerland, Bildarchiv und Dokumentation zur Geschichte der Arbeiterbewegung, Zürich, *1. Mai/1er mai: Mappe zur Geschichte des 1. Mai in der Schweiz* (Zurich, 1989).

26. Panaccione, *The Memory*, pp. 356–7.

27. Greussing, *Die Roten am Land*, p. 168.

28. Claude Willard, *Les Guesdistes* (Paris, 1964), p. 237n.; W. L. Guttsman, *The German Social Democratic Party, 1875–1933* (London, 1981), p. 160.

29. Cf. Renata Ameruso and Gabriela Spigarelii, 'Il 1° maggio delle donne', in Panaccione, *I luoghi e i soggetti del 1° maggio*, pp. 9–104.

30. Rivas Lara, 'El Primer de Maig', pp. 7–8.

31. Antonioli and Ginex, *Repertorio*, pp. 4–5. Ballester and Vicente, 'El Primer de Maig', p. 13 for the (typically) strong sense of the internationality of the 1890 demonstration in Barcelona. F. Giovanoli, *Die Maifeierbewegung. Ihre wirtschaftlichen und soziologischen Ursprünge und Wirkungen* (Karlsruhe, 1925), stresses the unexpected strength of this international feeling as revealed by the first demonstrations (pp. 90–1).

32. The anarchist poet Pietro Gori created his famous May Day hymn ('Sweet Easter of the Workers'), to be sung to the music of the chorus in Verdi's *Nabucco*, in 1896, as part of a one-act play on May Day. F. Andreucci and T. Detti (eds), *Il movimento operaio italiano. Dizionario biografico* (Rome, 1976), vol. 2, p. 526. See E. J. Hobsbawm, *Worlds of Labour* (London, 1984), p. 77.

33. Jules Destrée and Emile Vandervelde, *Le Socialisme en Belgique* (Paris, 1903), pp. 417–18. Giovanoli, *Die Maifeierbewegung*, pp. 114–15 notes the religious element in the language.

34. See Hobsbawm, *Worlds of Labour*, ch. 3, 'Religion and the Rise of Socialism'.

35. The sense of May Day as the *only* holiday exclusively associated with the workers, and its consequent effect in forming class consciousness, was noted from the start. 'This day is theirs. It is theirs alone': J. Diner-Denes, 'Der erste Mai', *Der Kampf* (Vienna), 1 May 1908. Diner-Denes, also notes the conquest of public space by the workers on this day.

36. Hobsbawm, *Worlds of Labour*, p. 73 and more generally ch. 5, 'The Transformation of Labour Rituals'.

37. Antonioli and Ginex, *Repertorio*, p. 23.

38. Greussing, *Die Roten am Land*, pp. 18–21.

39. The most interesting analysis of May Day symbolism is Giovanna Ginex, 'L'immagine del Primo Maggio in Italia (1890–1945)', in Comune di Milano, *Per i cent'anni*, pp. 37–41, and the same, 'Images on May Day Single Issue Newspapers (1891–1924): Their Function and Meanings', in A. Panaccione (ed.), *May Day Celebration* (Venice, 1988), pp. 13–25.

40. The role of May Day in advancing and catalysing the idea of the general strike – not only for universal suffrage – was already brought out in Giovanoli, *Die Maifeierbewegung*.

41. *Upp till kamp*, p. 12.

42. Panaccione, *The Memory*, p. 223.

43. Ibid., p. 363.

44. E. J. Hobsbawm, '100 Years of May Day', *Liber*, 8 June 1990 (distributed with *Times Literary Supplement*), pp. 10–11.

45. Ginex, 'L'immagine', p. 40.

46. The rise of the red carnation in Italy is most easily followed in Fondazione Giangiacomo Feltrinelli, *Ogni anno* (which includes the collection of Single Issues in the Feltrinelli Library, containing, it appears, some not listed in *Repertorio*) and has numerous illustrations. The first reference to the flower as 'official' seems to be a poem in an issue from 1898 (p. 94), though other flowers do not disappear until 1900. For *Il Garofano Rosso*'s explication, ibid., p. 105, and *Repertorio*, p. 130. For the Swedish rose, *Upp till kamp*, pp. 21–3.

47. At least, so Dommanget, *Histoire du Premier Mai*, pp. 361–3. But he himself traces the political use of the lily-of-the-valley back to an Austrian print of the early 1890s (pp. 175–6), i.e. a time when the political association was with spring flowers, not necessarily symbolically red ones. For a German May Day image of a small girl selling these flowers, which was taken up internationally, *Ogni anno*, p. 100 (*Der Wahre Jacob*, 26 April 1898).

48. The incident is vividly recaptured in Franco Rosi's superb film *Salvatore Giuliano*.

49. *Un altra Italia nelle bandiere dei lavoratori: simboli e cultura dall'unità d'Italia all'avvento del fascismo* (Turin, 1980), p. 276. This catalogue of an exhibition of workers' flags confiscated by the fascists is a superb contribution to the art history of popular ideology.

50. Ibid., p. 277.

51. Destrée and Vandervelde, *Le Socialisme en Belgique*, p. 418.

52. *L'Aurora del 1° Maggio* 1950 (Antonioli and Ginex, *Repertorio*, p. 290) Paradoxically this was anticipated by the Weberian bourgeois of Barcelona in 1890 who predicted, bitterly, that if the workers insisted on striking on May Day this would mean 'the addition of another holiday to the many which tradition and the Church have saddled the calendar with': Ballester and Vicente, 'El Primer de Maig', p. 14.

53. T. Ferenczi, 'Feastdays', *Liber*, 8 June 1990, p. 11.

54. *Victor Adler's Aufsätze, Reden und Briefe* (Vienna, 1922), vol. 1, p. 73.

CHAPTER 9: SOCIALISM AND THE AVANT-GARDE, 1880–1914

1. The massive exhibition of 'post-impressionism' at the London Royal Academy (1979–80) demonstrated this vividly.

2. Hauptmann's *Weavers* and *Florian Geyer* were frankly committed socio-political dramas and much admired as such.

3. *Gesammelte Schriften und Aufsätze*, ed. E. Fuchs, *Zur Literaturgeschichte* (Berlin, 1930), vol. 2, p. 107.

4. Cf. 'Was wollen die Modernen, von einem Modernen', *Neue Zeit*, 1893–4, pp. 132 ff., 168 ff.

5. Mehring, *Zur Literaturgeschichte*, vol. 2, p. 298 (originally published 1898–9).

6. For the same reasons a 'people's opera' never developed at all, though at least one operatic composer, the revolutionary Gustave Charpentier, tried his hand at a working-class heroine (*Louise*, 1900) and an element of *verismo* enters opera at this period (*Cavalleria Rusticana*).

7. E. P. Thompson, *William Morris: Romantic to Revolutionary* (London, 1955, 1977); P. Meier, *La Pensée utopique de William Morris* (Paris, 1972).

8. Stuart Merrill cited in E. W. Herbert, *The Artist and Social Reform: France and Belgium, 1885–1898* (Newhaven, 1961), p. 100n.

9. Subscribers to the anarchist *La Révolte* in 1894 included Daudet, Anatole France, Huysmans, Leconte de Lisle, Mallarmé, Loti and the theatrical avant-garde of Antoine and Lugné-Poe. No socialist review at the time was likely to attract such a galaxy. But even so early an anarchist as the poet Gustave Kahn deeply respected Marx and favoured a unity of all leftists. Herbert, *Artist and Social Reform*, pp. 21, 110–11.

10. B. Ermers, *Victor Adler* (Vienna, 1932), pp. 236–7.

11.. H. J. Steinberg, *Sozialismus und deutsche Sozialdemokratie* (Hanover, 1967), pp. 132–5.

12. C. Kohn, *Karl Kraus* (Stuttgart, 1966), pp. 65, 66.

13. Cf. G. Botz, G. Brandstetter and M. Pollack, *Im Schatten der Arbeiterbewegung* (Vienna, 1977), pp. 83–5 on Austro-German anarchism.

14. R. Luxemburg, *J'étais, je suis, je serai. Correspondance, 1914–1919* (Paris, 1977), pp. 306–7.

15. Ibid., p. 307.

16. L. Trotskij, *Letteratura e rivoluzione*, ed. V. Strada (Turin, 1973), p. 467.

17. G. Plekhanov, *Kunst und Literatur* (Berlin, 1954), pp. 284–5.

18. J. C. Holl, *La Jeune Peinture contemporaine* (Paris, 1912), pp. 14–15.

19. Plekhanov, *Kunst und Literatur*, pp. 292, 295.

20. W. Morris, *On Art and Socialism*, ed. Holbrook Jackson (London, 1946), p. 76.

21. Morris first appeared at a socialist meeting (to discuss the building of houses for the people) in 1883.

22. 'Considering the relation of the modern world to art, our business is now, and for long will be, not so much attempting to produce definite art, as rather clearing the ground to give art its opportunity': 'The Socialist Ideal', in *On Art and Socialism*, p. 323.

CHAPTER 11: PEASANTS AND POLITICS

1. Kazimierz Dobrowolski, 'Peasant Traditional Culture', in Teodor Shanin (ed.), *Peasant and Peasant Societies* (London, 1971).

2. Karl Marx, *The Eighteenth Brumaire of Louis Bonaparte* (1852).

3. Cf. a contemporary comment on a conflict between rural strata in sixteenth-century Germany: 'It is curious that the subjects of the Lordship of Messkirch should have rebelled against their lord, Gottfried Werner, because they

could give no valid or urgent reason for their action. They simply claimed that, in the villages, they were overrun by the cottagers and day-labourers who wanted to use the pasture-land, and that they could not live on their farms in the old ways. But, in fact, the majority of the labourers consisted of the sons, sons-in-law or close kin of the farmers': David Sabean, 'Famille tenure paysanne: aux origines de la guerre des paysans en Allemagne', *Annales: Economies, Sociétés, Civilisations* 27, 4–5 (July–October 1972), p. 904.

4. Teodor Shanin, 'The Peasantry as a Political Factor', in Shanin, *Peasants*.
5. Leonardo Sciascia, *La corda pazza: scrittori e cose della Sicilia* (Turin, 1970), pp. 80–3.
6. Jean de La Bruyère, *Les Caractères* (Paris, 1869), pp. 292–3.
7. Ramiro Condarco Morales, *Zarate, El 'Terrible' Willka: historia de la rebelión indigena de 1899* (La Paz, 1965), p. 290.
8. Pierre Gilhodès, 'Agrarian Struggles in Columbia', in R. Stavenhagen (ed.), *Agrarian Problems and Peasant Movements in Latin America* (New York, 1970), p. 445.
9. Teodor Shanin, *The Awkward Class: Political Sociology of Peasantry in a Developing Society: Russia, 1910–1925* (London, 1972), p. 161.
10. Wesley Craig, 'Peru: the peasant movement in La Convención' in H. Landsberger (ed.), *Latin American Peasant Movements* (Ithaca, 1969); E. J. Hobsbawm, 'Problèmes agraires à La Convención (Pérou)', in *Les Problèmes agraires des Amériques Latines* (Paris, 1967), pp. 385–94; E. J. Hobsbawm, 'A Case of Neo-feudalism: La Convención', *Journal of Latin American Studies*, 1/1 (1970).
11. John C. Hammock and Jeffrey A. Ashe (eds), *Hablan lideres campesinos* (Quito, 1970), pp. 19–20.
12. Ibid., p. 13.
13. Jean A. Meyer, *La Cristiada, el Estado y el pueblo en la Revolución mexicana (1926–1929)*, 3 vols (Mexico, 1973).
14. Edward Dew, *Politics in the Altiplano: The Dynamics of Change in Rural Peru* (Austin and London, 1969).
15. Hamza Alavi, 'Peasants and Revolution', in R. Miliband and J. Saville (eds), *The Socialist Register* (London, 1965), pp. 241–77; Eric Wolf, *Peasant Wars of the Twentieth Century* (New York and London, 1971).
16. Maureen Perrie, 'The Russian Peasant Movement of 1905–7: Its Social Composition and Revolutionary Significance', *Past and Present* 57 (November 1972), pp. 123–55.
17. Georges Lefebvre, *The Great Fear of 1789: Rural Panic in Revolutionary France* (London, 1973).
18. Nathan Wachtel, *La Vision des vaincus* (Paris, 1971).
19. Daniel Field, review of S. B. Okun and K. V. Sivkov (eds), 'Krestianske Dvizhenie v Rossii v 1857–mae 1961 gg.' *Kritika* 3/3 (Spring 1967), pp.

34–55; Juan Martinez Alier, 'Peasants and Labourers in Southern Spain, Cuba, and Highland Peru', *Journal of Peasant Studies* 1/2 (1974).

20. Field, review of Okun and Sivkov, p. 49. Field suggests that even the Russian peasants' monarchism was largely a defensive trick: they had enough problems without saddling themselves with a reputation for disloyalty to the state (pp. 49–50). This is probably pushing peasant pragmatism too far, but there is a grain of truth in such a view.

21. E. J. Hobsbawm, 'Peasant Land Invasions', *Past & Present*, 62, 1974.

22. Marc Ferro, *La Révolution Russe de 1917: la chute de tsarisme et les origines d'Octobre* (Paris, 1967), p. 186.

23. Martinez Alier, 'Peasants and Labourers'.

24. Field, review of Okun and Sivkov, p. 54.

25. Juan Diaz del Moral, *Historia de las agitaciones campesinas Andaluzas* (Madrid, 1967), p. 468.

26. Edward E. Malefakis, *Agrarian Reform and Peasant Revolution in Spain: Origins of the Civil War* (New Haven and London, 1970).

27. Perrie, 'Russian Peasant Movement', p. 136.

28. Maurice Duverger (ed.), *Partis politiques et classes sociales en France* (Paris, 1955), p. 225.

29. Ibid., p. 157.

30. Sidney G. Tarrow, *Peasant Communism in Southern Italy* (New Haven and London, 1967), pp. 134 and 144.

31. Marx, *Eighteenth Brumaire*.

32. John Duncan Powell, 'Peasant Society and Clientelist Politics', *American Political Science Review* 64 (2 June 1970), pp. 411–25.

CHAPTER 12: PEASANT LAND OCCUPATIONS

1. The main sources used, in addition to the press and a substantial number of Peruvian official and semi-official publications, are the documents held by Zone X of Agrarian Reform (Huancayo Office) and the 'Juzgado de Tierras', Huancayo, and the archives of several former estates, especially the former Sociedad Ganadera del Centro, Sociedad Ganadera Tucle and Compania Ganadera Antapongo. All these estates are in the Peruvian central highlands.

2. *La Prensa* (Lima), 7 August 1963. For earlier invasions (1924–6), see C.D.A., 'Inventario de los Fondos de la Sociedad Ganadera Algolan', t/s., pp. 45–61.

3. A. Aguilera Camacho, *Derecho Agrario Colombiano* (Bogotá, 1962).

4. *Prensa*, 27 August 1963.

5. 103 *invasioines* were reported in the Lima press from 1959 to 1966, including 77 in the period of maximum agrarian unrest, August–December 1963, the overwhelming majority being land recuperations. The reporting is, however, extremely defective. The only *complete* list I know is that

provided by the Civil Guard of the Cuzco Department for April to 11 November 1963, before *invasiones* in that department had reached their peak. It lists 70 cases, but details of the invaders are given in only 24 cases, the rest merely naming the property invaded. Of these:

Communities invading estates	14
Communities invading communities	4
Tenants invading estates	3
'Peasants of the locality' invading	3

Legislatura Ordinaria, *Diario de los Debates*, (Senado 1963), vol. v, pp. 481–5.

6. *En Torno a la Practica Revolucionaria y la Lucha Interna.* II *Pleno del Comité Central del Partido Comunista Peruano. Informe Politico* (Ediciones Bandera Roja, Lima, 1970, mimeo), p. 12. Dr Pareades is a lawyer with long experience of peasant work.

7. Pietro Laveglia, 'Lotte per la terra e prime tentativi d'organizzazioine contadina in provincia di Salerno', *Movimento Operario*, nos. 3–4 (May–August 1955), p. 599.

8. A. Basile, 'Il moto contadino nel Napoletano e il ministero del 3 aprile 1848', *Rivista Storica del Socialismo*, xi (1960), pp. 795, 799.

9. J. Diaz del Moral, *Historia de las agitaciones campesinas Andaluzas* (Madrid, 1967 edn.), pp. 85–6.

10. *Prensa*, 19 August 1963.

11. *Prensa*, 2 September 1963, 6 September 1963. Huamanmarca and Yanacachi referred to titles of 1825 in 1930: see C.D.A., 'Inventario . . . Algolan', p. 73.

12. Paredes, *En Torno a la Practica Revolucionaria*, p. 12.

13. John Womack, *Zapata and the Mexican Revolution* (New York, 1969), Epilogue, pp. 371 ff.

14. Interview with Sr. Oscar Bernuy Gomez, Huancayo, June 1971.

15. *Informe de la Comisión que investigó los sucesos sangrientos de Paquiló . . .* (Bogotá, 1932), p. 9.

16. Juzgado de Tierras, Huancavo: Expediente 70/1385/2 C, fj 468, 469.

17. Carlos Alberto Izaguirre, 'La transferencia de bienes comunales', *Peru Indigena*, vi, nos. 14–15 (1957), pp. 110–15.

18. Juzgado de Tierras Huancayo, *loc. cit.*, fj 105: 'the titles establishing this fact having gone astray'.

19. *Prensa*, 10 and 11 February 1964.

20. Cf. the report of a plan to invade the subtropical slopes of Hda. Runatullo: C.D.A., Archives Ganadera del Centro, Hda. Acopalca papers, File 'Runatullo', 27 January 1958.

21. *Prensa*, 11 February 1964, 12 November 1963, 30 November 1963: C.D.A., Arch. Ganadera del Centro, Acopalca papers: 'Informe sobre los sucesos

ocuridos en las Hdas. Tucle, Antapongo y Laive ...', by Ingeniero Alberto Chaparro (Correspondencia Confidencial, 25 January 1947).

22. Hugo Neira, *Cuzco, Tierra y Muerte* (Lima, 1964), p. 22.

23. C.D.A., Arch. Ganadera del Centro, Laive papers: Laive to Lima, 9 August 1931.

24. *Prensa*, 10 September 1963, 1 September 1963, 19 September 1963, 30 July 1963, 19 August 1963, 17 October 1963, 21 October 1963.

25. E.g. *Prensa*, 18 November 1963 (Hda. Inapi, Anta-Cuzco); 3 *haciendas* in Paruro-Cuzco, 30 November 1963; Hda. Mapi Florencia, Anta, 4 December 1963; Dist. Huacondo, 16 December 1963.

26. The theories justifying such urban squatting are evidently not the same as those justifying the recuperation of lost common lands, but we are not here concerned with the modifications of peasant jurisprudence among rural migrants to the cities.

27. Gerrit Huizer, *Report on the Study of the Role of Peasant Organizations in the Process of Agrarian Reform in Latin America* (ILO-CIDA, Geneva, 1969, mimeo), pp. 241, 243.

28. As in the arguments about the peasant claim in the Comarca Lagunera (Mexico) which turned on the question whether the claimants were capable of cultivating the land in dispute. Cf: 'Historical resumé ... written in 1936 by J. Cruz Chacon Sifuentes', App. 1 to Henry Landsberger and Cynthia Hewitt de Alcantara, *Peasant Organisation in La Laguna, Mexico* (CIDA Research Papers, 17, OAS, Washington, 1970), p. 129.

29. A. Affonso, S. Gómez, E. Klein, P. Ramírez, *Movimento Campesino Chileno* (Santiago, 1970), ii, pp. 127 ff. But political and trade-union organization was present in all cases.

30. Gerrit Huizer, *On Peasant Unrest in Latin America* (CIDA, Washington, 1967), pp. 217 ff.

31. A. La Cava, 'La rivolta calabrese del 1848', *Arch. Stor. delle Provincie Napoletane*, new ser., xxxi (1947–9), pp. 445 ff., 540, 552.

32. Laveglia, (see note 7 above), p. 601.

33. Basile, (see note 8 above), p. 795

34. Cited in Renzo del Carria, *Proletari senza Rivoluzione* (Milan, 1970), ii, pp. 78–91.

35. E. Malefakis, *Agrarian Reform and Peasant Revolution in Spain* (New Haven and London, 1970), esp. pp. 368–9.

36. This is contained mainly in the files of the Juzgado de Tierras, Huancayo, where I have consulted the voluminous Expedientes 69.831 and 70/1385/2C – the records of litigation between the community and Hda. Tucle, and the Subdirección de Reforma Agraria ZAX Huancayo, Expediente de afectación, Hacienda Tucle and Expediente, Comunidad Huasicancha. Juan Martinez Alier has been kind enough to consult these. For the fullest account of both the community and its land campaigns, see Gavin Smith,

Livelihood and Resistance (Berkeley, 1989). This excellent book amplifies and corrects my own earlier account.

37. The Expediente de Afectación for Tucle lists 13 communities in addition to Huasicancha, all of which asserted claims against the *hacienda* and recorded litigation against it.

38. Juzgado de Tierras, Huancayo, Exp. 70/1385/2 C Fj 17 ff.

39. Their energies were partly captured by the government through the 'Patronato Central de la Raza Indigena' (1922); but the more radical 'Comité Pro Derecho Indigena Tahuantinsuyo' (1920) was dissolved by the authorities in 1927. For these, see W. Kapsoli and W. Reategui, *El Campesinado Peruano 1919–1930* (Lima, 1972, mimeo), ch. v. The Patronato took up several cases concerning communities of our area in dispute with Hdas. Tucle, Antapongo and Laive-Ingahuasi.

40. Dr Carlos Samaniego, who has interviewed militants of the period in this region, assures me that the flag was a Peruvian national one (red-white), the headman of the community in question (Ahuac) being a policeman on leave who later advanced to the rank of sergeant. The report is in C.D.A., Arch. Ganadera del Centro, Laive papers: Laive to Lima, 9 August 1931.

41. What follows is based on the work of Dr Carlos Samaniego and his students at the Universidad Agraria, Lima, in Yanacancha.

42. Sociedad Ganadera del Centro, *Datos Estadisticos* (Lima, 1929), p. 13. This annual publication demonstrates the constant preoccupation of the estates with boundary disputes.

43. 'In the interview with the Subprefect of the Province it was agreed to detain the principal leaders of this movement, two individuals called Orellana and Sesa, who should have been transported to Lima, since communist documents were found in their possession. The situation now appears to have calmed down ...' (Laive Arch., Laive to Lima, 12 June 1931). 'On the 19th, 85 men of the 5th Infantry arrived in Huancayo and proceeded immediately to Chongos Bajo, where they have remained ever since, attempting to discover the culprits ... Enrique Llaca, Alcalde of the village, who was the official spokesman (*apoderado*) of the Community and signed the Agreement at the Ministerio de Fomento, Julio Muniba and the Gobernador Melchiades García and one Guerro, these four individuals will leave tomorrow with the troops for Lima': Laive to Lima, 25 September 1931. The people of Chongos refused to construct a demarcation fence and hid the posts.

44. Date of official recognition of communities in lower Mantaro valley (right bank):

1928	2	1939	3
1935	2	1940	1
1936	1	1941–50	5
1937	2	1951–60	0

1938	8		1961–9	0
	in process of recognition			3
	unrecognized			4

Source: *Proyecto Sociedad Ganadera del Centro, Datos Para Adjudicación*, pp. 7–7A.

On the left bank 6 communities registered before 1930, only 6 in the 1930s, 10 in the 1940s, 1 in the 1950s and 1 in the 1960s.

45. Paul L. Doughty, *Huaylas: An Andean District in Search of Progress* (Ithaca, N.Y., 1968), p. 143.

46. C.D.A., Arch. Ganadera del Centro: Laive papers, File I Comunidades, Camarena to Fernandez, 14 July 1937. The project 'has been thought up, they tell me, by one Sabini or Sabino Román who used to work on Ingahuasi and who has recently been made headman (*alcalde*)'.

47. *Boletín de la Dirección de Asuntos Indigenas*, 1940, p. 353. Tucle also thought it wise to settle some boundary disputes with Huasicancha: Juzgado de Tierras, Huancayo, Exp. 69.831, fj 197.

48. In the central highlands it was sufficiently powerful to force several large estates – Laive, Maco, Queta, San Francisco de Apicancha, Antapongo and doubtless others – actually to sign shortlived collective contracts with newly formed trade unions of estate workers: C.D.A., Arch. Ganadera del Centro, Laive papers, Arch. Soc. Ganadera Maco S.A.

49. C.D.A., Arch. Ganadera del Centro, Laive papers: File 'Comunidades', Memorandum, 'Comunidades colindantes con la Hacienda' (January 1963).

50. Interview with Sr. Oscar Bernuy Gomez, legal adviser to Huasicancha at this period. Cf. also Paul L. Doughty, *Huaylas*, pp. 144–5, for letters 'from a person residing in Callao' (Lima's seaport) seconding the request of Huaylas for registration as a community.

51. Floyd La Mond Tullis, *Lord and Peasant in Peru: A Paradigm of Political and Social Change* (Cambridge, Mass., 1970), pp. 63–6, outlines his biography. I have derived my information from interviews with Professor Jesus Veliz Lizárraga of Huancayo, who was associated with Tacunan in the Federation and other communal and political activities.

52. C.D.A., Arch. Ganadera del Centro, Laive papers: Laive to Lima, 16 October 1945.

53. Ibid., undated memorandum 'On the subversive plans of the Districts of Chongos Alto and Huasicancha' addressed to the General Manager in Lima, probably written between August and October of 1945.

54. Ibid.

55. C.D.A., Arch. Ganadera del Centro: Acopalca papers: 'Informe sobre los sucesos ocuridos en las Haciendas Tucle, Antapongo y Laive desde el 23 del mes de Diciembre 1946', by Alberto Chaparro, 25 January 1947.

56. The Hacienda went to enormous trouble to make this deed of sale binding by making it conditional not only on the completion of the demarcation

ditch, but on the personal agreement, verified by signature or mark, of every adult member of the community: Juzgado de T. Huancayo, Exp. 69.831, fj 39 ff. The community was to bind itself, on pain of a heavy fine, not to engage in further 'actos perturbatorios' or to make further claims. Sr. Bernuy Gomez, the community's legal adviser at the time, informs me that his clients only signed after his assurance that, for somewhat complex legal reasons, this did not in fact prejudice their other very large claims against Tucle.

57. C.D.A., Arch. Ganadera del Centro, Lima head-office: Minutes of Board of Directors, June–November 1963.

58. Expediente de afectación de Tucle (Suboficina Regional de Reforma Agraria, ZAX Huancayo).

59. Juzgado de T. Huancayo, Exp. 70/1385/2 C, fj 468.

60. Ibid., Exp. 69.831, fj 35.

61. Since for the peasants such devices had no organic connection with the 'real' community, but belonged to the world of state, state law and politics, they could be treated quite pragmatically. Thus at the peak of the social agitation of the early 1960s many communities organized themselves as trade unions (*sindicatos*) because this appeared to be helpful in their struggles. I understand that at present (1973) some in Central Peru are asking for the status of *pueblos jovenes* ('young settlements') which was devised by the military government for urban shanty-towns, because this promises advantages in obtaining access to electricity, roads, etc.

62. Instituto Indigenista Peruano, Subproyecto ... Mantaro 2 A, *Distrito Pucará* (Lima, 1968), pp. 58–62.

63. I am once again obliged to Dr. Samaniego for the information which follows.

64. C. Guillaguiros, Radiografía de las invasiones: *Prensa*, 11–13 February 1964.

65. Floyd La Mond Tullis, *Lord and Peasant in Peru*, pp. 94–5.

66. For Anta (Cuzco), *Prensa*, 5 December 1963.

67. *Prensa*, 8 October 1963.

68. I.I.P. Subproyecto ... Mantaro 2 A, *Distrito Pucará*, pp. 58–62.

69. Guillaguiros, (see note 64 above).

70. C.D.A., Arch. Ganadera del Centro, Laive papers: Laive to Lima, 9 August 1931.

71. C.D.A., Arch. Ganadera del Centro, Acopalca papers: Informe ... A. Chaparro, 25 January 1947, p. 2.

72. For the Corpacancha invasions, where students were present, *Prensa*, 19 August 1963; for an invasion by Yanacancha, *Voz de Huancayo*, 9 February 1961 ('headed by their authorities and an instigator').

73. Adriel Osorio Zamalloa, *La comunidad campesina, nivel micro-economico de desarrollo regional* (Fac. de Ciencias Economicas y Comerciales, Univ. Nacional del Centro de Peru, Huancayo, 1966, mimeo), pp. 279 ff.

340

74. The mixture is well illustrated by the alleged leadership of an invasion of the Cerro de Pasco *haciendas* (*Prensa*, 18 August 1963, 21 August 1963). The leader was said to be one Sergio Berrospi, a prosperous miner (or perhaps small mining entrepreneur) supported by Claro Huallanuay, *alcalde* of Pallanchacra, Juan Soto, *sub-alcalde*, Pedro Berrospi (a kinsman of Sergio?) and the student Zenon Najara, who had stood as candidate of the National Liberation Front the previous year.

75. Rodrigo Montoya R, *A Proposito del Caracter Predominantemente Capitalista de la Economía Peruana Actual* (Lima, 1970), pp. 110–11.

76. CIDA, *Tenencia de Tierra ... Peru* (Washington, 1966), p. 123.

77. Oficina Nacional del Desarrollo Comunal. Comité Zonal ZAC 1, *Sistema de Organización Campesina para el Desarrollo del Valle del Mantaro* (Huancayo, 1969, mimeo).

78. CIDA Peru, (see note 76 above), p. 134, finds half of its sample with disputes. Henry F. Dobyns, *Comunidades Campesinas del Peru* (Lima, 1970), pp. 57–8, records 44 per cent of a sample of 50 communities studied monographically but 64 per cent of the 640 communities investigated by the Peru-Cornell project with disputes. Two surveys of *all* the communities in a region show 50 per cent in Chucuito, Puno (with 46 out of 58 responding) and 61.7 per cent in Bolognesi, Ancash, with 14.7 per cent denying the existence of disputes and 23.5 per cent not answering. *Datos Basicos* for these provinces (Lima, 1970), pp. 19 and 29 respectively.

79. Dobyns, *Comunidades Compesinas del Peru*, p. 58. Of the Dobyns sample 54.4 per cent had disputes with landlords, 40.9 per cent with other communities, 4.5 per cent with both. Of the Peru-Cornell sample 64 per cent were in dispute with landlords, 60 per cent with other communities, 6 per cent within the community.

80. Min. Agric., Dirección General de Reforma Agraria y Asentamiento Rural, *Las Comunidades Integrantes de la SAIS Tupac Amaru* (Lima, 1971), p. 21.

81. Min. Agric., Dirección de Comunidades Campesinas, ZAC Mantaro 1, *Proyecto Sociedad Ganadera del Centro. Datos para Adjudicación*; and C.D.A., 'Inventario de los Fondos Sociedad Ganadera del Centro, Tucle y Antapongo' (MS., November 1971). It should be pointed out that the list of communities with disputes which can be compiled from the estate archives is much longer than that of the communities described as having common boundaries with the estate in the official survey of 1970.

82. Local insurrections to restore the Inca régime or expressing specific support for the Incas are not uncommon in nineteenth- and twentieth-century Peru, until the 1930s. For the Inca myth, see A. Flores Galindo, *Buscando vu Inca: Identidad y Utopia en los Andes* (Havana, 1986).

83. Henri Favre, *Changement et continuité chez les Mayas du Mexique* (Paris, 1971), pp. 269 ff.

84. For the 1712 rising see also Herbert S. Klein, 'Peasant communities in

revolt: the Tzeltal republic of 1712', *Pacific Hist. Rev.*, xxxv (1966), pp. 247 ff.

85. R. Portal (ed.), *Le statut des paysans liberés du servage* (Paris-Hague, 1963), pp. 248, 263.

86. Min. de Trabajo, Instituto Indigenista Peruano, Serie Monografica 17, *Sociedad y cultura en 10 areas Andino-Peruanas* (Lima, 1966), pp. 13, 36–8, for Andahuaylas.

87. Ibid., pp. 36–7, for Chuyas and Huaychao in Ancash.

88. The nature and extent of APRA's mass support outside the working class remains obscure. It is now generally agreed that in the past twenty years or more its support among, and interest in, Indian peasants has been far smaller than party mythology has claimed. In 1965 FENCAP, the party's peasant organization, organized precisely 13 communities, 6 of them in the Dept. of Lima and Callao. See Grant Hilliker, *The Politics of Reform in Peru* (Baltimore and London, 1971), p. 98. But the history of APRA at the grass roots during the period when it was, or was seen as, a revolutionary movement, remains to be seriously investigated.

89. Henri Favre, *L'évolution et la situation des haciendas dans la région de Huancavelica* (Paris, 1965, mimeo).

90. The exceptions which require investigation, are parts of the North (Cajamarca, Ancash and Huanuco) and that traditional centre of the 'native rising', Puno in the South.

CHAPTER 13: THE BANDIT GIULIANO

1. *Relazione della commissione parlamentare d'inchiesta sul fenomeno della mafia, testo integrale* (Rome, 1973), vol. 2, p. 1633.

2. *Girolamo Li Causi e la sua azione politica in Sicilia: scritti, ricordi e testimonianze a cura di Franco Grasso* (Palermo, 1966), p. 150.

3. Michele Pantaleone, *Mafia e politica* (Turin, 1962), p. 159.

4. Gavin Maxwell, *Bandit*; released in England as *God Protect Me from my Friends* (London, 1956; reissued in 1972 by Pan Books).

5. In fact, the police colonel commanding the group pursuing him was also a separatist. *Relazione*, vol. 2, p. 1700.

6. Ibid., p. 1658, and again p. 1665. See also the evidence of another (honest) cop, General Paolantonio, ibid., pp. 1700–1.

7. From a letter to the *Voce di Sicilia*, 20 September 1947, defending himself (insincerely) against the charge of having perpetrated a massacre on a communist demonstration. Cited in *Li Causi*, p. 147.

8. *Relazione*, vol. 1, pp. 111–12.

9. According to the well-informed Gaia Servadio, *Mafioso* (London, 1976), p. 130.

10. Thus, in 1947: 'You are a dead man, Giuliano, your life is finished. Either

you will be killed through Mafia treason ... or in a fight with the police, or you will be taken': *Li Causi*, p. 152.
11. 'I weep for you,' the Walrus said:
    'I deeply sympathize.'
    With sobs and tears he sorted out
    Those of the largest size.

CHAPTER 15: MAY 1968
1. Alain Touraine, *Le Mouvement de mai ou le communisme utopique* (Paris, 1969).

CHAPTER 16: THE RULES OF VIOLENCE
1. See A. Pigliaru, *La vendetta barbaricina come ordinamento giuridico* (Milan, 1959).
2. Between the wars the Royal Air Force resisted any plans to use it to maintain public order on the grounds that its weapons were too indiscriminate, and that it might hence be liable to prosecution under the common law. It did not apply this argument to the bombing of tribal villages in India and the Middle East...
3. The argument that these images cannot be proved to affect anyone's action merely tries to rationalize this contradiction, and cannot stand serious scrutiny. Neither can the arguments that popular culture has always revelled in images of violence, or that its images act as a sort of replacement for the real thing.
4. Rational revolutionaries have always measured violence entirely by its purpose and likely achievement. When Lenin was told in 1916 that the secretary of the Austrian social democrats had assassinated the Austrian prime minister as a gesture of protest against the war, he merely wondered why a man in his position had not taken the less dramatic but more effective step of circulating the party activists with an anti-war appeal. It was evident to him that a boring but effective non-violent action was preferable to a romantic but ineffective one. This did not stop him from recommending armed insurrection when necessary.

CHAPTER 19: THE CARUSO OF JAZZ
1. Sidney Bechet, *Treat It Gentle: An Autobiography* (London, 1960). It was published after a bumpy ride through publishers, lawyers, and collaborators such as John Ciardi.
2. Paul Oliver, Max Harrison, and William Bolcom, *The New Grove: Gospel, Blues and Jazz* (New York, 1987), p. 292.
3. However, Ansermet's negative judgement thirty years later ('The days of jazz are over. It has made its contribution to music. Now in itself it is merely

monotonous') has not been propagated by jazz-lovers or Bechet fans, though Chilton records it (p. 207).

CHAPTER 20: COUNT BASIE

1. 'He's been a hell of a man,' writes Basie of his discoverer John Hammond. 'And he has never asked for a nickel from me or any of those other people he's done so much for. And there have been quite a few of them. All he wanted to see was the results of what was supposed to be happening.'
2. Albert Murray, *Stomping the Blues* (New York, 1982), p. 166.

CHAPTER 21: THE DUKE

1. (New York, 1973).
2. Mercer Ellington with Stanley Dance, *Duke Ellington in Person* (Boston, 1978). In Mercer's account Duke Ellington was kind to him so long as he was willing to do his bidding and help him with the band. When the son tried to strike out on his own as a musician, the Duke, he writes, did everything he could to discourage him.
3. Martin Williams, *The Jazz Tradition*, new and revised edition (Oxford, 1983), p. 102.
4. Max Harrison, *A Jazz Retrospect* (New York, 1976), p. 128.
5. Alexander Coleman, 'The Duke and His Only Son', *New Boston Review*, December 1978.
6. *Music Is My Mistress*, p. x.
7. Surprisingly, Collier does not quite avoid the same pitfall in his praise of Ellington's three-minute pieces. The 78-rpm record, which provides us with so many of his surviving masterpieces, did not determine the structure of Ellington's compositions, but only that of the music produced for the recording studio, as the informal recording of his work in ballrooms demonstrates.

CHAPTER 24: JAZZ SINCE 1960

1. J. Skidmore in *Jazz Now* (London, 1976), p. 76.
2. Cited in S. Chapple and R. Garofalo, *Rock'n'Roll Is Here to Pay* (Chicago, 1977), p. 144.
3. Whitney Balliett, *New York Notes: A Journal of Jazz in the Seventies* (New York, 1977), p. 147.
4. Valerie Wilmer, *As Serious as your Life: The Story of the New Jazz* (London, 1977; 2nd edn, 1987), p. 27.
5. It also, incidentally, gave a virtual monopoly to singing groups, hitherto somewhat exceptional in jazz and blues, and – in spite of the overwhelming superiority of women in vocal blues, gospel song and jazz – to (young) men.
6. Their father, Ellis Marsalis, a New Orleans pianist and passionate supporter

of Ornette Coleman and the avant-garde, made a commercial living in order to bring up his family. In New Orleans, music is still often a family trade, as it was in the days of the Bachs.

INDEX

Abraham, William ('Mabon'), 70

Accati, Luisa, 105

Adams, John, 21, 43

Adderley, Julian ('Cannonball'), 290

Adler, Victor, 117–18, 127, 133

Adorno, Theodor W., 253

Ahuac, Peru, 178

Alexander, Willard, 252

Alexandre, Philippe, 217

Algeria, 207–9

Alianza Popular Revolucionaria
    Americana (APRA; Peru), 159, 179–
    80, 182–5, 189

American Federation of Labor, 115, 117

Americas (New World): aboriginal
    cultures, 295–7; conquest and
    colonization, 295–7, 302; influence
    on Old World, 295–303; new
    foodstuffs and commodities, 301, 303

Amis, (Sir) Kingsley, 270

Anabaptists, 51

anarchism: in France, 47; and May Day,
    119–20, 123; and progressive art,
    134–5; and village economy, 156;
    puritanism, 231

Angola, 206

Ansermet, Ernest, 241–2, 269

Applegarth, Robert, 78

apprenticeships, 77–8, 81, 84, 86–7

Arch, Joseph, 71

Argentina: unions in, 20

Armstrong, Louis, 236, 238, 240, 242,
    255, 281, 289, 294

art: images of women and men in, 94–
    112, 131; see also avant-garde

artisans see tradesmen (craft)

arts-and-crafts movement, 121, 131; see
    also Morris, William

Ashton, (Sir) Frederick, 270

Askwith, G., 68–9

Atlantic Records, 283

Attica Blues, 286

Attlee, Clement (*later* 1st Earl), 142, 145

Australia: sheep-shearers, 19; May Day
    in, 120

Austria: and May Day celebrations, 117–
    18, 120, 124

Austrian Communist Party, 42

Austrian Social Democratic Party, 116–
    17

Austrian Socialist Party, 41

avant-garde: and socialism, 128–39

Ayler, Albert, 288

Bahr, Hermann, 133

Baines, Sir Edward, 12

Baker, Josephine, 237, 239, 243

Bakunin, Mikhail, 133

Balliett, Whitney, 286

Balzac, Honoré de, 96

Bankhead, Tallulah, 237

Barbier, Henri Auguste: *La Curée*, 96

Barker, Paul, 229

Barnes, George, 88

Basie, Count: life and music, 246–53,
    280; politics, 278

Batista, General Fulgencio, 207

Beatles (pop group), 281, 284, 288

Bebel, August, 43, 116–18; *Woman and
    Socialism*, 107

bebop (music), 279–80, 285

Bechet, Sidney, 236–45, 260, 265, 269,
    278, 286

Bedlington, Durham, 8

Beerbohm, Sir Max, 266

Belgium: May Day in, 122, 124;
    labouring population exploited, 131;
    avant-garde art in, 133, 137

347

Wiltshire: machine-breaking, 7, 12–13, 16
Winckelmann, Johann Joachim, 102
Winks, W.E., 23
Winkworth, William, 21
Wolf, Howlin', 283
Womack, John, 183
women: working, 64, 88, 103–6; images and iconography of, 94–100, 107–8, 110, 121, 125; and marriage, 104–5, 109; militant action by, 105; trade union membership, 105–6; and socialism, 106–9; role, 109–10; liberation of, 230–1
Woods, Phil, 290
Woods, Samuel, 73
Woodstock (USA): 1969 rock festival, 285
Woolf, Leonard, 143
Workers' Congress of Curitiba (Brazil), 20
working class: and machine-wrecking, 6, 10; making of (1880–1914), 57–74; numbers and occupational composition, 60; dress and headgear, 62, 66, 69, 73–4; habits and interests, 63–8, 71, 73; housing and residence, 64, 67–8; standard of living, 64; educational standards, 68; alienation,

69; political orientation, 70–3; and class consciousness, 71–2, 149; leaders, 72; differentiation by skills, 78–9; iconography of, 98–101; *see also* labour
working day *see* Eight-Hour Day
World Peace Movement, 56
World Saxophone Quartet, 289
World War II: French resistance movement in, 54–5; popular music in, 279
Wright, Thomas, 79
Wrigley, Chris and John Shepherd (eds.): *On the Move: Essays in Labour and Transport History Presented to Philip Bagwell*, 113

Yanacancha, Peru, 178, 182, 184, 186
Yauri (Peruvian peasant leader), 184
Yaurivilca, Elías, 180
Young, Lester, 253, 294
Young, Trummy, 289

Zapata, Emiliano, 154, 157–8, 169, 183, 189
Zawinul, Joe, 282
Zeldin, Theodore, 19
Zola, Emile, 130